D0560069

F
289
.S78
1742a

v.2

Stephens

A journal of the proceed-

F
289 .V.2
.S78
1742a

AUTHOR Stephens

TITLE A Journal of the Proceed-
ings in Georgia

DATE LOANED	BORROWER'S NAME

Point Park Junior College
Wood St. and Blvd. of Allies
Pittsburgh, Pa. 15222

March of America Facsimile Series

Number 37

A Journal of the Proceedings in Georgia

VOLUME II

William Stephens

A Journal of the Proceedings in Georgia

VOLUME II

by William Stephens

F
289
.S78
1742a
975.802
S835
v.2
1/20/67
Publisher

ANN ARBOR
UNIVERSITY MICROFILMS, INC.
A Subsidiary of Xerox Corporation

POINT PARK COLLEGE LIBRARY

XEROX

COPYRIGHT © BY UNIVERSITY MICROFILMS, INC., 1966

ALL RIGHTS RESERVED

LIBRARY OF CONGRESS CATALOG CARD NO. 66-26311

MANUFACTURED IN THE UNITED STATES OF AMERICA

A Journal of the Proceedings in Georgia

VOLUME II

A

JOURNAL

OF THE

PROCEEDINGS

IN

GEORGIA,

BEGINNING

OCTOBER 20, 1737.

By *WILLIAM STEPHENS*, Esq;

To which is added,

A STATE of that PROVINCE,

As attested upon OATH

IN THE

COURT of SAVANNAH,

November 10, 1740.

VOL. II.

LONDON:
Printed for W. MEADOWS, at the *Angel* in *Cornhill.*
MDCCXLII.

JOURNAL

CONTINUED.

EDNESDAY. Wrote ſome Letters to the South, and ſent them, together with what came Yeſterday, to *Frederica*, St. *Simon*'s Camp, *&c.* by Mr. *Mace*, who took ſpecial Charge of what related in a more particular Manner to the General; and promiſed a ſafe Delivery of the reſt. Mr. *Horton*, on his Return from *Matthews*'s, acquainted me (with equal Satisfaction to us both) that he and his Wife had promiſed him to go forthwith, and wait on the General in the Camp, with Intent to ſhew 1739. May 2.

 their

1739. May their Readineſs, in whatever he required of them concerning the late Movement of the *Indians*; and that old *Tomo Chichi* would go alſo, and lay what Reſtraint on them he could, from proceeding any farther in what they purpoſed. In theſe three Days that Mr. *Horton* had been in Town, I could plainly diſcover what Sort of Sentiments he began to entertain of the Place, from ſuch Talk as we had together: And indeed a Man of much leſs Diſcernment, could not well miſs in that Space of Time, to find Demonſtration ſufficient to convince him what Miſchief an intemperate, ſelf-ſufficient Conduct, cloathed with Power, is capable of creating in the Publick.

3. *Thurſday*. In the Morning, Mr. *Horton* calling on me, it was thought a fit Time to enquire into another Affair, that he was charged with from the General, to learn the Truth of; relating to an Information made (as noted 23 *ult.)* wherein the General's own Safety ſeemed to be in Danger: In Order whereto, Meſſ. *Parker* and *Gilbert* (two Magiſtrates) aſſembled at my Houſe, Mr. *Chriſtie* the Recorder being out of Town; and the Informant *Green* being ſent for, together with his Boy *Cundal*, Mr. *Robert Williams* the Owner of the Sloop, and —— the Maſter of her, were alſo called: Then *Green* being aſked if he was

was ſure he knew the Men again when he ſaw them, with whom he had that Talk on *Saturday* Night was Se'nnight, on board the Sloop; and both he and his Boy affirming, that they ſhould know them upon Sight; they were ſent with a Conſtable on board the Sloop to find them; as they readily did, and came all together before the Magiſtrates; where, upon a ſtrict and careful Examination, the Informants *Green* and his Boy did ſeverally make Affidavit to this Effect, *viz.* That upon their going aboard the Sloop on the *Saturday* Night, as aforeſaid, and aſking what News from the South; the two Men now preſent, whoſe Names were *Nelſon* and *Conn*, the one Mate, and the other a Sailor belonging to the ſaid Sloop, anſwered him in theſe or the like Words: "The Soldiers at "the Camp told us they heard the Gene-"ral was laid hold on at *Charles-Town*; "which they ſaid they were glad to hear; "for if ever he came among them at the "Camp again, ſome of them would give "him a Pill; and if one did not ſhoot "him, another would; after which they "would go off to the *Spaniards*, &c." To which the two Sailors now preſent anſwered, That they utterly denied their having ever ſaid ſo much: They acknowledged the firſt Part of it, that the Soldiers

1739. May 3.

1739. May talked of the General's being in Cuſtody at *Charles-Town*; but farther than that, they never heard, nor did they ſay they had, which they offered to ſwear, if they might be allowed ſo to do; but that not being admitted, they objected againſt the Credit of *Green* the Informer, who they heard had a bad Character, and indeed he had not a good one; he having been formerly convicted of bad Crimes, and his Teſtimony on ſome Occaſions in our Court being regarded but very little by our Juries: Nevertheleſs, on ſuch poſitive Evidence, nothing could be done leſs than ſending them down to the General at *Frederica*, or confining them here till the General's Pleaſure ſhould be farther known: Whereupon they rather choſe to be ſent thither inſtantly, to make their Defence, leſt by delaying it, they might loſe the proceeding on their Voyage; and therefore making it a Requeſt of their own, the Magiſtrates allowed it, and Lieutenant *Horton* undertook to carry them down with him when he went.

4. *Friday*. Among other Things ſent from the Truſt by the Ship *America* lately arrived, was a Parcel of Vine-Cuttings, which with proper Care in packing would have been extreamly valuable, and are much coveted: But unhappily they came naked, without any Covering, and only bound up like

like a common Faggot; ſo that being in that Manner expoſed, and poſſibly thrown careleſly up and down in the Voyage, they had the Appearance of no other than a Bundle of dry Sticks; adding to all which, the uncommon Length of Time in their Paſſage, being ſeveral Months; I was very ſorry to ſee little or no Hopes left, of any Good to be expected from what was ſo truly deſirable: Nevertheleſs, that nothing might be omitted which could be done, I called *De Lyon* the *Jew* to my Aſſiſtance, who has the moſt Skill of any among us, and has planted ſome Hundreds of the *Portugal* Grape this Year, out in his Plantation, which he reared laſt Year from Cuttings and otherwiſe: And when I had ordered a Spot of freſh Ground, in the Swamp of the Garden belonging to the Truſt, to be cleanſed and dreſſed, I left it to him to put ſome of them into the Earth, that we might at leaſt try if any of them would haply make Shoot. *N. B.* He told me, that the Time they were cut in *(viz. December)* was a right Seaſon, and had they been rightly packt too, notwithſtanding ſo long a Paſſage, he believed moſt of them might have been ſaved: Wherefore for future Inſtruction, I learnt of him, that the proper Way of preſerving the Cuttings, is to fill a Caſk half full of good

1739. May 4.

1739. May Earth, wherein the Cuttings are to ſtand half their own Depth, and the Tops of them only bound with Straw, without any other Covering, by which the Air may come to them ſo much as is proper; but no Sprey of the Sea; wherefore they ſhould not be expoſed upon Deck. I found nothing elſe all Day, which I thought ſo much worth my regarding as this.

5. *Saturday.* Mr. *Horton* went off this Morning, on his Return to the General at *Frederica*, taking with him thoſe he deſigned. Mr. *Bradley*, I was informed, killed another Steer, which he called his own; but other People were of a different Opinion, and thought him making the moſt of what was in his keeping, before he ſurrendered all up.

6. *Sunday.* Mr. *Haberſham* read the Prayers of the Church, as before, in Mr. *Norris*'s Abſence; and two Sermons on the Working of God's Holy Spirit within us.

7. *Monday.* What I had to obſerve now principally was, the Diſlike which the Magiſtrates and Mr. *Jones* had conceived againſt each other, and which was every Day (as I thought) increaſing, notwithſtanding all the Endeavours I had a good while uſed to reconcile ſuch Differences, and to bring them into better Temper; that by uniting heartily, the publick Good might be the ſooner promoted: But all I could

could ſay began to be but little regarded on either Side; ſo keen was their Reſentment grown of late. What ſeemed to be the Ground-Work of all this was, that Mr. *Jones* thought he had not Deference enough paid him; and they thought what they had paid him was too much. He by Virtue of Power ſuperior to any (which he had, or appeared to have) expected the ready Attendance of the Magiſtrates whenever he pleaſed to ſend for them; and they complained of being treated in the Manner of ordinary Servants, to come wherefoever he pleaſed to call them; and moreover when met, they ſaid they were looked on as Cyphers, and hardly allowed to examine into Facts, but required to act in every Thing as Mr. *Jones* dictated, *&c.* This they had often expreſſed great Uneaſineſs at to me, thinking themſelves made contemptible to the common People; and I had frequently on ſuch Occaſions, when I ſaw Matters of Conſequence like to paſs too lightly over, made Uſe of an Expedient to bring them together, without Diminution of either of their Authority (ſo highly rated) by engaging them all to meet at my Houſe; which ſucceeded well, and I hoped a little Time would wear out theſe pernicious Jealouſies; till *Monday* the 23 *ult.* all ſuch Hopes began utterly to vaniſh; and from that Time they are grown

1739. May 7.

1739. May 7. more and more exaſperated on both Sides (*vide* the Notes of that Day.) Mr. *Chriſtie*, as I apprehend, was a little too dilatory then, in coming on that Occaſion ſo long after the Time appointed; in which to vindicate himſelf, he alledged afterwards, that he did not know it was a Matter of ſuch Importance, and believed it would make no Difference whether he came in a Quarter of an Hour, or ſtaid a whole one: But to have the Door ſhut againſt him in that ſcandalous Manner, was uſing him ſo as he could not bear: From whence aroſe that ſmart Tongue-Fight betwixt him and Mr. *Jones* at *Jenkins*'s ſoon after (as noted.) The ſame Afternoon, the Magiſtrates aſſembling all three at my Houſe, without ſo much as my knowing it, ſent a Meſſenger to find me, and very well pleaſed I was to be ſo ſent for, that the Truth might be enquired into of that Morning's Outrage: And I wiſh that Mr. *Jones*, who was in the ſame Manner ſent to, had gone as readily: But upon his returning that rough Anſwer, they all cried out immediately, "Now you "ſee how we are uſed;" and ſo breaking up, went their Way. The next Day Mr. *Jones* purſued his Deſign of going to wait on the General at *Frederica*; and there being two Steers killed before he went, for the neceſſary Support of ſuch as had any Dependance on the Stores; when the Meat

Meat was given out in ſmall Pieces the Day after, and every Body that had any Pretence, was deſirous of getting a Bit of freſh Meat (none ſalt at the ſame Time in the Store) Meſſ. *Parker* and *Chriſtie* each ſent to aſk for a little; but were anſwered, that Mr. *Jones* had left Orders there was none for *them*. This put them both into very ill Mood, and made them exclaim heavily to be ſo ſingled out. *Chriſtie* declared publickly his poſitive Reſolution of going ſoon for *England*, &c. &c. *Parker* grew ſullen, and ſaid, it could not be poſſible for him to act the Part of an honeſt Man, if he muſt be in Dread of the Store being ſhut againſt him, whenever in the Execution of his Office he differed in Opinion with Mr. *Jones*; and came to me this Day purpoſely to acquaint me, that he would be ready at any Time to come to me, or meet me when ſent for, on any Thing relating to the Publick, provided it was not to attend Mr. *Jones*; but whatever were the Conſequence, he never would wait on him again as a Magiſtrate, who ſhould expect Mr. *Jones* to come to him, if he had any Thing to ſay to him as ſuch. Which Declaration of his, was the Occaſion of this long Paragraph, reciting ſome Occurrences previous thereunto. 1739. May

Tueſday. Divers Servants being lately run away from their Maſters, which there 8.

was

1739. May 8. was Reaſon to believe were got the Length of *Charles-Town*, where they found Shelter, as Experience had too often ſhewn: At the ſame Time having full Information by Mr. *Shenton*, who had apprehended him, that *Iſaac Bradford*, that notorious Thief, who lately had committed ſo many Villanies here, was, at the Inſtance of the Perſon that took him, committed to Goal there by the civil Magiſtrate; it was thought proper to ſend a Boat with proper Inſtructions, as well to demand the Criminal, in order to his being brought to Juſtice, as alſo to diſcover and retake (if poſſible) ſome, if not all of thoſe Deſerters. Taking an Opportunity to talk with Mr. *Jones* on the Subject-Matter of the Magiſtrates Uneaſineſs; and letting him know what it was that they ſeemed moſt to ſtick at: He ſhewed no Concern about it; but told me, he ſaw what they would be at, was an unlimited Credit in the Stores: Which effectually ſtopt me from going farther; for as he had the Cuſtody of all, and muſt account for what he did, as well as others; he certainly ought to obſerve ſuch Rules as were given him, and it was not my Buſineſs to perſuade him to deviate from them, not knowing what Lengths they went: So I left it to him to do as he thought fit; but ſaw plainly, from many Inſtances,

Inſtances, he had ſet himſelf againſt them both. 1739.

Wedneſday. Mr. *Jones* being required to call on Mr. *Bradley*, to ſurrender up all Things in his Cuſtody belonging to the Truſt, purſuant to his Agreement with the General lately at *Charles-Town*; and deſiring me to be preſent at his demanding it, I was ſo: When Mr. *Bradley* made Shew, by his Words, of his Readineſs to do it; but at the ſame Time made Uſe of a little Chicanry (as I thought) to put it off for a while, by ſaying, that he ought firſt to have the General's Orders in Writing before he could be juſtified in ſo doing: And ſo we parted; Mr. *Bradley* appearing pleaſed at the Anſwer he had given to that Demand. May 9.

Thurſday. Lieutenant *Dunbar* arriving this Morning from the South in one of the Scout-Boats, he ſpent ſome Time with Mr. *Jones* in private; but as he was not pleaſed to ſee me, going on the ſame Day for *Palachocolas*, all that I could come at the Knowledge of was, that he was to take ſome Horſes there for the General's Service, which he was to convey over Land from thence Southward. Mr. *Jones*, in the Afternoon, calling on me, ſaid, he was quite empty of Meat in the Stores, having none to feed even the Truſt's Servants; and wiſhed to have two or three Steers killed for 10.

that

1739. May that Purpoſe: Whereupon knowing that Mr. *Parker*, who had the Care of thoſe Steers, had alſo Orders from the General to deliver at any Time to Mr. *Jones* what he needed of them; I told him, that he had no more to do, but to ſend Directions to Mr. *Parker* about it, who without Doubt would take Care they ſhould be brought up: But was ſurprized at his ſaying, whatever the Want was, he would neither aſk him, nor ſend him any Directions about it: However, that the publick Service might not thereby ſuffer, Mr. *Mercer* being preſent, I deſired him to acquaint Mr. *Parker* with it, who I was confident would readily ſee it done; and Mr. *Mercer* promiſed me to let him know it.——To ſuch a Height was Mr. *Jones*'s Reſentment grown ſince the 23d paſt.

11. *Friday.* Upon the Notice that Mr. *Mercer* gave, Mr. *Parker* took Care to ſee three Steers brought in this Day for the Uſe of the Stores; in which Service he got a ſevere Fall with his Horſe upon him, that had well nigh ſpoiled him. Moſt of my Time and Thoughts this Day were employed in promoting what was needful to be done about the Corn, *&c.* which I had planted this Spring; for unleſs continual Attendance was given, in houghing the Ground, and keeping down the Weeds, that grew apace, all our paſt Labour would come

come to Nought; and the villanous Falſhood of thoſe Servants I had, without frequent Inſpection, would not allow me to hope for any Good; neither with all the Care that my Son and I could uſe, was it in our Power to attain that Perfection we propoſed to ourſelves, almoſt in any Work: But if we could come up to, *cæteris paribus*, in keeping clean what Ground we had planted, we muſt not look for more. 1739. May

Saturday. Finding myſelf under a little Indiſpoſition, I kept home, and began preparing neceſſary Papers to make up another Packet for *England.* 12.

Sunday. Mr. *Norris* being yet in the South, Mr. *Haberſham*, as before, went on with the proper Service of the Day, in reading the Common Prayer, and after it ſome of Archbiſhop *Tillotſon*'s Doctrine, which is ſo univerſally admired. 13.

Monday, *Tueſday.* These two Days I ſpent wholly at the Mouth of *Vernon* River, having Mr. *Mercer* with me, whoſe Judgment in many Things relating to Improvements, I approved of very well, and therefore conſulted him ſometimes: Moreover, he had lately obtained from the General a Promiſe of a Grant of three hundred Acres upon Leaſe, under the ſame Covenants with ſeveral others; and as he had a View of being near the ſame Place, I was willing to promote it, and get him 14. 15.

fixed

1739. May fixed my next Neighbour, being aſſured in myſelf, that he would not be idle upon it: Our Buſineſs now was to look narrowly into, and make ſuch Obſervations, that we might, at our Leiſure, be contriving betwixt ourſelves at home, what was proper to be done as ſoon as it was ſurveyed, and Poſſeſſion given us. At my Return home on *Tueſday* Evening, what I met with for News was, that Captain *Shubrick*, in the *Mary Ann*, was newly arrived at *Charles-Town*; by whom Mr. *Verelſt*, in his laſt Letter, promiſed me I ſhould hear fully from the Truſt; but was now ſorry to hear it reported by ſome who came lately from *Charles-Town*, that Captain *Shubrick* was bound to *Frederica*, as ſoon as he had delivered what Merchants Goods he had aboard him for *Carolina*; and that he would deliver no Letters for *Georgia* till he came to *Frederica*, where he would deliver them himſelf: But when that would be, who could tell? Which gave me a little Uneaſineſs, being what I could not underſtand the Meaning of.

16. *Wedneſday*. *Samuel Lacy* arrived this Morning from *Charles-Town*, and brought with him four Letters from *England*, that were put under Cover for the General, and ſent to me by the Attorney-General; which Cover, when I had opened, I found three of the ſaid Letters came by Captain *Shubrick*,

Shubrick, and one of them by Captain *Gerald*; by whom alſo came other Letters, which I received (as noted) the 1ſt Inſtant; ſo that it appeared to me, that all theſe Letters came over from *England* in the common Bag, and were taken up by the Attorney-General at the Poſt-Office; which made me give the more Credit to what was ſaid laſt Night, of Captain *Shubrick*'s having with him a Packet from the Truſt not yet delivered: In the Afternoon Mr. *Purry* arrived from *Charles-Town*, and brought with him a Packet of more Letters for the General, and others at St. *Simon*'s, which came under Cover to Lieutenant Governor *Bull*, from whom Mr. *Purry* received them, and delivered them to my Care. Mr. *Jones* told me, that he had a Letter or two alſo for the General from *Charles-Town*; but did not acquaint me who it was that ſent it to him. By all theſe ſcattered Letters thus collected, and none from the Truſtees Office; it appeared now paſt all Doubt, that *Shubrick* had the Truſt's Packet with him, which he would not deliver till he arrived himſelf at *Frederica*, or ſome other Port in *Georgia*; which might be a great while yet to come. 1739. May

Thurſday. Mr. *Hird*, a Freeholder, and one of the Conſtables at *Frederica*, after two or three Days ſpent here on his own Affairs, intending to return thither this 17

1739. May Day; I delivered into his Care all the Letters that came to my Hands Yesterday, making them up in one Packet for the General; to whom also I wrote myself in Answer to one which I had through Mr. *Jones*'s Hands from him. Captain *Wood* from *Frederica*, in his Way to *Charles-Town*, came ashore here last Night, and called on me this Morning; but brought no Letters. Very heavy Rain came on in the Morning, and held all Day; which prevented both Captain *Wood* and Mr. *Hird* from setting out on their Passages North and South till another Day.

18. *Friday*. Little happening worth Notice abroad, stuck mostly at home to my Pen and Ink. Captain *Wood* and Mr. *Hird* went off their several Ways. In the Evening I was informed, that Bailiff *Parker* had received a Letter from the General, signifying his being informed by Mr. *Jones* of an Intention some Persons had to make Waste of certain Stores belonging to the Trust, and requiring him to look into it, and take Care that the Trust might not be injured in their Property: Wherein my Son apprehending, that Mr. *Jones* had again been doing him some ill Office with the General, relating to some Wines bought of Colonel *Cockran*; he now expected and wished that Affair might be thoroughly canvassed, so that it might appear with what

what Juſtice ſuch an Accuſation was brought against him: The Particulars of which ought not to be paſſed over, without a full and explicit Relation of the Whole, when Mr. *Jones* ſets forth before the Magiſtrates what he has to alledge. 1739. May

Saturday. Got forward with what Papers and Letters I had to ſend to *England*; and loſt as little Time as I could to make another Packet ready, not knowing how long it might be, ere we heard from Captain *Shubrick*, whether he had any Letters for us, or what they were; which I wiſhed to have learnt. My Son expected to have been called before the Magiſtrate, purſuant to what we were informed Yeſterday; but Mr. *Jones* had yet made no Step about it, and what he had to ſay, as well as when, was wholly in himſelf. Towards Evening Captain *Deſbraſſie*, and Enſign *Maxwell*, arrived from the South, by whom I had a Letter from the General, and one under the ſame Cover for Mr. *Jones*, which I delivered to him inſtantly; he accompanying thoſe Gentlemen to my Houſe. 19.

Sunday. This Morning two Letters were brought me by a Servant of Mr. *Cuthbert*, which his Maſter ſent him with, from his Plantation at *Joſeph's Town*, where they came to his Hands from Lieutenant *Willy* in the *Indian* Nations; the Contents of one of which would require my laying 20.

1739. May it before the General. Mr. *Habersham*, during Mr. *Norris*'s yet continuing in the South, performed the Duty of the Day in the ſame Manner he before had done.

21. *Monday*. Bailiff *Parker*, in Obedience to the General's Letter (as mentioned the 18th) calling the other Magiſtrates together; Mr. *Jones* at the ſame Time appearing, together with all Parties ſuppoſed to be concerned, *viz.* my Son and I, and Mr. *Bradley*; Mr. *Parker* read Extract out of the ſaid Letter from the General to him, in theſe Words: "Mr. *Jones* acquaints me, "that ſome Perſons have refuſed to deliver "to the Truſtees their Wines by them "bought, and the Poſſeſſion of their own "Cellar. I hope you will ſee Juſtice done "to the Truſtees, and that they are not "ſtript of their Properties with Impuni-"ty." Which Words, importing a grievous Charge, that without Doubt pointed particularly at my Son; it will be needful to look back, and trace this Matter from the Beginning, that the whole Truth may be underſtood. ——— When Colonel *Cockran* came hither with Part of the Regiment in *May* laſt Year, and brought a large Parcel of Wines with him, Part for the Regiment, and Part for his own Account; he found no Place in the Town ſo capable and fit to put them in, as a Cellar under the great Houſe that Mr. *Bradley* lived in,

 and

and was vulgarly called Mr. *Bradley*'s Houſe: Whereupon Colonel *Cockran* applied himſelf to Mr. *Bradley* for the Uſe of it on that Occaſion; who readily granted it; and when the Wine was all ſecured there; the Colonel knowing my Son, gave him the Cuſtody of the Wine, with the Key of the Cellar, *&c.* (for farther Information, *vide* 10th of *March* laſt.) After a whole Year paſt, and all the Wine diſpoſed of; the Cellar was now cleared of the Whole, excepting only two Pipes of Wine, which had been bought for the Uſe of the Truſtees Stores, and yet remained there: On which Account Mr. *Jones* demanded of my Son the Keys of the Cellar, intending to make Uſe of it for the Truſt; but Mr. *Bradley* had cautioned him ſome Time before not to deliver the Keys to any one but himſelf; from whom he ſhould expect them; for though he had lent the Uſe of the Cellar for a Seaſon, to anſwer a certain Purpoſe; yet he would not give up his Property in it: Which put my Son under ſome Doubt what Courſe he muſt take to be ſafe; often telling Mr. *Jones*, that he might ſend for the Wines when he pleaſed; but was deſirous to avoid having any Contention with Mr. *Bradley*, and only wiſhed to have Directions that were proper from one that would ſupport him. Matters thus depending, and my Son

1739. May 21.

1739. May 21. dreaming no Harm; Mr. *Jones* gave him this Wound in the Dark, ſetting forth theſe Tranſactions in ſuch a Manner, as ſhewed plainly the General was irritated, by what he had wrote to Bailiff *Parker*. But now on Enquiry before all the Magiſtrates (for I reſolved to have it diſcuſſed as publickly as might be) it appeared on full Proof, that my Son was perfectly blameleſs; that he had never refuſed delivering the Truſt's Wine; that there was not the leaſt Shadow of his being concerned in ſo vile an Act, as ſtripping the Truſt of their Property; and that the only Thing he boggled at, was whether he was legally cautioned or not by *Bradley* about ſurrendering the Keys: Which the Magiſtrates now gave their Judgment in, and made an Order, that the Keys ſhould be delivered up for the Uſe of the Truſt: This my Son was very glad of, being thereby freed from any farther Care about it: And this might have been done much ſooner, had Mr. *Jones* applied himſelf to the Magiſtrates, who would readily, at any Time, make Enquiry into Abuſes of ſuch Kind, if any there are, and rectify them: But that he ſeems to think is condeſcending too much, and wherever he apprehends his Will is obſtructed, he makes no Scruple of heaping Abundance on the General for Advice; a great deal more (as ſome think) than the

the General cares to be troubled with, unleſs where Matters of Difficulty and Importance require it. My Son could not help thinking this Act of Mr. *Jones*'s ſavoured of much Ill-will towards him, and muſt be repreſented in a very bad Light to the General, that it produced ſo ſharp an Anſwer; when he was conſcious of no Crime he had committed: And bringing freſh to his Remembrance the Diſpleaſure of the General, which he unhappily (tho' innocently) fell under in a former Affair (*March* 10.) it affected him deeply, and ſo diſcouraged him, that it became a Matter of great Concern to myſelf. Lieutenant *Delegal* arrived in the Evening, on his Way to St. *Simon*'s from *Port-Royal*. 1739. May

Tueſday. This Morning my Son delivered up the Keys of the Cellar for Mr. *Jones*'s Uſe; taking one of his Men with him, to ſee that the two Pipes of Wine there for the Truſt were perfectly full, and in good Condition. Captain *Deſbraſſie*, and Enſign *Maxwell*, who arrived here on *Saturday* from the South, taking a Tour up the River to viſit ſome Friends, and being not yet returned; and Lieutenant *Delegal* arriving here ſince, in his Way from *Port-Royal* Southward; he thought fit to wait their coming, not knowing what Orders he might meet with by them from the General. 22.

1739. May 23. *Wedneſday.* The General in a late Letter recommending it to me to ſettle the Matter amicably, between thoſe who hunt Cattle for themſelves, and the Pindar appointed by him, great Variance already ariſing among them; I got the Pindar, and two or three of the principal among the others, to my Houſe; where with a little cool Reaſoning, and ſoft Words, ſhewing them how much it was all their Intereſt to agree, and be aſſiſting to one another; I ſoon brought them to good Temper, and at length to (I hope) a perfect Unity. On which Occaſion I cannot help reflecting on the like Succeſs I have often met, in healing Diſcord among ſome that have been at Strife, by the like Means; and it is moſt certain theſe People pay more Regard to gentle Treatment, than to Menaces; which generally ſit ſour upon them, and often do more Harm than Good.

24. *Thurſday.* Expected to have ſent ſeveral Letters (ſome of which were from myſelf, and ſome from others) to the South by Lieutenant *Delegal*, who was going to wait on the General, but I was diſappointed; for he no ſooner ſaw Captain *Deſbraſſie* and Enſign *Maxwell*, but he met with ſuch Orders as obliged him to return to *Port-Royal* with them, on ſome particular Buſineſs of the Regiment; ſo that I knew no more when or how I ſhould have

have Opportunity of ſending them, than I did thoſe I had prepared to go to *England*. 1739.

Friday, *Saturday*. } The long continued Series of perfect Health, which had been ſo remarkable ever ſince the laſt Fall, throughout the Colony, began a little to alter with us: The great Viciſſitude of Weather, betwixt Thunder, Rain, and ſultry Heats (all violent in their Turns for a few Days paſt) catched many People unawares, and taught them to be more cautious hereafter, not to expoſe themſelves to ſuch Inclemencies more than Neceſſity required; from whence Fevers began again to grow rife among us all on a ſudden; and though I had been but little abroad of late at ſuch Seaſons, yet ſeveral ugly Symptoms began to tell me it was Time to take Care of myſelf; wherefore I thought it not amiſs to confine myſelf theſe two Days, when by Abſtinence, and a little Self-Defence, I began to hope the worſt was over. Mr. *Bradley* called on me on *Saturday*, to let me know that he was going again to make a ſhort Trip to *Charles-Town*, if I had any Service that Way; and that he intended not to ſtay there above three or four Days; how far he meant as he ſaid, he beſt knew himſelf; the common Talk of the People was, that ſome of his beſt and choiceſt Goods were ſent before; ſuch as Scrutores, fine Tables and Chairs, May 25. 26.

1739. May with other faſhionable Furniture, which was moſtly the Operation of an ingenious Workman, whom either the Truſt or Mr. *Bradley* paid (I know not which) and was employed many Months on ſuch Curioſities; and as he had now but a ſmall Remainder of his Family left here, which I knew not when he meant ſhould follow the reſt, I had no great Inclination to commit my Packet to his Care, that I deſigned for *England*; but would rather take another Chance.

27. *Sunday.* Mr. *Haberſham*, as before, continued to read the Prayers and a Sermon; whilſt the Return of Mr. *Norris* began now to be thought long. In the Evening by a trading Boat arriving, bound up the River, I had Opportunity of ſending incloſed, under Cover, to Lieutenant *Kent* at *Auguſta*, a Letter from the General to Mr. *Willy* in the *Creek* Nation.

28. *Monday.* Nothing ſtirring that was worth Obſervation; only a Difference happening betwixt Captain *Davis*, Owner of a Snow laden with Lumber for the *Weſt-Indies*, which now lay at *Tybee* ready for ſailing, and the Maſter which he had put in her; it produced great Controverſy before the Magiſtrates, where many People had the Curioſity to attend; and both of them pleaded their Parts ſo well, that there was great Difficulty in ſo uncommon a Caſe to decide

decide it to general Satisfaction; neither was it ended the whole Day. 1739. May 29.

Tueſday. The Contention yet continuing as Yeſterday betwixt Captain *Davis* and the Maſter, whoſe Name was *Pope*; it may not be improper to take ſome Notice of the Cauſe whence it aroſe; which from what I could collect, was thus: *Davis* had newly built this Snow at *Port-Royal*, where *Pope*, who was a good Carpenter, as well as a good Seaman, had a good Hand in haſtening the Work, and getting her out to Sea; when by Promiſe before made from *Davis*, he took to her as Maſter, and brought her to *Savannah*, where *Davis* had made his Abode for ſome Time, and now was ſettling in good Earneſt, having lately the Favour of one of the beſt Lots on the Strand granted him by the General, whereon he was intending to build a Dwelling-Houſe and Store-Houſe, *&c.* being a Man who in all Appearance traded with the moſt Money of any that uſed the Place, and had generally three or four Sloops, Snows, or ſuch like Veſſels, going and coming betwixt theſe Parts and *Auguſtin*, the *Weſt-Indies*, or elſewhere, that he found moſt to his Advantage: In which Capacity he was looked on, and regarded, by all who wiſhed well to the Colony, as an uſeful Man to promote Traffick. But his moſt viſible Foible, was keeping a Mulatto

1739. May 29. latto Servant (or Slave) who in Reality was his Miſtreſs: For he had in former Years, by trading much in the hotteſt Parts of *America*, contracted ſuch Diſtempers, as well nigh bereft him of the Uſe of both his Legs and Arms: And this Girl (who was of an exceeding fine Shape, and ſetting aſide her ſwarthy Countenance, might compare with an *European)* was of much Uſe to him; not only as an Helper to put on his Cloaths, dreſs him, and look after his Linen, *&c.* which ſhe did to great Perfection; but having very good natural Parts alſo, and by Length of Time having obtained good Knowledge of his Buſineſs, and learnt to look into Accounts; he ſuffered almoſt every Thing to paſs through her Hands, having ſuch Confidence in her, that ſhe had the Cuſtody of all his Caſh, as well as Books; and whenever he ordered any Parcel of Silver to be weighed out for any Uſe, whether it were two or three hundred Ounces, more or leſs, in Dollars, ſhe had the doing of it: And as this had been the Courſe of ſeveral Years paſt, wherein he had found her very faithful, and of great Service to him; it may eaſily be ſuppoſed the Life of ſuch Slavery was not a heavy Burden upon her, and that ſhe had Art enough to ſhew, all Perſons who had any Buſineſs with Captain *Davis*, were expected not to treat her with Contempt.

Contempt. It ſo happened, that *Pope*, who is a rough Tar, and naturally ſurly, upon ſome Difference with this Damſel, made Uſe of ſome Words ſhe did not like; and ſhe wanted not to return in ſofter Terms what was not a Jot leſs provoking; whereupon he gave her a Stripe croſs the Face with her own Fan; and having raiſed ſuch a Flame in the Houſe, left it. The Snow was now at *Tybee* ready for ſailing, and Mr. *Robert Williams*, who had a good Share with *Davis* in the Loading, was intending, together with his Brother, to go Paſſengers to St. *Kit*'s, where, upon their Arrival, it was agreed, that *Williams* ſhould have the Direction of all Things, and to freight her from thence as he ſaw good, to what Port he thought moſt likely to turn to Account. This (it ſeems) was what *Pope* neither expected or liked, depending on it, that on the Delivery of the preſent Cargo at St. *Kit*'s, the whole Direction of all was to devolve to him, and that he was to be both Maſter and Supercargo; on which Occaſion ſome Words falling from him, which *Davis* could not well reliſh, and the Abuſe of Madam being alſo freſh in Memory, *Davis* told him he diſcharged him from being Maſter of the Snow; and that he was ready, upon making up his Accounts, to clear with him, and pay him what was owing for Wages: To which the other replied,

1739. May 29.

1739. May 29. replied, it was not in his Power to diſcharge him from the Ship in ſuch a Manner, neither would he ſubmit to it; and thereupon went haſtily to his Boat, in order to go immediately on board, and keep Poſſeſſion: To prevent which *Davis* and *Williams* with ſome others, went to the Guard, and deſired them to ſtop the Boat as ſhe was paſſing by; for that *Pope* was running away with the Boat, and afterwards with the Ship, in a piratical Manner. And the Guard finding upon hailing the Boat, that they reſolved to keep on their Way, did their Duty, and fired a Gun to bring them to; whereat they came aſhore. This was on *Sunday* Night laſt about Eleven a Clock; and the next Day Complaint on all Sides was made to the Magiſtrates, when the Complainants inveighed heavily againſt each other; but it was too knotty a Point for them to determine upon haſte, being doubtful of their own Knowledge; and informed moreover, that it ought regularly to be brought before the Admiralty; wherefore they proceeded no farther, than to direct *Pope* to make up his Accounts with *Davis* as faſt as he could; in order to which, his Cheſt was to be ſent for aſhore with his Papers; but he was not permitted to go aboard himſelf, without *Davis*'s Knowledge, fearing the Conſequence might be his going to Sea

Sea as ſoon as he ſat his Foot upon the Deck. So ended this Affair on *Monday:* And this Day divers Meetings were had again about it; when all Expectance of accommodating Matters were given over on both Sides; and hard Speeches, with Threats, ſucceeded. By this Time it began to be the Opinion of moſt Folk, that foraſmuch as Mr. *Robert Williams*'s Brother was to go a Paſſenger, who was a good Seaman, and had been Maſter of ſeveral Ships; it was thought expedient by them, that it would be well, as one of them had the Diſpoſal of the Cargo, the other alſo might have the Direction of the Ship as Maſter; in order to which Captain *Davis* had been perſuaded to lay hold of this Quarrel, and put *James Williams* in Maſter, in the Room of *Pope*, at ſo ſhort Warning. 1739. May

Wedneſday. The ſame Controverſy ſtill increaſing, drew the Attention of many People, eſpecially ſuch as made themſelves Partiſans in the Diſpute; but I did not want Employment any Day ſufficient to take up my Time, about my own proper Buſineſs, without meddling of what did not belong to me. *Pope* was now ready to make up his Accounts; but having the Regiſter of the Ship in his Poſſeſſion, could not be perſuaded to give up that, alledging, that there were ſeveral Bonds out againſt him, 30.

1739. May him, which he had entered into as Maſter; beſide, that the Sailors, who were all ſhipped by him, might come upon him for Wages for the Time he had been Maſter, in caſe they had not a Mind to re-ſhip themſelves under a new Maſter: Whereupon our naval Officer, Mr. *Fallowfield*, being out of Town, was ſent for in order to get a new Regiſter; and Mr. *Williams*, impatient at theſe Delays, brought an Action againſt *Pope* of ſeveral hundred Pounds Damages, for detaining Veſſel and Cargo; to anſwer which, *Pope* not readily finding Bail, Mr. *Parker* withdrew, not apprehending how ſuch Damages could enſue, by a Veſſel delayed a few Days, that was only loaden with Lumber; and Mr. *Gilbert* being likewiſe away, Mr. *Chriſtie* took the farther Proceedings on himſelf; and, at the Inſtance of the Complainants, committed *Pope* to Priſon, for not offering Bail.

31. *Thurſday*. All pretty quiet this Day: *Pope* ſhut up faſt, made an open Field for his Adverſaries to triumph in; and Mr. *Fallowfield* provided them with a new Regiſter, to Content. Very near a Fortnight was now paſt, ſince I had prepared a Packet for the Truſtees, to go by the Way of *Charles-Town*, or any other, if I could find it; but no Opportunity offered in all that Time, to my Sorrow, which I had too often experienced.

Friday.

Friday. Very early this Morning Mr. *Williams* and his Brother went for *Tybee*, in order to bring the Snow to ſail, which they ſeemed more than ordinary hurried in, upon ſome Intelligence they had got, that the Admiralty, at the Inſtance of *Pope*, were intending to ſtop the Veſſel. *Pope* was now out of Priſon, upon offering Bail; and reſolved not to ſit quiet without carrying Matters as far as he could: Wherefore he in his Turn alſo brought an Action of Damages to the Value of *l.* againſt *Davis*, which he likewiſe was to find Bail to; and ſo for the preſent this Diſpute ceaſed. Mr. *Parker* with me this Morning, complaining of Mr. *Jones*'s dealing ſo intolerably with him, that he could not bear it, and that his Servants whom the Truſt had ordered to be provided for, would be obliged to leave him, and get their Bread where they could, Mr. *Jones* refuſing to allow any Thing farther towards their Support; I told him, that as I knew nothing of the Rules Mr. *Jones* went by, nor what Orders he might be under about the Delivery of Stores; it would not become me to be too officiouſly meddling; but his proper Way, was to apply to the General, who was now in the Province, and was the only Perſon to judge what was proper in this Caſe, as well as all others that required immediate Determination; and therefore I

1739. June 1.

adviſed

1739. June advised to put what he had to say in Writing, and send it to him, not doubting but he would take it into Consideration.

2. *Saturday.* All People most worth regarding, looked peaceably after their own Affairs, and attended what would conduce to their Benefit; especially the Planters, whose present Care was to subdue the Weeds from annoying the Corn, *&c.* in its Growth; which my good Folk would have been well content to have allowed, unless quickened by frequent Inspection.

3. *Sunday.* That notorious Rogue *Isaac Bradford*, who was lately taken at *Charles-Town*, and brought back to Prison here, that he might answer for his Crimes at our Sessions (which were on his Account adjourned a while, till the principal Evidence against him returned, who at present was in the South) this Morning early found Means to break out of Prison; which gave Cause of Uneasiness to many People, who knowing him to be so dextrous and accomplished a Villain, expected more Mischief would be done, unless he could soon be taken; which there were but little Hopes of. It was most probable, that his Escape was owing to the Negligence of his Keeper, who had suffered several to get off in the same Manner; particularly the Ring-leader of those three Deserters from the Regiment, as formerly noted, who could never since be

be recovered. Mr. *Norris*'s Abode in the South yet, ſhewed that he was welcome there; and though he found ſome Marks of a cold Reception here at his firſt Arrival, from Cauſes that having been formerly taken Notice of, need not be again repeated (*vide October* 22.) yet his Abſence now was generally regretted to that Degree, that moſt People wiſhed apparently for his Continuance among us, and no more Changes. Mr. *Haberſham* in the mean while read the appointed Service of the Day, *&c.* as before. 1739. June

Monday. Bailiff *Parker* called on me in the Forenoon again, and now told me, that his Caſe was become ſo deſperate, as not to admit of any farther Delay, for that his Servants were upon leaving him, which muſt end in his own Deſtruction; for that his Plantation now to be neglected, muſt occaſion his irreparable Loſs, it being the principal Dependance he had for the next Year's Support of himſelf and Family; wherefore he was ſeeking to get a Boat and two or three Hands, which ſhould carry him to wait on the General wherever he could find him. My Son, who was daily more intent on his intended Voyage to *England*, but had yet taken no Step towards it; upon hearing this, concluded it a lucky Conjuncture for him; foraſmuch as he would by no Means ſtir in it, till he had 4.

1739. June firſt paid his Duty to the General, and thought he now had the faireſt Opportunity he could wiſh: Wherefore he preſently laid hold of it; and Mr. *Parker* and he agreeing upon it together, whilſt I ſat ſtill and ſaid nothing; in the Cool of the Evening they both ſet out for *Frederica*.

5. *Tueſday*. Nothing particularly worth remembring happened this whole Day, that came to my Knowledge.

6. *Wedneſday*. *Peter Emery* arrived with his Boat from *Charles-Town*, and brought two ſmall Packets, which the Attorney-General ſent me, that he had by two Ships newly arrived; and wrote a ſhort Letter with them, adviſing me, that one of thoſe Ships came by Way of *Madera*, and the other in ſix Weeks from *London*; by which he found he might expect ſome more Letters by another Ship which ſailed ſome Days before *him*. In theſe Packets were Letters for the General, *&c.* and one for me from Mr. *Verelſt* of the 15th of *February*; incloſing Copy of the Minutes on Mr. *Cookſey*'s Petition, and referring ſeveral Reſolutions taken thereon by the Common-Council, for me to enquire into Facts, and report them to the honourable Truſtees. Mr. *Verelſt* was pleaſed alſo to ſignify to me, the favourable Diſpoſition of thoſe Gentlemen, to gratify my Requeſt formerly made, concerning *Joſeph Watſon*'s five

five hundred Acre-Lot; which I had wrote them he never had a Grant of, nor ſhewed any Regard to; and at that Time I had a great Inclination to fix upon, for Reaſons then given; wherefore they were now pleaſed to direct, that I ſhould ſtate the Caſe with reſpect to *Watſon*'s Pretenſions to it, or the Value of any Improvements made upon it. Mr. *Vereſt* farther added, that my Journals and Letters to *November* 21, were come to Hand, and would be anſwered by the *Mary Ann*, Captain *Shubrick*, who has been arrived at *Carolina* ſeveral Weeks ſince, and is now at *Frederica* (as I hear) but no News of any Letters by him for me yet. 1739. June

Thurſday. Underſtanding early in the Morning, that a Boat was ſetting out South by Order of Mr. *Jones*, who (it was ſaid) intended to go as far as *Skeedoway*, expecting there to find Captain *Deſbraſſie*, &c. on their Return to St. *Simon*'s from *Port-Royal*; and Information coming Yeſterday, that the Scout-Boat thoſe Gentlemen went in, was ſeen to turn in at *Auguſtin Creek*, making their Way South: Thereupon I would not let ſo fair an Opportunity ſlip, of ſending thoſe Letters to the General, *&c.* which I received Yeſterday; but putting them all under one Cover, directed to the General at St. *Simon*'s, I ſent my Packet to Mr. *Jones*'s Care; writing alſo therewith, 7.

1739. June a few Lines to the General from myſelf. Afterwards I went to make my People a Viſit, and ſee how well they followed their Work, in fulfilling the laſt Directions given them; and here I employed good Part of my Time this Day.

Friday. Mr. *Jones* returned this Morning from *Skeedoway*, where he miſſed Captain *Deſbraſſie*, who continued yet at *Port-Royal*; but found Lieutenant *Delegal*, who was going South with the Boat; to whom he told me he had given Charge of my Packet to the General, together with others Letters. What the Occaſion of this ſecret Expedition was, I could not learn. Mr. *Haberſham*, the School-Maſter, having received a large Packet of Letters from Mr. *Whitfield*, by the ſame Ship that brought thoſe I received on *Wedneſday* laſt, directed to many People in the Town; among whom I was one; he went with particular Delight to deliver them, and rejoice at the good News of Mr. *Whitfield*'s being appointed to return again to his former Charge at *Savannah*, which thoſe Letters from him imported. As to myſelf, I muſt own, that it was a Matter of more Indifference; for as I thought Mr. *Whitfield*, when among us, took great Pains in preaching God's Word, and doing his Duty; ſo I cannot ſay Mr. *Norris* was defective in his; and as he was particularly recommended by the honourable

honourable Truſtees, for being a Perſon of very good Qualifications, ſo I found him; and in Obedience to their Orders, gladly did what lay in my Power to promote a good Opinion of him among the People at his firſt coming; which by his good Conduct he had now well eſtabliſhed. 1739. June

Saturday. Captain *Hunt*, Maſter of a Brigantine that traded to theſe Parts from *New-York*, arrived from St. *Simon's* again, where he had been once before, offering his Cargo to Sale; but having (it ſeems) ſome Rum on board him, which he ſaid he was bound to *Providence* with; the General was ſo offended at his daring Preſumption to bring it into Harbour, that he would not allow him to diſpoſe of any other Goods among them; wherefore after having been and diſpoſed of his Rum elſewhere, he made this ſecond Offer to ſell the reſt of his Cargo; but in that, he did not yet ſucceed, the late Offence given being too freſh in Memory: Nevertheleſs, it was manifeſt (as I thought) that moſt of the Loading was diſpoſed of ſome how or another, by the Veſſel's appearing ſo much lighter in the Water, than ſhe formerly did. He brought no Letters, except one for Mr. *Jones*; nor any particular Advices, only that our Miniſter, Mr. *Norris*, was ſoon coming to us again, in order to take Leave of his Friends. 9.

1739. June 10. *Sunday.* Mr. *Haberſham* continued the publick Service of the Church, Morning and Afternoon; and took Occaſion to read an Epiſtle he had received from Mr. *Whitfield*, who had directed him to do it publickly to the Congregation; wherein he acquainted them with his being appointed their Miniſter, that he was returning to them ſoon, and exhorted them to bear in Mind the Doctrine he had formerly preached among them, *&c.* In the Evening arrived *Dondonald Stewart*, with his ſmall Sloop from *Frederica*; where he had been ſome Time to attend Mr. *Brownfield*, carrying divers Goods thither to diſpoſe of; and now Mr. *Norris*, our Miniſter, returned with him; who reported, that he had been exceeding kindly treated by the People there, in every Reſpect; and that the General had been pleaſed to give him great Countenance and Marks of Eſteem. He acquainted me, that Captain *Shubrick* had been there ſeveral Days, delivering what was committed to his Charge from the Truſt; and brought me a Packet from them, which was given to the Captain's Care; wherein I found divers Letters for ſeveral People, and one from Mr. *Verelſt* of *March* 3, which contained ſome weighty Matters that would require due Conſideration and Obedience, *&c.* But it was not in my Power to write any Thing immediately

diately about it to the Truſt, having delivered to *Peter Emery* a Packet, which he was to proceed with to-morrow Morning early for *Charles-Town* (on various Buſineſs of other People) and glad I was at laſt, after three Weeks Waiting, to catch this Opportunity; ſo uncertain and rare does any happen, to keep a due Correſpondence with *England.* The Packet that I now ſent, was directed (by a Letter I ſent with it) to the Care of Mr. *Hopton,* whom always I found very punctual in diſpatching whatever came to his Hand; and the laſt which I ſent, he had the good Luck to forward the ſame Day he received it, by Captain *Watts* in the *Greyhound,* dated *April* 21, as this was *May* 19. 1739. June

Whit-Monday. High Holy-Day among moſt of our common People in Town; but ſuch as were concerned in planting, could ſpare no Time from cloſe Attendance in dreſſing their Land, to preſerve the Fruit of the Ground from being over-run with Weeds. 11.

Tueſday. Captain *Wood* of *Frederica* having been ſome Time at *Charles-Town* on Account of Traffick; on his Return, ſtopt here ſince *Sunday* laſt; by whom I took Occaſion to write to the General, and ſend ſeveral other Letters, which I gave him before his Departure. *Duchee* the Potter, who I formerly took Notice had agreed 12.

1739. June with the General, to build a Wharf under our Bluff, for the better Landing of Goods, having framed moſt of it, began to ſet it up; but for many Days paſt, finding many Difficulties in fixing a certain Foundation in the looſe Sand, without Piles; and often altering his Purpoſe, now ſeemed determined how to proceed, in the Manner we ſaw; which from what I could judge, as well as many others of better Experience in ſuch Works, did not promiſe any long Duration, for divers Reaſons which I thought were apparent.

13. *Wedneſday.* Several *Indian* Traders began now to apply for Licences; ſome to obtain new, and ſome to renew their old ones: Wherein it was my Duty to acquaint the General with the Circumſtances as I found them, and take his Orders. I learnt by moſt of them, that divers of the Nations began to ſeek Occaſion of falling out with one another: Better ſo, than by too long Peace among themſelves, to differ with us, whoſe Buſineſs it is to avoid taking Part with one or the other, or meddling in their Quarrels (at leaſt openly.)

14. *Thurſday.* Devoted this Day almoſt wholly to my little Plantation; wherein falling ſo far ſhort of the Number of Acres I had laſt Year, through the Defect of bad Servants, that inſtead of fifteen, I could not reckon fully ten; I made it my Care, that

that what I had, ſhould be at leaſt as well dreſſed and cultivated as any of my Neighbours: And the Crop this Year generally promiſing very well, I concluded I ſhould have as great a Produce, at leaſt, as laſt Year, out of a larger Piece of Ground, when a dry Seaſon and bad Seed was a great Baulk to moſt People: And from hence alſo I concluded a pretty juſt Eſtimate might be made hereafter, of what might be expected by a diligent Planter, if the Land were reaſonably good, to pay him for his Labour. 1739. June

Friday. Little in Town worth Notice. In ſome Converſation with Mr. *Norris*, I found he was ſomewhat uneaſy at his Appointment here being ſuperſeded by the honourable Truſtees, to make Way for Mr. *Whitfield*, who (he ſaid) had found Means to ſupplant him; which he thought little agreed with that open Simplicity which was made ſo diſtinguiſhing a Part of his Character, by his Intimates at this Place; who with the like Candour had done what in them lay, to leſſen *him* in the good Opinion of the People, though not with that Succeſs they expected; for he muſt do them the Juſtice to acknowledge, he had found a kind Reception from the Generality, and a Readineſs to attend the publick Service; wherefore he was ſorry to leave them: Nevertheleſs he ſhould continue 15.

1739. June nue doing his Duty, till Mr. *Whitfield* ſhowed him his Authority to take his Place; and then (he ſeemed determined) upon quitting it, to quit *America* with it. I told him I was very ſorry to hear that; for indeed I thought him a valuable Man, of good Endowments, conſtant in his Duty, exceeding affable and courteous, and wholly inoffenſive in his Behaviour throughout: Wherefore I would perſuade him not to reſolve too haſtily in it, ſince I was confident the Truſtees meant it as no Diſfavour towards him, and without Doubt would have an equal kind Regard to him whatever Part of the Province he reſided in: Which he ſaid little to at preſent, and ſo we parted.

16. *Saturday.* Arrived a Pettyagua from *Frederica*, moſtly laden with Corn; which ſurely was the firſt Inſtance of that Kind; and it would have been indeed worth noting, had it been the Produce of the South; but that Time is not yet come, nor (it is to be hoped) will *Savannah* ſuffer her younger Siſter to contribute more to her Support, than ſhe has done for herſelf, or will do hereafter. This Corn (as the Maſter reported) came from the Northern Settlements in *Carolina*; and the Stores being pretty well provided in the South, it was ordered, without landing there, to come to the Aid of thoſe who ſtood in Need of it

it in *Savannah*; where (be it as it would) it was exceeding welcome, to People who at that Time were in Want of Bread. 1739. June

Sunday. Mr. *Norris* officiated regularly at Church, and adminiſtred the Sacrament; which he was prevented from doing the *Sunday* before, by a long Paſſage from *Frederica* by Water. 17.

Monday. Spent ſome Time again with my People abroad, giving what Directions were needful. The late Rains we had, which were ſo ſeaſonable and refreſhing, began now to come on in ſo great Abundance, having continued daily, more or leſs, for three Weeks paſt, that ſeveral of our Plantations in the low Lands were overflowed, and the Corn (we feared) was in Danger of ſuffering Damage. Mr. *Bradley* returned home from his late Expedition to *Charles-Town*, where his Buſineſs was known to himſelf only. In the Evening my Son alſo, and Mr. *Parker*, returned from the South; where I before took Notice of the Occaſion of their going (*vide* 4th Inſtant.) Mr. *Parker* found his Ends in ſome Meaſure anſwer'd, by ſome preſent kind Relief from the General, who promiſed him to take it into farther Conſideration, as ſoon as he came to *Savannah*, which he deſigned the Beginning of next Month; from whence he intended to take a farther Progreſs into ſome of the *Indian* 18.

Nations,

1739. June 18. Nations, where we heard he was earneſtly expected, and his Preſence would be of great Uſe, at this Time eſpecially, when the *French* and *Spaniards* were buſy infuſing what Miſchief they could, by endeavouring to alienate their Affections from us. My Son, I found, had little Satisfaction from his Journey; the General, he ſaid, retained yet a ſtrong Suſpicion of his being an Accomplice in ſome intended Fraud, about thoſe Wines of the Truſtees, remaining in *Bradley*'s Cellar; notwithſtanding that full and open Examination made into it, as related on 21 *ult.* when there appeared not the leaſt Room for any Suſpicion of ſuch a vile Practice; from whence my Son concluded his Character was ſo deeply ſtained by Mr. *Jones*, that he deſpaired of ever ſetting it right again with the General, which ſat very heavy upon him; and indeed affected me alſo now pretty much, to ſee a young Man (my Son) whom I knew to be endued with a virtuous Diſpoſition, and ſcorn'd to be guilty of baſe Acts, and uſing little mean Arts to conceal them; but was always open and honeſt, and dared be ſo, whomſoever he might give Offence to, through Want of Caution perhaps in his Words: To ſee him ſo ill treated by a Perſon whom he neither deſerved, nor expected it from (I mean Mr. *Jones*) it put me upon a little Reflexion

Reflexion on divers former Paſſages betwixt him and me; where he had too plainly diſcovered (as I thought) what an Opinion he had conceived of my Abilities, ſo far ſhort of his own, whoſe Vanity led him to imagine he ſaw clearly to the Bottom of other Peoples Capacities, whilſt his was unfathomable; which Conceit of his, he was welcome to enjoy; but when thoſe boaſted Talents, in Contempt of all others, are employed to the Injury of ſuch as have done no Ill, but perhaps ſtand ſuſpected by him, that they may poſſibly in Time be looked on too favourably; to get rid of ſuch, may, for ought I know, require the Skill of a Man of deep Reach (an Expreſſion he is very fond of) but I fear it will in Juſtice require another Name. In ſhort, I began to think it was Time for me no longer to look on Mr. *Jones* a Friend to me, or mine; which would have been no Ways incompatible, as I apprehend, with either of our Duties to the Truſt, whom we ſerved. 1739. June

Tueſday. Mr. *Obrien*, a Keeper of Stores at *New-Windſor*, coming to Town laſt Night, called on me, and brought with him ſeveral Licences from ſome of our *Indian* Traders, to be renewed in this Province; which I would lay before the General, together with ſome others of the like Sort for his Direction; to whom I 19.

wrote

1739. June 19. wrote in the Evening, and ſent it by Mr. *Phelps*, a Keeper of Stores with us, who was to ſet out early for the South, glad of ſuch an Opportunity, which I would not miſs, not knowing when I might find another. Mr. *Parker* came and told me, that he had been with Mr. *Jones*, to confer with him on what the General had ſaid at *Frederica*; when Mr. *Jones* took out ſome ſola Bills; (Part of them which the Truſtees wrote were to be iſſued by Mr. *Jones*, Mr. *Parker*, and myſelf, or any two of us) deſiring he would ſign them; which Mr. *Parker* ſaid he demurred at, aſking him if he had offered any of them to me for that Purpoſe; by whom he was informed of the Truſtees Orders; which were, that the Bills to be iſſued by any two of us three, were likewiſe to be accounted for by them that iſſued them, who were to certify what Uſes the Produce of ſaid Bills had been applied to; which he did not conceive was poſſible to be done, when the Bills ſo ſigned, were no longer within his Cognizance how diſpoſed of. Though I heard, that Mr. *Jones* had a conſiderable Quantity of thoſe Bills by him for ſome Days paſt, I was no Ways diſturbed at not being taken any Notice of about them, ſo far was I from coveting to meddle with Matters that were not well underſtood at preſent, and might ſubject me to great Inconveniencies hereafter, in accounting for. 1739.

Wedneſday. This Morning I underſtood that Mr. *Jones* went off very early for *Frederica*, to wait on the General; that he went out of Town on Horſeback, in Company with two or three others, among whom Mr. *Phelps* was one, to whom I had given my Letters laſt Night, knowing no better; that they intended to ride ſo far as Mr. *Fallowfield*'s Plantation, to which Place they had ſent a Boat round to meet them. About Noon Mr. *Upton* arrived from the South, who brought no Advice of any Kind for me; but had a Letter for Mr. *Jones*, whom he miſſed meeting by the Way: He had the Pleaſure to tell me, that the General had been very kind to him, in taking the Land off his Hands, which had been granted him near *Frederica*, and made him a new Grant on the Iſland called *Allhony*, lying a little beyond *Skeedoway* Southward: That what he had done on his other Plantation, he was to be paid for as ſhould be valued, which the General would convert to pious Uſes, *&c.* More *Indian* Traders were now frequently coming, this being the uſual Seaſon of the Year for granting Licences: Two ſuch were with me this Day, who were told by me, the General intending to be here very ſoon himſelf, it would be needleſs to write June 20.

to

1739. June to him any more about thoſe Matters, which he would give his Directions about when he came.

21. *Thurſday.* Heavy Rains continued to fall daily, which would admit of very little Attendance from any at their Plantations, and began to raiſe fearful Apprehenſions of much Damage. Time paſt ſince the Date of my laſt Packet to the Truſt, put me in Mind that another might be now expected; wherefore I began to prepare what was needful, and ſtirred but little from home, nor did I hear any Thing worth regarding abroad.

22. *Friday.* Buſy good Part of the Day in finiſhing my Diſpatches for *England.* It was currently reported about Town, that we might have had a little Money circulating among us, had not I been the Occaſion of the contrary, by refuſing to ſign the iſſuing of a great many ſola Bills, which had been offered me by Mr. *Jones:* Whereat I was the leſs ſurprized, expecting ſome ſuch malicious Turn might be given to what paſſed betwixt Meſſieurs *Parker* and *Jones* on the 19th, wherein I was no Party, nor had any Bills been offered me; but *Parker*'s refuſing was conſtrued by Mr. *Jones* my Advice; though in Truth I had not any Way conſulted *Parker*, nor knew any Thing that paſſed, till Mr. *Parker* informed me of it; when I muſt confeſs I told

told him that I thought the Anſwer he had given Mr. *Jones* was right. From hence I had Reaſon to imagine, that Mr. *Jones*'s ſudden Expedition South aroſe from theſe Grounds. 1739. June

Saturday. Nothing obſervable happened this Day; but late in the Evening arrived a Pettyagua, ſent by the Attorney-General, with two Men and five Women from *Saltzburgh*, together with ſundry Goods, which he wrote me were lately arrived *per* Captain *Harramond*, and conſigned to him by the Truſt, with their Direction to forward them to Mr. *Jones*; whereof he was to give me Notice, *viz*. eighty Barrels of Flour, thirty Caſks of Butter, fourteen of Cheeſe, and a Box of Books for Mr. *Norris*: With theſe came alſo a large Packet from the Truſt to me, wherein I found great Store of Letters; ſome for theſe Parts, and many more for the South; eſpecially divers for the General: What concerned me particularly was a Letter from Mr. *Verelſt* of the 2d of *April*, ſignifying the Pleaſure of the honourable Truſtees in divers Matters of Importance; wherein they required me to act in Conjunction with Mr. *Parker*, *Jones*, &c. *invicem*, as Occaſion required: And withal had ſent a Commiſſion, empowering us three to examine and ſtate the Truth of ſundry Accounts, certified by Mr. *Cauſton* to be owing from the Truſt: More- 23.

1739. June 23. over to examine and ſtate the ſeveral Debts owing by the Store in *Georgia* the 10th of *October* laſt; with which Commiſſion came alſo Inſtructions for executing it, and for examining and ſtating the Accounts of Meſſieurs *Cauſton* and *Bradley:* Theſe were Matters of ſo great Moment, that I had not Confidence ſufficient in my own Abilities, to acquit myſelf, as I wiſhed to do; but reſolved to ſhew my Good-will towards it as well as I could, in not declining to act as far as my Underſtanding would admit. By ſeveral Paſſages in this Letter, I was now fully convinced, that I had not miſconſtrued the former Directions ſent to Mr. *Parker* and me, relating to our joint iſſuing, together with Mr. *Jones*, divers ſola Bills; as *per* Mr. *Verelſt*'s Letter of the 3d of *March*; which Mr. *Jones* told Mr. *Parker*, we had no more to do with, than only to ſign our Names (*vide* 19th Inſtant;) for now we were plainly appointed to cheque the Delivery of not only thoſe Stores now ſent, but alſo the Remains of all others. As Mr. *Jones* was now in the South attending the General, and we ſhould probably (I thought) ſee upon his Return, what the General's Inſtructions to him were, relating to thoſe Bills, *&c.* and his Excellence being alſo expected very ſoon himſelf, I moſt heartily wiſhed to find the Way made plain wherein I was to walk, that I might

might not be ſubject to ſtumble ſo frequently, and in Danger of falling into Diſpleaſure, do what I could. 1739. June

Sunday. Mr. *Norris* did his Duty at Church as became a good Man; and after the publick Service was over, I thought it no Breach of the Sabbath, to divulge the welcome News I had received of the honourable Truſtees being about preparing an Act, to enable the Poſſeſſors of Land in *Georgia*, in caſe of Want of Iſſue Male, to diſpoſe of it by Deed or Will to their Daughters, or for Want of ſuch, to their other Relations, and their Iſſue Male, *&c.* Such Tidings ſoon ſpread thro' the Town; nor would it be unknown long in all Parts of the Province, to the great Joy of many People: And (if I may venture to ſpeak ſo plain, without giving Offence) I am fully perſuaded in myſelf, that the ſame Act of Grace a few Months ago, would have produced a hundred Acres at leaſt of Corn more than we can now find is planted in this Part of the Colony this Year; and I am very confident a viſible good Effect will ariſe from it in another. 24.

Monday. This being the Grand Anniverſary of the Free Maſons every where (as it is ſaid) the Brethren with us would not let it paſs without due Obſervance: Mr. *Norris* accordingly was aſked to give them a Sermon, which had been cuſto- 25.

1739. June mary with his Predeceſſors; and he made them an ingenious Diſcourſe, with a decent and proper Application: From Church they marched in ſolemn Order to Dinner at a publick Houſe, the Warden Dr. *Tailfer* (who likes Pre-eminence as well as any Man) attended by four or five with Wands, and red Ribbands in their Boſoms, as Badges of their ſeveral Offices, took Place foremoſt; but the Train that followed in white Gloves and Aprons, amounted only to about Half a Dozen more; which ſome, who are apt to burleſque the Order, turned into Ridicule. My principal Affair this Day was, to ſend off thoſe Packets and Letters to the General which I received on *Saturday*; wherein I met with no ſmall Trouble: None that I could apply to, would go without ready Money; till at laſt I prevailed with one to undertake it, upon my perſonal Engagement to be his Pay-Maſter, and then he went.

26. *Tueſday*. Meſſieurs *Samuel Brown* and *McBane*, two *Indian* Traders, came to Town from *Auguſta* laſt, and brought me a Letter from Lieutenant *Kent* there; together with one *Wright*, whom Mr. *Kent* wrote he had ſent a Priſoner; having lately taken him, and was the ſame who was taken up laſt Summer, committed to Priſon here, and broke out of Goal on the 25th of *July* with *Hetherington*, *Biſhop*, &c. But

But in their Way down the River now, a fatal Accident happened to one *Evans*, who was one of the two ſent to guard the Priſoner; his Gun by ſome Means unknown going off, killed him outright; which was the more to be lamented, for that he was a ſober, diligent young Man, well looked on by all that knew him, was lately out of his Servitude, and gave more promiſing Hopes of future Good to be expected from him, than too many do. A great Misfortune of another Kind, came to our Knowledge alſo; which was, that very much Damage was done to the Goods which came by the Pettyagua on *Saturday*, and which was now unloading: The Flour and Cheeſe eſpecially appeared ſo damnified, that it was feared little or none of it could be ſaved, the Wet having gone to the very Heart of the Caſks; from whence it was the Opinion of the moſt knowing People here, that the Damage was done at Sea; for it is univerſally agreed, that a Caſk of Flour well packed, though it ſtand ſeveral Days in the Rain (as this did in an open Pettyagua) yet will not take wet more than an Inch in; but this in general appeared muſty and ſtinking to the Centre of it, where they bored to try; from whence it is judged it muſt have lain in Water in the Ship's Hold. I adviſed, that two or three Men of honeſt Characters, and good

1739. June 26.

1739. June Underſtanding, among whom one to be a Baker, ſhould take a Survey of it all upon Oath: Such being found, and looking into ſeveral Caſks before they were ſworn, they reported to me, that the whole Cargo of Flour and Cheeſe was loſt; which I was not ſo ſatisfied in, but to tell them, that till they had ſtripped the Caſks off, and gone to the Heart of it, and reported then upon Oath as they found it, I thought it was of no Significance: Whereupon, as Mr. *Jones* was expected ſoon, who was not yet returned from *Frederica*, they were of Opinion it would be beſt to wait his coming; which I had no Objection to, the Goods being all carried into the Store, and a Receipt given to the Maſter of the Petty-agua for the whole Cargo much damaged, by —— *Harris*, who acts under Mr. *Jones*; as he told me himſelf. I fear no Care was taken at *Charles-Town*, upon taking the Goods out of the Ship, to ſee whether or not they came in good Order and well conditioned, as in the Bill of Lading: And if ſo, it is farther to be doubted if Satisfaction for the Damage will with great Difficulty be come at.

27. *Wedneſday*. Little to be done in Town; wherefore I took Occaſion to look again into what my few Hands were doing at my Plantation; which I found drenched with Water by the heavy Rains, which had

had fallen for ſo long a while paſt, and did not yet ceaſe in frequent Showers; but we hoped yet upon Change of Weather, to find the Corn recover. Fevers began now to grow riſe, occaſioned by a thick, unwholſome Air, and ſultry Heat; but they did not yet prove very mortal: Only Mr. *Bradley* lay dangerouſly ill, in one that he brought home with him. 1739. June

Thurſday. Not the leaſt Appearance this whole Day of any Thing worth taking any Notice of. 28.

Friday. The ſame. Mr. *Jones* ſtaying ſo long from home, gave Occaſion to many of thinking that he would return when the General came, and not before; and as I had good Reaſon to believe, that the Diſpatches from the Truſt, *&c.* which I ſent off on *Monday* laſt, were now before the General; I hoped he would ſo well conſider of thoſe Directions I had received from the Truſt, that I might be under no Miſtake in the Conſtruction of them, nor become liable to any Blame for not executing them. 29.

Saturday. All Things ſeemed at a Stand, and ſcarcely any Body ſtirring. The Stores had no Fleſh Proviſion of any Kind to give out to the *German* Truſt Servants, who were ill ſatisfied to live upon Bread Kind alone, till better could be; tho' it was too evident, that the Bread they eat, was more 30.

1739. June 30. than they earned; and many poor People in Town (that I knew) were hard put to it to provide *that* for themſelves. Some proper Courſe, without Doubt, would be taken by the General when he came, to make ſuch Proviſion for the future, as he ſhould think neceſſary. This proving a fine Day, and the only one without Rain for a long while paſt, we hoped good Summer Weather was coming ſeaſonably, to ripen the Fruits of the Earth.

July 1. *Sunday.* The publick Service was performed by Mr. *Norris* with due Decency: About Noon happened a moſt violent Tornado, with ſuch a Guſt of Wind and Rain, as we had ſcarcely ſeen the like, holding for about Half an Hour; in which Time ſeveral of the Huts and weaker Buildings about Town were blown down, and even the ſtrongeſt ſhook, ſo that we were apprehenſive of much Miſchief; and there was Reaſon to fear, that we ſhould find a great deal of the ſtrongeſt Corn blown down.

2. *Monday.* People upon a Review of what Damages the Storm Yeſterday might occaſion, had the Satisfaction to find it much ſhort of their Fear; ſo that the old Adage of being more afraid than hurt, was literally verified: And the Weather again promiſing fair in Appearance, we hoped the foul had taken its Leave in this laſt Effort.

Effort. Many *Indian* Traders were now in Town, in order to get Licences; for which End they waited the General's Arrival, whom, together with Mr. *Jones*, we looked for every Day. Several printed Papers (being Extracts of the *Weekly Miſcellany* in *London*, N° 320.) were ſent from *Charles-Town* by ſome Perſons there, to their Acquaintance here; in which Mr. *Whitfield* particularly, as well as the whole Sect of Methodiſts, were ſo animadverted on, that it was like to be the Entertainment of moſt publick Converſation, for ſome Time; and appeared to be an odd Preparative for Mr. *Whitfield*'s Reception, whenever he came. It is ſaid, that Mr. *Cookſey* brought over a Number with him when he came to *Charles-Town* lately; where I am informed he has taken up his Reſidence, and bid Adieu to *Georgia*, for ſome Time at leaſt. 1739. July

Tueſday. *John Penroſe*, whom I hired to go with his Boat on the 25th *ult.* for *Frederica*, and carry that Packet to the General, now returned, and brought me a ſhort Letter from Mr. *Jones*, ſignifying, that the General intended to ſet out from *Frederica* as Yeſterday, or this Day at fartheſt, in his Way hither, and thence up into ſome of the Nations; ſo that we looked for him now every Day. Hearing that one Mr. *Cattle* was in Town, who is 3.

1739. July a Merchant in *Charles-Town*, I found him, and aſked the Favour of him to carry a ſmall Packet, which I had for Mr. *Vereſt*, deſiring he would deliver it to Mr. *Hopton*'s Care, whom I alſo wrote to with it; and he readily promiſed me to do it, intending to be going very early to-morrow Morning. *N. B.* This was the Packet which I incloſed on the 22d *ult.* and this was the firſt Opportunity I could find ſince of ſending it.

4. *Wedneſday.* Rain ceaſing now for two or three Days, and hot Weather ſucceeding, as in this Part of the Year might be expected, the Waters began to ſink away, which had overflowed the low Lands, and done much Damage in ſome Places; but there remained ſtill an Appearance of a plentiful Crop in general, though ſome few might ſuffer Loſs. The printed Paper mentioned two Days ſince to have been made publick among us, began to ſhew the Effect that I expected it would produce; People of all Ranks engaging fiercely in Diſputes (as is too common in religious Matters) and it was pretty difficult for any one to avoid diſcovering his Sentiments therein, howſoever cautious he might be, not to meddle in Controverſy: Whilſt it afforded Sport, not only to *Jews* and *Deiſts*, but many of our Proteſtant Diſſenters from the Church of *England*, could not but

but ſneer at ſuch Diviſions. It ought nevertheleſs to be obſerved, that Mr. *Norris* manifeſted a meek Diſpoſition, and Deſire to promote Peace, without offering to blemiſh the Character of his Succeſſor, whom (he ſaid) he was ready to ſurrender to, as ſoon as he ſhewed his Authority from the Truſtees. This was what only I thought worth Notice this Day, and wiſhed it leſs, for I feared great Diſcord enſuing. 1739. July

Thurſday. An uncertain Report going about for two Days paſt, of a Man being drowned, or ſome how loſt, out of a Sloop lying at Anchor here; whereof Captain *Davis* had two now, which he intended to ſend abroad on ſome Trade or other; Providence ſo ordered it, that the Corpſe floated this Morning, and was brought aſhore, and left by the Tide very near us on the Strand: Whereupon the Recorder, who acted as Coroner, ſummoned a Jury, who upon Inſpection of the Body, with the Aſſiſtance of two experienced Surgeons that probed ſeveral Wounds given, brought in their Verdict *Wilful Murder*, by Perſons yet unknown to them. It appeared, that a certain Perſon who was ſaid to have had ſome Contention with the Deceaſed on board, ſome Days ago, was now miſſing, and gone out of the Way, ſuppoſed to be fled; and there were ſome Circumſtances by which divers were apt to imagine, that the 5.

1739. July the Maſter of the Sloop himſelf (one *Brixy)* was not wholly guiltleſs, but at leaſt knew of what was done, and never diſcovered it: No poſitive Evidence yet however appeared, ſufficient to found a Charge againſt him; but it was to be hoped by ſome Means or other ſo baſe a Murder would ere long come to Light, and the Authors meet with due Juſtice: In the Interim the Maſter of the Sloop, and two of his Men, who were under the ſtrongeſt Suſpicion, from what the Mate depoſed, *(viz.* that they had been all quarrelling) were confined, till it could be ſeen what farther Evidence might appear; and due Courſe was alſo taken, that ſuch Evidence as could be come at, ſhould be forth coming when required.

6. *Friday.* To-morrow being the Anniverſary of the Day, when the firſt Court was holden at *Savannah*, proper Care was taken to ſummon a Grand Jury, and to open it as cuſtomary at the ſtated Time. Nothing fell within my Knowledge, that I thought deſerved any Remark; and I reſolved not to meddle in any Contention touching our future ſpiritual Welfare, which at preſent was the Employment of more Tongues, than would be of any good Uſe, as I thought.

7. *Saturday.* The Court ſat, the Grand Jury was ſworn, received a proper Charge, and

and had divers Matters committed to their Conſideration: After which the Court adjourned till next *Thurſday*; before which Time we hoped to ſee the General, who was looked for with ſome Appearance of Certainty this Day; but in vain. 1739. July

Sunday. Mr. *Norris* officiated, and the publick Service was performed with due Decency. Information being made, late in the Evening Yeſterday, againſt a Perſon now in Town, for uttering ſome Words among the Soldiers (where he had been lately) magnifying the good Living of the *Spaniſh* Troops at *Auguſtin*, in Compariſon of the ſhort Allowance of ours here, *&c.* tending to their Diſcouragement; he was ordered into the Cuſtody of our Guard, where he was detained, in order to make a full Examination into it to-morrow. 8.

Monday. The firſt News I met with this Morning was, that the Fellow who was taken into Cuſtody Yeſterday (whoſe Name was *Kipp)* was gone off, and not to be found. Upon Enquiry I underſtood, that the Foundation of committing him, appearing doubtful, foraſmuch as it aroſe only from the Report of a Perſon in Town, newly returned from *Frederica*, and no Information given upon Oath; Mr. *Chriſtie* thought proper to give him the Liberty of walking about Town, upon one of the Freeholders engaging for his Appearance: 9.

But

1739. July But now his going off in ſuch a Manner, carried in it ſuch a Shew of Guilt, that a Hue and Cry was ſent out, to take him if they could. Our Expectations of ſeeing the General this Day were again baulked; but in the Evening Mr. *Jones* came, whom we looked on at this Time as his Forerunner; and told us he believed he would be with us to-morrow.

10. *Tueſday.* The Court ſat, and received from the Grand Jury ſuch Indictments and Preſentments as they had prepared; among which were three Indictments they had found againſt ſome of the Perſons concerned in the late Murder, whereof one was againſt *Brixy* the Maſter of the Sloop. In the Evening the General arrived from the South, and was received under a Diſcharge of the Cannon, and about forty of the Freeholders under Arms; which he was pleaſed to ſay, was more than he expected not run away.

11. *Wedneſday.* Upon my acquainting the General (among other Things) with what Circumſtances Matters appeared relating to the Murder, which were very ſtrong, but no poſitive Evidence of Fact; he was of Opinion not to proceed too haſtily on the Trial, but poſtpone it for a while, in Hopes of making the Proof clear; and I acquainted the Magiſtrates with it, who thereupon adjourned the Court to *Monday*

next. My Duty requiring cloſe Attendance on his Excellence, to learn his Pleaſure, moſt Part of the Day was ſo taken up; when he was pleaſed to diſcourſe freely, and lay open his Sentiments on divers Matters of great Importance. 1739. July

Thurſday. The General's Stay among us being very likely to be ſhort, many People ſucceſſively ſought Audience of him, on various Occaſions; whom he diſpatched in ſuch Manner as he ſaw good: But as he called on me pretty frequently, either to give Direction, or enquire into ſuch Matters as he thought proper; it behoved me to be near at Hand, ſo that I ſaw little of what paſſed elſewhere in Town. Upon a Survey of the Flour lately imported, it was found totally bad, and ſtinking; inſomuch that it was believed to be old caſt Goods when ſhipped, that were impoſed villanouſly on the Truſt: The Cheeſe eſcaped with ſome ſmall Damage, and the Butter with leſs. 12.

Friday. Several of the *Indian* Traders now in Town applying for Licences, and Mr. *Charles Weſley* having taken all the Books and Rules with him to *England*, relating to that Affair, which was his Care when here; I had the General's Orders to diſpatch four of them, by writing only ſhort Permits, inſtead of the regular Form to be obſerved at a proper Time; till when, 13.

1739. July 13. when, this Method would ſufficiently anſwer their Purpoſe, which limited their Power, and kept them under the ſame Regulations as their former Licences, whereunto Relation was had. I did ſo, and delivered ſuch a Permit to each of them. In the Evening, waiting on the General, when Meſſieurs *Jones* and *Parker* were alſo preſent, he was pleaſed very generouſly to call on Mr. *Jones*, to ſay *that* now to my Face, relating to my refuſing to iſſue thoſe ſola Bills of 500*l.* which he had told him at *Frederica*; from whence I made no Doubt of his ſetting forth that Affair without that Candour which I thought myſelf entitled to; and thereupon, taking Mr. *Verelſt*'s Letter out of my Pocket, of *March* 3, wherein the Truſtees Orders were fully and clearly delivered (as I thought) relating to that Matter; I read them as I had formerly done to Mr. *Jones*; when I told him, that I found myſelf therein farther concerned, than barely to write my Name, for the Reaſons ſo apparent; wherefore it behoved me to take Caution in what I did, and therefore was willing, before I took any farther Step in it, to be adviſed how to act by the General himſelf, who was expected ſoon: Which he called a Refuſal, (and had ſuggeſted it ſo to the General) and now upon referring to that Letter, the General readily ſaid, he could not blame me:

me: But as for thoſe Bills, he had taken it on himſelf to iſſue them; and as for that Part of the 710*l.* which was to be applied in cloathing and maintaining the Truſtees Servants, whoſe Service was to anſwer the Expence thereof, as far as 400*l.* towards building a Church at *Savannah*, &c. he had ſent thoſe Bills home again, with his Reaſons for ſo doing. Wherefore upon the Whole, I looked on myſelf, and ſo did Mr. *Parker* on himſelf, excuſed of any farther Trouble about iſſuing, or accounting for, any of the Bills that were ſent, as mentioned in Mr. *Verelſt*'s Letter aforeſaid. 1739. July

Saturday. The Evidence to prove the late Murder, not yet appearing ſo full and plain, as to leave no Doubt of Conviction; by Reaſon that moſt of the Perſons who belonged to the Sloop, were ſuppoſed to be concerned in the Fray that happened among them, when they had been drinking; and therefore, a Man being loſt, unleſs the particular Perſon who gave the mortal Wound could be diſtinguiſhed, they were all equally guilty; they ſtuck together, and the Truth was hard to come at: I had the General's Order to call upon the Magiſtrates, and together with them, to take a Re-examination of the Whole, as well thoſe who were in Cuſtody, as thoſe others who yet appeared leſs ſuſpected: Which took up the whole Day; neither 14.

1739. July 14. could we, after all our utmoſt Care, come at the Point we wanted: The Queſtion being, whether the Deceaſed voluntarily leaped out of the Veſſel, reſolving to go aſhore, againſt the Maſter's Will; and it being dark, miſſed the Boat, and ſo was drowned (which was what they all alledged) or whether he had received his Death among them, and then was thrown overboard; which there was great Reaſon to believe, from ſeveral Wounds that appeared on the Body, ſuppoſed to be done with a Fleſh-Fork, or a Pair of Compaſſes, which were found near the Place where they had been drinking; each of which anſwered to the Form of the Wounds, and appeared ruſty at the End, near about the Depth of the Surgeon's probing when the Coroner's Inqueſt ſat, whoſe Verdict was *Wilful Murder*. From ſo many concurring Circumſtances, every Body was perſuaded to believe the worſt; and the General, for the better Diſcovery of the Truth, ordered Publication to be made, that any Perſon concerned in that Fray, who would appear and give Evidence who it was that was the Author of this Man's Death, ſo far as that he might be convicted, except the Perſon himſelf who did it, ſhould not only have the General's Intereſt to be pardoned, but alſo receive a Reward of 40 *l.* to be paid

paid him in Sterling Money at the Stores upon ſuch Conviction. 1739.

Sunday. The ordinary Service of the Day was duly performed, with a full Congregation, where the General was one; and Mr. *Norris* afterwards adminiſtred the Sacrament to ſuch as were ſo well diſpoſed. July 15.

Monday. Great Crouding and Hurry of Buſineſs this Day; when it was expected the General would have ſet off in the Evening on his *Indian* Expedition; but ſuch Variety of Matters with-held him, that he was conſtrained to defer it till tomorrow. 16.

Tueſday. The General left us in the Forenoon, and proceeded up the River in his Cutter, with Lieutenant *Dunbar*, Enſign *Leman*, and Mr. *Eyre* (a Cadet) his Attendants, beſides Domeſticks and menial Servants: At the *Euchie* Town, about twenty-five Miles above *Ebenezer*, he purpoſed to quit the Water, having appointed ſome of our principal *Indian* Traders to wait his coming there, with a Number of Horſes, as well for Sumpture as Riding; and alſo ſome of our Rangers to aſſiſt; intending from thence to travel on to the *Creek* Nations, *&c.* The Court at *Savannah* now ſat, as *per* Adjournment, thinking themſelves fully prepared to enter on the Trials of the three Perſons under Commitment for Murder. Accordingly *Brixy* the Maſter 17.

1739. July was firſt brought to the Bar. The Trial laſted ſeveral Hours, though the Priſoner made but a poor Defence; but the Proof againſt him conſiſting of ſundry Circumſtances, which when put together left not the leaſt Room to doubt of his being a Principal in the Murder, the Court omitted not to produce all that appeared worth regarding; and the Jury were ſo fully convinced of the Fact, that they conſidered but a very little while, after being withdrawn, before they brought in their Verdict *Guilty*.

18. *Wedneſday*. The other two Sailors, —— *Cozens*, and *Levett*, came on their Trials ſeparately; and after a full Hearing of the ſame Evidence, and ſtrong Circumſtances which appeared Yeſterday againſt *Brixey*; and it being proved, that they were all together in Company at the Time of the Fact committed (as alſo one *Jones* who fled the next Morning) the Jury found them alſo *Guilty*. Two of our *Indian* Traders, coming for *Savannah*, and meeting the General on the Water, brought me a Note from him, with his Orders to continue their Licences, and ſome ſhort Directions in what Manner to diſtinguiſh ſuch others, as applied for Licences in his Abſence.

19. *Thurſday*. The Court proceeded to try other Indictments, for Miſdemeanours and other petty Offences; which being of no great Import,

Import, I could ill ſpare Time to attend till the Evening; when having gone through all Matters before them, relating to the Crown, I went again to hear Judgment given; and Sentence of Death was pronounced againſt the three Murderers; which they ſeemed little affected with, but appeared more and more hardened; as it was evident they had ſtuck cloſely together all along, from a Preſumption (as it was ſuppoſed) that the Evidence given was not ſufficient to take away their Lives: But they were adviſed not to flatter themſelves with Hopes of Mercy. *Wright*, who was ſent down a Priſoner from *Auguſta (vide June* 26.) and one or two more committed for Crimes of a high Nature, were allowed to find Bail (if they could) for their Appearance the next Seſſion, the Court not having yet ſufficient Evidence to try them. Adjourned to *Monday* next. 1739. July

Friday. Very little or nothing to be obſerved. Towards Evening Captains *Norbury* and *Deſbraſſie* arrived in a Scout-Boat from *Port-Royal*, intending to ſtop two or three Days with us in their Way South. 20.

Saturday. Early in the Morning a Meſſenger from the General, whom he left at the *Euchie* Town, and brought Letters to me and Bailiff *Parker* from him; requiring to be informed concerning the late Trials for Murder; that ſo in caſe the 21.

1739. July 21. Priſoners were convicted, and Sentence was given according to Law, he might bring it to Effect. About the ſame Time an Expreſs-Boat arrived from Mr. *Fallowfield* at *Tybee*, who was ordered by the General, as Naval Officer, to keep a good Look-out there for the Return of a *Spaniſh* Launch, which he was lately informed, came all the Way from *Auguſtin* within Land, and was gone for *Charles-Town*; which at this critical Juncture gave Occaſion to People to ſay, that his principal Buſineſs was, to ſound the Depths of the ſeveral Inlets of the Sea on this Coaſt; and which was not improbable. Hereupon the two Captains, with Mr. *Jones*, Captain *Davis*, and ſome others, took a Boat with a few Hands armed, and went to give Mr. *Fallowfield* Aſſiſtance; who had wrote, that the Launch was now returned thither, which he had prevailed with to ſtay there till ſhe was ſpoke with farther: On which Occaſion, I would gladly have made one; but my immediate Taſk was to fulfil the General's Orders, in giving him a full Relation of the late Trials, and the Proceedings of the Court thereupon; which would take up moſt of the ſhort Time allowed for the Meſſenger to ſtay. In the Evening the Gentlemen came back from *Tybee*, after ſpeaking with the commanding Officer of the Launch, who told them he had been at at *Charles-Town*, to deliver to the Governor there a Packet, from the Government of *Auguſtin*; and that he had another to deliver to the General (which by the Bye he might as well have delivered as he went, had he not imagined that he ſhould have been well watched) and that Packet he now gave to theſe Gentlemen, together with a Preſent of Sweetmeats for him: His whole Talk being of the Pacification agreed on between the two Crowns lately (though not ſo perfectly, we apprehended, as to put all Breach of it out of Doubt.) He ſeemed to be offended at his Reception at *Charles-Town*; where he ſaid he was only permitted to go aſhore alone, but none of his Men; wherefore he made but a ſhort Stay there. He was very earneſt to take the Inland Paſſage in his Way home, but was told it could not be allowed him. The two Captains wrote each a Letter to the General, to give him an Account of their Proceedings, and gave them to the ſame Meſſenger very opportunely that carried mine, and one alſo from Mr. *Parker*, the head Bailiff, incloſed in mine; with all which he ſet off about Midnight, with Deſign to make all poſſible Haſte, the General intending to wait his Return at the Place where he left him. 1739. July

Sunday. The publick Service of the Church was obſerved as uſual. Captain 22.

1739. July *Norbury* and *Deſbraſſie*, who had both been lately ill in Fevers, were each of them taken with the ſame again, and forced to ſubmit to proper Means uſed for their Recovery.

23. *Monday*. Received a Letter this Morning from Lieutenant *Kent* at Fort *Auguſta*, brought me by one *Morriſon*, who intended a very ſhort Stay, and was returning into the *Creek* Nation: And the Letter he gave me, containing ſome particular Relations of the Talk of the neighbouring *Indians*, as if the *Cherokees* were ready to fall out with the white Men among them (which I did not find any certain Foundation for giving too haſty Credit to) I thought it not ſo trivial, but that the General ſhould be acquainted with it: Wherefore I reſolved to write to him of it, and incloſe the Letter I had received; which I did, by the ſame Perſon; who returned in the Evening with Deſign (if poſſible) to overtake the General in his Progreſs. The Court met again, in order to go on upon civil Actions, which multiplied too faſt; and the Recorder being not well, the Magiſtrates made Uſe of it as a good Cauſe to adjourn farther to *Monday* next.

24. *Tueſday*. Moſt of my Employment this Day was in preparing Letters, and divers Papers for *England*. One of Captain *Davis*'s Sloops, which had lain here a long while,

while, fell down the River to *Tybee*, bound (as it was ſaid) for *Auguſtin*; but what her Cargo was, I did not learn; it was ſuppoſed moſt of it to be Proviſions, chiefly the Produce of *Carolina*, together with ſome Bale Goods for Cloathing; alſo Hats, Shoes, *&c.* 1739. July

Wedneſday. Followed the ſame Employ as Yeſterday, and made up my Packet; but left it yet unſealed, by which Means I had Opportunity remaining, to add any Poſtſcript I ſaw proper: And it well ſo happened, for late in the Evening arrived *Peter Emery* from *Charles-Town* (who with his Boat of late kept pretty conſtant going betwixt this Town and that, as often as he found ſufficient Freight) by whom I received a Packet from the Truſt, with divers Letters incloſed, and ſome looſe, for the General, and divers private Perſons, ſent me by the Attorney-General, who alſo wrote what Ship they came by from *England*, &c. *viz.* the *Prince Galley*, Captain *Bowles*. Mr. *Verelſt* was ſo kind to write me by the ſame Conveyance two Letters, one of the 27th of *April*, and the other of the 10th of *May*; in both which acquainting me with the favourable and kind Determination of the honourable Truſtees, in relation to me and my future Support; which was Matter of great Comfort to me, not doubting but it would be equivalent 25.

1739. lent to my Need; though the Particulars I was not yet acquainted with.

July 26. *Thurſday.* By the Return of the Boat which carried the General up the River, Letters came to Meſſieurs *Parker*, *Jones*, and myſelf, in Anſwer to what had been wrote him on the 21ſt Inſtant, adviſing us in what he thought proper, relating to the Execution of the Criminals: Upon which we met, and went to the Priſon; where we took *Levett* aſide, who was weak and ſickly, and had been ſo ſome Time before the Murder was committed; but it appearing at the Trial, that he was one among them when the Fact was done, and conſequently that he muſt be privy to it, though poſſibly he might not actually give any Wounds to the Deceaſed; whereby he was in Law equally guilty with the others; we let him know, that we had Leave to reprieve him, if he would ingenuouſly confeſs which of them gave thoſe mortal Wounds; which would give the greater Satisfaction to the Publick; and in ſo doing he would diſcharge his own Conſcience, and leave Room for Mercy to be ſhewn to himſelf: All that we could get from him was, that without Doubt the two Perſons under Sentence with him, together with *Lewis Jones*, who fled the next Morning, muſt be the Perſons who did it; but which of them particularly, he he could not tell; for that he was ill himſelf, and laid down to ſleep on the Deck: But that was not credited by the Jury, who thought it impoſſible for ſuch an Act to be done, wherein ſo many were concerned, all which muſt be in ſo ſmall a Veſſel, within the Space of a few Feet before the Maſt; and that any Man could, in the Midſt of all ſuch Confuſion, lie down quietly to ſleep, and not know what was done: As this was all the Defence he made at his Trial, ſo he yet perſiſted in the ſame; whereupon we left him, and ſpoke to Mr. *Norris*, who viſited them, to uſe his Endeavours in trying what he could prevail with him to ſay farther. 1739. July

Friday. Heavy Rains returning upon us again for ſome Days paſt, on this more eſpecially there was little or no ſtirring abroad: Fevers and Agues increaſed apace, and our two Captains could not yet get free of them, ſo as to proceed South: Nevertheleſs theſe Diſtempers hitherto were ſo far from proving mortal, that I ſcarce ever knew fewer People die here, than of late: Mr. *Weſt*, late Smith to the Truſt, died this Afternoon of a Conſumption, wherewith he had been waſting for near a Year paſt: Beſides this Occaſion, I hardly remember a Grave opened for any other, for ſome Months paſt; and it is generally remarked, that the catching theſe intermitting Fevers, 27.

is

1739. is moſtly owing to Peoples Unwarineſs in taking cold when they are hot.

July 28. *Saturday.* The Magiſtrates convened at my Houſe this Morning, to conſider of what was needful to be done about the Execution, which was agreed to be on *Friday* next the 3d of *Auguſt*; accordingly a Warrant was given out to the Conſtables for that Purpoſe, and Orders given for a ſufficient and proper Guard to attend it: It was alſo ordered, that a Gallows ſhould be erected on the Bluff, towards the Extremity of it, near the Water, as near as we could judge oppoſite to the Place where the Sloop lay, when this Murder was committed; which was agreeable to what we underſtood to be the General's Inſtructions: And if there was Room given by *Levett*, betwixt this and the Time of Execution, for him to find Mercy on the Terms adviſed by the General, he might yet obtain a Reprieve.

29. *Sunday.* The ordinary Service of the Day was regularly obſerved. In the Evening, upon Intelligence, that a Perſon had been ſkulking in Town, under the Character of a *Jew* practiſing Surgery and Phyſick, ever ſince *Friday*; and giving out, that he came from *North-Carolina*, intending to go for *Frederica*, and hoped to get Leave to ſettle there; it was thought proper to have him taken up, and examined

ned before the Magiſtrates; which was done: And it appeared by the Teſtimony of our principal *Jews* here, that he was not of that Religion: Then, upon aſking him what Country he was of, he ſaid, of *Germany:* But his Complexion not agreeing with that Climate, we could not preſently give Credit to it: And moreover it appearing he had his Pockets well ſtored, and that finding he began to be ſuſpected, he had agreed with ſome Hands to row him up the River in the Night to ſome convenient Place, from whence he might travel by Land as far South as *Darien*; we were more and more confirmed in our Opinions, that he was a dangerous Perſon; whereupon it was thought needful to have his Pockets well ſearched, where he had Abundance of Papers, *&c.* among which, though we could not make a plain Diſcovery of his Deſigns, yet many Tokens appeared of his deſerving to be taken good Care of: When he found that it was in vain for him to deny, what we ſhould quickly prove, he confeſſed himſelf born in *Old Spain*; that he had been rambling for a few Years paſt, farther Northward, in the Practice of his Profeſſion, particularly in *Virginia* and *North-Carolina*, &c. but had made no Abode in *South-Carolina*, nor ſeen *Charles-Town* for a long while paſt: But upon looking into his Papers, it

1739. July 29.

was

1739. July was evident he was in *Charles-Town* about a Fortnight or three Weeks ſince; which, as near as we could gueſs, was much about the Time that the *Spaniſh* Launch was lately there: It was plain, that he had gone by ſeveral Names; and in ſhort there was ſufficient Reaſon for ſuſpecting ſtrongly that he was no better than a Spy: Whereupon he was committed to the Guard, to be there ſecured till the next convenient Opportunity of enquiring farther, after having made as ſtrict an Examination as we could till Midnight.

30. *Monday*. The Court ſat again this Morning; and after determining ſome petty Cauſes, adjourned till to-morrow. In the Afternoon we made a farther Examination into the Affair of the *Spaniard*, who was brought before the Magiſtrates Yeſterday; and it was found needful to continue his Confinement till the General's Return. Arrived at *Tybee* a Brigantine belonging to the *Aſſiento*, Captain *Fennell* Commander; who, together with two other Gentlemen that were Paſſengers on board him, came up to Town in a Boat, out of Curioſity (as they ſaid) to ſee the Place: And as ſoon as they were houſed, I had the like Curioſity, to make them a Viſit of Compliment, hearing they came from the *Havannah*, to learn what News I could from thence: Mr. *Jones* accompanied me; and we ſoon found,

found, that Captain *Fennell* was a Man well known on this Coaſt; and though he had never ſeen this Town before, he had often been at *Charles-Town* and *Port-Royal*, near which laſt he had an Eſtate of his own. He reported, that he left *Havannah* twelve Days ſince, where all Things continued in their uſual Poſture; and as to Peace or War, they were under the ſame Uncertainty as we: So that the Captain ſaid he was not without Apprehenſions of being ſtopt; nor did he think himſelf ſafe, till he was out of Gun-ſhot from the Forts: That he was now bound for *England*, after having diſpatched ſome Buſineſs in *Carolina*, where he ſhould put aſhore a pretty many Men, who had been detained Priſoners at *Havannah*, and were making their Way now home, in ſuch Ships as they ſhould like: That the two Gentlemen with him were *Creolians* at *Jamaica* (one of whom had been a Writer in the *South-Sea* Company's Service) and were deſigning to take Paſſage home thither from *Carolina*. This Brig was ſuppoſed to have a rich Cargo, and carried twenty Hands or more: The Captain was a Man of courteous Behaviour, and agreeable Converſation: After paſſing away Part of the Evening with them, I took my Leave. 1739. July

Tueſday. The Court ſat again great Part of the Day, diſpatching ſuch Affairs 31.

1739. July 31. as were indiſpenſable, and poſtponing ſuch as well might be; importing rather Strife betwixt the Parties, than Benefit to either Plaintiff or Defendant; which ought to be diſcouraged: Nevertheleſs the Day was not ſufficient for what they had to do; but ſomewhat yet remained to take up Part of to-morrow. Nothing occurred to me worth Notice; but heavy Rains fell almoſt daily, inſomuch that it was much to be feared the Corn which was now in Ear, would ſuffer greatly, and rot, inſtead of growing hard, and ripening.

Auguſt 1. *Wedneſday.* This Forenoon the Court made an End of what they thought needful at preſent, and adjourned to the 22d Inſtant. My Son, who had waited a pretty while for a convenient Opportunity of making a Voyage to *England*, now thought that a better could never offer, than to go in this Brig commanded by Captain *Fennell*, now lying at *Tybee*, and bound directly for *Portſmouth:* Wherefore, applying to the Captain, he readily admitted him as a Paſſenger, intending the Ship ſhould ſail to-morrow, or next Day; which ſhort Warning muſt unavoidably create ſome Inconvenience to my Son and me both, by parting in ſuch a Hurry: And, as many Things were to be looked into, and well conſidered, before his Departure, it found us full Employment this Day, as it muſt

at

at leaſt another, ſo to adjuſt Matters, that no Defect therein might occaſion any Detriment to the Publick. The two Captains (though weak yet) went this Day South for St. *Simon*'s. 1739. August

Thurſday. This whole Day was found ſhort enough, for what Work my Son and I had to do, purſuing what we were upon Yeſterday; and I heard of nothing abroad, that required my Avocation from what I thought needful at home. 2.

Friday. This was the fatal Day, which called thoſe wretched Criminals for Murder, out of Priſon to Execution (which was appointed on the 28th *ult.)* and Gallows now were prepared, at the Place were Orders had been given about it. The Freeholders were called to Arms by Beat of Drum, and in an Hour's Time more than ſeventy appeared, well accoutred; which, conſidering the Abſence of ſome, who were occaſionally out of the Way, and others not well able to attend, being not in perfect Health, beſides Orphans, *&c. &c.* ſhewed that *Savannah* was not yet quite ſo much deſerted, as by ſome reported. Before the Hour of Execution came, the Magiſtrates met, to conſider farther of *Levett*'s Caſe; whoſe Sickneſs and Weakneſs at the Time when the Murder was committed, inclined Abundance of People to believe, that he was not one who actually gave any 3.

1739. August 3. of the Wounds to the Deceaſed; from whence he ſeemed to be an Object of Pity, though by the Law he was undoubtedly guilty, being privy to it, and not diſcovering it; for the Jury could not believe what he alledged in his own Defence, that he was aſleep all the while it was doing *(ut antea:)* All thoſe Circumſtances being now again debated, Pity prevailed; believing if it was an Error to ſhew Mercy, it was an Error on the beſt Side of the Queſtion: Wherefore it was reſolved to reprieve him for two Months, in which Time we might expect the General again, who would direct what farther he ſaw proper about it: It was ſo ordered nevertheleſs, that the Reprieve ſhould not be known, till the very Minute he was to ſuffer; whereby we thought it poſſible that he might make a fuller Confeſſion, than he had yet done, as before recited. At the Gallows, *Brixy*, the Maſter, behaved very reſolutely, confeſſed nothing, nor abſolutely denied any Thing: He had been of different Sects of Religion, conformable to the Country he was in; a Preſbyterian in the Northern Provinces, and at *Auguſtin* a Papiſt, as it was generally thought he died; though he received the Sacrament at the Hands of a Divine of the Church of *England*, who attended them ſince their Condemnation, and at the Place of Execution: He went up the

the Ladder more nimbly than the Hangman, and faſtened the Rope to the Beam himſelf: Then turning about to the Spectators, told them he was ſatisfied to die (which was interpreted variouſly by ſeveral) and after a ſhort Prayer, he was turned off. *Cozens* owned himſelf to have been a very wicked Man; for which, he ſaid, God's Vengeance had overtaken him: He behaved with Penitence in Priſon, and now alſo; but made no Confeſſion of the Guilt for which he ſuffered, nor ſaid any Thing in particular of it. *Levett* was conducted to the Foot of the Ladder, after the other two were turned off, before his Reprieve was declared: He made great Lamentation for his former Courſe of Life, and appeared under much Terror; but continued to deny that he ſaw the Wounds given; and was ſo affected with his unexpected Reprieve, that he was very near loſing his Life by an exceſſive Return and Flow of Spirits; after which he was returned in ſafe Cuſtody to the Priſon from whence he came. Theſe Things being over, I had a few Hours left to ſpend with my Son before his Departure; which was at Six in the Evening, when we took Leave of each other (for a ſhort Seaſon, it was hoped) and he went, in Company with a few others, for *Tybee*, where he was to embark immediately on board the St. *Francis* Brig, com-

1739. August 3.

1739. August manded thus far by Captain *Fennell:* But now the Captain had determined to ſend her for *England* under the Conduct of his Mate; intending, after a ſhort Stay in *Carolina*, to return to *Jamaica*, together with the other two Gentlemen that came with him: Wherefore he would only ſtay at *Tybee*, to ſee her under Sail over the Bar; which was intended early in the Morning, and then he would quit her, and make the beſt of his Way to *Port-Royal.* Sent my Packet of the 25th *ult.* by my Son.

4. *Saturday.* My Son being now gone, Mr. *Jones*, who had been a great while a Stranger at my Houſe, came and made me a neighbourly Viſit, ſitting an Hour with me in familiar Converſe on divers Matters relating to the Publick; which I was very glad of, and determined with myſelf, that I would not be behind him in all Kinds of Courteſy, to promote the Service, as far as in me lay; but could not avoid reflecting on his implacable Diſpoſition towards my Son; which had carried him ſuch a Length as to avoid my Houſe, during his Abode with me; and which I could no otherwiſe account for, than becauſe he would not tamely ſubmit to thoſe ſevere Imputations that came upon him through his Means; but thinking himſelf injuriouſly treated (as indeed I apprehend he was) uſed all proper Means to vindicate his Innocence;

nocence; and that was conſtrued by an angry Man of a haughty Temper, to be an Oppoſition of his Authority. Theſe Things I concluded would now blow over, and the Remembrance of them be extinct, by the Time of my Son's Return again. 1739. August

Sunday. The publick Service of the Church was duly obſerved. In the Evening I received Intelligence by a Letter from my Son on board the Ship at *Tybee*, that they were at the Time of his writing, weighing Anchor, in order to put to Sea with a fair Wind: Which Letter was brought me by the Pilot, who lives there; and after conducting the Ship over the Bar this Morning, left them about a League off Land. 5.

Monday. This Morning, at the Requeſt of *John Lyndall* (appointed Pindar) there was a voluntary Convention of the Freeholders, who had any Property in Cattle in theſe Parts; when the Orders and Inſtructions lately given to the Pindar, by the General, were read; and the Pindar requiring in Conſequence of thoſe Orders, that ſome other little Regulations ſhould be agreed on among themſelves, for the better enabling him to do his Duty; they readily agreed to them, and ſigned a Paper ſignifying their Conſent, *&c.* It was now thought high Time, to begin the Execution of the Commiſſion lately ſent by the 6.

1739. August Truſt to Meſſieurs *Parker*, *Jones*, and me; and we met accordingly in the Afternoon at Three a Clock, when we began with the Account of Meſſieurs *Montaigut* and *Purry* firſt, where we were apprehenſive of meeting with ſome Intricacy; eſpecially from what Mr. *Verelſt* had lately wrote in his Letter of *April* 22; and was likely to prove ſo; for after inſpecting it cloſely ſome Time, we adjourned the farther Conſideration of it till to-morrow Morning.

Tueſday. The Commiſſioners met again, and ſpent both the Forenoon and Afternoon in cloſe Application to the Matters before them, taking proper Minutes of what was thought worth Notice: Among ſome other Things, obſerving that Mr. *Williamſon* had Credit given, in the Account of Mr. *Purry* and Company, for about 13 *l.* which was now made Part of the Debt owing to him as Claimant from the Truſtees, and which was certified by Mr. *Cauſton:* Upon looking into Mr. *Purry*'s Books, it appeared Mr. *Williamſon* was made Debtor there for ſundry Goods bought of that Value: Upon which we examined Mr. *Purry* upon Oath, to know how he came to transfer that as a Debt in the Account of the Truſtees; and he ſaid he did it at Mr. *Williamſon*'s Requeſt, and by the Conſent of Mr. *Cauſton:* Mr. *Cauſton* alſo appeared Debtor in his own Name in Mr. *Purry*'s Books, for

for divers Goods ſold and delivered to him for his own private Uſe, in the Sum of about 70*l.* which he had likewiſe transferred to the Truſtees Account, and made Part of what was certified by him, as the Debt which Mr. *Purry* claimed, to the 29th of *September* laſt: Since which Time Mr. *Cauſton* appears Debtor to Mr. *Purry*, in his Books, for ſundry Articles, in the ſame Form and Manner as the foregoing Account ſhewed till *September* 29. How far Mr. *Cauſton* can exonerate himſelf of this Charge, is yet unknown, but looked for. 1739. August

Wedneſday. Continued our Examination: And Captain *M'Pherſon*'s Account, together with his Rangers, being before us; we could not but obſerve the exceeding great Difference we therein found, of what he claimed for the laſt half Year, from *Lady-Day* to *Michaelmas* 1738, from any preceding Account for the ſame Time; but having Recourſe to my Journal of *March* 24, and *April* 1, 2, 3, 1738, I perfectly recollected what I there found, and withal ſeveral other Particulars, not fully noted there: The Captain at that Time, when we could not be too much on our Guard againſt the *Spaniards*, took that Advantage, and in a great Meaſure extorted ſuch a Compliance with his Demands, as he thought we durſt not refuſe: Wherefore after exhorting him to be very watch- 8.

1739. August ful, and more than ordinary diligent in keeping a good Look-out; he was promiſed, that, as far as it was in our Power, he and his People ſhould have all their Demands fulfilled, which they then inſiſted on — which now is humbly ſubmitted to the Judgment of the honourable Truſtees. In the Courſe of this Enquiry, *William Elbert*, who at that Time, or very little before, was one of Captain *M^c^Pherſon*'s Rangers, was found to have ſold a Mare to Mr. *Cauſton* on his own Account, as he believed, together with two or three other ſmall Articles, which in the Whole came to 6*l.* 15*s.* 6*d.* for which the Truſtees are made Debtors in the ſaid *Elbert*'s Account certified to Mr. *Jones*.

9. *Thurſday*. In the certified Account of *Nunes Henriquez*, the Truſt is made Debtor for 5*l.* 15*s.* 7*d.* which we apprehended, from what we could diſcover, properly belonged to Mr. *Cauſton*, as alſo to ten Shillings charged to their Account, and owing by Mr. *Williamſon:* And in a ſubſequent Account with the ſaid *Nunes Henriquez*, he charges 2*l.* 14*s.* 6*d.* ½ to the Truſt for Table-Cloths and ſome Pewter, delivered to Mr. *Cauſton*'s Wife; and 1*l.* 14*s.* 2*d.* ½ to the Truſt for Pewter, which was delivered to Mr. *Thomas Upton*. Mr. *David Proveſt*'s Account, certified for one thouſand and eighty-five Pounds, was found unexceptionable; and ſo was Mr. *Thomas Ware*'s for

for 22 *l.* *Thomas Trip*, a Joiner, charging the Truſt, in a Bill delivered, with the Sum of 5*l.* 14*s.* 11*d.* was content to take 4*l.* 12*s.* 5*d.* of Mr. *Jones*; the remaining 1*l.* 2*s.* 6*d.* being for Work done for Mr. *Cauſton*. Upon finding that a continual, daily Attendance on this Work, would render each of us incapable of a due Regard to any other, we agreed unanimouſly, that for the future one Half of the Day, either Forenoon or Afternoon only, ſhould be alotted for that Purpoſe; and to appoint at parting, which would beſt ſuit our Purpoſe for the Day following, from Time to Time. 1739. August

Friday. Went through four Accounts more, *viz.* *William Woodrooffe*, *John Lloyd*, *Samuel Mercer*, and *Benjamin Adams*, wherein ſuch Errors as we found were moſtly to the Injury of the Claimants; eſpecially the latter of them; where it appeared ſo defective in due Entries of Credit given, that we poſtponed it for a Review ſome other Time. Meſſieurs *Jennys*'s and *Eveleigh*'s Accounts we much wiſhed to get over; but it was thought proper, that ſomebody ſhould appear in their Behalf when we went upon them; and therefore we muſt wait a little till we had Advice about it from *Charles-Town*. 10.

Saturday. Spent the whole Forenoon in examining Mr. *Brownfield*'s Accounts, relating to the Claims of Meſſieurs *Pyt* and *Tuckwell*; 11.

1739. August 11. *Tuckwell*; wherein many Difficulties occurred, from divers Articles charged to that Debt of the Truſt, which we apprehended they had nothing to do with; but upon farther Enquiry it appeared more and more intricate; and we found Mr. *Cauſton*'s Account in divers Places ſo blended with the Truſt's, that it was not an eaſy Taſk to ſeparate them: But Mr. *Brownfield* ſhewed a ready Diſpoſition to explain it fully, in a Manner more intelligible; wherefore we deferred the Conſideration of it to another Day. By a Boat arrived from Fort *Auguſta*, I received a Letter from Lieutenant *Kent*, informing me, that from ſome Intelligence they had lately received, there were ſome Reaſons to doubt the *Creek Indians* not to be ſo much our Friends as we took them to be: But the General being now himſelf among them, we did not doubt but he would beſt judge of their Sincerity, and take proper Meaſures to ſtrengthen their Fidelity. By the ſame Boat came a Priſoner, whoſe Name is *Shannon*, ſent down by the General, and committed by him to ſafe Cuſtody in our Priſon, for treaſonable Practices: He had been of the General's own Regiment, liſted and brought over from *England*; but was diſcovered to be a Villain, in endeavouring to ſeduce ſome of his Fellow Soldiers, *&c.* for which he was whipped, and

and drummed out of the Regiment; moreover, upon ſearching, he was found to belong to *Berwick's* Regiment, and had a Furlow in his Pocket from the ſaid Regiment: After which he went up among the *Indian* Nations, and was now found to have been practiſing his former Work, endeavouring to perſuade them into the Intereſt of the *French*; for which it was to be hoped he would meet with his Demerits. Spent the Afternoon at my little Plantation. 1739. August

Sunday. The Duty of the Day was obſerved as uſual, and the Sacrament adminiſtred by Mr. *Norris*, to ſuch as were ſo well diſpoſed. Mr. *Francis Moor*, who went South not long ſince, returned to us again, intending now to continue his Abode here till the Return of the General. 12.

Monday. The Commiſſioners met again, and proceeded in a farther Examination of the Accounts of Mr. *Brownfield*; which we found true in all its Parts of Credit claimed; but there were ſundry Articles, wherein we apprehended the honourable Truſt would not readily own themſelves Debtors, being ſuch as were placed to their Account by Mr. *Cauſton's* Orders, as Mr. *Brownfield* very readily acknowledged; and withal, that it was no more than what he had divers Times done before, not doubting but it would be approved of, 13.

as

1739. August 13. as it had been, and that Mr. *Cauſton* gave the Truſt Credit for it in his Accounts: Which, together with others of the like Sort, poſſibly might be better explained to us, before we made an abſolute Charge of them on Mr. *Cauſton*, whom it behoved to look to it. In the Afternoon the Magiſtrates aſſembled at my Houſe, to enquire into a Riot committed laſt Night *(Sunday)* by ſome drunken People, who had inſulted one of the Tything-men, a Peace-Officer then upon Duty, who required them to go peaceably home, and whom they had ill treated; wherefore he had confined them upon Guard: And the Matter appearing very heinous againſt them, they were three of them bound over under ſufficient Bail, to anſwer it at the next Seſſions: Which perceiving them much terrified at, I propoſed it to them to confeſs where it was they bought the Rum which had occaſioned it, and I would intercede with the Magiſtrates to be the milder in their Puniſhment, upon Conviction of the Offence which they had been guilty of; and they promiſed they would another Day; but why not now, I could not tell: Wherefore I doubted their Sincerity. *N. B.* Theſe three Men were not long ſince out of their Servitude, had each of them behaved well in their Services, as was acknowledged by their ſeveral Maſters; were all

all promiſing to be uſeful Men in the Co- 1739.
lony, and one of them lately married, at August 13.
whoſe Houſe they had thus debauched
themſelves. From whence it is an obvi-
ous Reflexion, how fatal this Exceſs of
Rum-drinking is likely to prove among the
common People; and how ineffectual all
Means have hitherto been found, for ſup-
preſſing the Sale of it by unlicens'd Per-
ſons, in all the bye Corners of the Town.
Mr. *Bradley*, who yet continued very weak
ſince his late Sickneſs, no ſooner began to
recover, but he returned to his former
Practice, of making Havock among the
Cattle which had been under his Charge;
and notwithſtanding his being abſolutely
diſcharged from meddling any more with
any of the Truſt's Goods or Effects (as
they were pleaſed to write me lately, and
which I made no Doubt but they had
ſignified to him in thoſe Letters which I
had delivered to him from them) I had In-
telligence of his having killed a Calf laſt
Saturday Evening, and ſelling three Fourths
of it; moreover, that he had fixed upon a
fat Heifer, which he purpoſed the ſame
Way to convert to his own Uſe the Be-
ginning of this Week: Wherefore upon my
taking Notice of it to thoſe who were now
with me of the Magiſtracy, and Mr. *Jones*
being alſo one with us; I propoſed it to
them, to go all of us in a Body to him, to
aſk

1739. August. aſk his Meaning, and when he intended to ſurrender all that appertained to the Truſt, into ſuch Hands as were appointed to receive it: Which we did; and he entertained us in his uſual rambling Way of Talk, very little to the Purpoſe, and not coming to any fixed Point, partly ſeeking by evaſive Anſwers to blind us, and chiefly preſſing our Forbearance till the General returned, who he would have perſuaded us to believe, would allow of what he had done, though we were convinced of the contrary; and moreover we could not expect him among us again yet awhile; in which Space of Time it was unknown what Miſchief might be done: We therefore were obliged to charge him at his Peril, not to touch a Hoof more, or offer to diſpoſe of any; which if he did, he might expect to be proceeded againſt as a Felon: So we left him.

14. *Tueſday.* Mr. *Jones* having received a Bruiſe by an accidental Fall over a Log in the Dark, could not well attend the Buſineſs this Day, which we were purſuing, in looking into what we were directed: Wherefore Mr. *Parker* and I ſpent ſome Hours upon it without him, comparing divers Accounts, *&c.* but we thought it beſt not to make Minute of any determinate Opinion relating to it, till we were all together, and agreed in the ſame. The Afternoon

ternoon I took to myſelf at home, where I never wanted Matter ſufficient to keep me employed; and heard of nothing abroad that I thought worth Notice. 1739. August

Wedneſday. Mr. *Jones* continuing yet unable to act in the Examination of what we were upon, it was thought proper to reſpite it for a Day or two longer, in Hopes of his Attendance to aſſiſt, as he now grew better: And I took this Opportunity of paying ſome Regard to my Plantation Affairs, where we might hope ſoon to reap ſome Fruit of what Labour had been beſtowed; eſpecially as the Seaſon was grown more favourable for bringing on Harveſt; and the Heats which this Month began with, made an agreeable Alteration in ripening the Corn: But I was not a little chagrined to think, that the Number of Acres planted near the Town I feared would fall ſhort of what the laſt Year produced; which indeed ſhould be imputed in a great Meaſure to the Diſtreſs which divers of the Inhabitants were driven to laſt Winter; which put them on the Neceſſity of earning their Bread by any honeſt Means they could uſe, at ſuch Time as their Labour might well have been beſtowed on their Lots, could the Stores have afforded them a few Months Credit: For I muſt again repeat (what I have elſewhere taken Notice of) that the major Part of the Freeholders 15.

remaining

1739. August remaining in *Savannah*, ſhew a good Diſpoſition to Work, and endeavour to maintain their Families: And the Alteration lately made in the Tenure of Lands by the honourable Truſtees, in their Favour, has had already ſuch an Influence, that ſeveral, even at this Time of the Year, have begun to give a Specimen of what may be expected from them when the Planting Seaſon returns. As for the out-lying Plantations that are diſtant from the Town, I have Reaſon to expect ſuch an Account may be returned of them, that I need not be aſhamed of; ſeveral of which are occupied by ſome of our Freeholders, who hold thoſe Lands upon Leaſe (they tell me) and where, by Reaſon of a convenient Situation, they are enabled to raiſe a live Stock of Cattle, and Hogs, *&c.* whereby their Subſtance increaſing, they will ſoon attain to a comfortable Way of living, and become downright Farmers. —— But theſe are ſuch as have a little Stock to begin with.

16. *Thurſday.* This Day paſſed over with very little or no Variation from the preceding.

17. *Friday.* The Commiſſioners met again early, and followed their Employment till paſt Noon; in which Time Captain *William Thompſon*'s certified Account came under Conſideration, which divers Exceptions were

were made to, having in it ſundry Articles, where Credits were given by him to particular Perſons, whoſe Accounts we thought ought to be charged with the ſame, as being accountable to him properly, and not inſerted in the ſaid Certificate: Several other Charges we thought unwarrantable, which we yet could find no Original of in the poſting Books belonging to the Stores, and muſt leave it to Mr. *Cauſton* to give a Reaſon for. Then we reconſidered the Accounts of Meſſieurs *Montaigut* and *Purry*, where ſeveral Exceptions were alſo made; among which we found the Sum of 26*l.* 13*s.* 4*d.* taken Notice of particularly in Mr. *Verelſt*'s late Letter, to ſtand thus: Mr. *Cauſton* had taken (*i. e.* borrowed) of Mr. *Purry* that Sum, for which he gave him a Bill on Mr. *Jennys*, and therewith debeted the Truſt; but upon that Bill being returned unpaid, we could no where find, that the Truſt had again any Credit given them; for which no Reaſon yet is given, why the Truſt ſhould find it ſo ſtated. 1739. Auguſt

Saturday. Stuck cloſe to the ſame Employment, and went through *Recompence Stenbury*'s Account, without any Objections that we could ſee Cauſe for; as well as one or two more of no great Moment: But looking into the Account of Meſſieurs *Pyt* and *Tuckwell*, which was ſaid in Mr. *Verelſt*'s 18.

1739. August *relſt*'s Letter not to be yet offered; we there found divers Articles to ſtick at, Mr. *Cauſton*'s Certification and Mr. *Brownfield*'s Books not agreeing in the Sums which the Truſt was made Debtor for: Which put us to a Nonplus for the preſent, and obliged us to defer a farther Enquiry till the Beginning of the Week, when we might hear what Mr. *Brownfield* could ſay to it, and how it came to paſs that the Account certified to be due, was in any Place more than he had charged in his Books; which we obſerved were very regular; and hitherto he had not (as far as we perceived) uſed any evaſive Anſwers, to whatever we queſtioned: He happened, at this Juncture, to be rode a few Miles out of Town. In the Evening arrived *Peter Emery* with his Boat from *Charles-Town*; but brought no Letters from *England*, no Ship being arrived thence ſince the *Prince Galley*, Captain *Bowles*. (*Vide July* 25.)

19. *Sunday*. The publick Service was regularly obſerved, as uſual. In the Afternoon two Sloops belonging to *New-York*, —— *Tingley* and —— *Ware* Maſters, laſt from *Frederica*, arrived at our Port; having diſpoſed of the greateſt Part of their Cargoes in the South; with whom came Monſieur *Thomas*, chief Engineer there, together with his Family: By whom we underſtood a Stop was put to the carrying on any

any Fortification for the preſent: He ſaid he was going to *Charles-Town*, to view the Fortifications there; and from thence probably he ſhould go for *England*. 1739. August

Monday, *Tueſday*. These two Days were wholly taken up in purſuing our Examination into ſome of thoſe Accounts which were expected from us: And in ſeveral of them we found Errors of the like Nature with ſuch as we had before obſerved, *viz.* making the Truſt Debtor for divers Sums which did not appear to us to belong to them, but properly ſhould have been charged to the right Owners; ſome to Mr. *Cauſton*, and ſome to others: Whereof though ſundry of them poſſibly might not be thought very groſs, yet in an aggregate Sum, probably would, in the End, be looked on otherwiſe. We began now to think of a proper Account being prepared, to be laid before the Truſtees, of our Proceedings, ſo far as we had gone, with our Obſervations thereupon, as we went on: To which we ſhould give Mr. *Cauſton* (as due to him in Juſtice) an Opportunity of exculpating, as far as he is able, ſuch Charges as now ſtand againſt him. This being the ſtated Time of the Court ſitting, the Magiſtrates met in Form, and adjourned to *Monday* next. Finding it impoſſible to ſit *de Die in Diem* on the publick Accounts, without great Detriment to other 20. 21.

1739. Affairs; we reſolved to dedicate to-morrow
August to our own private Uſes, and appointed to
meet again on *Thurſday* Morning.

22. *Wedneſday.* Plantation-Work required ſome looking into, which employed Part of my Time. An heavy Complaint being exhibited againſt the *Moravian* Brethren, by Mr. *Gilbert* (one of the Magiſtrates;) foraſmuch as the honourable Truſtees had ſeveral Times adviſed, that thoſe People ſhould be dealt tenderly with; it was thought proper to aſk Mr. *Jones*, Mr. *Francis Moor*, and me, to be preſent when it was enquired into: And it may not be improper to take Notice, how that Affair truly appeared. One *Robert How*, a Freeholder here, the ſame who had his Houſe burnt, and was ſo kindly holpen by the Truſtees to rebuild it again, though he never did; and moreover, being a Favourite of Mr. *Weſley*'s, had conſiderable charitable Collections made for him; by both which Means, his Gains abundantly overpaid his Loſs; from that Time laid aſide all Thought of Improvement of Land, but ſeemed rather deſirous of appearing an Adept in the Improvement of Grace: And being made Choice of by Mr. *Weſley* as a Clerk to ſet the Pſalms, and do other little Offices about the Church, he became a cloſe Attender on the Miniſter, and was looked on by many weak Folk, as a Per-

ſon

ſon of extraordinary Piety; ſuch as divers in thoſe Days ſought to be diſtinguiſhed by, and ſome others ſince have copied after. This *How* married a Daughter of Mr. *Gilbert*, that died, leaving two Children (Girls) behind her, whom their Grandmother ſhewed a kind Affection for; but their Father purpoſing to go for *England*, (ſince Mr. *Weſley* was no more expected, and Mr. *Whitfield*'s Return was impatiently waited for) he diſpoſed of his two Children (moſt unnaturally, as I conceive) and againſt the Will of their Grand Parents, to the Family of *Moravian* Brethren, under a Shew of their being brought up in a ſtricter Courſe of Religion, than the eſtabliſhed Church afforded, unleſs it were more purified; though what Kind of Religion theſe *Moravians* profeſs, nobody here knows, except themſelves: And to make Payment for the breeding up theſe two Children, of the Age of about ſeven or eight Years, their Father contracts for their Servitude in all Kinds of Work implicitly, till their attaining the Age of Twenty-four, and ſo leaves them. It pleaſed God to take away one of them a while ſince, by Sickneſs; which no great Notice was taken of, every Body ſuppoſing that due Care was taken of her in her Illneſs; tho' now, from what has happened to the other, many ſuſpect otherwiſe: For upon the

1739. Auguſt 22.

POINT PARK COLLEGE LIBRARY

1739. Auguſt 22. Grandmother's hearing accidentally of this Child's being not well, ſhe went to ſee her; but was denied that Satisfaction, which made her the more importunate; and taking one of her Neighbours with her, by ſome Means or other they got Admittance; when they found the poor Child in a moſt miſerable Condition, with cruel Uſage, and uncommon Severity; which occaſioned this Complaint, and the preſent Enquiry into the Matter. The Child was produced, and upon taking off her Cloaths, ſhe appeared to be ſcourged in a moſt terrible Manner, from her Neck down to her Heels, with Stripes laid on by a maſculine Hand, moſt piteous to look at, and her Fleſh torn, after the Manner of what a Criminal uſes to have, at the Hands of a common Executioner. Three of the *Moravians* owned it to be of the Brotherhood's doing, who appeared; that they held a Conſultation among themſelves (which is their ordinary Way in moſt Caſes) and that this was the Reſult of it; foraſmuch as the Child had fouled her Bed: In Conſequence of which Sentence, ſhe was thus inhumanly mangled; and that too not done by a Woman, but a Man of a cruel Diſpoſition. We ſent for a Surgeon to give his Opinion of it; who ſaid, he could not apprehend any Danger from the Stripes, farther, than if the Anguiſh ſhould throw her into

a

a Fever, he knew not what might happen; and the Child appeared very weak, with her Arms much emaciated. Upon the Whole, the Magiſtrates thought, that the leaſt they could do, was to require good Bail for the Perſon's Appearance at the next Seſſions, who had been the Inſtrument of inflicting ſuch Cruelty; and that the other two alſo ſhould be obliged, on their own Recognizances, to appear at the ſame Time. In the mean while, the Child was delivered to the Grandmother, to take Care of it, till it ſhould be farther conſidered at the Court.——From ſuch Marks of Sanctification, *libera nos:* And whether ſuch a Father, or ſuch Guardians, have the beſt Title to it, is not my Taſk to enquire. 1739. Auguſt

Thurſday, *Friday.* These two Days were wholly taken up in the ſame Manner as *Monday* and *Tueſday* laſt; when we found many abſtruſe Points to get thro' in divers Accounts before us, more eſpecially thoſe of *Abram Minis* the *Jew*, and *Patrick Graham* Surgeon; which we gave each of them Time till *Monday* next to unfold; to which Day we deferred the farther Conſideration of them. Meſſieurs *Jones*, *Parker*, and I, being together, took Occaſion to call again on Mr. *Bradley*, to know what he purpoſed about delivering up the Truſt's Goods and Effects in his Hands, 23. 24.

1739. August. purſuant to Order. We found him and his Son both indeed weak, which was admitted as ſome Excuſe for their not having yet wrote out an Inventory of all Particulars; but the live Stock (we told him) might be brought together, by his principal Director under him, without any Trouble to himſelf: Which he now promiſed ſhould no longer be delayed; and to make a Beginning, four Horſe Beaſts were delivered into Mr. *Jones*'s Cuſtody on *Friday*, which he ſaid was all he had, and they had been ſadly battered, and near worn out; but having lately found a little Reſpite, they appeared to be ſomewhat thriving. As for the other Cattle, we thought it beſt to commit the Care of them to the Pindar, who was firſt to take ſuch an Account of them in Writing as he could get, and then to ſee in the ſeveral Droves which ſhould be made, how well it agreed with what he found. Hard Rains came on again, ſince the Change of the Moon.

25. *Saturday*. Having by Agreement between ourſelves, adjourned our farther Conſideration of the Matter of Accounts from laſt Night to *Monday* Morning, we took each of us this Day to ſuch Uſes as we ſaw beſt: Wherein an Affair happened, which, though unwillingly, I cannot avoid taking ſome Notice of, not knowing what may be ſaid more of it another Time, when

poſſibly

poſſibly I might be called on to teſtify what I obſerved, *viz.* Mr. *Jones* ſitting an Hour with me in the Afternoon in Conference, upon ſeveral Points of the Service; it ſo fell out that Bailiff *Parker* called on me at the ſame Time; which would have been not in the leaſt amiſs, had he not brought Mr. *Cauſton* with him, who poſſibly might have it in his Intention to ſay ſomething to me, relating to his own Affairs at the Office; and it was a long while ſince he had been within my Doors, though I had never treated him but with Civility: Mr. *Jones* and he indeed had ſuch perſonal Animoſity one againſt the other, that ſuch a Convention (I feared) could forebode no Good: And as Mr. *Parker* was known to be ſo much a Friend of Mr. *Cauſton*'s, as to wiſh he might clear himſelf of all foul Practices; Mr. *Jones* always looked upon him in that Light, and ſometimes gave ſhrewd Tokens of his Diſeſteem; which the other was ready enough to remember: And in that Manner they both carried a mutual Ill-will, which ſooner or later would be ſmothered no longer, but muſt inevitably break out, as it ſometimes had done, and now again did. Mr. *Parker* and he ſoon fell into ſome Talk, about delivering of Stores to *Parker*'s Family; wherein he alledged, that he was uſed unkindly, his Wife lying in, and

1739. August 25.

1739. August 25. and one of the *German* Servants with him (by Order from the Truſt) had at the ſame Time a ſick Wife, for whom her Huſband, by his Maſter's Order, went to the Stores to beg a Bottle of Wine; but was told it would not be delivered without Money; which, Mr. *Parker* ſaid, was a ready Way to make Servants Thieves, and pilfer their Maſters Goods, to make Money: This Mr. *Jones* grew warm at; and *Parker* not a Jot leſs ſo; when throwing his Arm to and fro (as is common with him to do in any Vehemence of Expreſſion) Mr. *Jones* ſtarted from his Seat, and dared him to ſtrike; both then ſhaking their Fiſts at each other, but Care was taken to prevent Blows, and it ended in ſcurrilous Language on both Sides, each looking on himſelf as the beſt Man, and throwing out Ribaldry in Abundance, with ſcurvy Reflexions on one another's former Courſes of Life, before they came here: During this Hurly-burly *Cauſton* vaniſhed; and at length the Diſputants growing cooler, and coming in Appearance to better Temper, Mr. *Parker* alſo took his Leave, and left us as he found us: When Mr. *Jones* told me he could not but believe, that *Cauſton* had blown up *Parker* into that Heat before he came, aggravating his being denied a Bottle of Wine for ſuch Uſes, to be what the Truſtees would not well approve of; and that he brought him purpoſely

purpoſely to affront him: So at preſent it ended. 1739.

Sunday. The uſual Service was performed at Church. Monſieur *d'Beauſaine* brought me a Letter in the Afternoon, together with a ſmall Packet incloſing others, which Mr. *Montaigut* had received at his Plantation up the River in *Carolina*, near *Puryſburgh*, and now ſent it to Mr. *d'Beauſaine* (at preſent in Town) to deliver to me. It came *per* Expreſs from Lieutenant Governor *Bull*, who wrote me of what Intelligence he lately had received from Lieutenant Governor *Clarke* of *New-York*, concerning the *French* marching from *Mont Reall* near *Quebec*, with a Body of about two hundred *French* regular Troops, and five hundred *Indians*, who are to be inforced by *French* and *Indians* in their Journey: That this Army was deſigned againſt *Indians* who are now in Friendſhip with his *Britannick* Majeſty's Subjects of *Carolina* and *Georgia*, and who are ſituated near ſome Branches of the *Meſſaſippi* River: That a *Frenchman*, who was redeemed by General *Oglethorpe* (having been taken by thoſe *Indians)* and furniſhed with a Paſs, and Money, to go back to *Canada*, is with this Army: The Governor added, that he ſhould immediately diſpatch an Expreſs to the *Creek* Nations, to adviſe General *Oglethorpe* of the Contents of his Letters: Then

August 26.

1739. August. Then he added — " The Conſequence and " Event of this Undertaking cannot be " foreſeen, yet it may be neceſſary for us " to think of our Preſervation, and be " upon our Guard: And in a Poſtſcript " he wrote, that he ſuppoſed the Deſign " to be againſt the *Chickaſaw Indians*." — Thus far Colonel *Bull*. —— As to myſelf, I could not but think it a very lucky Incident, that the General was now up in the Nations himſelf, where he, upon receiving the Intelligence ſent him by Colonel *Bull*, would undoubtedly leave thoſe *Indians* who are in Amity or Alliance with us, confirmed without wavering, in their true Friendſhip and Fidelity: Which well effected, we ſhould have little Cauſe to be apprehenſive of Danger from the *French*; though moſt undoubtedly they were very buſy in fomenting Diſcord betwixt us and the *Indians* our Friends: And if the preſent Deſign of the *French* was againſt the *Chickaſaws*, whoſe Valour they had formerly experienced to their Coſt; on Condition the *Creeks* prove true to thoſe People, in an Alliance ſince made; the *Creeks* being a great Nation, it may be reaſonably hoped, that betwixt them they will make Monſieur once again pay dear for his Attempt.

27. *Monday*. The Commiſſioners met again, and Mr. *Graham* the Surgeon's Account took us up the whole Morning, to get

thro' what we had left undone on *Friday* 1739.
laſt, ſo much Incricacy was found ſtill re- August
maining in it, Debtor and Creditor often jumbled, and wrong placed, which occaſioned many Exceptions, and will not paſs without due Obſervation. Having a Piece of roaſt Meat for my Dinner, I engaged my two Aſſociates to take Part with me, hoping, by bringing them together again, they might grow better tempered: We ſat an Hour after eating, and nothing was offered by either that could give any Offence: And I declined touching upon what was paſt, hoping it might die away, and be no farther talked of; for it would not bear being revived, without Miſchief enſuing; which I well knew. The Court, which ſtood adjourned to this Day, was now again farther put off, and adjourned to the 7th of *October*, before which Time we expected the General's Return again; and there were ſome Priſoners in Goal, whom it would not be adviſable to try, before ſuch a Charge was exhibited againſt them, as he thought proper.

Tueſday. Another Day's Intermiſſion 28.
from meddling in Accounts, by Conſent. Mr. *d'Beauſaine* returning up the River to his Plantation, I wrote a Letter by him to Mr. *Montaigut*, acknowledging the Receipt of what Letters he had ſent me from the Lieutenant Governor, and alſo incloſed one

to

1739. August 28. to Colonel *Bull*, which I wrote in Return to his; and thought I could not chuſe a fitter Canoille, than the ſame which he had made Uſe of, more eſpecially as Opportunities of writing to *Charles-Town* were very rare with us. Mr. *Norris* coming to ſit an Hour with me, whom I had obſerved for a while paſt to be more reſerved and dumpiſh than uſual (as I thought, tho' not particularly ſo to me) ſeemed to wiſh for Captain *Thompſon*'s Arrival, by whom Mr. *Whitfield* was expected; ſaying, that he was determined to take the firſt Opportunity of returning for *England*; which I was ſorry to hear, and offered ſome ſuch Reaſons as occurred to me, why he ſhould lay aſide ſuch Thoughts; for that I was very confident he ſtood well in the Opinion of the Truſtees, and I did not doubt but all future Matters would be rendered eaſy to him: He replied, that he had met with many Diſcouragements, even from the Day of his firſt Landing, ſuch as none of his Predeceſſors had ever found, and ſuch as he truly believed the Truſtees never meant he ſhould; but they were far off, and it was not his Temper to be complaining often about little Things, which often repeated, were grown ſuch, as now he could not, with any Comfort of Life, bear any longer, *&c.* I obſerved, that one great Grievance (as he termed it) was, that he thought

thought himſelf ill treated at the Stores, where he ſaid he ſcarce ever met with civil Uſage: If he ſent for the Boys and Servants Allowance, who lived under the ſame Roof with him, they were worſe ſerved than any others: If at any Time he ſent for a few Bottles of Wine for his own Uſe, he had often ſuch brought him, as was not fit to drink; when at the ſame Time he knew, and had taken Part of what was given out to other Favourites, that was good. I told him, that poſſibly it might happen through the Careleſſneſs or ill Judgment of Servants, and therefore I would adviſe him to ſpeak with Mr. *Jones* himſelf of it, who I hoped would rectify any Miſtakes that might have happened: But he told me he had ſo often done that in vain, that he was abſolutely reſolved not to have any more to do with him, having found whatever he ſaid, always diſregarded, and plainly perceived he was to fare the worſe with him for his Function Sake, whoſe Averſion to the eſtabliſhed Church was too apparent; whilſt others were in a particular Manner careſſed: To which I offered in Reply, that I hoped he was miſtaken, and though he was a Diſſenter from our Church, yet ſurely he knew better than openly to throw any Obſtacles in the Way of promoting the publick Worſhip: Whereat, with more Marks of Reſentment

1739. August 28.

1739. August Reſentment than any I had before obſerved, he aſked me what I thought of his not allowing Candles (as always had been) for the daily Evening Service? Probably (ſaid I) there might be none in Store at the Time they were aſked: Then (ſaid he) they might have been provided ſince; for unleſs I had got ſome by ſeeking after them myſelf, there would have been no Evening Prayer for ſeveral Months paſt. I was willing to put an End to this Talk, which I found I could not turn to any Good; and after diverting it a little while to ſome other Point, he took his Leave with his uſual Complaiſance and Civility, which he had always ſhewn remarkably in his general Carriage to every Body; and I was concerned now to ſee what Impreſſion of Mind he was under.

29. *Wedneſday.* A Veſſel from *Philadelphia*, having a ſmall Quantity of Proviſions to diſpoſe of, ſuch as Mr. *Jones* thought neceſſary for preſent Uſe; Mr. *Jones* was in Treaty for them with the Maſter, whoſe Sloop lay at *Tybee:* And afterwards, Mr. *Purry* (whoſe Partnerſhip with *Montaigut* was ended, and he going to live elſewhere) having divers Remnants of Iron-work left on his Hands; among which were ſeveral uſeful Tools, often wanted, which Mr. *Jones* ſaid he could buy a great Pennyworth, *&c.* he dealt alſo for that: Mr. *Parker*

Parker at the ſame Time was gone up the River, by Invitation, out of Curioſity to ſee a Sloop launched at Mr. *Williams*'s Plantation; which was building by his Order before he went hence, and was the firſt ever known to be built on this River: So that no immediate Progreſs could be made on the Commiſſion of Accounts. Mr. *Cadogan*, in his Way from *Carolina* Southward, calling here, I took the Opportunity by him of writing to the Major (at preſent the Commander in Chief over the King's Troops in this Province) and tranſmitting to him thoſe Papers and Advices which I had received on *Sunday* laſt from Colonel *Bull*. By this Opportunity we had News from *Charles-Town*, that *Lewis Jones* was taken there, and committed to ſafe Cuſtody; being the Perſon who made his Eſcape by Flight the next Morning after that Murder was committed, which he was deeply a Party in, and for which two of them had been hanged. Spent the Afternoon at my Plantation. 1739. August

Thurſday. The frequent heavy Rains which had fallen this Summer, gave me ſometimes fearful Apprehenſions of great Damage enſuing: And the ill News we now received, ſhewed thoſe Apprehenſions not to be vain; for by a Letter from one *Tyrrel*, appointed Director of the Saw-Mill Work at *Old Ebenezer*, to Mr. *Jones* 30.

 laſt

1739. August 30. laſt Night, we were informed in few Words, that a great and uncommon Flood came down upon them, and had blown up the Mill; and therefore deſiring ſome Direction as ſoon as poſſible might be ſent, or given, what they muſt do. This was judged impoſſible without ſeeing it; wherefore it was propoſed, that ſome of us ſhould go up thither, and upon viewing it, give ſuch Directions as we then found neceſſary: Mr. *Jones* wiſhed that he and I might both go, as he had never ſeen the Place; which I readily conſented to, and withal, Mr. *Francis Moor* being at preſent (in Appearance) not overcharged with Buſineſs, it was aſked him alſo to go with us, that ſo our Enquiry into the Damage, and our joint Opinion thereon, might have the greater Weight with the General, when we ſaw him again. It being ſo reſolved, we ſet out in a Boat with five Hands, and one to ſteer, about Nine or Ten at Night, taking the Benefit of the firſt of the Flood, to carry us as far as it would help; which uſually is as far as *Puryſburgh*, and that is reckoned twenty-ſix Miles: But now by Reaſon of the great Stream that came down and overpowered the Tide, we had the Benefit of it no farther than about *Joſeph's Town*, which is ten Miles; and with very hard Labour againſt the Current, we made it it paſt Eight the next Morning before we reached *Puryſburgh*. 1739.

Friday. After two or three Hours Reſt and Refreſhment, about Eleven we ſet out again, having only fifteen Miles to *Ebenezer*; but now the Stream was grown ſo rapid, that after long Toil, we made it paſt Ten at Night ere we could reach it: From whence (having the Benefit of the Moon) we ſent away a Meſſenger immediately, to *Barker* the Cow-Pen Keeper by the Saw-Mill, to furniſh us with each a Horſe before Sun-riſing: After which we were kindly received by Mr. *Bolzius* the Miniſter, who has lately built a very good Houſe, where he lives; and Mr. *Groneau* another near him, of ſomewhat leſs Size. We lodged very commodiouſly with Bedding laid on the Floor, and ſlept comfortably. August 31.

Saturday. Horſes coming according to Appointment, we mounted very early, and got to the Mill about Seven, where we ſaw indeed a melancholy Wreck, and the Mill ſunk away and fallen all to one Side, but ſtill held entire, though impoſſible to be ſet ſo to right again: From whence it appeared, that the Work was of ſufficient Strength, as the Artificer had put it together; ſo was likewiſe the fore Bay, and the main Hatch-way, through which the ſpare Water was to be carried off, no Part Septemb. 1.

 of

1739. Septemb. 1. of it that we could diſcover, giving Way, or taking any Damage: But the Flood was ſo ſtrong, and ſpread ſo wide, that when it came, it covered the whole Ground near it, overflowing the whole Work, which was perfectly buried under Water, and thoſe Waters worked their Way from the Outſide of the Work underneath the Mill, which occaſioned its Ruin: For after it had once found Vent, thro' ever ſo ſmall a Cranny, it ſoon made it larger, the Ground waſhing away apace, being of a looſe, ſandy Nature, ſo that Cavities were quickly made almoſt every where round it; the Frame of the Whole yet holding together, after the greateſt Part of the Foundation waſhed away and gone. Wherefore we thought the only Expedient at preſent neceſſary was, that the Frame of the Mill ſhould be taken to Pieces as ſoon as poſſible, whilſt it remained whole, before it received any farther Damage; and that the ſeveral Parts of it ſhould be ſorted, and carefully laid together, as well as the Iron Work, and Tools, *&c.* in a Place of Safety, till the General's Pleaſure could be known; for which we gave Orders: And after ſpending what Time we had to ſpare there, in other Enquiries, we returned to *Ebenezer*, were kindly entertained there for an Hour or two, and taking Boat about One a Clock, we came to *Savannah* betwixt Eight and Nine,

Nine, performing that in ſo ſhort a Time with the Stream, which took up more than three Times as much againſt it. 1739. Septemb.

Sunday. Another exceeding heavy Rain began about Four in the Morning, which held till Afternoon; and many People began to expect ſo much foul Weather would end in a Hurricane at laſt. The publick Service of the Day was not neglected. 2.

Monday. We met again, to proceed on the Commiſſion of Enquiry into Accounts, and took Mr. *Minis*'s in Hand again, whereon we had ſpent ſome Time on a former Day, and was the more difficult to get through, from the looſe Way of Book-Keeping uſed by his late Partner *Colman Salamons*, who diſcovered himſelf guilty of divers Frauds in his Partnerſhip; which therefore was put an End to, and *Minis* was ſuing him; but he was fled and gone: *Minis* himſelf not being capable of keeping his own Books (which had been the principal Inducement of his taking *Salamons* into Partnerſhip with him) and ſince the Breach betwixt them, he hired an able Clerk to do his Buſineſs; by whoſe Readineſs we got ſuch Light as was neceſſary, and proceeding very warily, we made ſhift to get over the Whole: Wherein we found many ſmall Errors of little Moment, and no viſible Marks of any deſigned Fraud; unleſs it be charged to him as ſuch, that 3.

1739. Septemb. Mr. *Cauſton*'s private Account was blended with the Truſtees in ſome Articles, to the Value of about 40*l.* Sterling, in the ſame Manner as we had found it with ſeveral others. Confined myſelf at home the latter Part of the Day, and began to think it Time to prepare another Packet for the Truſt.

4. *Tueſday.* Spent good Part of my Time in copying my own Journal, *&c.* *Paſquin* began to appear again, in like Manner as laſt Year, and was very free with all Sorts of People, which was good Entertainment to many: But whether it was genuine *Savannah* Wit, or the Produce of ſome other Country, was not eaſy to diſcover. Mr. *Jennys* not appearing yet, or any one from him, we were at a little Stand in going on with our Examination of Accounts; but reſolved at our next Meeting to try how far we could penetrate of ourſelves, into that of Mr. *Jennys*'s, which carried the Face, ſo far as we yet ſaw, of much Perplexity.

Wedneſday. After a few Hours employed, looking into Mr. *Jennys*'s Accounts, which through Length of Time, and other Ways, required a cloſe Examination; upon finding myſelf under a little more than ordinary Indiſpoſition, I retired home, to compoſe my Diſorder, and laid aſide Buſineſs the reſt of the Day.

Thurſday,

Thurſday. Finding myſelf better, I returned to what we were doing Yeſterday; the ſame Account which then employed us, yet holding out to puzzle; neither could we get to an End of it, after a long Morning's Work. Copying Work at home was my Afternoon's Employment; and I found nothing of the Day more worth Notice, than the general Complaint which every Body made of the uncommon Heat they felt, which was attributed to a black, heavy Sky, without Thunder to clear it, as it commonly does, and without it is almoſt ſuffocating. 1739. Septemb. 6.

Friday. By Appointment with Mr. *Jones*, we were to have gone to the Truſt's Farm this Morning, which was under Mr. *Bradley*'s Management, to take an Inventory of what we ſhould find: But by Means of ſuch a Glut of Rain as had fallen of late (and particularly the Night paſt) ſome Swamp Lands in our Way were rendered unpaſſable at preſent; wherefore we deferred it for a few Days, and betook ourſelves again to what we were looking after in the Account of Mr. *Jennys*, freſh Matter ſtill appearing to ſtumble at: But we got through it, as well as we could, at laſt, making ſuch Obſervations in our going on, as will be beſt determined when laid before the Truſtees: And we purpoſed to ſtop our farther Enquiry for the 7.

1739. Septemb. preſent here, that we might methodize what we had done ſince we began, in order to ſend it away as ſoon as might be. In the Afternoon, by the Help of a Horſe that I borrowed, I made a Viſit to my little Plantation, which I found grievouſly drenched with the Wet; and I feared it might have a bad Effect upon our Potatoes and Roots under Ground; but the Corn being generally ripe in moſt Places, and the Stalks bent down (as the Practice of the Country is) thereby to defend itſelf, we hoped it would be ſafe till a proper Time offered to gather it; it being common among many old Planters, after their Corn is ſo bent down, to let it hang till the reſt of their Crop, whether Peaſe, Rice, *&c.* are all houſed.

8. *Saturday.* Very ſudden and unexpected News, of open War being declared with *Spain*, was brought us by a Sloop that arrived here this Day, with ſome Proviſions to ſell, from *Rhode-Iſland:* The Maſter of which reported, that the *Tartar* Pink ſailed out of *England* the 17th of *June*, by Order of the Government, being ſent Expreſs, to inform the Provinces in the Northern *America* of it, *&c.* That ſhe arrived firſt at *New-England*; from whence Packets, which ſhe brought, were immediately diſpatched by a Meſſenger over Land to *Connecticut*, *Rhode-Iſland*, *New-York*, *&c.* That

That the Meſſenger made no Stay, but went on in great Haſte: And that ſoon after, the Governor of *Rhode-Iſland*, together with his Council, went into the Balcony of a publick Houſe; from whence his Secretary read to the People, who aſſembled by Beat of Drum, what Orders he had received; whereby he was empowered to grant Commiſſions to all ſuch as were fitly qualified, to ſet out Privateers, and to take, burn, or deſtroy, any *Spaniſh* Ships that they could: That before he left *Rhode-Iſland*, there were accordingly three Sloops got ready, with eighty Men each, and preparing immediately to put to Sea, and three or four more were preparing to follow them: That he underſtood the *Tartar* Pink was deſigned to ſail, with as little Loſs of Time as might be, from *Boſton*, for *Carolina* and *Georgia*, with Packets from the Government for thoſe two Provinces; and that he expected ſhe was here before him. It was thought proper to require the Maſter's Affidavit to the Truth of this Report; which he readily complied with: And thereupon, Mr. *Francis Moor* being in Town, he went South in few Hours after, to acquaint the Major, who at preſent is Commander in Chief there, with theſe Things, taking a Copy of the Affidavit with him.

1739. Septemb. 8.

Sunday,

1739. Septemb. 9. *Sunday*. The publick Divine Service was duly obſerved at Church, and the Sacrament adminiſtred. In the Afternoon an Expreſs was diſpatched to the General (if haply he could be found, up in the Nations) to whom I wrote fully what occurred relating to the Affidavit, which I alſo ſent Copy of: And whereas in the laſt Packet that I received from the Truſt on the 25th of *July*, there were ſeveral Letters for the General, which at that Inſtant I delivered into his Secretary, Mr. *Moor*'s Hands; he now recommending the Care of thoſe Letters to ſuch as ſent the Expreſs, I made one Packet of the Whole: After which, I wrote alſo to the Lieutenant Governor of *Carolina*, incloſing Copy of the Maſter's Affidavit, as before; and alſo to the commanding Officer of the Company in the Barracks at *Port-Royal*, ſending it to the Care of Meſſieurs *Woodward* and *Flower* at *Port-Royal*, to whom likewiſe I wrote: All which I did, upon Advice newly received, by a Boat arrived from *Charles-Town*, that they had none of this News there at his coming away, and poſſibly might not have any certain Account of it, till the *Tartar* Pink brought it: Moreover, in caſe they had authentick Advice, before mine reached them, it would appear a Token of our Readineſs to impart any Intelligence we received, that either Province were intereſted in. In the Evening a trading Boat from *New-Windſor*, arrived in her Way to *Charles-Town*; the Patroon of which reported, that the General in his Travels, finding himſelf not well, was returning this Way, being not far from *Auguſta*, where it might be expected he was arrived before this Time; but how far this Patroon might be credited, I cannot ſay. 1739. Septemb.

Monday. Captain *Davis* having a Sloop laying here for ſome Time paſt, which was publickly known to be bound for *Auguſtin*, with the ſame Trade that he ſent hence by another not long ago; ſhe now fell down the River to *Tybee*, intending thence to purſue her Voyage: But as Affairs ſtood at preſent with the *Spaniards*, we were a little alarmed at it, and of Opinion, that no Veſſel ought to be permitted to ſail thither from hence, whereby they were to be ſerved in any Thing; and moreover we believed, that at *Auguſtin* they had yet no Intelligence of this Rupture, which could only be from the *Havannah*; and probably no Advice of it was yet arrived there from *Spain:* Wherefore we thought it would be wrong to allow this Sloop to ſail thither on any Account: And after a little Conference with Captain *Davis* thereon (who at firſt ſeemed to dare us to ſtop his Veſſel, at our Peril, but afterwards finding we were determined to do it) he wrote an 10.

Order

1739. Septemb. Order himſelf to the Man whom he had appointed to command her, to bring her up again, and come to an Anchor where ſhe lay before; which Order Mr. *Fallowfield*, our Naval Officer, was to carry down, and ſee executed; waiting farther the General's Pleaſure when he would be here.

11. *Tueſday.* Mr. *Fallowfield* returned from *Tybee*, and Captain *Davis*'s Sloop anchored again at her old Birth. What elſe happened worth Notice, was a malicious, wicked Act done by ſome Perſon yet unknown, either Yeſterday, or in the Night, upon Mr. *Parker*'s Cattle; two whereof, *viz.* a Milch Cow that had a Calf ſucking, and a young Heifer, were both cruelly maimed, and mortally wounded, by a Stroke with an Axe, or ſome heavy Weapon, croſs the Chine, which cut through the Back-Bone of each alike: For the Diſcovery of which vile Act, it was thought fit to publiſh a Reward of 5 *l.* Sterling to any who ſhould bring the Perſon to Juſtice that did it; which Mr. *Jones* has promiſed to pay upon Conviction of the Offender. This was the more remarkable, becauſe Mr. *Parker* had ſuffered divers Loſſes of late in his Cattle, and therefore it was pretty evident the Spite was at him particularly, and probably might ariſe from ſome Villain whom the Magiſtrate had found ſufficient Cauſe to deal ſomewhat ſharply with,

with, when he was in the Execution of his Office. 1739.

Wednesday. Notwithstanding what Precaution was taken on *Monday* last with Captain *Davis*, to hinder any Intelligence going to *Augustin*, we had now Notice, that he was preparing to elude it all, and determined, by some Means or other, to carry on his Design; which gave great Apprehensions to many People of the Consequence: Whereupon the Magistrates met again, and resolved to demand sufficient Security of him, by entering into a Bond of 500*l.* Sterling Penalty for himself, and his two Sureties in 250*l.* each, that he would not proceed farther in that Affair, till the General came: In Pursuance of which, the Recorder (Mr. *Christie*) was to see it done; and in the mean while Mr. *Parker* and I meeting the Captain, he seemed readily to agree to it: But the Recorder afterwards (either through Mistake, or rather designedly, as we had Reason to believe from what Temper he discovered) made the Condition of the Bond to be only for the Vessel's not sailing, and no Restraint on the Captain himself, who might go where he pleased: The Consequence of which was — Septemb. 12.

Thursday. About One a Clock in the Morning, we were alarmed again, at a fresh and unexpected Movement of the Captain's, who with several Hands was carrying 13.

1739. Septemb. 13. carrying divers Parcels of Baggage to the Water-Side; among whom was one *Foſter* a Tything-man, at whoſe Houſe the Captain lodged, and who was privy to the whole Intrigue (as we found afterwards) in Breach of his Duty to the Colony, and was to be one, among others, that ſhould accompany the Captain in his Expedition: Another Tything-man that happened accidentally to be ſtrolling about the Bluff at that Time of Night (on what Occaſion we know not) ſeeing what was about, went immediately and knocked up Mr. *Parker*, who in like Manner calling on me, I roſe, and called Mr. *Mercer* the Conſtable, and thence in our Way we alſo took Mr. *Jones* with us, making what Haſte we could to the Water-Side; where we found *Foſter* and the other Tything-man (whoſe Name is *Salter)* ſkuffling about putting the Baggage into a Boat: Whereupon the Guard was called, which we were at a good Diſtance from; and on their coming all was ſecured. Here it is to be noted, that a Skooner lay at Anchor hard by, which came with ſome petty Cargo for Sale, a long while ſince, the Maſter whereof was an idle, drunken Fellow, and had but newly taken out his Clearance to return to ſome Northern Plantation: It was ſo concerted now (as afterwards appeared) that upon the Captain's Sloop being ſtopt, he had hired, or (as (as ſome believed) bought this Skooner, to ſupply the Place of his Sloop, on board of which theſe Parcels were ſhipping, at this unſeaſonable Time in the Night; and the Captain, with his Followers, were alſo going in her; which the Captain himſelf acknowledged, but denied his Intention of going to Sea in her, telling us, that he was only going to *Tybee* for the Benefit of Change of Air, by the Advice of Dr. *Tailfer*, where he purpoſed to ſtay waiting the General's Arrival: Which we thought was not probable, *Tybee* being a Place ſo exceedingly peſtered with Muſketas, by Reaſon of the adjacent Marſhes, that no Perſon would ever be fond of taking his Abode aſhore there, as he pretended he meant to do in a Hut; where the Skooner, he ſaid, was to leave him. After looking into the Baggage at the Guard, where we then came, and finding that moſt of it conſiſted of Bedding, and ſome other Things uſeful, whether on board or aſhore, we diſmiſſed the Company, leaving with the Guard a ſtrict Charge, that they ſhould ſuffer no Veſſel or Boat to go off without a Permit from the Magiſtrates. Captain *Davis* growing very warm at theſe Diſappointments, and directing his Diſcourſe to me, told me I might expect a Proteſt, for Damages, *&c.* which I told him in Return, I valued not, and bade him do his worſt.

1739. Septemb. 13.

Soon

1739. Septemb. 13. Soon after, we ſent for the Maſter of the Skooner out of his Bed where he lodged; and upon Examination, found him groſsly prevaricating; but could not deny that Captain *Davis*, with other Company, was to go in his Veſſel to *Tybee*, whilſt he lay aſhore, and moſt of the Sailors were the Captain's own, which belonged to his Sloop that was ſtopt. Upon the Whole, therefore, it was pretty manifeſt what was intended; and it was judged neceſſary to ſtop the Skooner alſo in the River, as well as all other ſmall Craft: After which we all returned to our Reſt. Towards Noon an Expreſs arrived, with Letters of the 10th, from the Government at *Charles-Town*; and of Yeſterday's Date from the Magiſtrates in and near *Port-Royal*, confirming the War being actually declared, which they had Advice of by a Sloop alſo from *Rhode-Iſland*, that arrived ſince the other which brought the firſt News of it: But the *Tartar* Pink was not yet heard of. By theſe Letters we were farther informed, that at the coming away of the Expreſs, ſeveral Guns were fired, and Signals made at *Johnſon*'s Fort, in the Mouth of that Harbour; by which they underſtood ſeveral Ships were ſeen over the Bar, which they hoped came from *Europe*. But in the Midſt of theſe Hoſtilities from abroad, it was now their great Unhappineſs to have

a

a more dangerous Enemy in the Heart of their Country to deal with: For their Negroes had made an Insurrection, which began first at *Stonoe* (Midway betwixt *Charles-Town* and *Port-Royal)* where they had forced a large Store, furnished themselves with Arms and Ammunition, killed all the Family on that Plantation, and divers other white People, burning and destroying all that came in their Way; so that the Messenger who came, told us the Country thereabout was full of Flames: Our Letters also informed us, that they were fearful lest it should prove general; and that the Militia was raised upon them throughout the whole Province; a Party of whom, of about twenty, had met and engaged ninety of them in one Body, of whom they had taken four Prisoners, and killed ten, *&c.* They farther wrote us, they had Reason to believe, that many of them would bend their Course to the South, and endeavour to cross the *Savannah* River; from whence they intended to go on for *Augustin* to the *Spaniards:* Wherefore they hoped we would do what we could, in securing the Passes on that River, promising a Reward of 50*l.* Currency for every Negro taken alive, and delivered at *Charles-Town*; and 25*l.* ditto for every one killed. Upon these Advices, we dispatched Intelligence of it to the Major, commanding in the South, who

1739. September 13.

1739. Septemb. poſſibly might, by ſmall Parties, intercept ſome of them, if they eſcaped in croſſing the River *Savannah*, and purſued their March to the Southward by Land: And as we could ill ſpare any of the few Men we had, that were fit to bear Arms, and by ſo doing leave ourſelves more and more defenceleſs, we ſent immediately Notice of it to Mr. *Montaigut*, whoſe Plantation with Negroes is not many Miles diſtant, and who is alſo a military Officer himſelf; recommending it to him, to have a Guard at thoſe Paſſes beyond him, and to ſend proper Caution to the Fort at *Palachocolas*, farther than which would be needleſs: And we would do the beſt we could below, to the Mouth of the River.——Now it fully appeared, that the ſecuring that *Spaniard* ſome Time ago *(vide July 29.)* was not upon a groundleſs Suſpicion (as ſome People then termed it, who are rarely pleaſed with whatever is done, becauſe they have not the doing it) for it is more than probable, that he had been employed a pretty while, in corrupting the Negroes of *Carolina*; and was certainly with *Don Pedro* at *Charles-Town*, at the Time when he lately came thither with his Launch.

14. *Friday.* All appeared quiet, without any farther Diſturbance at preſent: And I was very glad to ſee the Storm compoſed alſo, which lately happened betwixt our firſt

firſt Magiſtrate and Store-Keeper; who both ſeemed deſirous, that what was paſt might be forgot; and they converſed with mutual Tokens of Friendſhip. Late in the Evening arrived Captain *Norbury*, and with him Enſign *Cadogan*, from St. *Simon*'s, being alarmed at the News of War, which we had ſent them from hence; the Captain now making his Way to his Poſt at *Port-Royal*, and *Cadogan* going for *Carolina* on Buſineſs of the Regiment, which was ordered him by the Major. 1739. Septemb.

Saturday. Mr. *Francis Moor*, who came with thoſe Officers Yeſterday as far as Mr. *Fallowfield*'s Plantation by Water, and lay there; rode thence this Morning, and returned to Town. Captain *Norbury* had an Expectation of taking a Sum of Money now with him that belonged to his Company, and was left, it ſeems, (on what Occaſion not known) in the Hands of Mr. *Upton*, by Lieutenant *Delegal*, when he went for *England*: This Money Mr. *Upton* had been trading with at *Charles-Town*, and was going to diſpoſe of the Goods in the South after his having ſtaid here two or three Days; and Captain *Norbury* thereupon ſent to ſpeak with him about it, underſtanding he intended to proceed next Day: But Mr. *Upton*, inſtead of ſeeing him, went off in the Morning very early with his Boat and Cargo; which the Cap- 15.

1739. Septemb. tain was ſo enraged at when he roſe, that he got a Warrant from Mr. *Parker* to ſtop him at *Thunderbolt*; which was done by Mr. *Mercer* the Conſtable: And Mr. *Upton* came to ſuch Terms with the Captain, by Aſſurance of the Money being paid into an Officer's Hands at St. *Simon*'s, as ſoon as the Goods were diſpoſed of; that at length he permitted him to go on, after a great Hurly-burly, and warm Controverſy, which the Captain had with Mr. *Jones*; who he thought took upon him to juſtify Mr. *Upton* farther than was right.

16. *Sunday*. The ordinary Duty of the Day was regularly obſerved.

17. *Monday*. Early this Morning died the Reverend Mr. *Edward Dyſon*, Chaplain to General *Oglethorpe*'s Regiment: He had been abſent upon Furlow ſome Time; moſt Part of which he paſſed away in this Town, where he ſickened a while ſince, and a Pleuretick Fever carried him off at laſt. Captain *Norbury*, with Mr. *Cadogan*, purpoſed to have gone off this Afternoon; and I took this Opportunity by them, of ſending my Packet of the 10th Inſtant to Mr. *Verelſt*; which they promiſed to take Care of, together with my Letter to Mr. *Hopton*, recommending it to him to ſend it off by the firſt fitting Occaſion: But being invited to Mr. *Dyſon*'s Funeral this Evening, where they attended, and did the Corpſe

Corpſe the Honour of firing ſome ſmall Arms in Token of his being one of the Regiment, they put off their Deſign till to-morrow. 1739. Septemb.

Tueſday. Mr. *Parker* acquainted me this Morning, that after Mr. *Fallowfield* (as Conſtable on Duty) had looked curſorily into Mr. *Dyſon*'s Cheſts, Scrutore, *&c.* wherein many Writings of various Kinds, and Accounts, were found; at which Inſpection we had deſired Mr. *Francis Moor* to be preſent, and alſo Mr. *Jones*; and they had locked and ſealed all up, to prevent any Embezzlement, till a proper Adminiſtrator was appointed: Mr. *Chriſtie*, the Recorder, had now applied to him *(Parker)* to join in putting the Seal to an Adminiſtration which he had prepared, wherein Mr. *Fallowfield* was appointed of Right (as he deemed it) to take that Office upon him: But Mr. *Parker* (knowing better than to commit the Truſt of ſuch Effects, that were ſuppoſed to be very conſiderable, to thoſe two) had refuſed him: And indeed it was well provided, that the Seal was never to be come at, without more Keys than one; otherwiſe it is to be doubted our Recorder might have gone ſometimes unwarrantable Lengths; and the Chagrin which ſat cloſe upon him for a while paſt, was generally imputed to the Defeats and Diſappointments he had met with in his At- 18.

1739. Septemb. 18. tempts. I told Mr. *Parker* what I thought, that he was much to be commended; and my Advice was, that every Thing being ſafe, under Locks and Seals, it would be beſt, for farther Security, to remove all into the publick Stores, and Mr. *Fallowfield* might keep the Keys till the General came, and a proper Perſon or Perſons were appointed by him to adminiſter. About Noon arrived *Peter Emery*, with his Boat from *Charles-Town*, after ſeveral Days Expectation; but brought no News of any Ship come from *England*, or any Letters thence: But I had one from Lieutenant Governor *Bull*, informing us, that what I had wrote him of the 9th, and the Affidavit incloſed, was verified in all its Parts; and that Captain *Warren* in the *Squirrel* was lately come in, who acquainted him of his having been at *Boſton*, and that he parted with Captain *Townſhend* in the *Tartar* Pink three Days before, who was ſtationed at *Carolina*, and was to follow him to the South after Delivery of the Orders he had brought; where he deſigned, with Captain *Laws* in the *Spence*, to viſit the Gulph of *Florida*, and the *Spaniſh* Coaſts: Moreover, Captain *Warren* aſſured the Lieutenant Governor (as he writes me) that he, with all his Majeſty's Ships on this Northern Station, have particular Orders, upon the firſt Notice or Suſpicion of the *Spaniards* intending

tending to invade either of theſe Provinces, to come to their Aſſiſtance immediately; and that he, as the ſenior Commander, upon due and full Information, would ſend for all his Majeſty's Ships aforementioned. This was good News indeed: But it occaſioned a little Obſervation to be made, that whilſt all the Northern Provinces had each of them one, two, or three ſtationed Ships always ready to protect them, poor *Georgia* had never any but the *Hawk* Sloop yet. Colonel *Bull*, after touching upon a few other Particulars, in Concluſion tells me, that all Matters which may concern the Safety and Advantage of either Province, ſhould from Time to Time be communicated to me: And he informed me likewiſe, that their Militia had attacked the rebellious Negroes, with that Vigour and Succeſs, killing ſo many of them, that they had put an End to their Deſigns; which was alſo happy News. But by ſome other Letters which came thence, a very terrible Calamity of Sickneſs had befallen them at *Charles-Town*, which proved exceeding mortal, great Numbers dying weekly, and it is termed a contagious, malignant Fever: Which among a Multitude of others, had carried off alſo ſome of our Freeholders, who preferred living there to this Place; namely, *Coates*, *Muer*, *Delgraſs*, and *Holmes*; whether any others of them

1739. Septemb. 18.

1739. Septemb. 18. or not, we are yet to learn. From ſeveral Inſtances it appearing, that Captain *Davis* was ſtill carrying on his Deſign, of getting ſecretly away, and to go to *Auguſtin*, in Spite of all Caution uſed to prevent it; which might be of moſt dangerous Conſequence to this Colony: And alſo receiving Information, that his Sloop which he ſent thither about two Months ſince, was returned, and coming up our River; but upon ſecret Advice ſent her, ſhe turned back, and was ſailed to ſome other Port, which we imagined was done to prevent any Examination being taken of her by the Magiſtrates here: It was now thought high Time to be no longer trifling, when we knew not but our All was at Stake; wherefore the Magiſtrates took him into ſafe Cuſtody: But in Conſideration of his being an infirm Man, would not commit him to the common Priſon; but at his own Requeſt, ordered him to be confined to his own Lodgings, with two Centuries over him. *N. B.* Mr. *Chriſtie* was not preſent, either at this, or any of the former Proceedings concerning *Davis*, though ſent to; but joined with the Cabal, which ſtill ſubſiſted at *Jenkins*'s, cenſuring and oppoſing every Thing, as far as they could, that was done, calling it arbitrary and tyrannical, againſt Law, *&c.* Nay, ſo far was he poſſeſſed with that Spirit of Contra-

 diction,

diction, that in my Hearing he declared it an unjuſt Act, to do what was before done, only on a groundleſs Suſpicion: Which I could not without ſome Indignation reply to, and aſk him, whether or not Captain *Davis*'s own Words of Defiance, which he uſed, and daring any one to ſtop him at their Peril, for to *Auguſtin* he was going, and thither he would go: Whether or not after ſuch a Declaration and Attempt to go off ſecretly in the Night, the Magiſtrates proceeded on *groundleſs Suſpicion:* For if he propagated ſuch Doctrine, there would be more than a groundleſs Suſpicion, that he himſelf was not ſo well affected as he ought. It was too remarkable, that for ſome Time paſt, he was become a cloſe Diſciple under our famous Demagogue, whoſe continual Practice for a long while had been to inſtruct his Hearers in being very circumſpect, leſt their Liberties ſhould be infringed; and that it was their Duty always to ſtand in Defence of them: So that from this Nurſery moſt of thoſe Evils have ſprung that have formerly been taken Notice of; and this poor, weak Man, having his Vanity tickled, and being perſuaded that his Knowledge in the Law was ſuperior to the others his Aſſociates in the Magiſtracy, which they ought to pay an implicit Regard to, but did not; he became peeviſh, and inſtead of giving any

1739. Septemb. 18.

Aſſiſtance

1739. Septemb. Aſſiſtance to the publick Affairs carrying on, he adviſed with none but thoſe, who never approved of any Thing which they had not the Direction of, or at leaſt were conſulted in: So that by his thus withdrawing himſelf, the greateſt Weight of civil Power to ſecure the Peace, fell to Mr. *Parker*'s Share almoſt totally for the preſent, Mr. *Gilbert* being incapable in many Things to take a Share abſtractedly to himſelf, though always ready to join in doing his Duty *ſans Reproche:* By which Means *Parker* has ſhewn fully a good natural Underſtanding, and clear Diſcernment of Juſtice, with a ſuitable Courage, not ſoon to be terrified from purſuing what he thinks ſo, like a right honeſt Man: And ſo Mr. *Jones* eſteems him, notwithſtanding their late Diſcord, which I hope is pretty well forgotten between them, and they will be better cemented hereafter: It would be pretty hard to determine which of them was in the right at that Time; I thought them both wrong.

19. *Wedneſday.* Our two Officers bound to *Port-Royal*, and not liking the Weather to croſs *Delfuſka Sound* Yeſterday, they went off this Morning: And this proving a Day of more Leiſure, every Body followed quietly their own Buſineſs; which among ſuch as had any Plantation, was to get in ſome of their Harveſt.

Thurſday.

Thurſday. This Morning I was knocked up about One a Clock by an Expreſs from the General, who wrote me of Yeſterday's Date from *Palachocolas*, that he was come thither; that his Health was pretty much recovered; that he ſhould ſtay there till this Day, to receive Advices of what was doing by the revolted Negroes; and that if nothing happened extraordinary, he intended to proceed to *Ebenezer* this Evening; then call at Mr. *d'Beauſain*'s, and ſo make all the Haſte he could down. By which we found the Report of his Sickneſs was too true; and all who had a due Value for him, when I publiſhed the News, as the Day came on, were very joyful to hear it. Towards Evening I received a large Packet, ſent by the Attorney-General from *Charles-Town*, which he wrote me of the 15th he received the Day before, by the *Tartar* Pink arrived juſt then, which had been earneſtly expected, and brought Orders from *England* to the Governor what he was to do, upon this War breaking out: On opening it, I found the Bulk of what was encloſed, was a diſtinct Packet to the General, and one of a ſmaller Size directed to me; both which had been put under one Cover by the Attorney-General, and came both to him from the Truſt: In that for me, were a few Letters for private Perſons, and one to myſelf from Mr.

1739. Septemb. 20.

1739. Septemb. 20. Mr. *Verelſt*, who wrote me of the 22d of *June* a ſhort Letter, but a very kind one, relating to my own Affairs, and the Truſt's Benevolence towards me; which gave me more and more Vigour: What elſe he had to ſay, he told me (being in a Hurry) I might expect by Captain *Thompſon*, who was ready to ſail, but a general Embargo at preſent ſtopt him, which it was expected the Truſtees would ſoon get a Licence from the Government to free him from, and then he would ſail. Theſe Packets were ſent from *Charles-Town* by the Way of *Puryſburgh*, under the Care of one Major *Bryan* who was going that Way, who had the Charge of another Packet, that came alſo by the *Tartar*, not from the Truſt, but ſuppoſed to be from ſome of the publick Offices of State, directed to the General; and by the ſame Conveyance likewiſe came another Letter of the 15th from Colonel *Bull* to me, ſignifying his having received Orders to grant Letters of Marque, *&c.* and to act offenſively againſt the *Spaniards*; and referring me farther to his Letter of the 13th, which I had received. All theſe Diſpatches coming to the Hands of Mr. *Montaigut* in the Neighbourhood of *Puryſburgh*, he ſent his Boat away with them immediately hither, where we alſo looked wiſhfully to ſee the General to-morrow.

Friday.

Friday. Took a Walk very early this Morning, and catched the Opportunity of a few Hours to ſpend with my Crew, and ſee what Advances they had made in the Work appointed them laſt. We were getting in Corn now, which *Jones* thought would have been exceeded by nobody in Goodneſs, on the like Quantity of Ground: But the long, heavy Rains that fell this Summer (more than common) and often covered the low Lands with Water, bred ſuch an Exceſs of Worms and Inſects, as did very great Damage, more than Half not eſcaping; which muſt reduce our Meaſure to the ſame Proportion: But the higheſt and dry Lands have produced ſuch a Crop for thoſe who have taken proper Care in Cultivation, as ought to encourage them. Theſe Accidents are not uncommon in all Countries; and in my Native of *England*, the Farmers in the up-land Parts ſeldom or never grieve, when they ſee their Neighbours in Vale almoſt drowned. I returned in Expectation of ſeeing the General ſome Time to Day; but upon his not coming, we concluded that he ſpent the Night enſuing with Meſſieurs *Montaigut* and *Beauſain*, agreeable to what he had wrote. Nothing ſtirring worth Note. 1739. Septemb. 21.

Saturday. Little Attention given to any Thing, beſides the earneſt Expectation that almoſt every Body ſhewed of the General's Arrival, 22.

1739. Septemb. Arrival, which drew many People to the Water-ſide, to wait his Coming; but it proved in vain yet. Captain *Davis*, with ſome of his principal Aſſiſtants of the Club, we underſtood was fully employed for two or three Days paſt in drawing up a Remonſtrance of the ill Uſage he had met with, to be preſented to the General as ſoon as he came; wherein it would appear ſo unexampled (as they gave out) that the Authors of it would have Cauſe to repent of what they had done: All which we were to ſee, and how far our Actions would be approved of by the General, or cenſured.

23. *Sunday*. The Service of the Church had due Obſervance. About Five in the Afternoon the Boat was eſpied coming down the River, wherein was the General, who landed ſoon after, under the uſual Compliment of our Cannon, and as many of our Freeholders, as could get under Arms in little more than a Quarter of an Hour, which was about fifty, to receive him; all glad to ſee him ſo well, and healthy, as he appeared, after ſo dangerous a Sickneſs as he had gone lately through. He was attended to his Lodging by the principal Officers and Magiſtrates of the Town; who after paying their Reſpects, and hearing what he was pleaſed to acquaint them with (briefly at preſent) all took their Leave, and withdrew. I delivered

vered him the Packet from the Truſt, which came to my Hands the 20th; and after he had opened it and read ſome of thoſe Advices he ſeemed to think of moſt Moment, I retired, and left him to his Reſt, which I thought he wanted. 1739. Septemb.

Monday. My Duty prompted me to a pretty cloſe Attendance on the General, which I gladly paid; and in Converſation he was pleaſed moſt agreeably to inform us, how unqueſtionably he had the Friendſhip of the Lower and Upper *Creek Indians* ſecured to us, which at this Time more eſpecially was of ſo great Value, when we were apprehenſive, thro' the ſecret Working of our Enemies, their former Amity began to wax cold: But as they were a very numerous and bold Nation, and lay immediately on the Back of this Province, we now looked on them as a Wall of Defence. After imparting to us what he thought proper, relating to his Travels, the next Thing deſirable was his Approbation of the publick Proceedings here ſince he left us; which he let us underſtand he was very well pleaſed with, particularly in bringing the Authors of that late Murder to Juſtice, for which two of them had ſuffered; and next, for being ſo watchful in guarding againſt any dangerous Correſpondence at this Seaſon with the *Spaniards*, commending the Spirit which appeared 24.

among

1739. Septemb. among us on that Occaſion, and confirming what was done relating to Captain *Davis*, as what the Exigence of Time required; whom he moreover ſent for in the Evening, and after a private Conference with him for a little while, he remanded him to his former Confinement, till he ſhould conſider farther of it another Day with the Magiſtrates. This was the more acceptable, becauſe it was a ſufficient Token to our Gentry of the Cabal, how vain and impotent their little Craft, mixed with much Malice, would appear, in Oppoſition to thoſe who purſued ſuch Steps as conduced to the Welfare of the Colony.

25. *Tueſday*,
26. *Weaneſday*,
27. *Thurſday*,
28. *Friday*,
29. *Saturday*.

The great Variety of Matter, which the General had under his Conſideration, during his Abode among us, at this important Juncture, made it impracticable for me ſo to keep Pace, as to make an exact Diary of all that paſſed: Wherefore it was only in my Power to note ſome of the moſt remarkable Tranſactions that happened during theſe five Days paſt, without ſpecifying particular Times. Captain *Davis*, by the General's Order to the Magiſtrates, was diſcharged from his Confinement, upon his entering into a Bond of 100 *l.* Penalty not to go to *Auguſtin*, or any *Spaniſh* Port, and to be of the good Behaviour: And afterwards he found

found Means of obtaining the General's Opinion of his Sincerity ſo far, that he undertook to turn his Sloop, which was intended for *Auguſtin*, into a Privateer, and the General would grant him a Commiſſion for that Purpoſe: So that he now appeared as earneſt to plunder the *Spaniards*, as before he was to ſuccour them: And it was well known, that through the long Intercourſe he had with them, and the Knowledge of all their Coaſts, he was capable of annoying them very much: Wherefore we were now to expect ſome Performances of thoſe Exploits which he propoſed, and due Diligence at preſent was uſed, to fit out this Privateer, and get her well manned. Frequent Diſpatches were ſent to divers Places, with Orders, as the General ſaw needful: And Lieutenant *Dunbar* being ſent on this Occaſion to *Charles-Town*, I wrote by him to Mr. *Vereſt* (to be forwarded by my Correſpondent Mr. *Hopton*) a Letter of the 25th; wherein I encloſed, by Order from the General, Copies I had taken of three Affidavits, made in the *Indian* Nation, by *Brown* and *Gardener*; ſetting forth the fatal Conſequence of Rum in ſuch Abundance, ſent from *Carolina* among the *Cherokee Indians*, &c. and it was not improbable but that this Letter might overtake at *Charles-Town* the former which I wrote of the 10th. Every

1739. Septemb. 25. 26. 27. 28. 29.

1739. Septemb. 25. 26. 27. 28. 29.

Body that we ſaw from *Carolina* confirmed the deplorable State they were in at *Charles-Town* (as before noted on the 18th) and the freſheſt News thence informed us, that *Saturday* and *Sunday* laſt they buried nineteen and twenty on a Day; ſo that it is deemed next to a Peſtilence; moſt of thoſe who are taken with it, dying in leſs than forty-eight Hours; and by a careful Computation among themſelves, they reckon the Small-Pox among them a little while ſince, and this dreadful Mortality now, have taken away at leaſt one Fourth of the white People of that Town: One or two more of our deſerting Freeholders are ſaid to be among the Deceaſed, namely, *Deſborow* the Carpenter, and his two Sons, both grown to Man's Eſtate; Mr. *Amiens*, Clerk of the Aſſembly; Mr. *Lewis*, a Lawyer, and Judge of the Admiralty; and old Monſieur *Thomas*, a noted Engineer, who left St. *Simon*'s lately, upon a Stop being put to any farther Fortifications there at that Time. Mr. *Eyre*, a Cadet in the Regiment, who with others attended the General in his Progreſs among the *Indians*, was now ſent back thither, with Inſtructions, and a Commiſſion, to one Mr. *Samuel Brown*, a noted and well eſteemed Trader among the *Cherokees*, to bring down a conſiderable Body of that Nation, and to march at the Head of them, expecting they

they would be ſeveral Hundreds, whom it is preſumed his Excellence purpoſes to make uſe of, as a Diverſion with the *Spaniſh Indians* in the Neighbourhood of *Auguſtin:* And he depends on a ſtrong Detachment from the *Creeks*, purſuant to their late Agreement; whom he will not keep idle. During theſe Preparations againſt the Enemy, which were carried on and directed by him alone, who beſt knew how, and in whom proper Powers were inveſted, our Juntillo, who ſought all Occaſions to diſtinguiſh themſelves at all Times, now projected to form themſelves into a Body, under the Title of Volunteers, who deſired to be regulated a Company for Defence of the Country, *&c.* but excluſive of any Commands from the ſtanding Militia of the Town where they lived: For which End, they believed it the wiſeſt Courſe to name their own Officers; and accordingly they choſe their Captain, Lieutenant, and Enſign among themſelves; who, all together, did not exceed ſix or ſeven in Number; but were looked on as Men qualified to conduct any Enterprize they took in Hand (though miſerably defeated hitherto in all their political Schemes) and having ſo laid this Ground-Work, they made no Queſtion but Gentlemen Volunteers would flock together, under the imaginary Command of Captain *Tailfer*, &c. till after two

1739. Septemb. 25. 26. 27. 28. 29.

1739. Septemb. or three Days Waiting, and ſeeing no Recruits come in, they then betook themſelves to ſollicit ſuch as they could prevail with, to be enrolled in a Piece of Paper; where at length they picked up about a Dozen more to be added to the former; and theſe were generally looſe Fellows, moſtly *Scotch* Servants lately out of their Time, or the like. Thus provided, they next addreſſed the General, by Petition, that he would authorize them to act conformable to what they conceived would render them uſeful to the Colony: But his Excellence not happening to think as they did, that an Independant Command in ſuch Hands would contribute to the Safety of the Colony, which required Unity, and due Obedience in all Things for our Preſervation; he received it with Contempt, and not without ſome Reſentment (it may be imagined) at their Inſolence, in conſtituting Officers of their own, in Expectation that he would give them Commiſſions, exalting them above all others. —— And ſo the Week ended.

30. *Sunday.* Due Obſervance was paid to the Day; and the General was pleaſed to attend Divine Service both before Noon and after.

October 1. *Monday.* The General ceaſed not from a continual Application to regulate every Thing that he thought expedient for us to govern

govern ourſelves by, in his Abſence, when he ſhould go for the Southern Frontier, which we now expected would be in few Days more. Towards Evening arrived Captain *Davis*'s Snow, under the Command of Captain *James Williams*, who ſailed hence with Lumber for the *Weſt-Indies* ſome Months ſince (*vide May* 28, 29, 30, and *June* 1.) and leaving the Snow at *Tybee*, he came up in his Boat, when he waited on the General, and made his Report, *&c.* His Loading was principally Molaſſes and Sugar; which unleſs he found a Market for here, he intended to look farther: His Brother *Robert*, who ſailed with him from hence, ſtaid at St. *Kitt*'s; and it was ſuppoſed was gone ere now for *England*. 1739. October

Tueſday. Nothing worth Note, unleſs a violent Rain may be thought ſo, which began with the Sun-riſing, and held all Day in an uncommon Manner; ſo that the Ground was covered with Water, even on the high Land where the Town ſtands; and there was no ſtirring out of Doors, neither did it entirely ceaſe at Bed-Time: But ſuch Rains being always looked for in other hot Countries, at this Seaſon of the Year, puts an End to any Admiration here. Tomorrow being the Day when the Reprieve would expire, which was granted to *Levett* (one of thoſe condemned for Murder) 2.

1739. October and he writing a Petition to the General for Mercy; wherein, inſtead of owning himſelf guilty of any Crime, he inſiſted on his Innocence, lamenting his Misfortune that he lay under *Suſpicion* of Murder; the General was much offended at it, and conſtrued it to be arraigning the Juſtice of the Place, and particularly of the Jury, who had found him *Guilty:* For how was it poſſible for them to believe what he alledged in his own Defence, *viz.* that he was not well, and laid down to ſleep, ſo that he heard nothing of it; when it was confeſſed by himſelf, and known, that the Place where he ſaid he lay, was upon the Deck, and within very few Yards of where the Fact was committed; which in the barbarous Manner it was carried on, muſt take up much Time, and could not be without Strife and Noiſe? The General farther obſerved, that he now fell ſhort even of that Confeſſion which he had made before, and found him prevaricating: Wherefore, to vindicate the Juſtice of the Court and Jury, and not to leave it in his Power, by a Pardon, to throw Reproaches on both hereafter, he reſolved he ſhould die; and ordered that he ſhould have Notice to prepare himſelf for it in four Days more.

3. *Wedneſday.* The General intending to publiſh the War with *Spain*, in due Manner

ner and Form; he gave Orders for all the Freeholders to be under Arms at Beat of Drum, and that the Magiſtrates, in their Gowns, ſhould be on the Bench at Noon in the Court-Houſe; whilſt in the mean Time he directed a proper Declaration to be wrote, ſetting forth the Orders he received from his Majeſty's Secretary of State, relating thereto; and alſo another Paper, cautioning all Perſons in this Province, to have a watchful Eye upon any Negroes, who might attempt to ſet a Foot in it; foraſmuch as many of them, at the Inſtigation of the *Spaniards*, had run lately away from their Maſters in *Carolina*, and found kind Reception at *Auguſtin:* And moreover, the late Inſurrection of them in that Province, which was but newly ſuppreſſed, gave Reaſon to apprehend, that ſome of ſuch as had yet eſcaped, might be lurking about in *Georgia*, in hopes to make their Way to the Enemy; and in paſſing on, might do great Miſchief among our Settlers; promiſing, as a Reward for taking them, what the Act here directs, and withal, what the Government at *Carolina* promiſes to pay, for every ſuch runaway Negroe, delivered at *Charles-Town*, alive or dead. When the General came to the Court-Houſe, where he found the Magiſtrates on the Bench, he took his Seat by them; and the Militia, who being drawn

1739. October 3.

1739. October up before the Court-Houſe, had grounded their Arms, and were all come within the Doors; his Excellence then made a Speech to them all, ſuitable to the Occaſion, commending that Chearfulneſs which he obſerved to be in all Ranks of People, aſſuring them, that effectual Care had been taken by him to prevent any Enemy coming on our Backs from the Weſt and South; and as we lay open only to the Sea, we had already ſome Frigates cruiſing on the Coaſt to protect us; and he had Aſſurance from the Government of more Strength at Sea; as alſo ſome Expectation of an additional Force by Land, to be ſent him in a little while. Then he put thoſe Papers into my Hands, which were prepared, directing me to read them to the People; which I did, as audibly as I could; afterwards the Conſtables read them again to the Men, on taking up their Arms; and next, they were affixed to the Doors of the Court-Houſe. Upon the General's Return to his Lodgings five Cannon were fired, and the Militia gave three handſome Vollies with their ſmall Arms, as it were in Defiance, without the Appearance of any Dread of the *Spaniards*.

4. *Thurſday*, 5. *Friday*, 6. *Saturday*. So little Intermiſſion was found theſe few Days from attending the General's Commands, which rather multiplied than

than abated, through his inceſſant Application,* that the moſt material Thing which happened abroad, and I thought worth noting, was the Death of the old *Mico Thomo Chichi*, ſaid to be upwards of ninety Years of Age: And as the General always eſteemed him a Friend of the Colony, and therefore ſhewed him particular Marks of his Eſteem, when living; ſo he diſtinguiſhed him at his Death, ordering his Corpſe to be brought down; and it was buried in the Centre of one of the principal Squares, the General being pleaſed to make himſelf one of his Pall-Bearers, with five others, among whom he laid his Commands on me to be one, and the other four were military Officers: At the Depoſiting of the Corpſe, ſeven Minute Guns were fired, and about forty Men in Arms (as many as could inſtantly be found) gave three Vollies over the Grave; which the General ſays he intends to dignify with ſome Obeliſk, or the like, over it, as an Ornament to the Town, and a Memorial to the *Indians*, how great Regard the *Engliſh* would pay to all their Nations, who maintain true Friendſhip with us. 1739. October

Sunday. Divine Service was performed in the uſual Manner. A Boat arrived from Captain *Thompſon*, juſt come to an Anchor without the Bar at *Tybee*: In the Boat was Captain *Hugh M^c^Kay*, who went as ſoon 7.

as

1739. October 7. as aſhore to wait on the General, to whom he carried a Packet: And at the ſame Time the Cockſwain of the Boat brought me a Bag ſealed, wherein I found alſo a Packet directed to me, and many Letters looſe in the Bag for divers People; beſides one from the Captain of the Ship to me, deſiring me to make haſte down to him, or to ſend a Reaſon why not: And moreover I received a Letter from Mr. *Verelſt* of the 16th of *July*, ſignifying the Orders the Truſt had given Captain *Thompſon*; as alſo importing the Truſtees Orders to me, to go forthwith on board the Ship, on her Arrival, and receive the Packet directed to me; in which Packet I ſhould find a Direction to a covered Box directed to me, N° 1. wherein were Bills General *Ogletborpe* would ſign and deliver to me, purſuant to the Truſtees Requeſt to him. With Leave of the General, about Ten at Night, I ſet off (the Tide then ſerving) together with Captain *McKay*, in the Ship's Yawl, which returned; and we had provided a ſmall Veſſel to follow us (a Skooner) ſufficient to bring away what Paſſengers were for this Place; likewiſe ſome few Goods that we were in great Need of, ſuch as could be readily come at, and by which I myſelf might be ſure of getting home again, with what Speed I could poſſibly; the General ſending his Orders by us us to Captain *Thompſon*, to make Sail for St. *Simon's* without Loſs of Time, apprehending that the Ship might lie in Danger where ſhe was, either from bad Weather ſuddenly riſing on the Coaſt, or poſſibly from the Enemy, by ſome of their Launches, or ſmall Craft well armed: So that there could be no Expectation of the Bulk of thoſe Goods conſigned to me, being delivered at *Savannah*, till the Ship returned thither; which probably could not be in leſs than four or five Weeks. The General granted a farther Reprieve to *Levett*, who otherwiſe muſt have ſuffered Death to-morrow. 1739. October

Monday. About Three in the Morning we got aboard, the Ship lying far out at Sea, where with great Impatience I waited the Skooner's Coming, all the fore Part of the Day, which gave Room for a little Chat what was doing in *England*, &c. And by Reaſon of an eaſterly Breeze, it was long ere the Skooner got out; ſo that ſhe came up to us late in the Day, and then we uſed all poſſible Diſpatch to put on board her four Pipes of *Madera* Wine (there being not a Drop to be had in Town) and ſeventeen Caſks of Flour, Part of the forty ſent; which alſo there was great Need of: And then putting the Paſſengers aboard, I took my Leave; but not without remembring to carry the Box N° 1. 8.

with

1739. October with me, and immediately both Veſſels made Sail, about Seven in the Evening, fine Moon-Light, with a ſmall Breeze at Eaſt, which anſwered equally our Purpoſes; but a ſtrong Tide with-held us from getting in
9. at *Tybee*; ſo that we were forced to come to an Anchor near the Bar till towards Morning; and then the Wind ſhifting to the North-Weſt, we made it a whole Tide's Work to reach *Cockſpur* Road, about two Miles within the Light-Houſe; and there (ſeeing Matters ſo croſs to my Deſigns) I got a ſmall Canoe, and rowing up againſt Tide, I came to *Savannah*, *Tueſday* Evening, juſt at ſhutting in of Day-Light; when I waited on the General, and made Report of what I knew.

10. *Wedneſday*,
11. *Thurſday*,
12. *Friday*,
13. *Saturday*.

The greateſt Part of my Time being taken up, as for a while paſt, moſt agreeably in attending the General's Commands, and executing ſuch as were required; I had only the Power of making a few ſhort Obſervations theſe four Days on the Temper of the People (as I could eaſily diſcover) ſince Captain *Thompſon*'s Arrival, and the great Alterations which came by the Letters he brought, that were to be made in the Magiſtracy of this Place: And I ſaw plainly, that they were in a good Diſpoſition to be well pleaſed, and pay all due Obedience to whatever the

the honourable Truſtees thought proper, for the good Government which they were to live under: But the Advancement of Mr. *Chriſtie* to the Place of firſt Bailiff, was a little ſhocking to almoſt every Body, even the beſt of the Inhabitants; that a Man, who for ſome Time paſt was grown ſo obnoxious among them, for his bare-faced Partiality, for his ſcandalous living in open Adultery with a Man's Wife *(Richard Turner)* who run away hence to the *Weſt-Indies* a while ago; and his cloſe Adherence to that miſchievous Aſſembly at *Jenkins*'s, who had been continually ſtirring up Strife and Sedition, inſomuch that, not without good Reaſon, they were apprehenſive his future Behaviour on the Bench, would ſhew manifeſtly under what Influence he acted; and it began already to appear, how far that Rump of an almoſt worn-out Party, were again elated, and pricked up their Ears at this News; for when it was underſtood by them, that Mr. *Chriſtie* was to take that Office upon him, as ſoon as he had made out Copies of the Proceedings of the Town-Court to the Time Mr. *Williamſon*, who was to ſucceed him, was ſworn in; when I was to deliver to Mr. *Chriſtie* his Conſtitution as firſt Bailiff, and not before; and likewiſe that I was to deliver Mr. *Williamſon*'s Conſtitution for the Place of Recorder, as ſoon

1739. October 10. 11. 12. 13.

1739. October 10. 11. 12. 13.

as Mr. *Chriſtie* had perfected his Copy of the Proceedings of the Court, to the Time of Mr. *Williamſon*'s taking upon him that Office, and not before; (the former of which was ſuch a Taſk, as was well known would employ him a long Time, if ever it could be perfected; in ſuch Confuſion and Diſorder were the Court Proceedings kept; and the latter no Man could foreſee when it would happen, Mr. *Williamſon* having left this Place, and being gone to *Charles-Town* to practiſe there as an Attorney, uncertain when, or whether ever, to return hither:) This ſo galled them, that they could not contain themſelves; but they gave a full Looſe to their Paſſions: And thereupon, after a Day or two whiſpering their Sentiments about Town, endeavouring to inveigle unwary People into an Opinion, that ſome Craft was at the Bottom to deſtroy their Liberties; it became an open Talk in the Streets, that it was determined, as ſoon as the Court opened, which would be next *Monday*, to ſet Mr. *Chriſtie* on the Bench, which was his Right, forcibly, if it could not be done otherwiſe. All this I took Care to inform the General of; who ordered me to put it into Writing by Way of Letter to him, and to give Notice to the Freeholders to make a full Appearance at the Time of opening the Court: I did ſo, and well knew

knew that the Orders the General gave, were ſufficient to defeat the Purpoſes of ſuch pigmy Enterprizers, ſhould they attempt any Violence: For how faulty ſoever we may have been at *Savannah*, I am very confident more than nine Parts in ten, would on ſuch, or any other Occaſion, oppoſe and defeat all Contrivances to annoy the Civil Power. —— But the Peace is beſt preſerved without ſuch Experiments. 1739. October

Sunday. Mr. *Norris* officiated at Church, in the publick Service, as uſual; and the General was pleaſed to attend it. 14.

Monday. The General having well conſidered the preſent Circumſtances of Affairs, was pleaſed to direct, that I ſhould deliver to Mr. *Fallowfield*, and Mr. *Jones*, their ſeveral Conſtitutions, appointing them to be ſecond and third Bailiffs; and alſo to Mr. *Chriſtie* his Conſtitution, appointing him to ſuperſede Mr. *Henry Parker* in the Commiſſion for examining Accounts, *&c.* But as to the Place of firſt Bailiff, he thought it not adviſable to inveſt him with that Authority immediately, without either of the Conditions performed on his Part: Wherefore he farther ordered, that Mr. *Parker* might very properly keep his Seat, as before, on the Bench, till the Pleaſure of the Truſtees was farther known. Purſuant to this, I gave to each of them the ſeveral Conſtitutions for the Uſes before-mentioned: 15.

1739. October mentioned: After which the two new Bailiffs were ſworn duly before the General; and then the Court ſat, when they took their Places; Meſſ. *Parker* and *Chriſtie* yet continuing in their former, till farther Orders, in a full Court, without any Interruption or Diſorder; the Abettors of all Diſturbance finding themſelves ſufficiently over-awed. A Grand Jury was called and ſworn, and proper Matters laid before them to conſider of; and then the Court adjourned till to-morrow.

16. *Tueſday.* Several Preſentments were delivered into Court by the Grand Jury, and Indictments for Miſdemeanours, *&c.* after which they were diſcharged: Then the Court proceeded to determine ſome little Matters; but there being ſome Actions of conſiderable Moment and Value commenced, carried on, and multiplied, by ſome Perſons in Trade, againſt each other, with the Appearance of much Rancour; it was the Opinion of the Court to poſtpone thoſe Trials a little, that ſome Means might be ſought, if poſſible, to bring them into better Temper, and ſee if they would be perſuaded to refer their Differences to Arbitration, eſpecially as they conſiſted chiefly of Matters in Accounts: Wherefore the Court adjourned to *Friday* Morning.

Wedneſday.

Wedneſday. The General obſerving, that ſince the Land of the Common being clear-ed of Trees, Abundance of Shrub-Wood was daily growing up, which filled the Ground; and that the publick Squares, and moſt open Parts of the Town, were filled with an offenſive Weed, near as high as a Man's Shoulders; both which were a great Annoyance, and beſides hindering Graſs from growing up, harboured and increaſed many troubleſome Inſects and Vermin; and moreover if ſet on Fire when dry, might endanger the Burning of the Town: For theſe Reaſons, he was pleaſed over Night to ſend out Orders, that upon Beat of Drum, this Morning, all Perſons inhabiting the Town, whether Freeholders, or Inmates, and Boys of a competent Age, ſhould appear at Sun-riſing this Morning, and go to Work in clearing this great Nuſance: Which accordingly they readily did; and all falling to Work heartily, before Night they had (ſome with one Inſtrument, and ſome with another) laid ſmooth ſome Hundreds of Acres: The General was pleaſed to be among them himſelf; and every Body, without Diſtinction, took Pains to do what he could; which gave his Excellence a double Pleaſure, it being not only a Trial of the Peoples Diſpoſition to obey, but hereby he ſaw plainly, under his own View, the Number

1739. October 17.

1739. October of People within this Town; which (allowing ſome Boys of good Stature and Strength, and reckoning Servants, and Inmates of all Sorts, living in Town) appeared to be very near two hundred Men, able, on Occaſion, to bear Arms. He ordered a Caſk of Bread, and another of Beer for them at Breakfaſt-Time in the Morning, and at leaving off Work in the Evening, another ſuch Refreſhment; highly delighted to ſee how large a Tract of Land they had cleanſed: And as there remained another Day's Work, but much leſs than this of the Day, which would compleat the Whole; the General ordered that ſhould be on the 5th of *November*; when at their finiſhing it, they were to be ſo again treated, and they might make a Bonfire of the Rubbiſh they had now under Foot.

18. *Thurſday*. The Affair of ſettling the Militia of the Town under proper Officers, was one Buſineſs of this Day, which took up great Part of it, in the General's enquiring after the Cauſes of many little Squabbles, which he found growing among the Tything-men, and the Conſtables alſo: As Things now ſtood with us, he was of Opinion, that inſtead of eighteen Tything-men, which we had, ten good ones would be ſufficient, and two Conſtables only: Wherefore he made Choice of ten ſuch Tything-

Tything-men as he liked, and appointed *Robert Potter* Conſtable (in the Room of *John Fallowfield*, now made ſecond Bailiff) to act in Conjunction with *Samuel Mercer*, the other Conſtable, formerly appointed.— But he reſolved to conſider of theſe Things a little farther. 1739. October

Friday, *Saturday*. } The publick Affairs now urgently calling the General Southward, theſe two Days required cloſe Attendance, from ſuch as waited for his Orders and Directions in many Caſes during his Abſence: So that I had little to remark elſewhere. 19. 20.

Sunday. The Divine Service was duly obſerved; and the General, as before, failed not to give a good Example in attending it. In the Evening, having obſerved that in Times paſt Diſputes had frequently ariſen among the Conſtables and other Officers, concerning their ſeveral Commands in the Militia, which in the preſent Situation of Affairs might prove to be of very dangerous Conſequence; and being of Opinion, that the beſt Way to prevent it, would be to lodge the principal Command in one Perſon, whoſe Orders all were to obey; he was pleaſed to entertain ſo good an Opinion of my Behaviour, as to make Choice of me for that Purpoſe; and accordingly delivered me his Commiſſion, appointing me to train, inſtruct, exerciſe, 21.

1739. October and govern, the Militia of the Northern Part of the Province, for the ſpecial Defence and Safety of the ſaid Province: To aſſemble in martial Array, put in warlike Poſture, the Inhabitants of the ſaid Northern Diviſion; and to lead and conduct them, and with them to encounter, expulſe, repel, reſiſt, and purſue, by Force of Arms; and to kill, ſlay, deſtroy, and conquer, by all fitting Ways, Enterprizes, and Means whatſoever, all and every ſuch Perſon or Perſons, as ſhall at any Time hereafter in an hoſtile Manner, attempt, or enterprize the Deſtruction, Invaſion, Detriment, or Annoyance of the ſaid Province, *&c.* Which Commiſſion (how unworthy ſoever I thought myſelf of it) it behoved me not to ſcruple the Acceptance of, leſt an Imputation ſhould follow, either of my ſetting little Value on the Honour conferred, or of ſuch a Sort of Baſhfulneſs, as at this Time would be very unſeaſonable, and might be conſtrued ſomething elſe, which I avoid naming: For which Reaſons I threw aſide any Marks of Reluctance, reſolving in all Things, as far as I was capable, to exert myſelf in promoting the publick Welfare.

22. *Monday.* This Day the General purpoſed to have left us; but upon Intelligence received, that a Body of *Indians*, partly *Chicaſaws*, and partly *Euchies*, had joined, to

to the Number of a hundred Men, and were coming down voluntarily, to attend, and ſerve againſt the *Spaniards*, and would be here in few Days; he thought it worth his while to wait their Coming, knowing of what Uſe they might be, and therefore would take them with him. *N. B.* Theſe *Indians* were no Part of thoſe much greater Numbers he expected from the populous Nations of the *Creeks*, and *Cherokees*, that he had ſent for, and ſhould expect to march to him at St. *Simon*'s directly. 1739. October

Tueſday. The Court having diſpatched what Buſineſs they thought neceſſary to be done this Seſſions, adjourned to the next orderly Time of their meeting again towards the latter End of *November*. The General granted a farther Reprieve for *Levett*, upon his altering the Stile of his Petition, and owning that he was juſtly condemned by the Law, for being privy to the Uproar which happened on board, when the Murder was committed, and not revealing it; for which he begged Mercy, perſiſting ſtill in ſaying he had no Hand in it, nor knew of his Death till he was overboard: And it was now expected theſe repeated Reprieves would end in a Pardon at laſt. 23.

Wedneſday. Finding a little Vacancy, from Buſineſs growing leſs urgent than hitherto, with the General; I devoted this 24.

1739. October 24. Day almoſt wholly to look into what my People were doing abroad, and what Product was to be ſeen off the Land that I had planted this Year, which now was pretty near got together: And what I before had obſerved, relating to the uncommon wet Summer we had, *(vide Sept.* 21.) appeared now too well verified; for all the low Lands had ſuffered extreamly; among which, thoſe Lots happened which I occupied, and Abundance of the Corn was utterly ſpoiled, partly by the Stalks rotting ere it came to Maturity; and moſt of that which ripened, was infeſted with the Worm, that did great Damage; whilſt the dry Lands threw out a plentiful Crop: Nevertheleſs, *communibus annis*, the Summer Heats here are ſuch, that I would, in my own Judgment, always prefer the low Lands to the high; and though it happened that they failed this Year, through ſuch exceſſive Wet, yet moſt undoubtedly they are leſs apt to do ſo than the other. The General having lately confirmed the Grant of five hundred Acres, which he partly put me in Poſſeſſion of on the 19th of *April* laſt, at the Mouth of *Vernon* River *(ut antea)* it was now my Deſire, with all convenient Speed, to ſet ſome Hands at Work there, and make what Improvements I could, as the Seaſon was proper; taking Care at the ſame Time, that

that thoſe Lots I had been cultivating for two Years paſt, ſhould be occupied; ſo that what Labour had been beſtowed, ſhould not be thrown away, till the right Owner came to poſſeſs it. 1739. October

Thurſday. Enſign *Cadogan* arrived this Morning from *Carolina*, whom I was very glad to enquire of, what came of the Packet which I delivered to his Care, together with Captain *Norbury*, on the 17th of *September* laſt, which I had for ſome Time ſince been very uneaſy about, not hearing a Word of any ſuch Packet coming to the Hands of my Correſpondent Mr. *Hopton*, who always had been very exact and punctual, and to whom (as uſual) I had wrote a Letter with it: Moreover he had adviſed me of the Receipt of another Letter of mine, to Mr. *Verelſt*, dated *December* 25, and what Ship he had ſent it by; but ſtill not a Word of my former, dated the 10th Ditto; till now that Mr. *Cadogan* brought me a Letter from him, informing me, that that former Packet was at laſt come to Hand, and juſt timely enough to ſend it away by a Ship bound for *Topſham*, which ſailed the ſame Day (*viz.* the 21ſt Inſtant) Captain *Ward* in the *Mary* Brig. Mr. *Cadogan* in Excuſe ſaid, that both he and Captain *Norbury* were taken very ill at *Port-Royal*, which continued a long while upon them, before he was able to proceed 25.

1739. October to *Charles-Town*; and he was not willing to put it out of his own Hands to the Care of another: By which Means it may be expected, that my Letter of the 25th of *September*, will find its Way ſome Time ſooner than that of the 10th. The reducing the Number of Tything-men, which the General had ſeveral Times under Conſideration, ſo as to leave a competent Strength for carrying on the Duties of that Office, and yet not to eſtabliſh an Expence more than could be anſwered, ſince no Proviſion was made in the Eſtimate for that Service; he now ſettled that Affair to his Liking, appointing only ten for it, *viz.* two for each of the old Wards, inſtead of four; and one for each of the new; and dividing the Town through *Broughton-Street*, from Eaſt to Weſt; he appointed two Conſtables only, one over the Northern Diviſion, conſiſting of three Wards; and the other over the Southern, conſiſting of the like Number; purſuant to which, he gave out the Tything-mens Warrants for me to deliver to them, and the Conſtables he delivered to them himſelf.

26. *Friday.* An Expreſs from the South, with Letters, *&c.* to the General; which brought ill News from the Camp, that they were grown very ſickly, and that they had not Officers ſufficient to do the common Duty; but the Sickneſs did not prove mortal,

tal, being a Sort of Ague and Fever with regular Intermiſſion, which pulled many down, both Officers and Soldiers, to a very weak State; ſuch as is pretty common in theſe Parts, at certain Seaſons, eſpecially among freſh People from *Europe*, and is uſually termed a Seaſoning. On this Occaſion the General immediately ſent off two or three Subalterns who attended him here, and began to grow impatient till he could go himſelf; but was very unwilling to leave the hundred *Indians* behind him, whom he looked earneſtly for every Day, as noted on *Monday* laſt. In the Afternoon I convened all the Officers, Conſtables and Tything-men, to whom I firſt read my own Commiſſion, and afterwards theirs; from whence I took Occaſion to exhort them all to lay aſide all little Picques and Animoſities among themſelves, and to unite heartily in promoting the publick Peace, and diſcouraging all Attempts to ſow Diſcord among them, eſpecially at this Time, when it behoved us to be on our Guard againſt all Enemies, whether open, or ſecret, the worſt of the two. I aſſured them of my ready Diſpoſition to conſult with them, and adviſe, upon all Emergencies; and in Caſe of any dangerous Attempt upon our Safety, my Command ſhould not expoſe them to ſuch Service as I would decline myſelf: And withal openly told them, that

1739. October 26.

1739. October that I muſt (in Juſtice to the Commiſſion I had the Honour to bear) expect due Obedience to be paid to ſuch Orders, as at any Time I ſhould iſſue, whether my Superiors or my own; and as I ſhould be a vigilant Obſerver of their ſeveral Deportments, ſo they might be aſſured of my repreſenting it without Partiality, to thoſe whoſe Favour was well worth deſerving. They expreſſed themſelves well pleaſed with my being at their Head, and ſeemed to be truly of Opinion, that all Occaſion of Diſputes about Priority was now removed, much to their Satisfaction (as they ſaid:) Mutual Aſſurances were given on all Sides, of an hearty Good-will towards one another; which I obſerved ſome of them were of Opinion would be beſt confirmed over a Bottle; wherefore taking the Hint, I willingly agreed to what they termed wetting my Commiſſion; and took a chearful Glaſs with them for an Hour or two in the Evening, to drink the King's Health, and the Royal Family, the honourable Truſtees, Succeſs to his Majeſty's Arms, and General *Oglethorpe* at the Head of them in theſe Provinces, *&c.* every Body, when we parted, going home in good Order, and good Humour.

27. The General now *(Saturday)* finding himſelf a little more at Leiſure than for a while paſt, diverted his Care about other Matters,

Matters, to look into the State of the great Lots of five hundred Acres; and ſome Doubts having ariſen about the Certainty of thoſe Lands, whether run out true or not, by the late Surveyor *Jones*; the General went himſelf to ſee the firſt original Lines, as they had been marked out; from whence, if due Obſervance was had, in running the traverſe Lines, it muſt unavoidably prove the Truth of the Whole: And this it was incumbent on the former Surveyor to demonſtrate, that ſo the Perſon whom the General ſhould think fit to appoint for the future aſcertaining thoſe Lands, to whom they belonged, might be well inſtructed by the preſent Plan how to proceed; which took up this whole Day, and was likely to be Work enough for another. During which Intermiſſion, I had Matter ſufficient to employ my Pen at home, and which I ſtuck cloſely to, to get forward what my Duty required, being unavoidably fallen much in Arrear, and it would coſt me ſome Pains to fetch up again. 1739. October

Sunday. The Divine Service was what called all People to the Performance of, and which it was to be wiſhed every one was alike careful to obſerve, as the proper Buſineſs of the Day: And nothing of any Moment happened to divert their Thoughts from it. 28.

Monday.

1739. October 29. *Monday.* The General, waiting only for his *Indians* coming now, before he left us, was intent upon looking carefully into the Plat of Lands formerly run out, to prevent any Miſtakes; and I was not leſs ſo in reducing my looſe Papers into right Order, tranſcribing what was needful, *&c.* which required ſome Time. Mr. *Bradley*, after too long trifling, and ſeeking many Shifts and Evaſions, not to quit the great Houſe belonging to the Truſt, which he had taken Poſſeſſion of; finding himſelf driven to the Neceſſity of it, now moved his Goods to another in Town that was vacant, at a moderate Rent, intending it for his Habitation no longer (as he gave out) than till he had provided a Place to be in, upon the five hundred Acres allotted him; which he had a long while raiſed many Objections to, and ſhewed himſelf diſſatiſfied about; but now thoſe imaginary Obſtacles being diſſipated by the General, it would appear ere long, how far he was in earneſt to cultivate that Farm.

30. *Tueſday.* Mr. *Norris* taking Breakfaſt with me this Morning, began again to complain very heavily of the unkind Uſage which he met with; and which for a pretty while paſt, he refrained from ſpeaking of to me (probably from his obſerving, that I ſhewed not an Over-readineſs to liſten to ſuch diſagreeable Controverſy, as far as I could

could well avoid it) but now, he ſaid, he could with-hold no longer, ſince it was God's Cauſe, and his Service was impugned; inſomuch, that for Want of Candles, the Evening Prayers now ceaſed; as they muſt have done a long while ſince, had not he himſelf, at his own Expence, bought Candles where he could get them, but now he could find none in Town to be ſold; and knowing Mr. *Jones* had ſome in the Stores, he ſent thither to buy, with Money to pay, but was refuſed: From hence he took Occaſion to expatiate largely on the Treatment he had met with, ſo different from any of his Predeceſſors, ever ſince his being here; particularly at the Stores, as he had divers Times before made known, and which he little expected, from thoſe Aſſurances he had, of kinder Regard being ſhewn him, before he left *England:* But as for the little malicious Stories ſpread of him, and the frequent Reproaches ſo baſely whiſpered about, by a Set of Men, who (he believes) think the Leſſening of his Character will conduce to aggrandize that of him who ſucceeds him; he prays God to forgive them, and they create him not the leaſt Uneaſineſs: At the ſame Time he was ſo juſt to acknowledge the Readineſs I had always ſhewn to do him any Service I could, and looked upon me as his true Friend. To all this I had little to ſay: The

1739. October 30.

1739. October 30. The Want of Candles, and thereby the Want of Evening Prayers, I know was too true: But as Mr. *Jones* and I were (I hoped) in a mutual good Underſtanding with each other, in all Things that our Duties required us to act jointly together, I was not fond of entering into any Arguments with him, knowing his teſty Temper: Wherefore I told Mr. *Norris*, that as the General was now here, the beſt Way undoubtedly for him, would be to lay open any Grievances there, where it was moſt likely to find a Remedy: But at the ſame Time, underſtanding the General had engaged him to go with him to *Frederica*, where for Want of a Miniſter, the moſt neceſſary Parts of a Prieſt's Office were wanting, more eſpecially Baptiſm and the Lord's Supper; I hoped with myſelf, that finding Things more agreeable to him where he was going, would make him forget what he took amiſs here, from very few; for the Generality of the People ſhewed him the Reſpect which his truly unblameable Behaviour among us deſerved: And it was probable, that Mr. *Whitfield*'s coming ſoon hither (whom we now looked for) might prevent any future Cauſe of Complaint from him hence. After he left me, I betook myſelf to my own Work, the ſame as Yeſterday.

Wedneſday.

Wedneſday. The General doing me the Favour of aſking me to dine with him, was pleaſed afterwards to engage my Stay there the remaining Part of the Day; when, free from all other Company, moſt Part of the Time, I had the Pleaſure of a long Converſation with him, and of knowing his Sentiments in many Things, which might be of Uſe to me in my future Conduct: Divers Matters he gave me a particular Charge in, which he ſeemed to think of great Conſequence; and among others, he required me not to fail laying before the honourable Truſtees, a true State of the whole Affair relating to the late Change of Magiſtrates, and the Reaſons why their Orders concerning *Parker* and *Chriſtie* had not yet been entirely fulfilled: I told him, that I never miſſed noting in my Journal every Thing of Moment that came to my Knowledge, and there it would be found; but he ſaid, he did not think that ſufficient, without a Letter; for Journals might, or might not, be read; but Letters to be ſure always were: And tho' he was more and more confirmed in Opinion, that what Orders he had given in that Affair were needful, till the Pleaſure of the Truſtees could be farther known; yet it would be neceſſary, for his Honour's Defence, to have that Buſineſs laid open, as clear as poſſible: Which I promiſed to do

1739. October 31.

1739. do as well as my Capacity would allow; and then took my Leave.

Novemb. 1. *Thurſday*, } Being ſeized with ſome
2. *Friday*. } ſharp Pains in my Breaſt, and divers other Parts, I was bound to keep in, hoping by Warmth, and good Kitchen Phyſick, to get the better of it: As I did; for in twenty-four Hours it began to wear off, and plainly ſhewed me it was no more than a Cold; which might reaſonably be expected from the ſudden Change of Weather in very few Days paſt; in which ſhort Time, the great Warmth we had, by Means of a Southerly Wind and clear Sky, was changed into a North-Weſt Wind and thick Clouds, which made as great a Difference in the Temper of the Air, as is uſually found in *England* between the Months of *June* and *December*: And theſe ſurprizing Alterations ſome Times happen at any Seaſon of the Year. All that I could learn worth noting in theſe two Days was, that Captain *Fennel*, whom I gave ſome Account of, in my former Notes of the 30th of *July* and the 1ſt and 3d of *Auguſt*, was now come in from *Carolina* to *Cockſpur*, with a new Sloop of his own, carrying ten Guns and twenty Men, and bound for *Jamaica*; where he ſhould alſo have another Sloop; and with thoſe (being now diſingaged from the *South-Sea* Company and *Spaniſh* Trade) he purpoſed

to carry on a private Trade of his own, betwixt the *Weſt-Indies* and the Northern Provinces, being well armed, and provided for Attack or Defence, as he ſhould ſee needful. With him came Mr. *George Saxby*, and Mr. *William Williamſon*, as Paſſengers from *Charles-Town*; the firſt on his Pleaſure, more than any Buſineſs; and the other we ſuppoſed might come on Account of the Recorderſhip of this Place, which he underſtood was his Appointment, and which now would ſoon be conſidered of by the General, *&c.* —— By whom they were all courteouſly received. 1739. Novemb.

Saturday. Finding myſelf pretty well at Eaſe, I went abroad again and waited on the General, where I found the Strangers at Breakfaſt with him: And Captain *Fennel* being a ſenſible, genteel Man, beyond the common Level of ſome unpoliſhed Tars; he ſeemed pleaſed with the Opportunity of ſuch a Conference, with ſuch an intelligent Perſon, who could ſatisfy his Curioſity in divers Things which he thought fit to enquire into: Wherefore on their withdrawing, he engaged them both to dine with him, as he did afterwards Mr. *Williamſon* alſo. Nothing could fall out more opportunely for me, than ſuch a Conjuncture; for having a Bill ſent me from the Truſt, drawn by Mr. *Hammerton*, for 200*l.* Sterling on this ſame Gentleman (Mr. *Saxby)* 3.

1739. Novemb. for Value received of the Truſtees, for his Majeſty's Service; and Mr. *Saxby* being Deputy-Receiver of the King's Quit-Rents in *Carolina*, I now preſented the ſame to him, together with Mr. *Hammerton*'s Letter of Advice; but was a little ſurprized at his telling me he could not accept it, for that he had not half ſo much of the King's Money in his Hands; which was all that paſſed betwixt us then: But in the Evening I thought it proper to take Mr. *Jones* with me to *Jenkins*'s, where thoſe Gentlemen quartered; and there in a civil Manner, over a Glaſs of Wine, I again preſented the Bill for Acceptance, before proper Witneſs, acquainting him, upon his Refuſal again, that I ſhould be obliged to proteſt and return it; which he ſaid he was ſorry for, but could not help it.

4. *Sunday.* Young Mr. *Vernon*, who had ſailed under Captain *Gaſcoigne* in the *Hawk* (which was gone for *England*, as was alſo Captain *Gaſcoigne* in another Ship) having been ſome Time at *Charles-Town*, waiting in Expectation when his Uncle the Admiral would come to the *Weſt-Indies*, now took the Opportunity of a Paſſage with Captain *Fennel* to *Jamaica*; and coming up to Town this Morning from *Cockſpur*, firſt waited on the General, and afterwards did me the Favour of a Viſit; which I took very kindly, and wiſhed any little Ci-

vilities

vilities I could ſhew him here, might be rated as a Reſpect due from me to his Father. The Church Service was orderly obſerved, which the General was pleaſed to attend, as did alſo the two Strangers. In the Evening Mr. *Saxby* diſcovered a little Uneaſineſs at my Intention of returning that Bill, knowing how great Coſt muſt attend it; wherefore he ſaid he ſhould take it as a Favour, after my proteſting it, if I would defer returning it a little while, till he got home to *Charles-Town*, from whence he would write me poſitively, whether he could pay it or not; for that he wiſhed to do it if he could: Wherefore, preſuming no Damage could enſue, by a ſhort Delay, I agreed ſo to do. Soon after, I attended the General, together with Mr. *Jones*, where we met Mr. *Williamſon*; and the Affair of the Recorderſhip was the Subject Matter to be conſidered; which Mr. *Williamſon* ſaid he was ready to accept of, and was what brought him hither at this Time from *Charles-Town*: But in his Converſation and Diſcourſe elſewhere, he diſcovered different Sentiments; and talking with me of it in particular Yeſterday, he ſaid plainly it was a Thing of great Indifference to him, whether he had it or not; for that the Buſineſs which he was falling into at *Charles-Town*, was likely to be of much greater Value to him; and indeed the

1739. Novemb. 4.

1739. Novemb. 4. principal Motive which induced him to came now after it, was his knowing that his Uncle *Taylor* had obtained it from the Truſtees; and now for him not to accept of it, would be giving Offence to his Uncle, to whom he had lately wrote to procure him either the Place of Judge of the Admiralty (if he could) void by the Death of Mr. *Maurice Lewis*; or that of Clerk of the Aſſembly, void by the Death of Mr. *Amiens*; either of which would be of abundant greater Value to him than this; but his Uncle having procured him this, before he had heard from him about the other; he would not be thought to make light of it: I then ſaid it looked to me as if he meant to make this a Sort of *Sinecure*, which he might execute by a Deputy; but I preſumed the Truſt would not allow of any ſuch Appointments, nor ſuffer their Favours to be undervalued: To which he told me in plain Words, that when he was once poſſeſſed of the Place, he would ſee who could hinder him, or to that Effect: And now in this Conference with the General, the chief Topick of the Whole ſeemed to ſavour much of the Reſtrictions, which it was expected a Perſon occupying that Place muſt ſubmit to; and to lay aſide all Imagination, that the ſame Power which created him ſuch an Officer, could not in the ſame Manner take it away

way from him again at Pleaſure, without Regard to *quamdiu ſe bene geſſerit:* Then it was ſhewn to Mr. *Williamſon*, what the Truſtees had been pleaſed to direct me, relating to the ſeveral new Conſtitutions lately ſent; and therein particularly, what I was to do in this preſent Affair now before us, and what was required to be done by Mr. *Chriſtie* before a Succeſſor could take Place; which Mr. *Williamſon* finding little Room to ſay any Thing to, he then aſked me peremptorily, whether I would deliver him his Conſtitution or not; and upon my ſaying that I ſhould do it as ſoon as Mr. *Chriſtie* enabled me, by performing his Part, and not ſooner, unleſs I had new Commands from my Superiors; he appeared not diſappointed in the leaſt; and ſo that Diſcourſe ended. 1739. Novemb.

Monday. Upon my ſeeing Mr. *Williamſon* this Morning, I aſked him how he reliſhed the Anſwer he preſſed me (againſt my Inclination) to give him laſt Night; and he told me frankly, that had he been in my Place, he did not ſee how any other could be given; which he ſaid he was very eaſy at, telling me, at the ſame Time, that he ſaw no Likelihood of the preſent Recorder's quitting that Place in haſte; for he had ſworn deeply to him, that he would never deliver up any Copy of his Records to me, nor to any one elſe, but the Truſ- 5.

1739. Novemb. 5. tees only; which I only ſmiled at, and wiſhed he had it in his Power to do *that* compleat, as it was expected; but I feared it was not: At parting ſoon after, he told me, that he had wrote, and ſent in to the General, a Letter, wherein he begged he would pleaſe to remember, that he had been to offer his Acceptance of the Recorder's Office, *&c.* intimating, to preſerve his Uncle's good Opinion: But the General conceived ſomething farther meant in it, and ordered his Secretary to take particular Care, and keep it ſafe. And now the Time was come, when the General would not ſtay longer waiting for his *Indians*, who muſt come after: For having received a Letter from Captain *Warren* (the oldeſt Sea Commander of all in theſe Northerly Stations) that he was upon ſailing to St. *Simon*'s, to confer with him for the better Protection of this Province; he left us about Three in the Afternoon, having ſpent ſix Weeks here in doing what he thought needful; and going off in the Scout-Boat, with three or four *Indians* that he had a ſpecial Value for, Mr. *Norris*, and his Secretary Mr. *Moor*, went in another Boat that attended, making the beſt of their Way South. The only Matter in Town that I had to obſerve, was, that the Inhabitants at Beat of Drum early in the Morning aſſembled, and went on vigorouſly with the

the Work of clearing the Common of all that ſhrubby Matter which it was over-run with; and what they could not accompliſh at their laſt Meeting (the 17th of *October)* they put an End to now, under the Direction of the Town-Officers, *&c.* 1739. Novemb.

Tueſday. All now in Appearance huſht and quiet. The General was gone, and every Body at Leiſure to mind their own proper Buſineſs; which I made as good Uſe of as I could, that another Packet might be ready ſoon to ſend to the Truſt. Mr. *Williamſon* (I was informed) diſcovered what Diſpoſition he was in plainly, by joining in cloſe Council with the Committee, which continued to ſit at *Jenkins*'s (Dr. *Tailfer* in the Chair) to enquire into Grievances, in order to get them redreſſed, by ſuch Means as their Wiſdom ſhould deviſe: Thither reſorted at all Times, as to an Oracle for Advice, every Malecontent, who believed himſelf more deſerving than his Neighbours; and this knotty Point how to get over, of ſettling the Recorderſhip and Magiſtracy, immediately to their better Liking, was now thought worth their Conſideration; from whence I did not doubt I ſhould ſoon hear ſomewhat more about it: And, as I expected, 6.

Wedneſday, in the Morning, Mr. *Williamſon* came again, bringing Mr. *Fallowfield* with him as Witneſs (I underſtood it) 7.

1739. Novemb. 7. of what paſſed betwixt us: And then Mr. *Williamſon* again renewed his Demand of being put in Poſſeſſion of the Place of Recorder, *&c.* To which I anſwered (as I had before done) that when Mr. *Chriſtie* had fulfilled the Truſtees Orders, of making out Copy of the Court Proceedings to this Time, I ſhould be then ready to obſerve on my Part, their Orders likewiſe of delivering their Conſtitution to him (Mr. *Williamſon)* and not ſooner, without freſh Orders: He then told me, that Mr. *Chriſtie* had informed him he was ready with his Copy of the Court Proceedings; but ſwore he would deliver them neither to me, nor to any one, except the Truſtees themſelves (the ſame he had ſo ſolemnly ſworn before) with this Addition now, that I was an old Fool to expect it: Such dirty Compliments gave me not the leaſt Diſturbance; but I then replied, that if he thought me not worthy the Sight of them, though upon this Occaſion I apprehended, by the Office I had the Honour to execute under the Truſt, I might inſiſt upon ſeeing them; yet I was very ready to wave that Point, to facilitate the Affair as much as I could: But I hoped, and expected, that he would ſhew his Work to the Magiſtrates at leaſt, who ſurely had a Right to it; and upon their certifying the Truth of it, I would be ſatisfied; But to ſpeak plainly, he was grown

a

a Man of ſo little Veracity, that whatever he ſaid, found little Credit with almoſt any Body: And as I well knew, that the Books he had made out the laſt Year, and ſent to the Truſt then with my Packet, was the Work of Mr. *Cauſton* and him together at *Ockſtead*, where they ſat cloſe about it ſome Weeks, Mr. *Chriſtie* having then Notice from me, that it was expected from him; and if he had not found that Help, it is moſt probable he had been nonpluſs'd: For theſe, and divers other good Reaſons, I was fully perſuaded to believe him as much and more at a Loſs now, unleſs he had the Skill of collecting *Sybils* Leaves. It ſo happened, that Mr. *Jones*, calling at my Houſe, was preſent at this Conference; which I was very glad of, to be as well prepared as the Complainer, with Evidence of what was ſaid and done. After ſome little Wrangling, which I gave no great Heed to, they walked away; and Mr. *Williamſon*, in few Hours more, took Boat to return to *Charles-Town*; but not till he had firſt paid his Reſpects to Dr. *Tailfer* (as Care was taken to obſerve) at his own Houſe, where no Doubt but he made Report of what he had been doing, in Purſuance of that Reſolution which Yeſterday brought forth: And their farther Operations we are next to wait for.

1739. Novemb. 7.

Thurſday.

1739. Novemb. 8. *Thurſday.* Ill News came to Town this Morning of Mr. *Montaigut*'s Death, who ſickened in a Fever of the worſt Kind, about eight Days ſince, at his Plantation up the River in *Carolina*, whereof he died Yeſterday in the Evening. Mr. *Chriſtie* not thinking it convenient (I ſuppoſe) to be obſerved going out, and coming in, ſo frequently to his Doxy Mrs. *Turner*, at her Houſe here, thought it beſt to remove to his Hut on the Lot, about two Miles off: So he ſent her with Bed and Bedding, *&c.* before, following her ſoon after.

9. *Friday.* Little worth obſerving till the Afternoon, when Mr. *Montaigut*'s Corpſe was brought down and decently buried, the *French* Miniſter of *Puryſburgh* performing the Funeral Rites, in the Abſence of Mr. *Norris*, who was now gone to the South: Moſt of the principal Inhabitants (who were particularly invited) attended him to the Grave; and in Regard to the military Command, which he had in *Carolina*, thinking it a Reſpect due, I ordered twelve Minute Cannon to be fired, during the Time of his Interment; to anſwer which Purpoſe, having not Powder ſufficient in Store, Monſieur *d'Beauſain* ordered ſome to be provided. It is to be hoped we ſhall ere long be furniſhed with what is neceſſary of that Kind, when Captain *Thompſon* arrives from the South, where he yet

yet continues; and without it indeed, we ſeem among ſome Folks to be a Subject of Ridicule. *N. B.* This I wrote upon what Information the Gunner gave me: But Mr. *Jones* has ſince told me, that he got ſome Powder for that Uſe from Mr. *Brownfield.* 1739. Novemb.

Saturday. This Day I converted to my own peculiar Uſe, and ſpent moſt Part of it at my little Plantations, forming to myſelf new Schemes of what I propoſed next Year, which according to the Planters Way of reckoning, began about this Time. At my Return home, hearing accidentally of a Boat going South, I wrote to the General, acquainting him with what I apprehended he ought to be informed of from hence ſince he left us. Mr. *Chriſtie*, I underſtood, had been expoſing to publick Sale a few of his own old Goods of little Value; ſuch as two or three ordinary Chairs and Stools, a Table, one Pewter Diſh, a few common *Dutch* printed Pictures coloured upon Paper, and the like; by which it was intended to be underſtood, that he purpoſed ſoon to leave the Colony; but moſt People were of a different Opinion, and took it rather to be an Experiment made by his truſty Adviſers, to ſee whether or not we would ſuffer ſo valuable a Man to quit the Place, through the ill Treatment he found, in not meeting with 10.

1739. Novemb. with the Promotion intended him, ſo readily as he expected. As to myſelf, I gave little Heed to it, having, to the beſt of my Underſtanding, and not without proper Advice, acted in that Affair, as I have now done; neither could I readily believe his real Deſign to be leaving the Colony, from what was ſaid; having ever ſince I knew the Place, been frequently giving it out, that he was determined to go ſoon for *England*, for that he found not Encouragement to continue in that Office; though it is well known, that *he only* took Fees in many Caſes, when the other Magiſtrates never pretended to make any Demand; and I myſelf have heard him in the Height of his Vanity boaſt, that he made a hundred Pounds a Year of it.

11. *Sunday.* In the Abſence of Mr. *Norris*, Mr. *Haberſham* read the Prayers of the Church.

12. *Monday.* Early this Morning arrived an *Indian* trading Boat, bound for *Charles-Town*, by which came *John Rea* (a Freeholder here) from Fort *Auguſta*, with divers Letters for the General, importing (among other Things) that the *Chicaſſaw Indians*, our good Friends, whom the *French* had attempted ſeveral Times to deſtroy, had lately, by a ſmall Party in Ambuſcade, attacked a large *French* Boat, in her Way on the *Meſſaſippi* to *Moville*, from the Mouth

Mouth of that River, laden with many very valuable Goods, and Letters to the *French* Governor at that Place: That they had killed ſeveral of them, and taken ſome Priſoners; then plundered the Boat of what they thought moſt valuable, namely, fine Woollen, Linen, Plate and Ammunition, which by them is moſt prized; and (what we apprehend to be of more Value to us) a Packet of Letters for that Governor, which they ſent as a Preſent to our General, whereby probably ſome Diſcovery might be made of the *French* Deſigns; and after taking with them what they could carry off, they ſunk the Boat with the Remainder. Which Packet and Letters to be ſure we loſt no Time in ſending forward to the General. 1739. Novemb.

Tueſday. The Seaſon now requiring every one to be buſy on his Lands, who had any Deſign of improving them; and my chief View the enſuing Year, being towards my five hundred Acres (as before noted *October* 24.) I employed what Hands I could poſſibly, to ſet about that Work; and it being a conſiderable Diſtance from Town, which would not admit of my Eyes being over them frequently, I choſe, on that Occaſion, to allow myſelf the whole Day. At my Return in the Evening, Mr. *Jones* informed me, that the Report of Mr. *Chriſtie*'s Intention to quit the 13.

Colony,

1739. Novemb. Colony, began to find a little more Credit than hitherto; and ſome People were inclined to believe it; as alſo that he would take his Beloved with him.—A little Time probably might bring to Light what his Purpoſes were. He farther told me, that Mr. *Bradley* having applied for a Permit to go in a Boat for *Carolina* (as no Boat, now for ſome Time paſt, was allowed by the Guard to put off hence, without ſuch Leave under one of the Magiſtrates Hands) which was denied him upon divers Applications from Perſons he was indebted to, or had Diſputes with; who apprehended that he deſigned never to return: He privately took Horſe, and rode up the River, with Deſign to paſs it at the firſt convenient Place he could come at, leaving Part of his Family at the Houſe he had lately taken in Town, when he went out of that great one belonging to the Truſt. His real Intention alſo, as well as the other's, will require a little more Time to unfold.

14. *Wedneſday*. Upon Enquiry after what became of the Effects of *Wiſe*, *Clarke*, and others, after their Deceaſe; in Purſuance of the Orders I received from the Truſt; I learnt, that there had formerly been ſome Care taken in it by the Court, who had directed the Jury to make Inquiſition ſtrictly into that Affair; and they found, that there was publick Sale made of *Wiſe*'s Goods,

Goods, an Account whereof was returned to the Recorder Mr. *Chriſtie:* Since which Time I could not find that any farther Notice was taken of it; nor could I get any Information, whether the Money ariſing by that Sale, or any Part of it, was paid to Mr. *Chriſtie*, or any other: Wherefore I applied to the Magiſtrates, and told them, that as there was a Box in Mr. *Chriſtie*'s Cuſtody with two Locks upon it, whereof he kept one Key, and one of the Magiſtrates another; it would be very needful for them all together to look into that Box, and ſee what Papers were in it that might be of Value, *&c.* and they appointed ſo to do to-morrow; and in the mean while to give Notice to Mr. *Chriſtie* to be there with them. In the Evening Enſign *Maxwell*, and Quarter-Maſter *Wanſell*, arrived from St. *Simon*'s; by whom I received a Letter from the General of the 11th Inſtant, relating to Mr. *Douglaſs*'s having Leave to ſell his great Houſe which he had built here: The former in his Way to *Frederick* Fort at *Port-Royal*, from whence he was to detach ten Men to go with him to the South; and the other came to look into the Goods and Stores that had been lodged in this Town by Colonel *Cockran* at his firſt Coming, and lay here ever ſince: But now the General had ordered them all to be taken hence, and carried to the South.

1739. Novemb. 14.

1739. Novemb. 15. *Thurſday.* The Magiſtrates met, and together with Mr. *Chriſtie* opened the Box, wherein were found divers Papers, giving an Account of the Effects of ſeveral Perſons deceaſed; and among others, thoſe of *William Wiſe*, which had been moſt of them ſold, as before-mentioned; and the Particulars charged to ſundry People; whereof a Return had been made to Mr. *Chriſtie* by the Jury that was directed to make Enquiry into it; and the Sum amounted to 20*l.* and odd; but how to come at the Knowledge of what had been paid, and to whom, was not to be eaſily diſcovered; Mr. *Chriſtie* pleading Ignorance of it, and denying that he had ever received any Money on that Account: Wherefore that Nut was a little too hard for us to crack yet, and required our farther Endeavour to come at what we wanted. After ſo wet a Summer, the Air was ſo thin and purified, that our Winter began earlier than common, with ſharp Froſts for ſome Days paſt; which made it very delightful, and probably would conduce much to the Health of the People: But it behoved ſuch as were nurſing up Vines, and Oranges, *&c.* to take good Care of thoſe eſpecially which were young and tender: And it was now evident from Experience, that all ſuch Kind of Plants thrived the better, the nearer they

they grew to the Sea, where the Froſt is leſs ſevere. 1739. Novemb. 16.

Friday. This Day paſſed over without any Thing notable: But late in the Evening we received the ill News of the Death of Captain *John Cuthbert*, by the Arrival of *Scroggs* from *Carolina*. The State of War which we were now in, occaſioned the General to revive the Company of Rangers, which Captain *M^c^Pherſon* before had the Command of, till broke: And now they were to conſiſt of thirty Men, well horſed, and armed, whom this Gentleman was to command; and he was lately ſent into *Carolina*, together with his Lieutenant *Scroggs*, by the General's Order, to buy Horſes, *&c.* being furniſhed with Money for that Purpoſe; but he unhappily ſickened and died in that Country: Whereupon Mr. *Scroggs*, after ſecuring his Papers, Money, and Effects, and ſeeing him buried, now returned; and the News of his Death occaſioned Grief to many People, being a good-natured, ſprightly Man, generally beloved; and it was believed by all, that he would have acquitted himſelf well in that Poſt. He had made conſiderable Improvements upon his five hundred Acres up the River *Savannah*, and was judged to have one of the beſt Plantations yet in the Colony: He died unmarried, leaving a Siſter (who took Care of his

1739. Novemb. Houſe) dangerouſly ill here, inſomuch that her Death was feared, when we little expected to hear of his; and whether ſhe will ſurvive him long or not, none can tell.

17. *Saturday.* All that I found material to be obſerved, was, that ſome of our wiſe Reformers (who would in all Things be meddling) thought it worth their peculiar Care, to be providing ſuch an Adminiſtrator, to the Effects of our deceaſed Friend, as *they* judged fit for that Purpoſe, and in the ſame Manner as was attempted when Mr. *Dyſon* died *(vide Sept.* 17 and 18.) all was to be done in a Hurry: But it happened, that every Body did not agree with them in that Opinion; for which Reaſon it was thought proper to defer the farther Conſideration of it to another Day.

18. *Sunday.* Mr. *Haberſham* read the Service of the Day, and a Sermon after it, ſetting forth the Operation of the Spirit upon a new Birth, *&c.* (out of what Author I know not) which was a Subject ſome of the Audience were pretty well tired with heretofore.

19. *Monday.* The Affair of an Adminiſtrator was renewed by ſuch as began it the other Day; and Mr. *Jones* being applied to on that Occaſion, he ſent to Mr. *Parker* and me to be preſent at the Time it was debated: When in Anſwer to what was urged in Behalf of the Creditors (of whom Dr.

Dr. *Tailſer* and Mr. *Jenkins* alledged they were the chief, one a Victualler, and the other a Diſpenſer of Phyſick) they were told, that the Truſt alſo were Creditors, and muſt be looked on as ſuch; but it appeared very ſtrange to us, that they ſhould offer at it, when they knew the Deceaſed had a Siſter yet living, who undoubtedly claimed a Priority; and if ſhe ſhould fail, poſſibly ſome other near Relation might be found, who had a Right of Preference to either of *them*; moreover, that it was the univerſal Practice of the Civil Law Courts, to allow a certain limited Time in ſuch Caſes, for any Perſon concerned to offer a Claim, if they had any to make in their own Behalf, or to enter a Caveat againſt any other. For the Satisfaction of all then preſent, it was thought not amiſs, that a Liſt and ſhort Inventory ſhould be taken of the ready Money, Notes, Bills, or the like, found upon him at the Time of his Deceaſe, and now in Cuſtody of Mr. *Scroggs:* Which appearing to be no inconſiderable Sum, and being well known to be Part of what the General had advanced for the Purpoſes aforeſaid; it was thought proper to commit it to the Care of Mr. *Scroggs* again, to carry to the General where he was to go: And in the Evening I wrote what I thought needful to the General; as Mr. *Jones* alſo did, to be ready for the

1739. Novemb. 19.

1739. ſame Bearer, who was to ſet off in the Morning.

Novemb. 20. *Tueſday.* Mr. *Scroggs* went off early for St. *Simon*'s. In the Afternoon arrived Lieutenant *Dunbar*, and Captain *Æneas Mackintoſh*, whom the General had ſent to Fort *Auguſta*, to enquire after ſome *Chicaſſaw Indians*, that lived in that Neighbourhood remote from their own Nation, in a vagrant Manner; but were looked on by all as a daring, bold People: And ſome of theſe the General had expected before he went hence. Theſe Gentlemen now told us they were coming, and we might expect them to-morrow or next Day; that they were but few (under thirty) but were pickt Men, all Warriors, led by experienced Chiefs, and might be eſteemed more than equal to a hundred common Men.

21. *Wedneſday.* Nothing occurred to my Knowledge this whole Day, that I thought deſerved any Notice here.

22. *Thurſday.* What happened moſt remarkable this Day, was the Receipt of a Packet from the General, brought me by Mr. *Upton*, who came from *Frederica* laſt *Sunday:* Encloſed in it I found a ſmall Packet directed to the Truſt from his Excellence, together with one to Lieutenant Governor *Bull*; one to Mr. *Pinkney*, Speaker of the Aſſembly; one to Captain *Warren*, commanding his Majeſty's Ships at

at *Charles-Town*; and one to Colonel *Palmer*, at his Plantation in *Carolina:* All which I was to ſend forward by the firſt Opportunity. The Letter to Colonel *Palmer*, I gueſs, might be in Return to an handſome Offer which I heard the Colonel had made to his Excellence; that in Caſe he had any Deſign upon *Auguſtin*, he (the Colonel) would attend him with an hundred and fifty good Men, and himſelf at the Head of them, under the General's Command, on that Enterprize. Such a ſeaſonable Complement (if punctually performed) might be a good Example to others in that Province to do the like: But from the Behaviour of too many of them towards this Colony, I doubt we have little Reaſon to expect much Aſſiſtance from them; though it is evident, that whatever good Succeſs may attend our General's Toil in Arms, they will be ſure to find the Benefit of it in *Carolina.* The firſt Blood ſpilt, that we heard of in theſe Parts, ſince the War broke out, unhappily fell to our Lot: The General acquainting me, in a Letter he was pleaſed to write me by this Packet, that the Enemy had attacked and murdered two Highland Men in *Amelia*; and from Mr. *Upton* I gather ſome particular Circumſtances thereto relating: But firſt it is to be underſtood in what Poſture we were there, when this happened. *Amelia*

1739. Novemb. 22.

1739. Novemb. 22. *Iſland* is the fartheſt Look-out we have againſt the *Spaniards*, where a Scout-Boat was ſtationed with ſixteen Men belonging to her, who were to relieve one another as the Service might require; they who ſtaid aſhore employing themſelves in cultivating Land, whilſt the reſt were upon Duty: To theſe the General added a Serjeant's Guard of twelve Men; and as ſome of each Sort had Wives and Children, they might be computed at near forty in all; who were fortified with a Paliſade, *&c.* and two or three ſmall Pieces of Cannon, to command any Boat paſſing that Way. It happened (as I am told) that three of the Scout-Men, ſtraggling unwarily into the Woods, were attacked in the Manner aforeſaid, when two of them were thus ſlain; and the third being miſſing, it is believed he is carried off Priſoner: One of thoſe killed being ſcalped, and the other's Head taken off, it is not doubted but the Authors of it were *Spaniſh Indians*, who landed unſeen at the Back of the Iſland, and ſtole their Way thus privately to do it. At the Hearing of ten or eleven Guns fired (which diſcovered them to be at leaſt that Number) our People were alarmed, and made all the Haſte they could to come up with them; but they fled in ſuch Haſte, that they got off unſeen, before we could intercept them. The General, on the firſt Hearing

Hearing of it, got what Boats he could find, and went in Purſuit, with about fifty Men, hoping ſome where or other to repay them: And it is ſuppoſed he went for the River St. *John*'s, where there is a *Spaniſh* Settlement: But as this is known to himſelf alone, it is only gueſſing his Deſigns at Random. 1739. Novemb.

Friday. As the greateſt Danger we imagine ourſelves expoſed to in this Colony, may be from ſuch *Indians* as are in the *Spaniſh* Intereſt; whom it is pretty hard to diſtinguiſh from our Friends, in Caſe they ſtraggle far Northward; though our neighbouring *Indians* know them well: The General's Orders to me in Yeſterday's Packet, were to give out in Orders here, that no Perſon ſhould preſume to go into the Woods in theſe Parts without Arms, at their own Peril; which I took Care to publiſh accordingly. 23.

Saturday. The *Indians* (partly *Chicaſſaws*, and partly *Euchies)* who Meſſieurs *Mackintoſh* and *Dunbar* told us, were coming to us on *Tueſday* laſt, arrived here this Day; and we received them with all Demonſtration of Friendſhip: They appeared highly pleaſed to hear of Action began by the *Spaniards*, and ſeemed to thirſt for ſome of their Blood in Requital. 24.

1739. Novemb. 25. *Sunday.* The Prayers of the Church continued to be read by Mr. *Haberſham.* It was with great Uneaſineſs I waited to ſend off the General's Packet to the Truſt, with other Letters, which had been ever ſince *Thurſday* laſt in my Cuſtody; and not doubting but they were of the greateſt Importance, I feared the Blame would fall on me for ſuch a Delay; for which Reaſon I had ſeveral Times applied to Mr. *Jones* (who had all Boats and Servants at his Command here) to aſſiſt me in ſending away that Packet; but he ſtill put me off, in telling me there was no Boat or Hands to ſpare; for that they were all employed in the Service, ſome one Way, and ſome another: But had the General ſent his Packet to *him*, I well knew he would have ſhewn his Diligence, and loſt no Time in it; though he was in no Care what Reflexions might fall on me.

26. *Monday.* Mr. *Bradley* having abſented himſelf ever ſince the 13th, when he went off in the Manner then ſet forth; and having a little before bought a ſmall Skooner, under Pretence of trading with it to the Northward; but ſince his Departure, it being obſerved, that divers of his beſt houſhold Goods were privately put on board by his Son, from the Houſe he was removed to, near the Water-ſide; his Creditors grew alarmed at it; and two of them having

having before got Judgment for their Debts, now made haſte to take out Execution (which hitherto they had delayed) and ſtopt the Veſſel from proceeding, intending to make Sale of Effects ſufficient to pay what was owing to them. No Token yet appeared how, or when, I might diſcharge my Duty, in ſending off the General's Packet to the Truſt, with other of his Letters; which threw me into the utmoſt Impatience, and I could not forbear remonſtrating it to Mr. *Jones* in ſuch a Manner, that he muſt perceive I was determined to acquit myſelf of whatever ill Conſequence might attend it. 1739. Novemb.

Tueſday. Mr. *Jones*, with Mr. *Upton*, acquainted me, that a Boat would be provided this Evening, wherein Mr. *Upton* was going to *Charles-Town*; and if I thought proper, it would be a good Convenience for me to ſend what I had in my Care: I thought ſo too, ſince I could come at none ſooner, and reſolved ſo to do: But as Mr. *Upton* told me, when he brought me that Packet laſt *Thurſday*, that he deſigned ſoon to go to *Charles-Town* on Buſineſs of his own; I could not avoid ſurmiſing, that either this Delay was contrived to accommodate Mr. *Upton* when he was ready; or elſe that Mr. *Jones* had Letters to write by him which were not ſooner perfected: Whereas I had not allowed myſelf to write 27.

more

1739. Novemb. more than a few Lines to Mr. *Verelſt*, dated the 25th; every Day and Hour expecting to be called on in haſte, for what I had ready at a Moment's Notice; and now delivered into Mr. *Upton*'s Hands immediately the General's Packet, together with one from myſelf; writing to my Correſpondent Mr. *Hopton*, at the ſame Time, to take ſpecial Care (as indeed he had always done) to forward them by the firſt Ship for *England*.

28. *Wedneſday*. Mr. *Upton* went off for *Charles-Town* very early in the Morning; and in an Hour or two after, the *Indians* under the Conduct of Lieutenant *Dunbar*, accompanied by the Quarter-Maſter *Wanſel*, after refreſhing themſelves here a few Days, made the beſt of their Way to the General in the South. The late Accounts we had from *Charles-Town* acquainted us, that that Place was growing pretty healthy again; but the Numbers ſwept away by Death in ſome Months paſt, during that grievous Sickneſs, occaſioned a melancholy Appearance of the Inhabitants, who were much thinned; and that it was hardly known, when ſo few Ships were there, as at preſent; but that probably might be owing to the preſent State of War we are in, it being ſuppoſed that few *Engliſh* Ships would put to Sea, but as they found

found Opportunity of Convoy, the firſt Part of their Voyage. 1739. Novemb. 29.

Thurſday. The Court now ſat again, according to the ordinary Courſe; when a Grand Jury was ſworn; and leaving them to preſent what was properly cognizable when the Court met again, they adjourned till to-morrow. More ill News of People wrecked and loſt at Sea, came to Town by a Boat which arrived this Day from *Charles-Town*; who reported, that in his Way hither, he ſaw the Wreck of a Boat upon a ſmall Iſland, with her Stern beat out, but her Maſt and Sail ſtanding, the People that were in her being ſuppoſed to be drowned; for that it appeared ſhe had ſtruck on the North-Breakers off St. *Helena Sound*, in attempting to go without all: From whence it was feared it could be no other than a Boat of Mr. *Upton*'s, which was laden at *Charles-Town* by his Order, and which he had impatiently expected here for ſome Time, wondering why ſhe ſtaid ſo long; and it was moſt likely, that good Part of the Buſineſs which he went hence about Yeſterday Morning, was to enquire after her: And in few Hours after this, we were more confirmed in the Belief that this Report was true: For as it was known the Cargo was of conſiderable Value, being partly Butter, Soap, Candles, *&c* for his own retailing (which were all much wanted

1739. Novemb. wanted in this Town) and partly ſeveral Coils of Rope and Cordage, belonging to the General, for rigging ſmall Veſſels in the South, together with ſome Caſks of Pitch and Tar, and a Parcel of Saddles for equipping the Troop of Rangers; we had it now certified to us, that what Goods remained yet in the Wreck, were ſome Caſks of Butter, and ſome of the Coils of Rope; being ſuch as were not liable ſo immediately to be loſt, as the other Part of the Loading; and the Owner of the Iſland was taking an honeſt Care, to ſave what could be ſaved; but the Perſons in her, nobody doubted their being loſt; which were four Hands, whereof *Andrew Barber*, as Patroon, had the Direction, who was looked on as a pretty good Pilot within Land; and I fear his attempting to go without, at this Time of the Year with a Boat loaden, hardly can be juſtified.

30. *Friday.* There remained now no farther Queſtion of the Truth of Yeſterday's News, which came confirmed from all Hands, and withal, that two of thoſe Men loſt were ſaid to be Soldiers belonging to Captain *Norbury*'s Company at *Port-Royal*; which we wiſhed might not prove as true as the reſt. The Court ſat again; but the Recorder being taken ſo ill, that he ſaid he could not avoid going home, they broke up, after doing little Buſineſs, and

and adjourned till to-morrow. This being St. *Andrew*'s Day, which the *Scotch* never fail to celebrate annually, and look on it as a friendly Act in ſuch as join them; I went in the Evening to ſhew the Regard I had to their Society; as Mr. *Jones* alſo did, and ſeveral others; when we paſſed it away inoffenſively, with Chearfulneſs, without entering into any political Arguments, which could not well take Place at this Time; the uſual Committee at *Jenkins*'s well knowing, that divers of their own Countrymen were poſſeſſed of Sentiments very different from theirs; as alſo were ſeveral others then preſent. 1739. Novemb. 30.

Saturday. Once again the Court ſat to little Purpoſe; for the Recorder did not appear, by Reaſon of his Indiſpoſition, who had the moſt material Papers relating to what was to come before them at this Court: Wherefore the Grand Jury was diſcharged, after delivering into Court what Preſentments they had to offer; and then the Court adjourned farther to *Monday* the 10th Inſtant, in Expectation they might by that Time find all Things ready to proceed on. The Magiſtrates, as well as Mr. *Bradley*'s Creditors, having Reaſon, from good Information, to believe that he was actually buying ſome Sows, and other Stock in *Carolina*, with Deſign to return hither; that no Diſcouragement might be given him Decemb. 1.

1739. Decemb. him in it, they took off the Attachment that was on the Skooner, allowing her to proceed, and his Son in her, to his Assistance; taking Care at the same Time, that no ill Use was made of this Indulgence, by carrying off hence any of his best Goods and Effects. *(Vide Nov. 26.)*

2. *Sunday.* Mr. *Habersham* read the Prayers of the Church, as he used to do, during Mr. *Norris*'s Absence in the South.

3. *Monday.* Mrs. *Matthews* calling here on her Way to the General at St. *Simon*'s, and seeing Mr. *Jones*, he had the Opportunity of writing Letters thither; which I missed, for want of timely Notice: However, Mr. *Eyre* coming to Town soon after, in Company with one Mr. *Holmes*, an *Indian* Trader from the *Cherokee* Nation, whither he was sent so long since by the General, as the 29th of *September* last (see the Notes of that Day) and was now on his Return to the General; I could make good that Defect. He was so kind to call upon me immediately on his Arrival, when I delivered him the Packet that was committed to my Care, which came with the other Letters by Captain *Thompson*, and which I received about a Week after Mr. *Eyre* was gone, from his Kinsman, one of the honourable Trustees; and it was Matter of great Joy to him, as therefore it was a Pleasure to me: For he was esteemed

by every Body as a good-natured Gentleman, very active in his Duty, and wanted not Reſolution and Spirit ſufficient to carry him through all Parts of it with Bravery. He had not the good Fortune to meet with that Succeſs immediately which he expected, in Execution of the Commiſſion he carried; which was occaſioned partly through the great Mortality among them, which had ſwept away great Numbers of their beſt Men; whereof the Cauſe was ſet forth in ſome Affidavits I ſent by the General's Order in my Letter of the 25th of *September* to Mr. *Verelſt*, as it is alſo noted in my Journal of that Date; and their chief Warriors now happened to be all abroad upon their Hunt, which is carefully and duly obſerved by all *Indians*, and generally holds two or three Months at a Time, when perhaps they wander on that Employment ſome Hundreds of Miles: But Mr. *Eyre* had now with him one of their principal Leaders, who would attend the General with him, and give his Excellence Aſſurances of a great Body of choſen Men, that would certainly join him early in the Spring: But as for the common Run, Mr. *Eyre* wiſely choſe to meddle with none of them: For ſuch as ſtay at home, on theſe appointed Seaſons of being abroad, are looked on by their own People, as good for nothing; and he rightly judged,

1739. Decemb. 3.

1739. Decemb. judged, that the General wanted none ſuch as muſt be fed and cloathed, without any good Service to be expected from them.

4. *Tueſday.* This Day I laid hold of, to make another Viſit to my People, and provide for their intended Movement to my other Plantation near *Vernon* River. At my Return my Ears were preſently filled with the Talk which almoſt every Body had at their Tongue End, of Mr. *Scroggs*'s being defrauded of a great Sum of Money, which it was ſuppoſed was done by picking his Pocket of a Letter-Caſe, wherein were Notes to the Value of about 70*l.* Sterling, and was Part of that Money which the General had advanced to Captain *Cuthbert*, to buy Horſes, Mr. *Scroggs* having waited on the General, from whom he was newly returned with this Sum for the Purpoſe aforeſaid *(vide* 16 and 20 of *November*;*)* but now in all Appearance was thus cheated: Which occaſioned various Conjectures, but all at Random: It was certain that the Letter-Caſe, with the Notes in it, was ſeen in his Hands, in an honeſt Man's Houſe in Town; where he was alſo ſeen to put it up again, about an Hour or leſs before it was loſt: The next Queſtion then was, what Company he had been in ſince; and it did not appear that he had ſat down any where, nor could he remember that he had aſſociated himſelf with

with any one, only as he might accidentally, in common with others; three Perſons he particularly remembered he had talked with, in that caſual Way: But as they were all well known in Town, and lay under no ſuſpicious Character, there could be no Accuſation againſt them: Mr. *Jones* (who had good Experience in detecting Roguery) told me he had made uſe of the beſt Skill he had, in his Enquiry; but it was paſt his finding out yet: And ſo it remained till ſome lucky Accident or other poſſibly might give us more Light another Time. 1739. Decemb.

Wedneſday. What I had ſeveral Times before heard as a flying Report only, I had ſuch farther Information of, that I now took it for Truth, *viz.* that Meſſieurs *Sterling*, *Baylie*, *Grant* and *Douglaſs*, ſeeing no Hopes left of obtaining Negroes, or Proſpect of ſettling in *Georgia* to their own Liking, were determined, and preparing, to try their Fortune on the Banks of the River *Savannah*, in *Carolina*, about fifty or ſixty Miles by Water ſhort of *New-Windſor*. This by ſome few, very few, was looked on and talked of as a conſiderable Loſs to the Colony; but People of more Diſcernment could not think ſo; for what Loſs can it be to any Place, if ſuch leave it, who will put their helping Hands to no Good in it? Which theſe Perſons 5.

1739. Decemb. have evidently ſhewn they had no Intention of: The Committee at *Jenkins*'s will indeed hereby loſe ſo many truſty Members, who never failed conſtant Attendance; and I conceive the total Diſſolution of that mutinous Aſſembly is approaching, Diſcord of late being crept in among them, and ſome of them now thinking themſelves pretty good Adepts in the political Way, ſometimes differ in their Sentiments, about what they have been ſo long forming Schemes in vain for, and refuſe paying implicit Obedience to the Dictator any longer; who, if Fame is to be credited, or he himſelf believed, is alſo threatning to leave us to ourſelves, and remove to ſome Iſland or another in the *Weſt-Indies*. —— May *Georgia* ſuffer no greater Loſs, and all will be well.

6. *Thurſday*. Meſſieurs *Eyre* and *Holmes*, lately arrived from the *Cherokee* Nation, preparing to ſet off for the South this Day, and attend the General there; I wrote by them to his Excellency, incloſing divers Letters and Papers that came to my Hands, deſigned to be ſent him. I had no ſooner finiſhed what I had to do, and delivered it to Mr. *Eyre* juſt taking Boat, when a Packet was brought me from the Truſt, forwarded by the Attorney-General at *Charles-Town*; who ſent me a Letter with it, dated *November* 5, wherein he wrote me, that he

he had juſt then received it by Captain *Nicholſon*, newly arrived in the *Minerva* from *London*, who had a tedious Paſſage of twelve Weeks: And the Paſſage which this Packet had from *Charles-Town*, was much after the ſame Rate; the Fellow who had the Charge of it, though a Freeholder here, loitering at *Port-Royal* by the Way, on Buſineſs of his own; ſo that it was a full Month in coming from *Charles-Town*. I luckily ſtopped the Gentlemen a few Minutes, and the Tide preſſing them away, I had juſt Time to deliver to them for the General, what I received for him from *England*, together with other Letters that came with it from *Charles-Town*; but had no Time to write him any more than that I had before done. Afterwards I had Leiſure to peruſe Mr. *Verelſt*'s Letter to me, dated the 10th of *Auguſt*; which was ſo near after the Date of the former *per* Capt. *Thompſon*, that the Purport of it chiefly was, to inform me of the Subſtance of the Act, which the honourable Truſtees had prepared for his Majeſty's Approval, and which, when printed, would be ſent hither. 1739. Decemb.

Friday. Enſign *Maxwell* having finiſhed what he had to do in *Carolina* by Order, returned with the ten Soldiers detached from the Gariſon at *Port-Royal*: And in the Evening Mr. *Upton* alſo came back from *Charles-Town*; who found all that 7

1739. Decemb. had been reported here, too true, concerning the Loſs of his Boat and Cargo; but was of Opinion there was Roguery in it, and that the Men were not drowned, but run away, after plundering the Boat of what was moſt valuable and portable; which they might do eaſily, he ſaid, and go to ſome remote Place on the Coaſt, by the Help of a Canoe they had with them: And what induced him the more to ſuſpect it was, that ſome Trunks, which had the moſt valuable Things in them, were found broke open, and ſtript: The Truth of which might in Time be diſcovered. He brought me a Letter from Mr. *Hopton*, informing, that he had received the Packets which I committed to Mr. *Upton*'s Care the 27th *ult.* and that they came in very good Time to go for *England*, in the Ship *Endeavour*, Captain *Alexander Hope*, who was juſt upon ſailing, and to whoſe Care he had committed it.

8. *Saturday.* Enſign *Maxwell* proceeded South, together with his Detachment of Soldiers. News came in the Evening of another ſad Accident, that happened to a poor Man, who was at Work (among others) for Mr. *Haberſham*, by his Appointment, on a Tract of upwards of five hundred Acres of Land, which was newly run out by the General's Order, next adjoining to mine near *Vernon* River; and in the

the falling of a Tree, the Man was killed by a ſmall Branch of it. The Intent of this Land being run out, was, that it might be ready for Mr. *Whitfield*'s converting to a proper Uſe whenever he came; and whatever Uſe that ſhall be, this that Mr. *Haberſham* purſues is preparatory to it. Nothing more worth noting; but ſufficient for this Day, may be ſaid, was the Evil thereof. 1739. Decemb.

Sunday. Mr. *Haberſham* continued, as he had done, to read the Prayers of the Church, and a Sermon. 9.

Monday. Captain *Davis* having now got his Snow ready for ſailing, after a pretty deal of Time ſpent in equipping her for the Deſign of privateering; ſhe fell down to *Tybee* in order for a Cruize; but not being yet ſufficiently manned, he would wait there for more Hands, which he expected: She was a neat-built Veſſel, ſailed well, and of good Force, if well manned, carrying about twenty Guns mounted on Carriages, beſides Swivels; and required at leaſt a hundred Men. A Jury of twelve Men were impanelled, and ſent to ſit in Inqueſt on the Body of the poor Man, who loſt his Life on *Saturday*; who found it *Accidental Death*, and ſaw the Body buried: His Name was *Gardener*, had ſome Land allotted him at *Skeedoway*, where he lived a little while, and cleared a ſmall Piece 10.

1739. Decemb. of two or three Acres; but grew weary and deſerted it, more than two Years ſince, as divers others have done; and lived of late by letting himſelf out to Hire.

11. *Tueſday*, } Nothing more than com-
12. *Wedneſday*. } mon requiring my Attention in Town, my principal Care theſe two Days was, to promote and haſten forward the Work I had begun at my new Plantation; which at firſt ſetting out was attended with many new Expences; and I found it neceſſary to begin *de novo* with thoſe Hands which I was to employ there, by providing them with new Axes, Houghs, *&c.* and a new Set of Cloathing from Head to Foot, both Linen and Woollen, to be added to what they were now wearing out, of what was laſt provided for them: And as they were henceforward to be employed at ſuch a Diſtance from hence, that they could not be ſupplied ſo frequently as formerly with what they might want, it would be alſo neceſſary to lay in ſuch a Store of Proviſions, as might be ſufficient for their Wants a while to come, of all Kinds.

13. *Thurſday*. A little Diſorder, occaſioned by a Cold coming upon me, made it adviſable to keep home; where I could always employ myſelf uſefully, when well.

Friday.

Friday. The ſame: Nothing interrupting me from abroad, I made what Advances I could with my Pen and Ink; and found myſelf much better as the Day ended. 1739. Decemb. 14.

Saturday. Mr. *Jones* having a Deſire to ſee *Abercorn* (which he never had) at his Requeſt I went up the River with him; and the rather, becauſe one *Bunyon*, a Builder of Boats and a Settler there, had newly, by the General's Order, built a large Ferry-Boat, fit to carry about nine or ten Horſes at a Time, which was intended to be kept at *Palachocolas*, it being a proper and convenient Paſs on this River from that Fort: Here we found the ſaid Boat newly finiſhed, and by her Appearance on the Water, we judged ſhe would well anſwer the Purpoſe ſhe was intended for. As there was no Place in the whole Province, of the like Allotment of fifty Acres each, which in my Eye ſeemed ſo deſirable, being a moſt pleaſant Situation on the Banks of ſuch a River, with as good Land belonging to each Lot, as is readily to be found in moſt Parts of the Province; I never ſaw it but with Regret, that there never yet had been a Number of Settlers there deſerving it; but generally they happened to be looſe, idle People, who after ſome ſhort Abode wandered elſewhere, and left it: It conſiſts of twelve Lots, the two Truſt-Lots bounding each Extream; and 15.

1739. Decemb. there are at preſent five Families only remaining there, nor has there often been more at one Time. As the Truſt-Lands ſeem to be now in ſome better Way of cultivating by their own Servants, than hitherto; I propoſed it to Mr. *Jones* to ſend down a few *German* Families to work on the Truſt-Lots there; which by helping to fill the Place, very probably might induce others the ſooner to occupy Lands there alſo: He agreed with me in Opinion, and ſaid he would write of it to the General.

16. *Sunday.* We made what haſte we could home; but the Tide not favouring us in due Time, it was paſt Noon ere we reached *Savannah*; and a wet Day.

17. *Monday.* Moſt Part of the Day employed with Mr. *Jones* in methodizing Accounts, which were preparing as faſt as we could to ſend to the Truſtees. In the Evening I had once more an Inclination to make a Viſit to our nightly Club; where in this Time of Scarcity of News from all Parts, I thought I ſhould not fail of ſomething, either true or falſe; for rather than want, they could coin: I found them now reduced to a very ſmall Number, three or four only; who upon my coming in (whatever Subject they had been upon before) turned moſt of their Diſcourſe into a doleful Story of the ſad State they ſaw poor *Georgia* fallen into, and how People

ple were deſerting it Day by Day: Which not having Sagacity enough of myſelf to diſcover, I ſaid I wiſhed to know who they were: And after a pretty long Pauſe upon it, they named two or three, adding to them all the *Jews* in general; which I ſaid little to then, intending to be better informed: And by Degrees paſſing from one Point to another, at length the Truſtees Anſwer to their Repreſentation was to be animadverted on; which with Patience I heard them a pretty while take in Pieces, and reaſon upon in their own Way as they liked, offering ſometimes a Word or two myſelf in Vindication of what needed none: Till at laſt they came to that Length as to tell me, in plain Words, they thought it not a fair Anſwer, nor Way of proceeding in the Truſt, to publiſh an Anſwer in Print, to what ſo very few in *England* had ſeen in Writing; and that in Juſtice they ſhould have ſet one againſt the other, and printed them both together, whereby the World would then judge who was in the right: Which I thought ſuch a Piece of Impudence, that I could no longer bear; and ſo I took my Leave, not likely to trouble them, or myſelf about them again in haſte. 1739. Decemb.

Tueſday. After diſpatching ſome neceſſary Buſineſs at home, being pretty eagerly whetted at what paſſed laſt Night; I 18

went

1739. Decemb. 18. went out with a Reſolution to diſcover, as far as I could, what Foundation appeared for ſuch a Talk of Deſertion, as I was then entertained with: And I was very well aſſured, that not one of the *Jews* who were People of Induſtry, or of any Value among us, had any ſuch Thoughts or Deſign, being eaſy and contented in the preſent State they lived; ſome of them Planters, and others in a Way of Trade; only one, who was a Barber, and lived wholly by Shaving, but never improved his Lot; another who neglected his Land wholly, and followed no viſible Buſineſs; and a third, who had not the leaſt Property among us, but was a Wanderer; theſe three I underſtood had received lately ſome Advice from their Friends in *Jamaica*, inviting them to come thither; which they were pondering upon, and unreſolved in: And among the common Freeholders, I could hear of none except *Robert Potter*, who was an elderly Man, lately made one of the Conſtables, by the General's Favour, to encourage him; from whence he ſeemed to expect a Maintenance, that he had no Title to otherwiſe; and therefore could not obtain it: He (it is confeſſed) had of late ſhewn ſome Tokens of Uneaſineſs, and given it out, that he would not ſtay here and ſtarve, but rather try his Fortune with Captain *Davis* in his Privateer;

teer; who being now upon ſailing in few Days, we ſhould ſoon ſee how far he was in earneſt. 1739. Decemb.

Wedneſday. My chief Employment great Part of the Day, was to haſten on the Work I had taken in Hand, of a new Plantation; wherein I was not willing to admit of loitering. Towards Evening I received by a trading Boat juſt arrived, Letters from Lieutenant *Kent* at Fort *Auguſta*, informing me, among other Things, that it was currently reported in the Nations near us, the *French* were once more marching with a great Body of Men to attack the *Chicaſſaw Indians*, whoſe Fidelity to us, and whoſe Bravery againſt their Enemies, had been thoroughly experienced: Wherefore we could not but be in ſome Pain for their Defence: Incloſed I found a Letter alſo for the General, which I made no Doubt imported the ſame News, and I ſhould forward with all the Diſpatch I could. 19.

Thurſday. Often in Conference with Mr. *Jones*, and buſy in Accounts; when between while we fell into Diſcourſe about thoſe who were ſaid to be leaving us; the Principal of whom being *Robert Potter*, and he having now declared openly his Reſolution of ſeeking his Fortune in privateering, I aſked Mr. *Jones* to tell me freely his Opinion of him, that (without telling him 20.

1739. Decemb. 20. him mine) I might know how well our Sentiments agreed: And without Heſitation, he anſwered plainly, that he knew him to be a ſly, old Knave, and that he only wiſhed he might hold his Reſolution of going; which rather than he ſhould not, he would give Money out of his own Pocket, that the Colony might be rid of him: Which Opinion of his, I entirely concurred in; the ſame Reaſons inducing us to think ſo; among which ſome we ſpecified.——As to his Religion, he put on at Times a Shew of conſtant Attendance on the publick Worſhip of the Church, perhaps for a Month; and then would abſent himſelf from it more than twice as long, profeſſing himſelf a Diſſenter; but it is generally ſuſpected he had no Title to the Word Proteſtant, for it is certain he was bred a *Roman Catholick* in *Ireland*, and many People do not ſcruple to ſay, that he is actually in Orders under that Church, even now: He is univerſally looked on as a great Hypocrite, affecting to go in a tattered Habit, and complaining of Poverty; whereas it is well known, he has good Store of better Apparel in his Cheſt; and as to his Pretence of Want, ſcarcely any one gives Ear to it, believing rather that he has a Miſer's Hoard, which he dares not make proper Uſe of: Nevertheleſs, utterly to deſtroy all ſuch Shams, it is well known

known Mr. *Jones* employed him ſeveral Months at the Rate of nine Shillings *per* Week, as a conſtant Guard on the Office were the publick Accounts were examining, and where all the Books were ſecured, to take effectual Care leſt any unfair Dealing ſhould be uſed, or Embezzlement made to the Detriment of the Truſt; and upon the late Promotion of Mr. *Fallowfield* to the Magiſtracy, a Vacancy of one of the Conſtables happening, the General made him a Conſtable, to which was annexed a Payment of 10*l.* *per Annum*, intended as a Mark of his Favour for not ſubſcribing the late Repreſentation, his Excellence kindly overlooking all other Defects: But Mr. *Jones* had ſome Time before diſcharged him from his Employment at the Office, upon diſcovering ſome evident Tokens of his Infidelity: This 10*l.* of itſelf, however, was ſufficient for feeding him, and only one Daughter, which he had (a Girl of about ten Years of Age;) and if he would have added any Thing to it, by cultivating a little Land, as he had formerly done, and with Pleaſure he now might, having a few Acres well cleared, he had a fair Proſpect of living comfortably; but this laſt Year he wholly neglected that, and now thought himſelf hardly uſed, for not being maintained as he expected. This being the true State of Mr. *Potter*'s Caſe, I cannot apprehend

1739. Decemb. 20.

1739. Decemb. 20. apprehend the Colony will ſuſtain any Damage for the Want of him. Two others likewiſe, that a pretty while ſince engaged in the Privateer Service, would as little be miſſed: One of them, whoſe Name is *Eliſha Foſter*, and by Office a Tythingman, at whoſe Houſe Capt. *Davis* lodged, was perſuaded to think he could not miſs making his Fortune in that Way, and entered as Quarter-Maſter, whoſe Office was, upon taking a Prize, to ſtand between the Captain and his Men, and ſee that every one had his Dividend right: What Improvement he has made aſhore on his Lot, is, a pretty good little Houſe to live in; but in five or ſix Years that he has lived here, he never cultivated one Acre of Land, chuſing to get Money any other Ways, if he could, by ſome Traffick; which from the little viſible Appearance of, was generally thought to be unwarrantable, being ſtrongly ſuſpected to be one of the Number of ſuch as furniſh this Place with Spirits; and whereof he took ſo plentiful a Share himſelf, that it was common with him to appear publickly drunk in the Streets in open Day. The next to be named is one *Garrett*, a Sort of Quack, who had little Skill and little Practice, ſettling here about three Years ſince, or more; had a Freehold Lot granted him in this Town, which he kept not long, and then threw it it up, refuſing to do the Guard Duty, or diſcharge it by another: But both he and *Foſter*, we now hear, are already wavering whether or not to purſue their intended Voyage. Theſe were ſome of the good People, whom the Company I kept laſt *Monday*, were perſuading to believe the Loſs of, would be of ſad Conſequence: But we happened not to think alike; and I had good Reaſon to believe, that if they ſtopped ſhort from proceeding to Sea, it was not for Want of Encouragement from *them*, who delighted in nothing more than to ſeduce all they could from continuing among us. 1739. Decemb.

Friday. Early this Morning arrived a ſmall Boat from the South (*John Rea* Patroon) with ſeveral Paſſengers, moſtly belonging to this Place and Neighbourhood: We all ſought eagerly for News, having not had any freſh Intelligence of late; but they could tell us little more than that the General was juſt returned ſafe, from the Expedition he had been upon near St. *Juan*'s, where the *Spaniſh* Guard Sloop lately lay that was ſtationed there; but now was gone, and no Enemy appeared: The General, we were told, advanced with his little Body of about two hundred Men, partly Mariners, and ſome Landmen, with a few *Indians*; but ſcarce any of the regular Troops, except ſome Gentlemen Ca- 21.

1739. Decemb. 21. dets, and three or four Commiſſion Officers, who obtained the Favour to attend him; and with theſe he advanced within a little Way of *Auguſtin*: In marching, our *Indians* ſet up the War Whoop; which thoſe of the Enemy's Side underſtood ſo well, that they who were near took to their Heels, and ran into the Town for Safety; only one of our *Indians* overtook one of their Negroes with a Ball, which ſtopt his Flight and killed him. After reconnoitring thus far, and finding none to oppoſe, his Excellence probably did not think it prudential to wait, and ſee whether or not they would take Courage and intercept them with a ſtrong Body: Wherefore he retreated homewards, but not in ſuch haſte as to neglect taking in Fort St. *George* by the Way; which was the utmoſt of our Limits for a while, and given up again upon ſome Terms of Accommodation as were then agreed to: Here the General replaced now a few Men, as a Look-out, to keep Gariſon, and obſerve what the *Spaniards* are about.—This was what we could pick out from theſe Paſſengers, who ſaid they came off in half an Hour's Time after the General's Arrival, who was much fatigued, and went to take his Reſt: Wherefore we next hoped for ſome more authentick Advices thence by the next Opportunity. This being his Excellency's Birth-

Birth-Day, was obſerved by firing ſome Guns, and his Health was drank under the Flag, without any Profuſeneſs of Powder or Wine; which he forbid upon any publick Solemnity. 1739. Decemb.

Saturday. Upon Advice received, that a ſmall Skooner had been obſerved lurking for ſeveral Days paſt within *Uſſybaw Sound*, and ſome that belonged to her had been aſhore at one of our Plantations in that Neighbourhood, where by making Shew of their being in want of many Things, they gave good Cauſe of Suſpicion that they had no good Deſign; Captain *Davis* was applied to, to ſend out his Sloop, now at *Tybee*, to prevent her getting away by Sea: At the ſame Time a Boat well armed went within Land, to lay hold of her; and Meſſieurs *Parker* and *Jones* (two Magiſtrates) required the Maſter, as well as the Men belonging to her, to be brought aſhore at the neareſt and moſt commodious Place of landing, where they might be examined; for which Purpoſe the ſaid Magiſtrates rode thither; and finding their Orders punctually executed, by *Noble Jones*, who had a Plantation near the Place, they there examined them, and found her navigated by four or five Hands only, without any Appearance of Arms: Nevertheleſs, as ſhe came from *Hiſpaniola*, laden with *Spaniſh* contraband Goods, con- 22.

1739. Decemb. 22. ſigned to Meſſieurs *Woodward* and *Flower* at *Port-Royal*, ſhe was ſeizable; and moreover her lying there ſo many Days, gave Grounds of Suſpicion, that they were ſounding the Depths of that Inlet, or ſomething elſe was in their View, which they would not own, but pretended that they miſtook their Port: She was ordered round to *Tybee*, and to be ſecured, till we had the General's Orders concerning her. This Afternoon Mr. *Chriſtie* came to my Houſe, and brought with him Meſſieurs *Fallowfield*, *Theo. Hetherington*, and *Andrew Grant*, as Witneſſes to his peremptory Demand of the Conſtitution appointing him firſt Bailiff; having, as he ſaid, fulfilled the Conditions required of him, in making out a Copy of the Proceedings of the Court to this Time; and putting into my Hands a Packet with ſeveral Sheets of Paper written, the Contents to me unknown, which he put into a Cover of brown Paper immediately; and being then ſealed with divers Seals, he delivered it to me, directed to the honourable Truſtees, and told me he expected I would ſend it: To which Mr. *Fallowfield*, in a moſt inſolent Manner (as it is his uſual Way) added many rude Expreſſions in a Sort of menacing, which I little regarded; but directing my Anſwer to Mr. *Chriſtie*, I told him, that it was my Duty to tranſmit faithfully to the Truſt what-

whatever was put into my Hands for that Intent, and accordingly would take Care of this; but what Name to give it I could not tell, unleſs I was better informed; for it did not appear to me, that it was a full Copy of the Court Proceedings; to which he replied, that Mr. *Hetherington* then preſent could teſtify that it was examined by his Book; but I alledged, that Mr. *Hetherington* could be no Judge whether or not that Book was duly kept, or contained what ought to be recorded; for it was known, that the Book itſelf, as well as this now called a Copy, were all made out ſince the late Stop put to delivering him the Conſtitution of firſt Bailiff; and it was out of ſuch Fragments, as it was to be feared were never to be reduced into perfect Order; moreover, that it was well known alſo there were ſeveral Fines due to the Truſtees, and other Sums paid into Court, which he never yet accounted for, or charged himſelf with; which none could ſo well diſcover how well they were taken Notice of, as the Magiſtrates themſelves, who I apprehended had a Right at all Times to call for that Book, and have Recourſe to it: To which he replied poſitively, that neither the Magiſtrates, nor any one living, ſhould look into his Book: And to conclude, I told him my laſt Orders from the General were, that all theſe

1739. Decemb. 22.

1739. Decemb. Matters ſhould remain as they now ſtood, till the Truſtees Pleaſure was farther known; that nevertheleſs I would write to the General who was near, for his Advice as ſoon as he pleaſed; and that I would not fail to lay before the Truſtees what now paſſed, by the next firſt Packet that I ſent for *England:* And ſo they left me.

23. *Sunday.* Mr. *Haberſham* continued to read the publick Prayers, *&c.* during the Abſence of a Miniſter. Some Perſons came up to Town from *Tybee*, belonging to a Sloop Privateer which came from *Providence Iſland*, that anchored at *Cockſpur* laſt Night: Their Buſineſs was with the General, to get their Commiſſion improved and ſtrengthned by him; but miſſing him here, they would loſe no Time in going to find him at St. *Simon's*: They had taken ſome ſmall Prizes from the *Spaniards* (as they ſaid) which they ſent home; but they told us a Privateer belonging unto *Rhode-Iſland* had the good Fortune lately, though but a ſmall Sloop with forty Hands, to take a rich *Spaniard* lately on the *Spaniards* own Coaſt, with ſuch a Quantity of Silver aboard, that they ſhared four hundred Dollars apiece, beſides ſolid Plate for the Uſe of a Church, and many rich Brocades, *&c.*

24. *Monday.* The moſt remarkable Occurrence of this Day was the Arrival of a Sloop

Sloop from *Philadelphia*, belonging to Mr. *Whitfield*, which he had bought, and ſent hither, filled with great Variety of Neceſſaries for ſuch as were to ſettle here: She brought ſeven or eight ſuch (Men, Women, and Children) beſides two that had been here, and now returned from *England*, namely, a young Son of Mr. *Bradley*'s, and one *Robert How*, who it might be hoped from Mr. *Whitfield*'s Inſtruction was become a new Man; for he carried but a bad Character with him from hence. They made Report, that Mr. *Whitfield* was coming, in Company with two or three to attend him, by Land, thro' *Maryland*, *Virginia*, *North* and *South-Carolina*, hither; which is computed at leaſt ſix hundred Miles; and that we might expect him here in about a Week more. 1739. Decemb.

Tueſday, *Chriſtmas-Day*. Publick Divine Service was obſerved, as at other Times. 25.

Wedneſday. The Skooner that was taken on Suſpicion of unwarrantable Practices laſt *Saturday*, and apparently loaden with *Spaniſh* Goods, being ordered round hither, arrived; and Col. *Flower*, of *Port-Royal*, who was the Owner, having Intelligence what a Situation ſhe was in, thought it Time to beſtir himſelf, and came hither alſo; who alledged many Things in his own Favour, plauſible and fit to be conſidered; but as the General was now in the 26.

1739. Decemb. Province, no Judicature here would venture to decide ſo nice an Affair, without firſt taking his Opinion and Advice: Wherefore Colonel *Flower* determined to wait on his Excellence at *Frederica* with all convenient Speed; when at the ſame Time the Magiſtrates, who had acted in it ſo far, would inform the General of all Proceedings. By Colonel *Flower* I received the Packets ſent from the Truſt by Captains *Ayres* and *Gregory*, with Letters of *September* 14, and *October* 6; together with a Letter from Mr. *Hopton* (as he never failed) now informing me, that Captain *Ayres* made eleven Weeks Paſſage of it, by whom he had the large Packet, and alſo a Box for the General: And Captain *Gregory*, who arrived in eight Weeks, and was within very few Days of the other, brought him the ſmall Packet: All which he forwarded to me by Mr. *Jonathan Bryan*, who was to deliver it to Mr. *Wyre*, his Correſpondent at *Port-Royal*; and who accordingly took this firſt Opportunity of ſending it to me by the Colonel: But Mr. *Bryan* being on Horſeback, could not take the Box with him; wherefore Mr. *Hopton* waited the firſt Convenience of ſending it.

27. *Thurſday*. The whole Day taken up in writing Letters, and preparing many Things which required being ſent to the South, wherewith a Pettyagua was now loading, and

and a ſmall Boat was ordered alſo at the Colonel's Requeſt and Expence; by which he purpoſed to make quick Expedition tomorrow Morning; and I deſigned, by the ſame Conveyance, to tranſmit to the General what I had received for him Yeſterday. 1739. Decemb.

Friday. Colonel *Flower*'s Deſign of ſetting out for *Frederica*, being baulked by a very wet Day, which prevented his going on Horſeback as far as *Noble Jones*'s Plantation, who was to accompany him in his Paſſage thence, for which Purpoſe the Boat was ſent round thither Yeſterday; I delivered the General's Packet, and other Letters for him, to Mr. *Parker*, who had engaged to ſhew the Colonel the Way to *Noble Jones*'s, his own Plantation alſo lying in that Neighbourhood; and he promiſed to put what I gave him the Charge of, into *Noble Jones*'s Hands, to deliver it all ſafe to the General. Bad Weather and *Chriſtmas* Holidays meeting, occaſioned a Conjunction alſo of Friends at one another's Houſes, and ſcarcely any one to be ſeen abroad, nor any Thing paſſed worth Note. 28.

Saturday. Took Horſe, and rode to my Plantation (intended) at the Mouth of *Vernon* River, being the firſt Viſit I made my People ſince I ſent them to begin there, after they had firſt fenced in the full Quantity of Land allotted; which was the ſooner 29.

1739. Decemb. 29. done, by Means of an Iſthmus of near a Mile extent, that we ſet our Fence on, and ſo parted it from the Wilderneſs. I found them well covered from the bad Weather, by a ſtrong Palmeta Hut, which they had made as ſoon as they arrived; to which in the next Place they would add a convenient Enlargement with Clapboards in few Days more, and then to work in falling Trees, clearing Ground, *&c.* I had five Hands there, beſides one that I had hired for an Overſeer, on ſuch Terms as would make it his Intereſt to take Care they all did their Duty; and that he alſo put a helping Hand to it himſelf. As this was the very utmoſt Settlement in the Northern Diviſion of this Province, towards the Sea-Coaſt, and required their keeping a good Look-out that Way againſt the *Spaniards*; as well as backwards againſt any ſtraggling *Spaniſh Indians* that ſhould attempt to come upon them unprovided; I furniſhed them with two Fuſees and Bayonets of my own, and a Couple of Muſkets I got from the Stores for them, with Powder and Ball ſufficient; telling them, that in Caſe of any Danger, I hoped they would behave like Men; which they promiſed me very chearfully; and I aſſured them they ſhould want for no Encouragement from me, that they deſerved. Returned home in the Evening; and being informed

informed by the Tything-man upon Duty, that there was like to be a weak Guard to-night, through ſeveral Peoples Neglect, *&c.* I gave him Charge to make a particular Return to me, of all that was fit to be taken Notice of, when he went off his Guard; reſolving to ſee the late Orders left us by the General, relating to thoſe Affairs, ſtrictly obſerved. 1739. Decemb.

Sunday. Mr. *Norris* not yet returning, the publick Service, and a Sermon upon Juſtification, was read by Mr. *Haberſham.* 30.

Monday. The Year ended without any Thing remarkable, after too many that I would gladly have taken no Notice of, had it been conſiſtent with the Duty required of me: But while ſome among us were too buſy in promoting Diſcord, and tempting divers to think they might live happier elſewhere (which few here of real Value would give Ear to; but on the contrary ſaw ſome returning; heard of others who were become very miſerable, not knowing how to get their Bread, and had no Reaſon to expect much Countenance here, from their former ill Courſe of Life; beſides what Accounts we frequently had of ſeveral of them that were taken away by Death, in the late common Calamity of Sickneſs, which fell upon the People of *Carolina*, and *Charles-Town* eſpecially) kind Providence beſtowed the Bleſſing of Health 31.

in

1739. Decemb. 31. in ſo large a Share upon this Province, that ſo few were not known to have died in one Year, ſince the planting of the Colony. The Camp nevertheleſs at St. *Simon*'s grew ſickly, about the Fall of the Leaf, and the Soldiers were addicted to Agues, which rendered many of them weak; but very rarely proved mortal, they that had taſted of the current Diſtemper recovering apace.

January 1. *Tueſday*. Great Part of this Day ſpent with Mr. *Jones* in adjuſting divers Accounts which had been examined ſome Time paſt, in order now to haſten them away with what Speed we could to the Truſtees; who by their laſt Letters required us ſo to do; wherein we had found great Intricacy: And it is a Piece of Juſtice due to Mr. *Jones*, to acknowledge, that without his Application to that Buſineſs, I ſee little could be done in it by either of thoſe Colleagues joined in Commiſſion with him: For as to myſelf, who have no Pretence to the Rank of an Accomptant, I only tread in the Path that he firſt traces out, very often through many Turnings and Windings; and when the Light opens, ſo that Truth may be more eaſily diſcovered from Error, whether by Accident or Deſign, I then make uſe of what little Capacity I have, to inform my Judgment, in ſuch Manner that I may not ſet my Hand

Hand blindfold to I know not what; in which Purſuit I never fail to join him, whenever he calls upon me ſo to do, and tells me he has Leiſure. 1739. January

Wedneſday. In Conference with Mr. *Jones* on ſundry Affairs, he acquainted me in what Manner he was accoſted by Mr. *Chriſtie*; who bringing two Witneſſes with him, namely, *Andrew Grant* and *Theoph. Hetherington*, in the ſame Manner as he did to me on the 22d *ult.* he produced an Account which he ſhewed; wherein he made the Truſtees Debtors to him in a large Sum upwards of 100*l.* Sterling; and he (Mr. *Jones)* looking on it as what there was no juſt Foundation for, told him in a ſatirical Way, that they would have done well, if they had brought their ſeveral Concubines with them, as a farther Evidence of what paſſed; wherein *Grant* and *Chriſtie* were moſt barefaced and ſcandalouſly culpable; the firſt of them having two Baſtards by one Woman, who all cohabit with him; and the other with as little Shame had taken to his Bed another Man's Wife (who was run away ſome Time) with whom he lived in open Adultery *(vide* 10, 11, 12, 13 of *Oct.)* *Chriſtie* then aſked him how he dared iſſue any Money without his Privity; to which the other replied, that he was not looked on as a Man fit to be truſted in thoſe Affairs, who was known to 2.

1739. January have made ſeveral Concealments of Money belonging to the Truſtees, which had come to his Hands; and withal he let him know in plain Words, that his Character was grown ſo bad, the General declared he would never ſuffer his Name to ſtand on the ſame Paper with his. The Time drawing near of our Court ſitting again next Week; from theſe ſeveral Attacks lately made, it was imagined ſomething was intended by them when that Day came, theſe Proceedings being well known to be the Reſult of our Committee of Safety; which though reduced now to a ſmall Number, yet like Vipers near expiring, continue to ſhew a Diſpoſition to Miſchief as long as they can: Of which Number Mr. *Chriſtie* (as before obſerved) has for a conſiderable Time paſt made himſelf one; and I wiſh I could wholly clear one of our new Magiſtrates (Mr. *Fallowfield)* from any the like Imputation, who has been obſerved to be a pretty frequent Attender on that Club; but how far a Partaker of their Counſels, Time will beſt ſhew; Facts, and not Suppoſitions only, being the Guide I muſt follow.

3. *Thurſday*. The Day at length came, that had been long expected, when Captain *Davis* and his People took Leave of this Place for a while, *Potter* and *Foſter*, two of our Officers (before mentioned) making Part

Part of their Crew; and both the Snow and Sloop lay at *Tybee* ready for ſailing, fitted out by *Davis*, who took the Command of one of them himſelf, and *James Williams* had that of the other: It was expected they would find good Hands, and enough, at *Providence*, where they were bound firſt; but they were yet poorly manned, neither could it be expected they were to be found here. A *New-York* Sloop that had been at *Frederica*, and diſpoſed of moſt of her Cargo of Proviſions there, —— *Tinley* Maſter, ſtopt at Anchor in our River; and the Maſter brought no Letters, but reported, that the General was preparing, when he came thence on *Tueſday* laſt, to ſet out on another Expedition againſt the Enemy, much ſtronger than before, reſolving (as it was believed) at any Rate to drive the *Spaniards* out of two Forts they had on St. *John*'s River: Wherein it ſeems ſome Attempt had been made a little while ſince, by a ſmall Party, under the Command of a Subaltern or two, who found the Forts ſo fortify'd and gariſon'd, that it was impracticable to attack them with Succeſs, by naked Men, under no Defence or Cover; for which Reaſon they then returned *re infectâ* after one (a Serjeant) being mortally wounded, who is ſince dead: What this Maſter farther reported was, that a Duel was fought lately between Meſſieurs

1739. January 3.

Leman

1739. January *Leman* and *Sutherland* (two Enſigns) and that Mr. *Leman* lay dangerouſly ill of his Wounds.

4. *Friday*. *Samuel Lacy* coming in his Pettyagua from *Charles-Town*, brought Letters with him thence for the General, to be forwarded for his Majeſty's Service; ſome Letters alſo for me, but of no great Import; and ſeveral for other People; but no Ship arrived from *England* ſince Captain *Gregory*, nor any farther News than what *he* brought with him.

5. *Saturday*. Moſt of my Time this Day, as well as for ſeveral preceding, was taken up with Mr. *Jones*; in getting forward ſuch Accounts as we poſſibly could, of thoſe which had been examined ſome Time paſt, but had not been yet put into due Order: And what yet remained to be examined, ſuppoſing them to be alike perplexed (at leaſt ſeveral of them) it was not in our Power to foreſee with any Certainty, what Time it would take to finiſh them: In the mean while I was unwilling my next Letters ſhould go without ſome Specimen of what we had been doing; which on the other Hand muſt occaſion a Delay more than uſual in ſending away my Packet.

6. *Sunday*. No News yet of Mr. *Norris*'s Return from the South, or of Mr. *Whitfield* from the North: Wherefore Mr. *Haberſham*

berſham continued, as he had done, to read the Service of the Church, and a Sermon after it. 1739. January

Monday. This being the ordinary Day of the Court's ſitting, the Magiſtrates met, and opened it in due Form; but upon calling over the Names of the Perſons ſummoned, both on the Grand and Petty Jury, ſo many failed to appear, that they could not make out a Number ſufficient for either; and obſerving that the Perſons on thoſe Liſts, were many of them ſuch as were well known to be at preſent far out of Town, they conceived that the Recorder (who had always taken that Part upon him of giving out thoſe Liſts to be ſummoned) had now picked out enough Abſentees to prevent the Court's proceeding any farther: Wherefore being now aſſembled together, they took Care that other Liſts ſhould immediately be made, of the Freeholders, ſufficient to prevent any ſuch Defect when they met again; which by Adjournment they appointed this Day Fortnight. Mr. *Jones* returned, and I with him, to haſten on, as faſt as might be, ſome of thoſe Accounts the Truſtees expected. 7.

Tueſday. The ſame: And I learnt nothing material from without. A *New-York* Sloop with Proviſions, *&c.* came up the River, —— *Ware* Maſter; who after privately higgling about among our Keepers of 8.

1739. January of Stores, and furniſhing them with what they beſt liked, offered the Remainder to us; which we rejected with Scorn.

9. *Wedneſday.* Colonel *Flower* returned from the South, where he had been to wait on the General, about his Affair before-mentioned *(Dec.* 26 *& ſeq.)* and brought Letters from the General: In one of which to Mr. *Jones*, he gave ſome Directions relating to that Skooner, which he communicated to Mr. *Parker* and me; Copies whereof he promiſed to ſend to the Truſtees: And this Evening, at Colonel *Flower's* Requeſt, the three Bailiffs and I met him, in order to conſider what to be done therein; when it was propoſed by Meſſieurs *Jones*, *Parker*, and ſelf (in order to make the Colonel as eaſy as could be, in ſo difficult an Affair, which we were not fond of deciding) that the Caſe ſhould be ſtated, and ſent to Mr. *Rutledge*, a Lawyer in *Charles-Town*, whom the General has employed on ſeveral Occaſions; deſiring him to adviſe with the Officers of the Cuſtoms thereon, and to let us know how far we might proceed without Blame: But the Colonel thereupon ſaid, that if that was the Reſolution to be taken, he would ſave us that Trouble; for he well knew, that as he could not deny but there were ſome contraband Goods aboard, *viz.* a ſmall Parcel of Coffee and Soap, that alone would, in

in the Opinion of the Lawyers and Cuſtom-Houſe Officers, condemn the Veſſel; but he hoped we ſhould not carry Things on with that Rigour; ſince (as he ſaid) thoſe Things were taken in by the Maſter, without Direction from him; and the Bulk of the Cargo was Molaſſes and Sugar, which if ſuffered to be entered, would be of Service to the Colony. Hereupon Mr. *Fallowfield* declaring, with his uſual Warmth, that the Affair was properly cognizable by him as Naval Officer, and none elſe; that he would enter the Molaſſes and Sugar; and as for thoſe Goods that were contraband, he would take them into his Cuſtody till farther Order; and the Blame (if any) he would take upon himſelf; that he knew what he did, being a better Judge of thoſe Matters than any one here, *&c.* and appearing ſo very poſitive in it, Meſſieurs *Jones* and *Parker* were of Opinion not to enter into any Controverſy with him, but to let him take his own Courſe; and if any new Difficulty ſhould ariſe, they would meet upon it again to-morrow Morning: In the mean Time Meſſieurs *Jones* and *Parker* deſired I would note what paſſed, that they might be juſtified. 1739. January

Thurſday. The ſame Perſons meeting again this Morning, continued in the ſame Opinion as Yeſterday; and Mr. *Fallowfield* undertook the Whole of what was to be done: 10.

1739. January 10. done: But upon its being urged by us, that thoſe contraband Goods could no where be ſo ſafely and properly lodged, as in the Truſtees own Cuſtody; Mr. *Fallowfield* thought fit to yield that Point, and promiſed they ſhould be brought to the Truſt's Stores; and as for the reſt, he undertook the Colonel ſhould give his Bond to the Truſtees, for paying the Duty on thoſe Goods, which Bond he would deliver to me. —— *Ware*, Maſter of the *New-York* Sloop, going to the South, to ſee if he could diſpoſe of the Reſidue of his Cargo there, I took the Opportunity of ſending by him a Packet to the General, wherein were encloſed ſundry Letters that came to my Hands from different Parts of the two Provinces for him, ſince the laſt I ſent on the 28th *ult.* In the Afternoon arrived Mr. *Norris* (long wiſhed for) from the South, and with him Mr. *Eyre* the Cadet, in his Way again to the *Cherokee* Nation, by Order from the General: By whom I found the Story confirmed in all its Parts, as related to me, and noted the 3d Inſtant; Mr. *Eyre* having been one at the Attack of thoſe Forts: He told us, that Mr. *Leman*, who had been ill in a Fever, occaſioned by the Wound he received in that Duel, was upon Recovery; and confirmed likewiſe the other Enterprize the General was intending, and which he actually was ſet out on, on, upon *Tueſday* the 1ſt Inſtant, with about two hundred good Men, Soldiers and Volunteers, for the Purpoſe before related. 1739. January

Friday. Towards Noon arrived Mr. *Whitfield*, accompanied by three or four in his Travels; and it luckily happening, that Mr. *Norris* arrived Yeſterday from the South, it was quickly ſeen with what Temper they met: When, to the Diſappointment of ſome People, who are pleaſed beſt with Contention, upon Mr. *Whitfield*'s ſhewing the Authority he brought with him, Mr. *Norris*, without the leaſt Emotion, told him, that he ſhould by no Means enter into any Diſputes to diſturb the Peace of the Church; nor had he ever wrote once to the Truſtees concerning it, from the firſt Notice he had of what was in Agitation; wherefore it was far from his Intention to enter into any Controverſy with him; but on the contrary declared, that his Miniſtry at *Savannah* ceaſed from that Inſtant, declining to officiate at Evening Prayer this Night, but left it to Mr. *Whitfield* to take Poſſeſſion of the Church immediately; who accordingly did ſo, when a greater Congregation than uſual moſt Days were met, many (I fear) more out of Curioſity than Devotion. He delivered to me in the Afternoon a Letter from Mr. *Martyn*, Secretary to the Truſt, dated *June* 1, relating to the Land appointed for 11.

1739. January his Uſe, and whereon to ſet the Orphan-Houſe, *&c.* which after I had read, he alſo did; and I told him I would not be wanting in any Thing on my Part to promote what the Truſt appointed, and to give him what Aſſiſtance I could; but as to the five hundred Acres, Mr. *Haberſham*, without conferring with me upon it, when the General was here, applied himſelf to him, who approved of the Place he had made Choice of, ordered it to be run out, and then ſigned a Warrant, which he directed me to give the Conſtable, empowering him to give Poſſeſſion of it to Mr. *Haberſham*; which was done accordingly in ſome ſhort Time after: And that Mr. *Haberſham* had already began fencing and clearing upon it. After his reading the Letter from Mr. *Martyn*, he deſired me to let him take a Copy of it; which I would not refuſe him.

12. *Saturday.* Mr. *Whitfield* loſt no Time in ſetting forward the Work which he profeſſed to have much at Heart, about an Orphan-Houſe; and rode out to view the Land which Mr. *Haberſham* had taken Care to provide againſt his coming, conſiſting of five hundred Acres, that he had taken Poſſeſſion of in his own Name; where Mr. *Whitfield* gave ſuch Orders and Directions as he thought proper. I met with very little Interruption from abroad in what I had

had to do at home; ſo that I ſtuck to it pretty cloſely: Only Mr. *Fallowfield* called on me, to ſhew the rough Draught of a Bond which he was preparing for Colonel *Flower* to execute, purſuant to what was agreed on laſt *Thurſday:* But I ſoon found it differed pretty much from what I expected; for it was not made to the Truſtees, but to the King; which he ſaid, upon conſidering of, he thought moſt proper: I then aſked him, whether or not he knew that all Recognizances, either for the Peace or otherwiſe, which in *England* were made to the King, were here always taken in the Name of the Truſtees; and that he had little to ſay to, but he thought it not a parallel Caſe: Then I aſked if he did not intend to deliver the Bond, when ſigned, into my Cuſtody; which he plainly told me he ſaw no Occaſion for: But as I had the Honour to ſerve the Truſt in the Station appointed me, I apprehended all Things of that Kind, which ſo immediately concerned the honourable Truſtees, and their Intereſt, would be properly lodged in my Hands: Then I aſked him whoſe Servant he thought himſelf to be? from whom he received the Powers by which he acted? and to whom he believed he was accountable? To all which he ſeemed to turn a deaf Ear, and only wiſhed I would inform him, whether the Form of the

1739. January 12.

1739. January Bond was right or not: But as he had not fulfilled the Promiſe and Engagement he was under, I thought it my wiſeſt Way not to meddle, or offer to mend what he had ſo warmly taken on himſelf, excluſive of all others.

13. *Sunday.* Mr. *Whitfield*'s Name, which of late had made ſo much Noiſe in *England*, could not fail drawing all Sorts of People to Church, who profeſſed Chriſtianity, to hear what Doctrine it was that he preached: When both in the Morning and Afternoon, he made our Juſtification by Faith only, the Subject of his Diſcourſe; taking thoſe Words in St. *Matthew* for his Text, "What think you of Chriſt?" Which he preſſed home with great Energy, denouncing Anathema's on all ſuch as taught otherwiſe. In the Evening, at his Requeſt, I drank Tea with him; where Mr. *Norris* alſo came; and delivering back to me Mr. *Martyn*'s Letter from the Truſt, which he had taken Copy of, he told me he was ſo well ſatisfied with the Situation of the five hundred Acres, which he found provided for him by Mr. *Haberſham* againſt his coming, that he would lay aſide all farther Thought where to build his Orphan-Houſe, being determined to fix it on that Land, and not meddle with what *Robert Hows* had reſigned up to the Truſt (which Lot therefore now became void.) As this five hundred

hundred Acres was about ten Miles from the Town, after ſome Pauſe, he reflected a little upon ſome Inconvenience which he ſhould thereby bring upon himſelf, foraſmuch as he purpoſed, where the Orphan-Houſe was, to have a Chapel (or Oratory) and alſo an Apartment for himſelf, intending to make it pretty much the Place of his Reſidence, when in theſe Parts; Wherefore he ſeemed to wiſh for ſome Help in diſcharging the Office of his Miniſtry at *Savannah*, whilſt he carried on the good Work he was upon; and for the better effecting whereof, it would be expedient for him, after ſome Months Abode here, to take another Travel, in order to get the Fund augmented for that End: And addreſſing himſelf to Mr. *Norris*, he made him an Offer of exerciſing his Function here with us, at all Times when he pleaſed, and did not ſee (he ſaid) but it might be done very well, by his being ſometimes here, and ſometimes at *Frederica*, as formerly it had been done by Mr. *Weſley*, &c. But Mr. *Norris* replied, that ſince the Truſt had been pleaſed to appoint him ſpecially at *Frederica*, he thought himſelf bound not to neglect his Charge, which next under God he was accountable for to the Biſhop, who for his future Encouragement, had obtained a Stipend of 50*l.* *per Annum*, to be paid him by the Society for

1739. January 13.

1739. propagating the Goſpel in Foreign Parts, additional to what the Truſt allowed.

January 4. *Monday.* An exceeding heavy Rain kept every body within Doors all the Day; which Mr. *Jones* and I ſpent good Part of nevertheleſs together; and upon my aſking (now Colonel *Flower*'s Skooner was unladen) whether or not Mr. *Fallowfield* had put thoſe contraband Goods into the Truſt's Stores, as he engaged; Mr. *Jones* told me, that there was no ſuch Thing done; to which I replied, that then he had not kept his Word with me in any one Thing inſiſted on, which he had promiſed.

15. *Tueſday.* What I thought moſt worth preſent Obſervation, aroſe from the extraordinary Preparations making to build the Orphan-Houſe, *&c.* wherein Mr. *Whitfield* indeed ſhewed himſelf much in earneſt; and it may be preſumed, he expected it would be finiſhed in few Months; in order to which, there was hardly one Sawyer of any Value in Town, but all hired, and engaged by him to go over and work, where he meant to erect that Building: Moſt of our Carpenters, Bricklayers, *&c.* were likewiſe engaged by him, and a great Quantity of Scantling Timber, ready ſawn, was coming (as I heard) for the more Expedition, from *North-Carolina.* The Houſe that Mr. *Bradley* had lived in, being empty, Mr. *Jones* complimented the firſt Com-

ers

ers with the Uſe of, for the preſent; and Mr. *Whitfield* choſe, upon his Arrival, to carry thoſe Friends that came with him thither alſo, as well as to be with them himſelf, leaving Mr. *Norris* in Poſſeſſion of the Parſonage-Houſe (which could not hold more than two or three) till he could conveniently move what he had there, and carry it with him to *Frederica:* But the great Houſe not being finiſhed within, and incommodious on many Accounts, eſpecially by letting the Rain come through the Roof, which was flat; Mr. *Whitfield* agreed with *David Douglaſs* for the Uſe of his Houſe (much the largeſt of any private Lot in Town) at the Rent of 20*l.* Sterling for half a Year only; when I heard he might have rented it for a whole Year under 30*l.* which plainly ſhews (in my Opinion) that he depended on the new Building to be ready for him within that Time; and *Douglaſs* took the Advantage of exacting ſo unreaſonable a Rent on that Occaſion. 1739. January

Wedneſday. This Day was moſtly taken up in rectifying many Things relating to our Militia, and the Guard Duty; which, without good Looking into, too many were apt to be negligent in: Wherefore I thought it my Duty to examine particularly into all ſuch Neglects, as I apprehended were growing among us, ordering a Return to be made 16.

con-

1739. January 16. conſtantly to the Conſtable every Morning, by the Tything-man going off Duty, giving an exact and true Account how many, and who were upon Guard of his Tything, and who were abſent; as alſo to certify what Occurrences he met with in the Night; what Boats came, or went (by Permit) and who were in them: And foraſmuch as in theſe dangerous Times, it was not improbable but ſome Incendiaries might be employed by the Enemy, ſecretly to make what Deſtruction they could; I gave Orders, that there muſt be a punctual Obſervance of the Patrol walking the Rounds on the Skirts of the Town, once in two Hours at leaſt: And as I found by an Inſpection, which I had before ordered to be made, that ſeveral Arms were wanting, eſpecially among ſome who had Freehold Lots lately granted them by the General; I took Care this Inſtant they ſhould be furniſhed out of the Stores, where they muſt be accountable, and produce them again when required: Then I recommended it to the Conſtable *Samuel Mercer* (who ſince *Potter*'s going off to Sea, was the only one, till the General ſhould appoint another) that he would be frequent in viſiting the Guard at uncertain Hours in the Night, that they might not know when to expect him, and to ſee if they were alert, or not; which I told him I ſhould think it my my Duty alſo to do ſometimes: He promiſed me to obſerve it; and I did not doubt it, for a more diligent Officer in that Poſt I never knew in *Savannah*. 1739. January

Thurſday. Mr. *Whitfield* going again to his new Plantation, took Mr. *Mercer* the Conſtable with him, to ſhew him the Way; but when he came there, what he aſked of him, was to give him Poſſeſſion of that five hundred Acres, as he had before done to Mr. *Haberſham*, who was now ready to ſurrender it to him, for the Uſe of the Orphan-Houſe: But *Mercer* deſired to be excuſed, giving his Reaſons for it: Whereat Mr. *Whitfield* was much diſpleaſed; and as ſoon as he came home in the Afternoon, he ſent, deſiring me to come to him; and when I came, he complained much of his being ſo dealt with; but I explained the Cauſe of it to him as well as I could, which in Subſtance was thus.— Mr. *Haberſham* (his Agent here) from the Time of Mr. *Norris*'s firſt Arrival by Appointment from the Truſt, had ſhewn many evident Tokens of Diſreſpect to him, and was (not without good Reaſon) ſuſpected of ſtirring up, and abetting, a little Party of angry Zealots; from whence idle Stories were frequently ſpread abroad, tending to leſſen Mr. *Norris*'s Character, which they put in Contraſt with Mr. *Whitfield*'s, to make *his* appear with the greater Advantage, 17.

1739. January 17. vantage, whom they expected to return again, with more Power than ever. Be that as it would, I had the Truſtees Orders to countenance Mr. *Norris*, and to join with the Magiſtrates in giving him all the Aſſiſtance we could, for the Support of his Miniſtry, *&c.* I did ſo; and in ſome of my Letters to the Truſt, vindicated him for his unblameable Conduct: Whereupon Mr. *Haberſham*, finding me an Advocate for Mr. *Norris* (I perceived very plainly) appeared ſhy in Converſation with me, and never uttered ſo much as one Word to me about his Intention of running out any Land for Mr. *Whitfield*'s Purpoſe, till the Work was began; tho' I then had by me the Commands of the Truſt of the 14th of *July*, ſignifying, that Mr. *Whitfield* was to conſult me in that Affair: But the General being here a while after, Mr. *Haberſham* rather choſe to go to the Fountain's Head (wherein no one can blame him;) and the firſt Notice I had of what was doing, was from the General himſelf, who ordered me to make out a Warrant for giving Mr. *Haberſham* five hundred Acres of Land, in ſuch a certain Place, under the uſual Reſtrictions, as I had done to others; which I did; and when the General had ſigned it, I delivered it to Mr. *Haberſham*, who by Virtue of it, in a ſhort Time after, got *Mercer* the Conſtable,

ſtable, whom it was directed to, to go and give him Poſſeſſion of it; after which, Mr. *Mercer* re-delivered the Warrant endorſed, as duly executed, for me to keep among many others. This being really the Caſe, I told Mr. *Whitfield*, that I could not think but *Mercer* had acted very cautiouſly, and with Prudence, in ſtopping where he did: For how could he juſtify it to the General, to give Poſſeſſion of the ſame Land to another Perſon, without the ſame, or equal Authority? Mr. *Whitfield* ſaid little more to it, but I ſaw he was pretty uneaſy; and thereupon I told him, that nothing ſhould be wanting in me to clear the Way with what Expedition I could, and give him what little Aſſiſtance I was able. 1739. January

Friday. This whole Day produced nothing obſervable, but that the late heavy Rains which had fallen this Winter, as well as the Summer foregoing, rendered our Ways to the ſeveral Lots almoſt unpaſſable. We began now to look with ſome Impatience for ſome News from the South, and to hear what Succeſs the General met with, in the late Expedition he went upon the 1ſt Inſtant. 18.

Saturday. Little to obſerve, more than Yeſterday; only hard Rains continuing, occaſioned ſeveral People travelling on Horſeback, to be in great Danger of drowning, their Horſes ſwimming in ſome Places, 19.

which

1739. January which had ſcarce ever before been known under Water; and all the low Lands were ſo flooded, that it was feared we ſhould hear of great Loſſes of Cattle; the like having not been known (as it was ſaid) ſince the firſt planting of the Colony. I attended Mr. *Jones* again about the publick Accounts, being urgent (as often) to ſend away ſuch as were gone through, and wiſhing that I might not be obliged to ſend away my Packet at laſt without any.

20. *Sunday.* Mr. *Whitfield* did the Duties of the Day, with more than ordinary Diligence, by reading Prayers at Seven in the Morning; at Ten again, with a Sermon after it; at Three again, the ſame as at Ten; and a Lecture at Seven in the Evening; beſides the Sacrament, which he adminiſtred to betwixt thirty and forty People after the ſecond Morning Service: His Sermons both before Noon and after, in the ſame Manner as on *Sunday* laſt, were wholly on the Doctrine of Juſtification and Regeneration; which we hoped would ere long be followed by an Exhortation to the Practice of all Chriſtian Duties, that ſo our Faith might be ſhewn by our Works; otherwiſe a dry and inactive Faith, it is to be feared, might prove a dangerous State. This Evening Mr. *Bradley* returned from *Carolina.*

Monday.

Monday. The Court now ſat again, when upon calling over the Names of thoſe that had been ſummoned to ſerve upon the Grand Jury, ſeventeen appeared: And whereas it had been frequently complained of, as well by Mr. *Norris* in his Time of Miniſtry, as now of late by Mr. *Whitfield*, that ſeveral Perſons in this Town lived moſt ſcandalous Lives with their Whores, and went on *impunè* in open Defiance of all Laws both divine and human, to the great Reproach of the Place in which they lived; and therefore hoping that the Magiſtracy would take Notice of it, ſince there could be no Proceſs againſt ſuch notorious Offences, by any eccleſiaſtical Law, where thoſe Offences were committed: The Court now ſitting thought it high Time to take ſome Cognizance of it; and Mr. *Parker* (who ſince the Time of the Truſtees Appointment of a new Set of Magiſtrates, declined as much as poſſible taking upon him to act, but in ſuch Caſes only where it was unavoidably neceſſary) deſiring to be excuſed from giving the Charge as uſual to the Grand Jury, looking on himſelf in no other Light, than as one ſubſtituted by the General to fill that Place on the Bench, till the Truſtees Pleaſure was farther known (as noted on the 15th of *October* laſt) and Mr. *Fallowfield* declining to take that upon him, which he knew

1739. January 21.

1739. January 21. knew himſelf not well qualified for: Mr. *Jones* undertook that Part; and among other Things proper to be recommended to their Conſideration, inſiſted ſtrongly upon it as their Duty, to make a Preſentment to the Court, of all ſuch Offences as came to their Knowledge, either through common Fame, or ſuch Evidence as might be produced, which were committed againſt the known Laws of God and Man, or were *contra bonos mores*; particularly ſpecifying Adultery, and Incontinency: After which, Mr. *Whitfield*, ſitting near the Bench, roſe, and made an Oration, ſetting forth the Heinouſneſs of ſuch Crimes, in very pathetick Terms; ſhewing that we muſt never expect a Bleſſing on this Colony, unleſs the civil Power would give all poſſible Aſſiſtance, in rooting out this accurſed Thing; concluding, that it was his firm Perſuaſion, the ſlow Progreſs that was made in the Advancement of the Colony, was owing to God's not permitting it to proſper whilſt ſuch barefaced Wickedneſs was, through Neglect, ſuffered to remain among us; which every good Man was ready to allow: But I found a pretty many who thought ſo, ſeemed not well pleaſed at his taking upon him to harangue the Grand Jury with what would more properly have come from the Pulpit; and I myſelf then feared, it would have

have a different Effect upon the Grand Jury from what was hoped and expected. 1739. January 22.

Tueſday. What I feared came to paſs; for upon the Court's adjourning Yeſterday to give Room for the Deliberations of the Jury, they fell immediately into warm Debates on what had happened; which held all that Day, and came to nothing; and it was late in the Afternoon this Day, ere they agreed upon any Thing; when they came into Court, and delivered in a few Preſentments of ordinary Matters; but not a Word concerning what was of much greater Conſequence: Whereat the Majority of the Court appeared diſpleaſed, and adjourned to a long Day, namely, the 4th of *February*, to take Time and conſider what Expedient could be attained, how to bring their good Deſigns to paſs. In the Evening the Magiſtrates all aſſembled at my Houſe; and in Obedience to the Commands of the Truſtees, knowing Mr. *Bradley* to be returned to Town, they ſent for him; who readily came; and was given to underſtand what the Truſt expected from him, *viz.* that he muſt find Security for his not leaving the Colony till his Accounts were made up: Which he ſeemed ſomewhat ſhocked at, and plainly told them, he muſt then conclude himſelf utterly loſt; for that he knew not one in the whole Town who would be his Bail;

1739. January which indeed we all thought alike in: But that occaſioned a ſorrowful Reflexion, what Sort of Behaviour then he muſt have ſhewn among them, not to find one Friend in this Time of Need, who would appear to give him kind Aſſiſtance: The Magiſtrates were all unwilling to puſh Matters againſt him with the utmoſt Severity, and immediately commit him; wherefore in great Tenderneſs, they allowed him till to-morrow to get what Security he could.

23 *Wedneſday.* In Conference with Mr. *Jones* this Day, about the Affair of ſending off to the Truſt ſo many of the Accompts as had paſſed Examination; I found him, I thought, a little doubtful in himſelf concerning it, whether or not we ought to ſend them in ſuch a Manner by piece-meal, or defer it a little longer, till the whole Liſt of Debts ſent us by the Truſtees, to be examined and looked carefully into, could be perfected; which it was to be hoped in Time we might ſee an End of: But as to Meſſieurs *Cauſton* and *Bradley*'s Accounts, he plainly told me, he almoſt deſpaired of getting to the Bottom of either. And if he had ſuch Thoughts of his own Inability in ſuch Work, much more Reaſon was there for me to think ſo of mine, who never pretended to judge of Accompts, which were ſo intricate eſpecially: But my Opinion was,

was, that it was incumbent on us to ſend what was ready, that thereby the Truſtees might ſee, and make ſome Judgment of what we had done; and to haſten forward the Remainder as faſt as we were capable: Moreover I told him, that I had deferred writing a pretty while longer than uſual, which I could offer no Excuſe for, excepting my great Deſire, that another Letter might not go from me unaccompanied with ſome of thoſe Accounts, which had been fully looked into: And he promiſed me it ſhould be ready ſome Time next Week, to take out of the Clerk's Hands. Mr. *Bradley* failed in getting Security this Day, as was ordered; and it was to be feared, another Day's Indulgence on that Occaſion, would produce nothing better; which I was ſorry to ſee. 1739. January

Thurſday. Since it ſo happened, that Mr. *Whitfield* was miſtaken in his Expectation on laſt *Thurſday*, in the Manner I then noted; at his Requeſt I went with him and Mr. *Haberſham*, attended by two or three more of thoſe who followed him hither, to ſee what he had begun to do on the five hundred Acres, and to know whether any Means could immediately be uſed for giving him Poſſeſſion; which he appeared very uneaſy at, to find any Delay; telling me, that as the Truſt had recommended him to me to ſee it done, he 24.

1739. January 24. would apply no where elſe: In Anſwer to which, I told him I was ready to attend him this Day, and any other that he ſhould aſk, and would readily do the Thing required; but his own Agent Mr. *Haberſham*, by the precipitate Meaſures he had taken, had put it out of my Power to do it inſtantly: For as Mr. *Haberſham* had obtained a Grant of that particular'd Land from the General, which I knew nothing of, till the General himſelf ordered a Warrant to be made out, for giving Poſſeſſion of that Tract to Mr. *Haberſham*; which Warrant the General ſigned; who ſhall dare take upon them, of thoſe that ſerve the Truſt, to make void that Act of his, but he himſelf? who undoubtedly would ſet all right, as the Truſt intended it, as ſoon as he is informed truly of the Caſe. This Argument (however) did not ſo ſatisfy, but that Mr. *Whitfield* ſhewed plainly he was uneaſy: Wherefore, to give him all the Satisfaction I could, I propoſed it to him, that his Friend *Haberſham* might make a Surrender to him of all that Tract of Land for the Uſes intended, reſigning thereby all the Right, Title, and Property, which he has, or ever had in the ſame; which I would be preſent at, and ready to teſtify: Accordingly when we came there, Mr. *Haberſham* did ſo in Form, delivering to Mr. *Whitfield* a ſmall Shrub,

Shrub, which he plucked up, and therewith declaring, that he ſurrendered all his Right, *&c.* in thoſe Lands, to him, for the Purpoſe intended: Which though I knew could not be deemed taking a legal Poſſeſſion, foraſmuch as no Surrender of any Lands (as I apprehend) can be made to another Perſon, without being authorized by the Truſt, or ſome Perſon to whom ſuch Power is delegated; yet they appeared content with it for the preſent; and I had only farther to obſerve, that I found the new-intended Work already carrying on with a good Number of Hands, Artificers and Labourers; which Mr. *Whitfield* not thinking yet ſufficient, he was ſending for Men out of other Provinces, to haſten it as faſt as poſſible. In our Way home, falling into ſome Talk of the ill Succeſs our Attempts met with on *Monday* laſt, in getting Preſentments from the Grand Jury, againſt ſuch Men as were become ſcandalous for their Debauchery; I underſtood Mr. *Chriſtie* had been with him, and promiſed him to put away his Houſe-keeper (as he called her) that there might be no farther Occaſion of Scandal; inſinuating, that thoſe Reports which were ſpread of him, were very injurious, and without any real Foundation: But I fear rather, his Guilt gave him Apprehenſions, that Truth could not be withſtood, when Proof could

1739. January 24.

1739. January be produced, from more than one poſitive Evidence, of his Houſe-keeper and himſelf having only one Bed between them, which they made uſe of together for a long while, and were ſeen ſo to do by a Man and Boy Servants, who then lived with him.

25. *Friday.* Mr. *Whitfield,* having at his firſt Coming, given Notice in Church, that he would adminiſter the Sacrament there conſtantly on all *Sundays* and Holidays; there was a Communion early at Morning Prayer, being the Feſtival of St. *Paul.* The Occurrences of the Day were no more than common, and therefore not worth obſerving.

26. *Saturday.* The great Rains ceaſing for ſome Days paſt, a ſmart Froſt ſucceeded, with a clear Sky, and pleaſant Weather; but being attended with a freſh North-Weſt Wind, it was piercing cold, and the Ice, which generally goes off in the Day, returned at Nights with more than ordinary Rigour. Theſe ſudden Extreams of Weather, nevertheleſs, had no ill Effect on the Inhabitants of this Place, which was never known more healthy, having ſcarcely one ſick Perſon in it; nor did any Thing happen this Day deſerving more Notice than the preceding. Capt. *Thompſon* now was expected daily with his Ship from St. *Simon's.*

Sunday.

Sunday. Mr. *Whitfield* called a Congregation again, four Times, at the ſame Hours as on *Sunday* laſt; and in his Sermons before Noon and after, purſued the Doctrine of Juſtification and a New Birth. Capt. *Thompſon* arrived at *Tybee* in the Evening, and came up in his Boat, late at Night, together with Lieutenant *Horton*, from *Frederica*; Mr. *Horton* having the General's Leave to go with *Thompſon* for *England*; and to return again, after he has diſpatched what Buſineſs calls him hence. 1739. January 27.

Monday. A Boat was ſent down to *Cockſpur*, to bring up Capt. *Heron*, and Mr. *Carteret*, with their Ladies, who all came with Capt. *Thompſon* from *Frederica*; and the Ladies were bound for *England* with him; and I allowed myſelf the Liberty of being pretty much with them this Day, where I had the Pleaſure of hearing the whole Relation of the Manner wherein the General proceeded, in his late Expedition againſt the *Spaniſh* Forts, on the River St. *Juan's*: One of which (it ſeems) was deſerted by the Enemy, ſince the late Attempt againſt them; who judged it not tenable, in Caſe we returned with another Viſit: But the other they defended with good Reſolution, till our Forces played three or four ſmall Pieces of Cannon upon them; which going thro' and thro', they then ſent out a Flag of Truce, in or- 28.

1739. January

der to treat of ſurrendring; but the General would allow of no other Terms, than at Diſcretion; which they were obliged to ſubmit to: It was held only by twelve Men, but ſo fortified with Logs of Timber, as to be Proof againſt Muſket-Shot; and he who commanded, told the General, that had he not brought Ordnance with him, he would have withſtood any Attack that could be made, if there had been double the Number againſt him there was. The General cauſed ſome new Works of Fortification to be made, and left a Gariſon of thirty good Men, under a proper Officer, to defend it. This Fort is eſteemed of great Conſequence, as being a Paſs where all muſt come, who would go to *Auguſtin* by Land, whether they are diſaffected *Indians* out of the Nations, or runaway Negroes from *Carolina*; which is ſuch a Benefit to that Province, that it is hoped they will contribute handſomely to ſtrengthen the General's Hands, ſo as to enable him to put theſe Provinces out of all Danger from *Auguſtin* in Time coming; for nothing now ſtands in our Way thither, and it is currently talked, *delenda eſt Carthago.* Began my Letters to the Truſt, but had not Time to finiſh them.

29. *Tueſday.* Capt. *Heron* proceeded early to *Charles-Town*, on the Affairs which he was charged with from the General; and in

in the Afternoon Mr. *Eyre* took his Way up the River in Purſuance of the General's Orders, making what Speed he could to the *Cherokee* Nation of *Indians*; which the great Floods we had lately, forbad him to attempt, ſince his Arrival here the 10th Inſtant, till now. Meſſieurs *Horton* and *Carteret* continued here with the Ladies, and probably might for a while, waiting the Time when *Thompſon* would be ready to ſail. A Boat being upon going to the South, it took me up Part of this Day in writing Letters to the General and others, and preparing ſeveral Papers to be ſent. 1739. January

Wedneſday. From Mr. *Whitfield*'s giving Notice in Church laſt *Sunday*, that this Day was to be publickly obſerved; it was expected he would have officiated himſelf; but he choſe rather to viſit his People at the new Settlement, leaving Mr. *Norris* to perform the Duty at Church, who read the appointed Service, and a Church Homily after it, againſt Rebellion: In the Evening Mr. *Whitfield* read the uſual Prayers, and expounded on the ſecond Leſſon, as conſtantly at other Times; but took no Notice of any Part of the Service appointed for the Day; from whence every body concluded he had no Regard to it. 30.

Thurſday. I delivered my Letters, *&c.* this Morning, which I had prepared on 31.

Tueſday,

1739. January 31. *Tueſday*, to the Care of Mr. *Upton*, who was going South in a Pettyagua of his own, which he had bought lately, and was now loaden moſtly with Corn, for the Uſe of the Camp and Gariſons, under the Conduct of a proper Patroon; he himſelf going as Supercargo, and carrying on a Traffick in various Commodities, betwixt *Charles-Town*, this Town, *Frederica*, &c. which has often been a Matter paſt my Comprehenſion to dive into, knowing him to have very little or no Fund of his own; and it muſt be not a trifling Sum, that can enable him to do what he does: The General (it is well known) has ſhewn him Favours, ſince his quitting what he had in the Neighbourhood of *Frederica*; and given him the Grant of an Iſland called *All-Honey*, Midway betwixt this and that, where he purpoſes to keep a large Stock of Cattle, Hogs, *&c.* which muſt require alſo a Purſe, at firſt ſetting out; but whence that comes, may poſſibly be better known hereafter, than at preſent: In the mean while that Mr. *Upton* has the good Fortune to find ſuch Aid, he is certainly not to be blamed for making as good Uſe of it as he can: People very often advance their Fortunes by joining with an able Partner. The Day produced nothing material relating to the Publick.

Friday.

Friday. This being the Anniverſary Day of the Colony's firſt Landing here, under the Conduct of *James Ogletborpe*, Eſq; the Gunner aſked me whether or not he ſhould fire any Guns, as had been formerly accuſtomed; to which Mr. *Jones* (then with me) anſwered, no; but I was of a different Opinion, and thought the Anſwer would more properly have come from me, as the General had left the Command of all the Militia with me, in his Abſence: Who when here laſt, told us, that now in Time of War, Powder ought not to be waſted in needleſs Salutes, *&c.* Upon which Mr. *Jones* made that the Foundation of his Opinion, calling it a Saving; which I had before ſhewn a particular Regard to, by divers Reſtrictions made, where I thought it proper; which would be found Savings indeed, worth Notice; but to ſhew a Contempt of this Day, by ſuch a poor Pretence, which in Effect was a bad Compliment to the General himſelf too, I thought a mean Act, and might carry ſuch a Reflexion, as could not eaſily be juſtified: Therefore the leaſt I could do, was to order five Guns to be fired; which I did, as a Memorial; hoping that Ages to come will celebrate this Day annually here, in a better Manner. In the Evening a ſelect Company of ſuch as had Confidence in one another's ſincere Diſpoſition towards promoting

1739. February 1.

1739. February moting the Colony's Welfare, met, and took a chearful Glaſs to its Founders, Protectors, and Benefactors Healths, Meſſieurs *Carteret* and *Horton* (now in Town) joining us; and nothing appeared among us but Love and Good-humour.

2. *Saturday.* After the Fore-part of the Day ſpent with my Pen and Ink at home, the Remainder of it I dedicated to Improvement of Land; and having now moſt of my Strength employed upon my five hundred Acres, unwilling nevertheleſs to throw up what I had been doing for two Years paſt nearer home, I reſolved to try what I could do with one Hand, upon the five-Acre Lot, which was perfectly cleared, but had made a very poor Return hitherto, for the Labour and Coſt beſtowed upon it: My Deſign now being to dreſs and cultivate ſuch Parts of it, as I hoped for any Benefit from, and by Degrees to make an Orchard of it all, conſiſting chiefly of Mulberries; whereof I had already planted a pretty many the laſt two Years, and now was preparing a good Number more for the preſent Seaſon. In this Amuſement I paſſed away a few Hours, and returned home as Night came on.

3. *Sunday.* Mr. *Whitfield* performed the divine Offices as before; but being taken with a ſudden Diſorder upon me, during the Service at Eleven, I was obliged to go out

out of Church home; where, after a few Hours, with a little Help of warm Things inwardly applied, I quickly found Relief; and at the Seven a Clock Evening Lecture, I went again, having never yet been there; when the Work he took in Hand, was expounding on a Chapter in St. *John*'s Goſpel; and, indeed, he did it, I thought, with great Perſpicuity; but when he came towards a Concluſion, he could not ſhut up without a Touch on his darling Topick of Regeneration, which muſt ſpring from a vital Principle in the Heart, infuſed by the Holy Spirit; till which is made ſure to us, we are all in a State of Damnation: And the Way to attain this, is by a ſtrong Faith, without Regard to good Works; which will occaſion great Pangs in the New Birth; and when by ſtruggling with God in Prayer, we have obtained his Grace, we ſhall find the Holy Spirit ſenſibly moving upon our Hearts, as it did upon the Face of the Waters: Which if any one denies, in plain he told us he lied; for that the Warmth of the Spirit was as ſenſibly felt, as the Beams of the Sun upon our Bodies: But this, he ſaid, was a Doctrine which very few of our modern Clergy approved of; whom he inveighed againſt terribly, as ſlothful Shepherds, dumb Dogs, *&c.* who led their People dreaming on in a carnal Security to Deſtruction; and that

1739. February 3.

1739. February that he was firmly perſuaded in himſelf, very few great and rich Men, and as few of our learned Doctors, for an Age and more paſt, could ever ſee Heaven; among whom, the Author of the *Whole Duty of Man*, he verily believed, had ſent Thouſands to Hell: Then he exhorted ſuch of his Hearers as were true Converts, to be on their Guard againſt all Temptations, which they muſt ſurely expect, to try them, whether or not they were ſtedfaſt; telling them they muſt meet with Contempt and Deriſion, on their thus ſetting out in their Way to Glory; and by and by Perſecution would follow: For Men in high Places would be offended at all Oppoſition made to their Deluſions, and then we might expect undoubtedly it was at hand. Theſe Things were very ſhocking to many People, who were otherwiſe well diſpoſed.

4. *Monday*. The Court ſat again, as *per* Adjournment; diſpatched ſome little Affairs, and farther adjourned to the 22d Inſtant, not finding any Means to revive what they were diſappointed in at their laſt Meeting: Some little Good, however, came to paſs, if true what was ſaid, that Mr. *Chriſtie* in the Fright, put off his Houſekeeper. In the Afternoon the Magiſtrates and Mr. *Whitfield* (by their own Appointment) met at my Houſe, to conſider of the Orphans Affair; when Mr. *Jenkins*, the

the only ſurviving Truſtee, ſhewed a great Deſire he had to be quit of that Buſineſs, as he had indeed deſired many Times before; and now upon Mr. *Whitfield*'s telling him, that he was ready to take all that Trouble off his Hands; he promiſed to bring, and deliver into his Care, all that he had been accountable for, to-morrow; from which Time Mr. *Whitfield* engaged to free him from accounting any farther, and his Accounts hitherto were to be looked into as the Court ſhould direct. During this Convention, in diſcourſing on the Subject-Matter of their Meeting, a little Diſputation aroſe betwixt Mr. *Whitfield*, and Mr. *Parker*, who had two Orphan-Boys with him (their Name was *Tondee)* the eldeſt of which being a well-grown Lad of fifteen or ſixteen Years of Age, Mr. *Parker* ſaid, he thought it would be a great Hardſhip to have that Boy taken from him, now he is grown capable of doing him ſome Service, after living ſo long with him when he could do him none: To which Mr. *Whitfield* ſaid, that the Boy would be ſo much the better for him and his Purpoſe, as he could be employed for the Benefit of the other Orphans: But *Parker* took that to be no Anſwer, to what he thought himſelf aggrieved in, and ſhewed a little more Warmth than I thought ſeaſonable at that Time; which I blamed him for: His Argument

1739. February 4.

1739. February gument was, that where the Child was taken Care of as he ought, by a good Maſter (which the Magiſtrates might judge of) and without any Charge to the Truſt; he did ſuppoſe ſuch a Boy not to be reckoned an Orphan that Mr. *Whitfield* was entitled to by the Truſt: Mr. *Whitfield* then produced the Deed he had from the Truſt; which was the firſt Time I had ſeen it, though I obſerved my own Name to be mentioned in it for divers Purpoſes.——But enough of that.

5. *Tueſday*. Nothing of any Conſequence occurred this Day. Wrote to the General by *George Cuthbert*.

6. *Wedneſday*. Capt. *Thompſon*'s Ship having been detained at *Cockſpur* ever ſince the 27th paſt by contrary Winds, came up this Day, in order to deliver what remained in her, of ſuch Things as, *per* Advices I received, were deſigned for this Place; which I had heard nothing more of ſince my being on board at *Tybee* the Beginning of *October* laſt: And we would make no Delay now in clearing the Ship, that ſhe might return home again, which was intended directly from this Place, where ſhe would find a Loading of Rice from the neighbouring Plantations in *Carolina*, without going to *Charles-Town*. Having ſome Notice, that there was like to be a thin Guard this Evening, I went about Bed-Time

Time to look into it, and found it ſo indeed, ſcarce half the Number upon Duty that ought to be: Which was ſuch a Neglect, as gave me much Diſturbance in my Mind, and I chiefly imputed it to the Advantage they took, of our having but one Conſtable at preſent to act, ſince *Potter*'s going off *(viz. Mercer)* who was vigilant, whenever he could be ſo; but by reaſon of his new Plantation at a Diſtance, muſt neceſſarily be out of Town ſometimes, or it would come to nothing: So that I was every Day in hopes of receiving from the General, a Conſtitution of another Conſtable, which by taking their Turn, would make it eaſy to them both. I could at preſent only give it in ſtrict Charge to the Tything-man, to ſee and keep a good Look-out, with thoſe Men he had; and to make a particular Report to me to-morrow Morning of all that happened: And it was incumbent on me to uſe all Means, pleaſing, or diſpleaſing, that might oblige all Perſons to perform that fundamental Duty required upon Guard, which was ſo eſſential to the common Safety of all. While I was at the Guard, a Scout-Boat from *Frederica*, as the Officer told me, arrived, whom I ſent to enquire; and he farther acquainted me, that the Patroon was gone with Letters to Mr. *Jones*; but if he had any for me, I believed he would

1739. February 6.

1739. February think to morrow Morning Time enough to deliver them: Such was the Cuſtom, and ſuch the Difference.

7. *Thurſday.* As I imagined, ſo it was: About Eight this Morning, the Maſter of the Scout-Boat gave me a Letter from the General; wherein, among other Things, he was pleaſed to give a particular, and very pleaſing Detail, of his late Proceedings againſt the Enemy, deſcribing the Situation of all thoſe Parts near *Auguſtin*, with the ſeveral Forts, moſt of which had been abandoned; but one which he had attacked and taken, was of very great Importance, to ſecure a Paſs there, which would prevent any Annoyance from the *Spaniards* upon the Back of this Colony: He moreover ordered a Deſcription to be ſent me, of the Fortification of the Town and Caſtle of *Auguſtin*, and the Strength of the Gariſon, how many and what Troops they conſiſted of: All which I could communicate with Delight to ſuch as wiſhed to hear it. Spent the Day in frequent Conference with Mr. *Jones*, tending to haſten on the Accompts.

8. *Friday.* Met the Magiſtrates at Breakfaſt with Mr. *Whitfield*, by his Deſire; where the Affair of the Orphans was again reſumed; and two or three of ſuch as had any in their Keeping, having ſhewn an Unwillingneſs to deliver up thoſe who were now grown up

up pretty well in Years, and therefore capable of doing them good Service, eſpecially as the planting Seaſon was coming on; it was the Opinion of all preſent, upon having Recourſe again to the Truſt's Deed to Mr. *Whitfield*, that there was not any Exception made; but all Orphans were included, who either were, or had been, chargeable to the Truſt: One Exception only was allowed, *nem. con.* nevertheleſs, to be juſt; and that was in the Caſe of one *Little*, an Orphan, under the Care of *Samuel Mercer* (Conſtable) who having a particular Friendſhip for the Father, and ſeeing the Child in bad Hands, by Leave of the Magiſtrates at that Time, took him into his Keeping; and though he was very young, promiſed he ſhould be a Charge to nobody; wherein he has not only kept his Word, but having no other Children, beſides what came with his Wife, who was a Widow; he has taken the ſame Care of him as of a Son; and from a Cow and Calf, which the Child had at his Parents Death, he has ſeen them ſo well looked after, that from the Increaſe which he has in few Years paſt, probably before he comes to Man's Eſtate (and he is yet not more than eight or nine Years old) he may be looked on as a Man of good Subſtance to begin the World, and make no contemptible Freeholder: This, 1739. February 8.

1739. February therefore, all agreed to be a ſingular Caſe, and fit to remain as it was. In the Afternoon arrived *Peter Emery*, in a trading Boat, bound for *Auguſta* from *Charles-Town*, whereof he was Patroon, and brought with him a Letter from Mr. *Hopton*, dated the 1ſt Inſtant, and encloſing ſeveral Letters thence to the General; among which one from himſelf: With this he alſo ſent a Box for the General, which I took Notice of in my Notes of the 26th of *December*, and which he had attempted to ſend to St. *Simon*'s by the *Tartar*; but that Ship being driven back to *Charles-Town* by foul Weather, he now took this Opportunity of ſending it to me thus, to be forwarded from hence.

9. *Saturday*. *Samuel Lacy* being ready to ſail for *Charles-Town*, with his Pettyagua, I was glad to ſend my Packet and Letters by him, dated ſo long ſince as the 28th of *January*; and to accompany it, I ſent one other Packet alſo from Mr. *Chriſtie*, which he had left to my Care; writing at the ſame Time to Mr. *Hopton*, to forward them *per* firſt Opportunity for *London*. Wrote Letters to the South, and encloſed ſeveral to the General, which had come to my Hands ſince the 5th, when I wrote by *George Cuthbert*, intending to ſend theſe off by the Scout-Boat that came hither from thence on laſt *Thurſday*, and was to return

turn on *Monday*. Mr. *Parker*, I under- 1739.
ſtood, had delivered up *Tondee* the Orphan February
to Mr. *Whitfield*'s Care; which he did, he ſaid, leſt the Truſtees ſhould be offended at him more and more; but complained, that it was a great Loſs and Diſappointment to him; as indeed it muſt be in his planting, to be deprived of the Benefit of ſuch an Youth's Labour, now grown to a good Stature, ſo as to do conſtant Guard-Duty for his own Lot. *(Vid. Feb.* 4.)

Sunday. Mr. *Whitfield* took Care that 10.
the Day ſhould be duly obſerved, by performing Divine Service four Times, as before; and with great Vehemence, which ſome call Power, inforced his Doctrine of Juſtification by Faith, which good Works would follow of courſe; ſeeming determined to lay down this, as a Foundation for Chriſtians to reſt on; and therefore allowed himſelf little Variation in handling his Subject, which he moſt ſolemnly pronounced to be ſo eſſentially neceſſary to Salvation, that without a firm Belief of its Truth, no Perſon ought to make uſe of the Lord's Prayer, and call God his Father, when he was undoubtedly a Child of the Devil. From henceforth I reſolved not to turn Obſervator, or be at any Pains in endeavouring to collect, what poſſibly in his Warmth might ſometimes drop from

1739. February him: Nevertheleſs I ſhould ſtill think it my Duty to attend the publick Worſhip, whatever my Sentiments were of the Preacher: But I feared every body would not be of the like Mind.

11. *Monday.* *Samuel Lacy* went not for *Charles-Town* till this Morning early, to whoſe Care I had delivered my Packets for *England:* And this Afternoon I delivered my Letters for the General, to *John Latter*, Maſter of the Scout-Boat, together with the Box that I received on *Friday* by *Peter Emery*; the Boat being to ſet off this Evening: Which Mr. *Whitfield* made a ſeaſonable Uſe of, having it lately in his Thoughts, to go and pay his Reſpects to the General at *Frederica:* Wherefore he rode to his new Plantation, where the Orphan-Houſe was building, intending to ſtay and reſt this Night among his Workmen, there, or thereabout, in that Neighbourhood, probably at Mr. *Burnſide*'s; where the Scout-Boat, that was to go round, might take him in to-morrow Morning. This being the right Seaſon for planting Mulberries, wherein the General had given me Direction to deliver out of the publick Garden, what Seedlings or Suckers could be had thence this Year, to all ſuch as I judged would make a good Uſe of them; I made that my Employment good Part of this Day.

Tueſday.

Tueſday. After little more than a Month paſt, ſince Capt. *Davis* went out a privateering with two Veſſels (*vide Jan.* 3.) they were now both returned to *Cockſpur*, and the two Commanders come to Town again; in order to get their Ships refitted, having been terribly buffeted in a long Continuance of bad Weather, which drove them quite off the Coaſt, more than one hundred and fifty Leagues; ſo that their Sails and Rigging were utterly ruined; and for want of able Sailors, they were almoſt out of all Hopes of getting into Harbour again, having not found Men to add to their Strength, ſince they went ſo weakly out; and it may be ſuppoſed our two brave Officers, *Potter* and *Foſter* (who not content with the Station they were in, imagined they ſhould ſoon become great Men) have taken a Surfeit of going to ſeek their Fortunes at Sea, which we may ſoon expect they will confeſs: At the ſame Time it is to be feared, that unleſs ſome Means can ſoon be found of getting able Men, to carry on ſuch an Enterprize, it cannot be to good Effect. 1739. February 12.

Wedneſday. Scarce any Thing to obſerve. Capt. *M^c^Intoſh* from *Palachocolas* arrived, on his Way to the General in the South, in order to clear his Accompts, and take his Leave of theſe Parts, after ſeveral Years Continuance, purpoſing to take the 13.

1739. February first Opportunity of going for his native Country in *North Britain*, upon Advice he had received, that his Brother the Chieftain of that Clan was dead, or near dying; and whom, as next Heir, he was to ſucceed in Title and Eſtate. Wrote Letters to the South, to the General, Mr. *Hawkins*, *&c.* and incloſed ſeveral which I had lately received for the General. In the Night arrived *Jacob Matthews* from the *Alatamaha*, where he and his Wife were ſettled far up in that Country, by the General's Approbation, to keep a Store; and he was now come to ſpend a few Days at their former Habitation on this River, and then to return again.

14. *Thurſday*. Capt. *M^c^Intoſh* going off this Morning for *Frederica*, I ſent my Letters by him, which I had prepared Yeſterday; and attended Mr. *Jones* good Part of the Day in getting forward the Accounts; as indeed moſt other Days, what ſpare Time I had from other indiſpenſable Buſineſs, was that Way employed; that we might be ready againſt Capt. *Thompſon* ſailed, to ſend what was poſſible for us to do, wherein he could not always be alike intent. In the Afternoon he came to me under a great Diſorder of Mind, complaining of a moſt outrageous Inſult made upon him at the Stores by *Jacob Matthews:* Who having been among our incendiary Gentlemen at

Jenkins's

Jenkins's (which is the Company that he always kept, when in Town formerly, and *Robert Williams*, and he, and *Tailfer*, were never long aſunder) he got very drunk, and it is too probable was ſpurred on now, by thoſe continual Miſchief-makers, to do ſome Exploit, that might ſhew what he dared; and (as Mr. *Jones* told me) it was in this Manner.—At firſt he picked a Quarrel with one of the Truſt's Servants, who was attending a Waggon drawn by Oxen, for the publick Work; aſking him how he dared to drive his Oxen? and, without farther Words, knocked him down with his Fiſt; when Mr. *Jones*, being near, interpoſed, and aſked him what he meant, by thus abuſing a Servant of the Truſt, whom he was bound to protect? telling him, he muſt expect to anſwer it in another Place: Whereat *Matthews*, curſing and ſwearing, told him he would beat him too; and immediately coming at him, in Spite of two or three with-holding him, gave him a Blow in the Face, and a Kick in the Belly: After which he was huddled away by ſome of his Friends, put into his Boat, and ſo ſent off to his Dwelling up the River. Enquiring of Mr. *Jones* what Pretence *Matthews* had to call the Oxen his; he informed me, that thoſe Oxen were aſſigned by the General for common Draught, to the Care of *John Mellidge*, a young Fellow,

1739. February 14.

1739. February 14. low, Son to one of them that came firſt over; who being a diligent Youth, the General had, among other Marks of his Favour, given him this farther Encouragement; and the better to be aſſured of the Uſe of thoſe Oxen, *Mellidge* had branded them with the two firſt Letters of his Name, *J. M.* which *Matthews* now ſaid was *Jacob Matthews*; though he knew moſt undoubtedly they were not of his branding. It is moſt likely the Venom lay next his Heart, ever ſince the former Diſpute about Cattle; when he thought a ſcandalous Aſperſion was caſt at him, and his Friend *Williams*, by Mr. *Jones*, which he kept in Memory (*vid. April* 23.) but whoever was in the Right then, it is certain that *Matthews* was much in the Wrong now. In the Afternoon arrived Mr. *Cadogan* (Enſign) from *Charles-Town*, where he had been ſent ſome Time ſince, with divers Diſpatches to the Governor, Council, *&c.* demanding ſome Aid from them againſt the *Spaniards*; on which Occaſion Capt. *Heron* alſo followed him (as noted *Jan.* 29.) and Mr. *Cadogan* was now on his Way South, Expreſs to the General, with Letters from the Government at *Charles-Town*, ſignifying, that the Council and Aſſembly had agreed to raiſe 120,000 *l.* Currency (15,000 *l.* Sterling) for his uſe in carrying on the War: Which was within

a

a Trifle, I hear, of what the General aſked: And they have agreed alſo to aſſiſt him with a conſiderable Number of white Men (ſome ſay five hundred) well appointed for Action, together with ſome Hundreds of Negroes for Pioneers. So far is well; but with it (if it is true what we hear) there comes a Stain which takes away the Luſtre of a good Act being done with an hearty Unanimity; for it is ſaid, the Affair was carried on by the Majority of only one Vote: So cloſe does their Ill-will to this Province ſtick to many of them. After a few Hours ſtopping here, Mr. *Cadogan* made what Expedition he could to the General at *Frederica*. 1739. February

Friday. Nothing came to my Knowledge worth obſerving: My own Time was ſufficiently taken up in purſuing the Work I was daily upon, to get forward ſuch Matters as it was intended to ſend by Capt. *Thompſon*. Mr. *Whitfield*'s Sloop, Capt. *Gladman*, arrived with more Stores from *Carolina*. 15.

Saturday. Gave myſelf a little Vacancy from other Buſineſs, to attend what was doing abroad, and ſpent good Part of the Day at the five-Acre Lot, in planting Vines, Mulberries, *&c.* reſolving (as before noted) to try if I could not make that little Spot turn to ſome good Account, which hitherto had 16.

1739. had diſappointed me in what I might reaſonably have expected from it. *(Vid. Feb. 2.)*

February 17. *Sunday.* Upon Mr. *Whitfield*'s going South the Beginning of the Week paſt, Mr. *Norris* took Care of the Church here in his Abſence, and read the Morning and Evening Service; as he alſo preached this Day twice: But he told me, he had not ſo much as any Knowledge given him of Mr. *Whitfield*'s Intention to be abſent: So ſtrangely were they diſpoſed towards each other. Another unhappy Accident fell out to-day to be added to divers of the like Sort formerly: A Boy that belonged to Capt. *Thompſon*, and attended in the Cabbin, was drowned: The Ship lying at the new Wharf, in order to take in her Loading, People went in and out, on a Couple of Planks laid for that Purpoſe; and this poor Boy misſtepping, fell in, and was loſt. Mr. *Upton*, with his Pettyagua, arrived, in order to carry more Proviſions to the South; as Mr. *Perkins*, who arrived Yeſterday with his Pettyagua, came on the ſame Errand, both from *Frederica*; where (it is to be preſumed) a large Magazine is neceſſary, for the Maintenance of ſuch a Number of Men, as the General ſhall think proper for any Enterprize.

18. *Monday.* Nothing particular to obſerve; but it was too evident in general not to obſerve that there was yet but a poor Appearance

pearance of planting likely to be this Spring, from the Inhabitants of *Savannah:* I mean from ſuch, as have no other Dependence but their own Labour; whereof I purpoſe to make ſome neceſſary Remarks occaſionally, as the Year advances; that ſo the full Truth and Cauſes being laid open, the Conſequences will naturally follow, which either promote or retard the Progreſs of this Colony in Agriculture: Such as are going on with it, have divers of them applied to me for Mulberries; which by the General's Order I got what Quantity of we poſſibly could; and I take Care to deliver out ſuch a Number of Plants, whether twenty, thirty, forty, fifty, or to an hundred, for their Uſe, in ſuch Proportion as I know they have laboured in clearing their Land. One Thing here I cannot but take Notice of with ſome Pleaſure, which is, that I find an uncommon Tendency lately ſprung up among our People of all Ranks, towards planting Vines; wherein they ſhew an Emulation, if they get but a few, of out-doing one another; and I would be glad to encourage them in that, or any Thing commendable; more eſpecially where cultivating Land has its Share, whatever be the Product: And I tell them, that againſt another Seaſon, I make no Doubt but Proviſion will be made, in ſuch a Manner, to get the choiceſt of Vine-

1739. February 18.

1739. February Cuttings for their Encouragement; that with their own Diligence added to it, they may reaſonably hope in a ſhort Time to be each of them Maſter of a Vineyard: To promote this, nothing ſeems to be wanting but Store of Cuttings, from Vines beſt eſteemed; which may be procured, I hope, againſt another Seaſon: In the mean while, I expect this Year to ſee a very conſiderable Increaſe of this Plant, and the Fruit of it ſhewing ſome Tokens of a large Recompence to the Planter in due Time.

19. *Shrove-Tueſday.* After diſpatching what I thought needful at home the firſt Part of the Day; in the Afternoon I applied myſelf to the Magiſtrates, for their Aſſiſtance in promoting the Guard Duty, wherein great Neglect had been from ſundry Perſons, as appeared by ſeveral Reports made to me, from divers of the Tything-men, on coming off their Guard; which Reports I ſtrictly required always: And upon our preſent Enquiry, finding there was juſt Cauſe of Complaint, we fixed upon a few of the moſt culpable, to make Examples of, by the Magiſtrates iſſuing their Warrant, to levy by Diſtreſs two Shillings for every ſuch Neglect committed by each of them; hoping it would be a Means of Reformation, when they found that paying the Penalty of two Shillings, was double to what it would coſt any of them, who

choſe

choſe rather to hire a Man in their Stead, than perſonally to perform it themſelves, that Duty coming about once in eighteen Nights: And the Magiſtrates, at my Requeſt, iſſued ſuch Warrant accordingly. 1739. February

Wedneſday. Mr. *Patrick Houſton* coming to Town from his Plantation near *Vernon* River, whom I looked on as a good Neighbour there, and who had made good Improvements, by cultivating a conſiderable Tract of Land, *&c.* called on me this Morning; and knowing he had been lately at *Frederica*, we naturally fell into ſome Talk about what was doing there, and how great Things the General had in view: Among other Matters, telling him, that I had heard from ſeveral, there was a Box directed to me from the honourable Truſtees, wherein were ſaid to be many Papers, which I had no Advice of by any Letter; that the Box came by the Ship St. *George*, which arrived at St. *Simon*'s ever ſince the Beginning of *January*, and was now gone again; but that I had never heard what came of that Box (if any ſuch was come) nor any Letter relating to it: He readily told me, that there was ſuch a Box directed to me, which he ſaw lying in the Stores at *Frederica*; that what was in it he knew not; but it was generally ſaid to be full of Papers, and it was believed, of ſome Value; for that the 20.

Maſter

1739. February Maſter of the Ship ſaid he had given his Receipt for it in *London*, and therefore he muſt have a Receipt for it again, upon his delivering it; which Receipt he underſtood Mr. *Hawkins* had given him, and taken the Box out of the Ship. Upon hearing this ſo particularly, it was indeed a Matter of Admiration to me, what could be the Meaning of ſuch dark Work; and I began to think what a notable Correſpondent I was likely to find in him whom the Truſt had appointed: Many Things occurred to my Thoughts on this Occaſion.——But no more of that now.

21. *Thurſday*. A Letter came to the Magiſtrates from Mr. *Chriſtie*, now at *Thunderbolt*, acquainting them, that he was not well, and therefore could not attend the Court that was adjourned to to-morrow. It was generally talked of, and believed, that he and Mr. *Hetherington* were preparing both to go for *England*; and as his Houſekeeper and he yet ſtuck cloſe together, it was imagined, that he purpoſed to take her alſo with him, notwithſtanding what was given out of his Intention to part with her; that Fright being pretty well over. Spent as much of the Day as I could with Mr. *Jones*, in getting forward what we could, to go by Capt. *Thompſon*.

Friday.

Friday. The Court was opened, and adjourned farther to the 10th of *March.* This Evening the Company returning home, that had been on their Pleaſure up the River, this very cold Weather, at Mr. *Matthews*'s for two or three Days and Nights paſt; I cannot well let it paſs unobſerved, having the Appearance in it to many People, of ſomething pretty particular. The Invitation was from *Matthews*, not many Days after the Inſult he had made on Mr. *Jones*; and the Company was of a very odd Mixture: Firſt, Dr. *Tailfer* and his Lady; next, Mr. *Carteret* and his, together with Capt. *Heron*'s Lady and her Daughter (the Captain not being yet returned from *Charles-Town)* then Mr. *Upton* and his; Capt. *Thompſon*, and Mr. *Norris*, making alſo Part of the Company ſome of the Time. I could not learn from any of them, that they dealt much in Politicks; the very oppoſite Way of thinking (ſo well known among divers of them) forbidding it; but what People thought remarkable was, that it looked like a Piece of Daring in *Matthews*, to ſhow the World he had no Concern upon him, for that violent Outrage he had been ſo lately guilty of; for which Mr. *Jones* (if he had thought fit) might have ſent an Officer, and ſpoiled their Entertainment, by taking mine Hoſt into Cuſtody, *&c.* but he rather

1739. February 22.

 choſe

1739. February 22. choſe to ſend a Narrative of it to the General, and leave it to him in what Manner to reſent it. The Truth is, *Matthews*'s Wife has always been in great Eſteem with the General, and not without good Reaſon; for being half *Indian* by Extract, ſhe has a very great Influence upon many of them, particularly the *Creek* Nation, our next Neighbours; ſo that there always has been a frequent Reſort of thoſe People to her Houſe; and the General would adviſe with her in many Things, for his better dealing with the *Indians*; taking her generally for his Interpreter, and uſing her very kindly on all Occaſions. A few Years ſince, after her late Huſband *Muſgrave*'s Death, ſhe thought fit to marry this Man, a hail, luſty, young Fellow, an *Engliſhman*, and her Servant: Such a Promotion from Obeying to Commanding, had the uſual Effect, which ſeldom fails; and he ſoon grew vain, dreſſing gaily (which ill became him) and began to behave inſolently among all he kept Company with, looking on himſelf at leaſt equal to the beſt Man in the Colony, from the Subſtance he was poſſeſſed of with his Wife: And Mr. *Williams*'s Plantation lying contiguous to his on this River, by Degrees there grew an Intimacy betwixt them, as Neighbours; and in Proceſs of Time, when Mr. *Williams*, unhappily with others in in Conjunction, began to ſow Diſcord, and draw as many as they could, of the People in Town, into a Diſlike of their Tenure, with many other ſuppoſed Grievances which they wanted the Power to rectify to their Humour; *Matthews* made one among them: And at that Time our Malecontents ſo blowed up their new Favourite among them, that he was taught to believe he ought to be diſtinguiſhed, and gratified in whatever he aſked; and that he ſhould look upon himſelf, as a Man capable of doing great Service to the Colony, or reſenting it ſeverely, in Caſe he found himſelf ſlighted, having ſuch a powerful Body of Men to ſtand by him: But whatever Credit he gave to that, he has ſeveral Times experienced that he was ſadly miſtaken; for when in his drunken Frolicks, he has ſometimes attempted any Sort of Authority or Command, over ſuch as came occaſionally that Way from the Nation, he ſeldom has failed of a good Thraſhing from them, to convince him of his Error: For though they ſhew ſome Regard to *Mary* (as they call his Wife) they ſhew none to him: And yet it is ſuppoſed, the good Company he came from drunk the other Day, when he did that Exploit, had filled his Head again with ſome of their former Doctrine, that he was not to be in Awe of any Man he had to do with.

1739. February 22.

1739. February

From hence ſome Eſtimate may be made of what may be at any Time neceſſary to obſerve, of the future Behaviour of Mr. *Matthews*.

23. *Saturday*. Being ſomewhat cloyed with the cloſe Application, I tied myſelf down to, of Buſineſs with my Pen and Ink, the Week paſt; I gave a Looſe to my Inclination this Day, and paſſed away good Part of it very agreeably, at my little five-Acre Lot, in planting more Vines, Mulberries, *&c.* and walking among ſome of the adjacent Lots, to ſee what Preparation was made by any towards planting Corn, or the like: A few ſuch I found, but wiſhed it had been many more; it being high Time now to get ready for that Work; and it would be ſoon ſeen who intended it, and who not.

24. *Sunday*. Mr. *Whitfield* not being yet returned from the South, Mr. *Norris* continued to do the Office of the Day; and preached ſuch orthodox Divinity to his Hearers, as they might well underſtand, and ought to put in Practice.

25. *Monday*. Followed what I had to do, and loſt no Time at home, where I ſpent moſt of the Day, and found nothing ſo remarkable in it, as the exceeding ſudden Change of Seaſons; the Weather for a pretty while paſt, being moſtly froſty, ſince thoſe heavy Rains, and extream cold, thro'

a

a ſtrong North-Weſt Wind, which continued preciſely till this Morning, the very laſt Night being as ſevere as any paſt: And after the Sun aroſe, the Wind getting round to the Southward, the Weather became immediately as warm as we ordinarily find it in *England* at *Midſummer*: From whence I reckon Winter is now quite over; and it is to be wiſhed, that the Summer Heats may not come on ſo faſt upon us, as to cut our Spring ſhort. 1739. February

Tueſday. Capt. *Æneas McIntoſh*, who went hence the 14th to wait on the General, returned this Day, and brought Letters from his Excellence at *Frederica*, importing various Directions to Mr. *Jones* and me, ſo ſuited to each as he ſaw proper. I was very ſorry to hear what the Captain, and the Maſter of the Boat which brought him, reported had lately happened in the South, *viz.* that Lieutenant *Dunbar*, being ſent out with a Party of Men, in a well-armed Pettyagua, and a Scout-Boat to attend him, in order to reconnoitre the Coaſt, and ſeveral Creeks which fall into the *Alatamaha*; they came to Anchor, where the commanding Officer ſaw good; and the Scout-Boat, with ſome Soldiers in her, was ſent off, to make what Diſcoveries they could, of the Banks of the River, and to know how far it was to any convenient Place of Landing: But at the ſame 26.

1739. February 26. Time ſtrict Orders were given, that at their Peril they ſhould not offer to go aſhore, or come any where within Muſket-Shot of it: Nevertheleſs theſe poor infatuated People ſeeing great Plenty of Oranges in the Woods, growing naturally, and full of Fruit; they went aſhore to gather ſome, but very ſoon found the Conſequence: For eſpying ſome *Spaniards* and *Indians* coming towards them, they retreated to their Boat, and were put off; when the Enemy fired upon them, and killed two Men; one of whom was a Soldier ſhot in the Breaſt, and the other was the Maſter of the Boat (appointed by the General) who was ſhot into the Hind-part of his Head: Which ſhews the Situation they were in, the firſt at the Oar, the other at the Helm; whoſe Loſs is particularly lamented by his poor Wife, and two ſmall Children that live here; where the Man was a Freeholder, and his Name *Francis Brooks*, formerly a menial Servant of the General's. It was farther reported by the ſaid Perſons, that they met with a *Spaniſh* Launch, that had nobody in her; which they took, and might have been ſufficient to ſhew them, there were ſome that belonged to her not far off. The General was not pleaſed to mention it in his Letter to me; but told me, he ſhould write me farther by Mr. *Whitfield*, who was upon his Return hither; and who I found,

found, by what he wrote me, he thought had gone beyond what the Truſt intended, in taking ſome Orphans into his Keeping, who were well grown, and might have been of good Service this planting Time, to the Maſters they lived with. I cannot paſs over this Circumſtance of the Oranges, without a little Obſervation, having frequently heard the ſame related, of their growing common in the Woods: It is agreed by all, that no Beaſt will feed on them, or crop them; neither will the Dropping of any Trees annoy them, except the Pine, which will ſuffer no Tree to grow by him: Wherefore I purpoſe to make an Experiment this Seaſon of putting ſome Hundreds of good Orange-Seeds into the Ground, two or three in a Hole, in ſuch Places as I judge proper, in my new Plantation by *Vernon* River; which differs not a great deal in Latitude from the *Alatamaha:* And whereas the ill Succeſs we have hitherto had with Oranges in this Part, is ſaid to proceed from being too remote from the Salt; as well for the Influence of that Air, as that the Froſt is never ſo ſevere, as here farther up on the Freſhes; the Situation of my Land is open to the Sea: And from all this put together, I am not without Hopes that Oranges, by ſome lucky Incident or other, may in Time be the Product of *Georgia*; though this ſevere

1739. February 26.

1739. February 27. Winter has left very few young ones alive, either in the publick Garden, or in any private about us, in Spite of all our Care.

Wedneſday. Capt. *M^c^Intoſh* made the beſt of his Way this Morning for *Palachocolas*, in order to ſurrender the Command of that Fort to his Brother, whom the General had given a Commiſſion to ſucceed him: Before his going hence, we learnt another Piece of News, that he brought with him from the South, far more agreeable than the other Account which he gave, of that unhappy Diſaſter, *viz.* that a Party of the Enemy lately, having a Packet of Letters in their Charge, from St. *Mark*'s, and not knowing that the Fort of St. *Francis de Pupa* was taken by us, went directly thither; where they found themſelves Priſoners: And it is ſaid, the Letters they had with them, were of the greateſt Conſequence; diſcovering a Deſign of a great Body of *French*, and *Spaniards*, to join ſomewhere near that Place, and march about the Middle of *April* towards the *Savannah*; which they were to croſs, either at *Auguſta*, or *Palachocolas*, and ſo come upon the Back of both theſe Provinces. We could learn no farther Particulars, nor make any certain Judgment what Credit was to be given to this Report: But it certainly behoved us to be on our Guard; and we did not doubt, if if the General got ſuch Intelligence, we ſhould be adviſed of it from him, and receive his Orders thereon. A ſudden Report went about Town this Evening (whence it aroſe I know not) that he would be here in two or three Days. 1739. February

Thurſday. My preſent Thoughts being pretty full of Contrivances, how to improve that little domeſtick five-Acre Lot, which lay ſo near under my Eye (while that of much more Importance was far remote, where my chief Strength was employed) I went thither early in the Morning, and after entertaining myſelf there ſome Hours, when the Heat of the Day came on, I returned home to my ordinary Employment, where I had little to obſerve at preſent. Mr. *Whitfield*, with his Friend *Seward*, came to Town in the Afternoon, not having it in their Power to accompliſh their Intention ſooner, ſince they went South on *Monday* the 11th Inſtant: By them I received a Letter from the General of the 18th Inſtant, ſignifying, that he had given 150 *l.* by his Bill on Mr. *Verelſt*, as Money advanced towards building the Church; and recommending it to me to aſſiſt in forwarding that Work; having at the ſame Time Regard to the Seaſon of the Year, in not diſcouraging planting, by hiring labouring Hands, *&c.* and in his Letter to me *per* Capt. *Mc Intoſh*, which I received 28.

1739. February received on *Tueſday* laſt, he was pleaſed to tell me his Opinion freely in relation to the Orphans, by ſending me a Paper incloſed, which was a Duplicate of what he had ſent Mr. *Jones*; at the ſame Time adviſing me to acquaint the Truſtees with what is done relating to the Orphans, the Orphan-Houſe, and the Church: Which I have noted moſt commonly in the foregoing Pages, particularly on the 4th and 8th of this Month; and ſundry other Places, ſince the Time of Mr. *Whitfield*'s Arrival on the 11th of *January*; and ſhall for the future be obſervant not to fail therein.

29. *Friday*. A Negro Slave that belonged to the late Mr. *Dyſon*, whom he kept in a clandeſtine Manner to and fro betwixt the two Provinces, being laid hold on by the Magiſtrates, after his Maſter's Deceaſe here, and kept in Cuſtody; the General ſent Orders to Mr. *Jones* to ſell him; wherein conſulting me, I was of Opinion it ſhould be at a publick Sale by Auction: In Purſuance of which, publick Advertiſements being fixed up Yeſterday, that the Sale would be this Morning; it was ſo; and among ſeveral Bidders, Captain *Thompſon* advancing higheſt, he bought him for 23*l.* 5*s.* Sterling. The reſt of the Day produced nothing extraordinary.

Saturday.

Saturday. I could not learn any Thing this Day fit to take Notice of here. Capt. *Thompſon* began to think of falling down the River, Part of the Way to *Tybee*, for more Depth of Water, doubting, as he was far advanced now in his Loading, leſt he might be taken up by ſome Shoal; and being paſt ſuch, he would take in the reſt of his Loading there. Wherefore I was now, together with Mr. *Jones*, to get ready with all Diligence, what Papers we meant to ſend by him. 1739. March 1.

Sunday. Mr. *Whitfield* went on without ſlackening his Rate of four Times a Day, weekly, in praying, preaching, expounding, and adminiſtring the Sacrament: Wherein he took great Pains, exhorting his Hearers to a ſtedfaſt, ſaving Faith; the ſame as when he preached here laſt, on the 10th of *February*, and before: Wherein I wiſhed he had ſpared his Invectives againſt the Clergy. 2.

Monday. Divers of our Pieces of Artillery lying uſeleſs, either without Carriages, or ſuch as were unfit for Service; I had for ſome Time paſt given Directions, to remount as many as needed it on Ship-Carriages (or Trucks) which would be far leſs expenſive than Field-Carriages, and as proper for the Uſe intended them here, as the other: Which being now prepared, I ranged them in decent Order under a Shed, 3.

1739. March from whence on any Occaſion they might with Eaſe be immediately run out, and in the mean while the Carriages be preſerved from the Weather. One of the ſmarteſt Pieces on a Truck-Carriage, I choſe out to place commodiouſly on the new Wharf under the Bluff; where it might be brought ſo to bear, as to command the River upwards and downwards, whenever there was preſent Cauſe for it; and all the reſt were under the conſtant Care of the Guard, at their uſual Place of Duty; which indeed was now ſo open and expoſed, that I hoped the General would grant Leave, when I ſaw him again, to let it be incloſed with a ſlight Paliſade at leaſt, at very little Coſt; which would keep idle People among ourſelves from committing any Annoyance, and playing Tricks, as ſometimes they were too apt to practiſe: And all Strangers coming and going would ſee that we were diſpoſed to be in earneſt.

4. *Tueſday.* Mr. *Minis* going South this Morning, in order to diſpoſe of the Proviſions which arrived lately in a Sloop there, Capt. *Tingly* from *New-York*; which Goods were conſigned to *Minis*; I wrote Letters by him to the General, in Anſwer to thoſe I received by Capt. *M^c^Intoſh* and Mr. *Whitfield.* A Boat arrived from *Frederica*, wherein were two Cadets (Meſſieurs *Wemys* and *Goldſmith)* ſent by the General for

for *Charles-Town*, whither they were haſtening without Delay; by whom we learnt, that the General was coming quickly after, and bound to the ſame Place; which we judged was in order to confer with the Government of that Province, concerning the future Attempts intended againſt the Enemy, now the Council and Aſſembly had voted ſuch an Aid. Another Boat came in from the South this Morning, which was alſo bound for *Charles-Town*, on Traffick; in which was one Mr. *Ramſay*, who brought me a ſmall Packet from Mr. *Hawkins*, in Return to what I wrote him of the 13th *ult.* and incloſing ſeveral Liſts, which by the Truſtees Order I had called on him for: But as to the Box ſent me from the Truſtees by the Ship St. *George*, which arrived the Beginning of *January* at St. *Simon*'s, and which Box I had ſo particular an Account of very lately by Mr. *Patrick Houſton (vide Feb.* 20.) and I had wrote to Mr. *Hawkins*, to be careful in ſending it to me *per* firſt Opportunity: The Anſwer I now received from him was this, in a Poſtſcript. " I have incloſed one of the Pa-
" pers from the Truſtees, not being cer-
" tain whether the Box is come to your
" Hands: About forwarding the ſame I
" have ſpared no Pains." This carries with it ſuch a Show of ———, that I know not what to make of it, or what to call it:

1739. March 4.

1739. March it: By his ſaying that he had ſent me one of the Papers, I ſuppoſe I am to underſtand, that the Box contained them and nothing elſe: If ſo, why are they not ſent me? or how can I believe him at ſuch an Uncertainty, whether the Box is come to my Hands or not, after what I have heard from Mr. *Houſton*? Theſe are Myſteries too deep for me to fathom.

5. *Wedneſday.* Capt. *Thompſon* looſed his Ship from the Wharf, got up her Anchor, and attempted to fall down the River, in order to take in the reſt of his Loading below: But through the Negligence of the Pilot (as it is ſaid) the Ship ran aground on the Edge of a Marſh near the Town, tho' there was Water more than ſufficient in the right Courſe, and the Wind very fair, an eaſy Breeze at Weſt: What makes it the worſe is, that it happened to be juſt at high Water, and the Top of the Spring Tide; ſo that when the Water ebbed, the Ship laid faſt on the Mud, and there remained but little Expectation of her floating again till next Spring Tide. It muſt not, however, be inferred from hence, that the Navigation of this River is attended with uncommon Difficulties, Ships that draw as much or more Water than this, having frequently paſſed up and down, without any Obſtruction, as I well know; and the Entrance in at *Tybee* over the Bar is allowed

to

to exceed all on this Coaſt, many Leagues Northward and Southward; beſides the great Advantage of ſo fine a Land-Mark there, which it is to be hoped will ſhortly be well repaired and ſtrengthned, before it is too late to mend it. Mr. *Patrick Graham*, Surgeon, who has made very conſiderable Improvements in building on his Lot in this Town, as well as been a conſtant Planter for two or three Years paſt, having Mrs. *Cuthbert* (Siſter to the late Capt. *Cuthbert*, deceaſed) for his Patient, dangerouſly ill in a Fever, at that Time a Lodger in his Houſe; the Doctor took the Opportunity of preſcribing Matrimony to her, as a Specifick which he was ſure would compleat her Cure; and on conſenting to take his Advice in it, they were married at her late Brother's Plantation: Mr. *Jones* and I (only) were preſſingly invited to the Wedding; which we complied with; though we could hardly perſuade ourſelves to be ſo long idling; and we rowed up to *Joſeph-Town* this Forenoon, timely enough to take Part of a good Dinner with them; but the Ceremony of the Wedding was over, the Marriage performed Yeſterday by Mr. *Norris*, and conſummated the ſame Evening: So after two or three Hours ſpent, we returned to the Place whence we came. 1739. March

Thurſday. Meeting Mr. *Fallowfield* this Forenoon, he ſhewed me a Letter he had received 6.

1739. March received from Mr. *Williamſon* at *Charles-Town*, and pointed out a Paragraph for me to read (by Direction I ſuppoſe from the Writer) full of Scurrility and Abuſe; aſking how I dared with-hold Mr. *Chriſtie*'s and his Conſtitutions, which were ſent them by the Truſtees? That I ought to know my Duty to my Maſters better, and ſhould be taught to know the Superiority of the Magiſtrates, under whom I was to act only as Secretary and Letter-Carrier to the Truſt; with Abundance more ſuch polite Strokes of his Wit: Which I only ſmiled at, and told his Crony who imparted it to me, that I hoped I needed not him for an Inſtructor in my Duty; that the State of that Affair was, by Order from the General, laid before thoſe whom I thought it an Honour to ſerve as my Maſters, which I ſhould endeavour to do with Fidelity; nor would I be terrified from ſo doing: And that as ſoon as I knew their Pleaſure, I ſhould moſt undoubtedly obey it; which Mr. *Fallowfield* made no Reply to; and ſo we parted, at the Stores; where, with Mr. *Jones*, I ſpent great Part of the Day, in perfecting thoſe Accompts which were intended to be ſent by Capt. *Thompſon*.

Friday. The common Talk of the Town Yeſterday, being of what paſſed between our two Miniſters on *Wedneſday*, whilſt Mr. *Jones* and I were at the Wedding-

Wedding-Houſe abroad; Mr. *Norris* thought proper to give me a verbal Relation this Day of the principal Parts of their Conference; which being *ex parte* only, I muſt not take upon me to judge betwixt them: But as he deſired me to take in Writing what he related, and his Credit ſhould ſtand at Stake for the Veracity and Impartiality of what he deſired might be noted; I would not refuſe him, nor would I to do the ſame on the other Side, in Caſe it ſhould be aſked of me at any Time; which I had the leſs Reaſon to expect, becauſe Care was taken when they met, that two Witneſſes, namely, Mr. *Haberſham* and Mr. *Brownfield*, were to be preſent, that they might teſtify what they heard; whilſt Mr. *Norris* was not ſo guarded, who told me as follows.—" That on *Wedneſday* laſt, under-" ſtanding Mr. *Whitfield* had a Deſire to " ſee him, he went to wait on him; when " he was received with common Civility, " and a Cup of Tea, *&c.* That he had " been there but a very little while, ere " the two Perſons above-named came in " as Witneſſes of what was ſaid; when " (all farther Ceremony laid aſide) he was " flatly charged with having preached falſe " Doctrine here, during the Time of Mr. " *Whitfield*'s being abſent in the South: " Wherein Mr. *Norris* finding himſelf ſo " ſtruck at, confeſſed he was pretty much

1739. March 7.

1739. March 7. " ſtartled, and aſked what Teſtimony " there was of it? To which he was an- " ſwered, the two Perſons before-men- " tioned were Witneſſes of it, as alſo the " following named, *viz.* *Gladman* (Maſter " of Mr. *Whitfield*'s Sloop) *Hunter* (an A- " pothecary that came with Mr. *Whitfield)* " the Widow *Vanderplank*, and laſtly Mr. " *Jones*, who lodges at her Houſe. Mr. " *Norris* then required, that they ſhould " give him ſome Particulars in Writing, of " what they alledged; but they ſaid they " ſhould not do that; nevertheleſs they in- " ſiſted upon it, that his Foundations in " general were falſe: Then Mr. *Whitfield* " preſſed him to produce his Notes; but " he ſaid he did not think it proper to do " that, which might give them an Advan- " tage over him, as they were maliciouſly " diſpoſed to wreſt every Thing he had " ſpoken, to a wrong Meaning; but upon " their pointing out what they had ta- " ken ſuch Offence at, he would ſtand or " fall by what appeared in the Sermons he " had preached: Then he told them, that " he had preached here eighteen Months " among them, and never was ſuſpected of " falſe Doctrine till now; that he would " appeal to the moſt competent Judges in " this Town, or Neighbourhood, touching " the Orthodoxy of his Sermons; but ex- " cepted particularly againſt Mr. *Jones*,

" who

"who was bred a Diſſenter, and had ever "ſince his being here, ſhewn an utter An- "tipathy to him; and more particularly "when he preached that Sermon on *Matt.* "vi. 23. (which is what he ſuppoſes they "are ſo angry at) as ſoon as he had named "his Text; Mr. *Whitfield* ſaid, Mr. *Jones* "had told him himſelf, that he took a "Book, and read, during the whole Ser- "mon; which muſt incapacitate him to "obſerve the Connexion of his Diſcourſe, "and render him an incompetent Judge: "And from that Time Mr. *Jones* never "came near the Church whilſt he ſupplied "it. Mr. *Norris* farther alledged, that "he had received double Orders from the "Biſhop of *London*; and upon a ſtrict "Examination before his Lordſhip and his "Arch-Deacon, had given a full and ſa- "tisfactory Account of his Faith: To "which Mr. *Whitfield* replied, that he be- "lieved ſo; but that he took the Biſhop "of *London* to be no better a Judge, or "knew more of Chriſtianity, than *Mabo-* "*met*, or an Infidel; and that he was "now proving him to be ſuch, having "wrote two Letters, which he had ſent to "*Charles-Town* to be printed: Then Mr. "*Norris* aſked him, whether or not he "had read that Biſhop's Œconomy of our "Redemption? Which he ſaid he had; "but that he was quite wrong, and that

1739. March 7.

1739. March "that Book was ſufficient to ſend Thou-
"ſands to Hell; as alſo Archbiſhop *Til-*
"*lotſon*, and the Author of the *Whole Du-*
"*ty of Man:* Mr. *Whitfield* alſo told him,
"that he was at Work for the Devil, and
"capable of doing abundantly more Hurt
"than *Dyſon*, or any ſuch immoral
"Livers: Which Saying of Mr. *Whit-*
"*field*'s, proceeded from Mr. *Norris*'s aſk-
"ing him, what he had to alledge againſt
"him, as to his Way of Life and Con-
"verſation? When all he had to object,
"was that he played on the Fiddle, and
"at Cards with the Ladies, and kept po-
"lite Company; adding this for a Con-
"cluſion, that he (Mr. *Norris)* had aſſiſted
"him twice in adminiſtring the Sacra-
"ment, but that he never ſhould again,
"or receive it at his Hands." I found nothing fit to make any Remark on, of the ordinary Occurrences of the Day; nor ſhall I offer any on this that I have wrote: But I wiſh it may ſtop here, without any farther Diſtraction among us.

8. *Saturday.* Good Luck, and a ſtrong eaſterly Wind, having beyond Expectation lifted up Capt. *Thompſon*'s Ship from where ſhe lay, by the Help of a high Tide, he was now got down lower in the River; ſo that what Mr. *Jones* and I could get ready to ſend by him, would admit of little Delay. It was currently reported about Town, that

that Mr. *Chriſtie*, together with Mr. *Hetherington*, were gone off privately for *Carolina*, in their Way to *England*; but I was not readily inclined to believe it, for he had more than a Year paſt frequently given out ſuch Speeches himſelf, of his Intention ſo to do; all which coming to nothing, few People now gave Credit to any ſuch Talk: And a particular Eſteem which he had for *Hetherington*, with whom he ſpent a Day or two ſometimes at *Thunderbolt*, occaſioned his going thither lately, to give no Umbrage: But about Evening we had certain Advice of it, that they were both gone, and had taken their Bedfellows with them (one his Wife, formerly *Roger Lacey*'s; and the other his famous Houſe-keeper, whom he had for a good while ſtuck cloſe to.) By this Flight I fear *Thunderbolt* is now almoſt deſerted. 1739. March

Sunday. In my Way to Church this Forenoon, Mr. *Andrew Grant* met me, and ſhewed me a Letter he had juſt received from Mr. *Chriſtie*, of Yeſterday's Date, from a Plantation on this Side *Port-Royal*; where he and his Companions ſtopped a little, as they were going for *Charles-Town*: Incloſed he had one from him to deliver to me, wherein were ſome Keys; wherefore I forbore opening it immediately, but deferred it till we came from Church, reſolving with myſelf to have 9.

1739. March 9. ſomebody with me, as a Witneſs of what the Contents of it were; more eſpecially as this Mr. *Grant* was employed by Mr. *Chriſtie*, to be a Witneſs (among others) of what paſſed, when *Chriſtie* made his late Demand on me, to deliver him that Conſtitution, which appointed him firſt Bailiff, *&c.* (*vide Dec.* 22.) and I well knew, that all Steps taken in ſuch Affairs, were the Reſult of that wiſe Council at *Jenkins*'s, whereof this *Grant* was a ſtedfaſt Member. After Church, I took with me Mr. *Jones*, together with Mr. *Grant*, to my Houſe; and opening the Letter (which was very ſhort) I found three Keys, which he wrote me were the Keys of the Office, Records, and the Orphan-Box: I ſaid little about it to Mr. *Grant*, but locked up the Keys, intending to give them to-morrow to the Magiſtrates; when (as it happened) they were to aſſemble, *per* Adjournment of the Court. Capt. *Norbury*, and Lieutenant *Horton*, came to Town both this Morning; the latter from *Charles-Town*, in order to proceed for *England* with *Thompſon*; and the other from his Command at *Port-Royal*, with ſome of his Family, whom he purpoſed to ſend by the ſame Ship. Mr. *Whitfield* preached, and prayed, as hitherto, ſticking fervently to the Doctrine of a New Birth, and Juſtification by Faith, provided it be ſuch, as to produce an Evidence within ourſelves, that the Spirit of God is working in our Hearts; which he inſiſts on, we may feel with a real Senſation; and till that is wrought within us, we are in a State of Damnation. 1739. March

Monday. The Magiſtrates met at the Court-Houſe, *pro formâ*, according to their laſt Adjournment; but not finding any Matters deſigned to come before the Court, to be ſuch, as by being deferred would bring, or occaſion, any Loſs or Damage to any Complainant, they adjourned farther to the next Day, which muſt have been otherwiſe their ordinary Time of ſitting in *April:* But before they did ſo, they looked (at my Requeſt) into the many Defaults that were made by ſeveral, in not obſerving their Guard Duty; divers of whom were fined, to pay double the Money which they might hire a Man for, to have done Duty in their Stead; and it is hoped they will take more Care hereafter. The Wind changing ſuddenly from Eaſt to North-Weſt, with much Lightning, betokened Storms. 10.

Tueſday. We found ourſelves not miſtaken in Yeſterday's Prognoſticks of the Weather; for a furious Wind from the North-Weſt blowed all this Day, and ſo piercing cold, that no Day in the paſt Winter exceeded it, which it was apprehended would 11.

1739. March produce a ſevere Froſt. An old Woman of Mr. *Whitfield*'s Houſhold, who came hither, among others, when he did, dying laſt Night, was buried this Evening, with a ſolemn Funeral; thirty or forty little Boys and Girls walking in Pairs, partly Orphans, and others, whom with their Parents Requeſt or Conſent, he had taken under his Care, ſung Pſalms as they went on to the Church; then followed Mr. *Whitfield*, and after him the Corpſe, half a Dozen diſtinguiſhed, choſen Men holding up the Pall; and a Number of mixed People, to cloſe the Proceſſion, joined them as they came by: Many People were gathered together at the Church, waiting; where after the uſual Prayers, Mr. *Whitfield* gave them a Sermon, *à propos*, on the Words *Watch and pray:* After which, the Corpſe was carried to the common Place of Burial, and there interred in the ordinary Manner. This was all that came to my Knowledge of this Day's Production, which I thought worth Notice, if it can deſerve any.

12. *Wedneſday.* Mr. *Whitfield* intending for ſome Days paſt, to take a Paſſage for *Charles-Town* in his own Sloop, bound that Way, but with-held by contrary Winds, went off in her this Morning very early, the Wind at Weſt, and a cruel Froſt; which it is to be feared may prove pernicious again to the Vines, and all Kinds of tender

tender Plants. *Robert Potter*, late Conſtable, who ſo lightly eſteemed the Promotion the General had given him to that Office, as to go a privateering, and came lately ſick aſhore, died at the Widow *Montaigut*'s Plantation, where he was deſigned by her for an Overſeer of her Negroes; and his Corpſe was brought down from thence, and buried here this Evening. 1739. March

Thurſday. The Rigour of the Weather abated, but continued froſty ſtill. Allowed myſelf little Intermiſſion this whole Day, from attending with Mr. *Jones*, to examine carefully thoſe Accompts which had paſſed our Enquiry, that no Errors might eſcape uncorrected. 13.

Friday. Kept cloſe at home, copying my Journal, *&c.* (heavy Work! but ſuch as I dared not commit to another.) Mr. *Minis* returned home about Noon from *Frederica*; by whom I wrote to the General when he went thither (as noted the 4th Inſtant) but he brought me no Letter, except one from Mr. *Houſton*; who remembring what Converſation we had together when he was here (as noted the 20th *ult.*) was ſo kind to enquire of Mr. *Hawkins* at *Frederica*, why that Box was not ſent me? To which Mr. *Hawkins* replied, it was conſigned to the General, and was in his Cuſtody: So Mr. *Houſton* now wrote me: And the ſame Anſwer, I apprehend, would have 14.

1739. March have been more ingenuous from Mr. *Hawkins* before, than ſuch Trifling as he then uſed (*vide March* 4.) I then ſhould have ceaſed from aſking any farther after it; which poſſibly I may have given Offence in, to his Excellence, by ſuch repeated Enquiry: But I would not incur his Diſpleaſure knowingly; and conceiving it to be my Duty to aſk after any Thing that I hear is directed to me by the honourable Truſtees, and meets with Accidents or Delays by the Way; I ought to hope it will not be imputed to me as a Crime. Wrote my Letter to the Truſt, expecting Capt. *Thompſon* would ſail in a Day or two.

15. *Saturday.* It was Work enough for this Day, to finiſh what we had been preparing to go by Capt. *Thompſon*, who intended to take his Leave to-morrow.

16. *Sunday.* Mr. *Whitfield* not returning yet from *Charles-Town*, Mr. *Haberſham* read the Prayers at Church, and a Sermon after it: Mr. *Norris* determining with himſelf not to meddle any farther here, ſince the Treatment he had lately received; ſome Particulars whereof he had related to me on *Friday* the 7th Inſtant.—Capt. *Thompſon* not yet come.

17. *Monday.* This Morning Mr. *Norris* took his Departure hence; and bringing me the Keys of the Houſe he had lived in, deſired I would not deliver them to any of Mr.

Mr. *Whitfield*'s Followers, but to Mr. *Whitfield* himſelf, when he came home; for that he did not know how far the Malice which they bore towards him, might prompt them to farther Injuries. I took all poſſible Care to avoid interfering with any of their Diſputes on either Side; but kept my own Thoughts to myſelf, not ill pleaſed that he was going; for it was evident, ſo long as he ſhould continue in this Place, there was like to be no Peace among us.—Delivered my Packet now to Capt. *Thompſon*. 1739. March

Tueſday. Having now ſeen every Thing to the beſt of my Power diſpatched, that was to be ſent by this Ship for *England*; I was very glad of a little Reſpite from that Employment, and went in the Morning early, to ſee how Things ſtood at the five-Acre Lot, which I cultivated, at a little Diſtance from the Town: There I ſpent the greateſt Part of the Day moſt agreeably, in ſeeing my planting go forward, and putting various Seeds, with my own Hands, into the Earth, partly experimental, and partly with Expectation of the Uſe of them hereafter in my own Kitchen. At my Return I was informed, that Capt. *Thompſon* went off in the Forenoon; and taking with him ſome of his principal Paſſengers that yet remained here, namely Mr. *Horton*, and ſome Ladies, who had 18.

1739. March had lived at *Frederica*; he purpoſed to ſail as ſoon as he got aboard his Ship at *Cockſpur*. In the Evening Mr. *Norris* came back to Town again, diſappointed in his Paſſage South, by reaſon of the Pettyagua wherein he was going being laden; and meeting with croſs Winds, they were obliged to lie at Anchor, uncertain when to proceed farther.

19. *Wedneſday*. By a Boat which came up the River this Morning, we were informed, that Capt. *Thompſon* was not ſailed, the fair weſterly Wind that we had Yeſterday, ſhifting to the North-Eaſt, ſo he could not get out at *Tybee*, till veered again to ſome more favourable Point: In the Afternoon the Captain came again up to Town, to look after a runaway Sailor, that had left him very injuriouſly, at this Time eſpecially: But little Hopes appearing of his being retaken, he returned to *Tybee* in the Night Tide, very intent upon ſailing the firſt Offer of a Wind.

20. *Thurſday*. Early this Morning, by an Expreſs Meſſenger we were informed, that the General was on his Paſſage from *Frederica* to *Charles-Town*, and would ſtop an Hour or two at *Thunderbolt*, where he would be glad to ſee Mr. *Jones* and me: Accordingly we ſet out immediately on foot, not waiting till Horſes could be got; and found him where he had appointed:

From

From whence, after an Hour or two's Conference, and receiving his Commands in divers Matters, he proceeded; and we returned home about Noon. Capt. *Thompſon*, I underſtood, lay yet windbound at *Tybee*. 1739. March

Friday. Not having had it in my Power for a good while paſt, to ſee how my Affairs went on at my new Plantation by *Vernon* River; I took this Day to myſelf for that Purpoſe, and rode thither: The extream Point of which, Southward from *Savannah*, is near about twelve Miles; where I deſigned the Place of Habitation to be. Here indeed I was much pleaſed, to ſee what Progreſs they had made, ſince I ſaw them laſt; having now built ſeveral good Huts, ſufficient to withſtand any Weather, and for various Uſes; the principal one being made with whole Logs, very ſtrong, and capable of ſome Defence, in Caſe of any ſudden Attack made by vagrant Enemies, whether *Indian* or *Spaniards*; with ſeveral Loop-holes for the Diſcharge of ſmall Arms; and my Servants there, every one provided by me with ſuch; which I found clean, and in good Order; and the Appearance of a ready Diſpoſition in them all to make a good Uſe of thoſe Arms, if Occaſion required: Another Hut made of Clapboards for the Servants to reſt in: Another to keep Stores of all Kinds needful: Beſides proper Receptacles, 21.

for

1739. March 21. for my Poultry, Swine, *&c.* which I ſaw an Increaſe of in each Kind happily begun; and a very reaſonable Cauſe of hoping, that Multiplication may take Place next after Increaſe: Near adjoining they had ſunk a Well, the Sides of which they had ſupported with a ſtrong Timber Frame; and at about ſeventeen or eighteen Foot Depth, they came at excellent Water, not in the leaſt brackiſh, though within the Space of a hundred and fifty Yards of the Salt: There was an Opening made of about ſeven Acres, wherein Abundance of large Trees were fallen, and the Ground in a good Forwardneſs of being cleared; which, together with ſome more that we hoped to add to it, was intended to be planted with Corn, and Potatoes: So that it appeared from the Whole, they had not been idle ſince their being there; for it was after *Chriſtmas* they began Plantation-Work at that Place, where it was intended to ſettle: And herein appeared the Uſe of a good Overſeer, who will both direct, and alſo employ his own Hands in carrying on the Work. I was now called upon, to give the Place a Name; and thereupon naturally revolving in my Thoughts, divers Places in my native Country, to try if I could find any that had a Reſemblance to this; I fancied that *Bewlie*, a Manor of his Grace the Duke of *Montague* in the *New Foreſt*,

Foreſt, was not unlike it much, as to its Situation; and being on the Skirts of that Foreſt, had Plenty of large Timber growing every where near; moreover a fine Arm of the Sea running cloſe by, which parts the *Iſle of Wight* from the main Land, and makes a beautiful Proſpect; from all which, Tradition tells us it took its Name, and was antiently called *Beaulieu*, though now vulgarly *Bewlie*; only by leaving out the *a* in the firſt Syllable, and the *u* in the End of the laſt. After a few Hours ſpent at *Bewlie*, my direct Way home (which I took) was through the five hundred Acre Tract of Land, taken up by Mr. *Whitfield* for the Uſe of the Orphan-Houſe; which Land adjoins to mine, as we return northerly: And here I found the Building of that Houſe carrying on with great Application, and Abundance of Hands; which it is expected will in few Months effect the Deſign: But I conceive it would have turned to as good an Account for the Publick, if a little leſs Haſte had been made in that Work, which takes up ſo many People at this Seaſon, when one would wiſh to have ſeen them as intent upon planting: Some among them probably might have taken a little to it; but I could not promiſe for many, ſuch a Backwardneſs ſtill appears among the ordinary, labouring People, who are apt to let them-

1739. March 21.

ſelves

1739. March ſelves out to Hire, preferring that at all Times when they can, to Cultivation of Land; telling us plainly, that they are ſure of Pay for their Pains, when they work that Way; but if they truſt to planting, their Families may ſtarve. The Day ſo ſpent, I returned home in the Evening.

22. *Saturday.* Mr. *Whitfield*, and his Companions, returned from *Charles-Town* in his own Sloop; by whom I learnt, that during the few Days he ſtaid there, he had preached nine Times in various non-conforming Meeting-Houſes, and collected good Sums of Money towards the charitable Work of an Orphan-Houſe being promoted; at one Sermon particularly, upwards of 70*l.* Sterling: The *Carolina* printed News-Papers coming with them, I could not but obſerve an Advertiſement in one of them, ſignifying, that Mr. *Whitfield* had publiſhed two Letters there; one of them ſhewing that Archbiſhop *Tillotſon* knew no more of Chriſtianity than *Mahomet*; and the other ſhewing the fundamental Errors of a Book, entitled, *The Whole Duty of Man*; which confirmed my Belief of what I before doubted the Truth of, when it was told me, that he made one of his Boys throw that Book into the Fire, with great Deteſtation. Mr. *Hopton* ſent me by this Opportunity, a few private Letters from my Friends, which came by a Ship lately arrived

arrived from *Cowes*, to his Hands; but none from *London*; whence ſeveral Ships were daily expected. What I found wrote me (as reported) relating to the honourable Truſt, was ſo exceeding ſhocking, that I dare not commit it to Paper, hoping it will prove to have no Foundation, and deſerve not the leaſt Credit: Nevertheleſs, the hearty Zeal which muſt always attend my Actions, in the Station wherein I have the Honour to ſerve them, leaves me under great Impatience till I receive their farther Commands; when I will not doubt but ſuch an Ecclairciſment will appear, that no Room will be left for Jealouſies and Fears. Capt. *Thompſon* ſailed out at *Tybee* this Day for *England*. 1739. March

Sunday. The Church Service was performed by Mr. *Whitfield*, without any Variation from his uſual Method of enforcing the Neceſſity of a New Birth. 23.

Monday. A frightful Story was publiſhed this Morning, of the *French*, and *Indians* in their Alliance, having fallen upon the *Chicaſſaws*, cut off divers of our *Engliſh* Traders among the Nations, particularly *Thomas Andrews*, one of the moſt noted of them; and were going on with a View of farther Miſchief, *&c.* But I had now ſo long experienced the Uſe which I found was made of theſe bugbear Tales, that I was reſolved to trace it as far as I 24.

1740. March could, to its firſt Source; which at length I diſcovered to be from that Mint of Scandal and Lies, which has for ſo long Time paſt created that Uneaſineſs in many People of this Colony; and who made it their Buſineſs ſtill to terrify weak Minds, infuſing ſad Apprehenſions of the Dangers that ſurrounded us, and ſticking at nothing they thought would make the Place odious to the Inhabitants: Inſomuch that it appeared evidently, it was a peculiar Pleaſure to them, whenever they knew any Deſertion of a Family likely to happen; which very probably alſo was by their Advice and Perſuaſion. As for the preſent Story, I could not find any Foundation for it.

25. *Tueſday.* It may be proper here to inſert a Copy of what the General wrote to Mr. *Jones*, as his Sentiments, relating to Mr. *Whitfield*'s Proceedings concerning the Orphan-Houſe: Extract whereof, the General was pleaſed to order, ſhould be given me, that I might make it known to whom it might concern, *viz.*

SIR (Mr. *Jones*)

" As for *Mellidge*'s Brothers, I think " your Repreſentation is very juſt; that " taking them away to the Orphan-Houſe " will break up a Family, which is in a " likely Way of living comfortably: Mr. " *Whitfield*'s Deſign is for the Good of the " People, and the Glory of God; and I " dare

" dare ſay, when he conſiders this, he will 1740.
" be very well ſatisfied with the Boy and March 25.
" Girl's Return to their Brother *John Mel-*
" *lidge*, ſince they can aſſiſt him: Upon
" this Head I am to acquaint you, that
" I have inſpected the Grant relating to the
" Orphan-Houſe; Mr. *Seward* ſaid, that
" the Truſtees had granted the Orphans to
" Mr. *Whitfield*; but I ſhewed him, that it
" could not be in the Senſe he at firſt
" ſeemed to underſtand it: It is moſt cer-
" tain, that the Orphans are human Crea-
" tures, and neither Cattle, nor any other
" Kind of Chattels; therefore cannot be
" granted: But the Truſt have granted the
" Care of the helpleſs Orphans to Mr.
" *Whitfield*, and have given him five hun-
" dred Acres of Land, and a Power of col-
" lecting Charities, as a Conſideration for
" maintaining all the Orphans, who are in
" Neceſſity in this Province; and thereby
" the Truſtees think themſelves diſcharged
" from maintaining of any: But at the
" ſame Time the Truſtees have not given,
" as I ſee, any Power to Mr. *Whitfield* to
" receive the Effects of the Orphans, much
" leſs to take by Force any Orphans who
" can maintain themſelves, or whom any
" other ſubſtantial Perſon will maintain:
" The Truſtees in this, act according to
" the Law of *England*; in Caſe Orphans
" are left deſtitute, they become the Charge

1740. March 25. " of the Pariſh, and the Pariſh may put " them out to be taken Care of; but if " any Perſon will maintain them, ſo that " they are not chargeable to the Pariſh, " then the Pariſh doth not meddle with " them: And ſince taking away the Court " of Wards and Liveries, the Guardian- " ſhip of Orphans is in their next Rela- " tions; or themſelves, at certain Age, can " chuſe their Guardians; and the Chan- " cellor, Judges, Magiſtrates, *&c.* have the " ſame Inſpection over the Effects and " Perſons of the Orphans, as they have " over thoſe of his Majeſty's other Sub- " jects: And the Effects and Perſons of " Orphans are as much under the Protec- " tion of the Laws, as thoſe of any other " of his Majeſty's Subjects."

In Purſuance of his Excellency's Opinion thus ſignified, *John Mellidge* was adviſed to wait on Mr. *Whitfield*, and deſire that he would permit his younger Brother and Siſter to go home to him, that they might be helpful to one another: But upon his ſo doing this Day, he told me, that Mr. *Whitfield* gave him for Anſwer, his Brother and Siſter were at their proper Home already, and he knew no other Home they had to go to; deſiring him to give his Service to the General, and tell him ſo.

Wedneſday.

Wedneſday. I betook myſelf again to Agriculture, and paſſed away a few Hours at the five-Acre Lot very agreeably, in improving it to various Purpoſes, as my Inclination or Fancy led me to conceive, hoping to come at an experimental Knowledge of what would turn to moſt Advantage, and be therefore worth my chiefeſt Care hereafter. Beſide the uſual Sorts of Bread-Kind planted, I thought Cotton deſerved a Place not too ſcanty; at leaſtwiſe I would try, whether it would turn to any Account or not; for the *Weſt-India* Cotton, which is perennial there, dies here every Winter (as I have found) and the annual Plant which will grow in this Country, produces Plenty enough; and the Cotton is at leaſt equal to the other, if not better; but ſo full of Seeds, that it cannot be cleanſed by the ordinary Way of a Gin, nor by any other Means than picking out with Fingers; which is Work only for decrepid, old People, and little Children; for which Purpoſe Mr. *Whitfield* intends (he ſays) to provide a good Stock of it, for Employment of the leaſt of his Flock. Some Hundreds of Mulberries and Vines I had before planted, for two Years paſt, beſides of this Seaſon; to which I added now, upwards of fourſcore of Vine-Cuttings more, which I received the latter End of the laſt Week by a Ship arrived lately at *Charles-Town* 1740. March 26.

1740. March from *Cowes*, all freſh, and ready to put out; ſo promiſing, that I hope few or none of them will fail; and if they are taken from thoſe Vines of my own former planting (as I expect) I have almoſt Vanity enough to promiſe myſelf they will hardly be exceeded by any that are brought into this Colony from foreign Countries: Sir *William Bowyer* of *Bucks*, who was curious in Gardening, eſpecially in Vines, brought ſome choice Cuttings himſelf out of *Italy*, which he was pleaſed to make me a Preſent of a few of; and they proved excellent in two or three Kinds: Wherefore I hope the nearer Approach of the Sun will not make them degenerate here, after more than forty Years flouriſhing in a more Northern Climate.

27. *Thurſday*. The Town was now grown ſo thin of People, that few were to be met with in the Streets, except ſome ſmall Remains of the political Club, who commonly aſſembled in the Evening in the moſt publick Parts, making a tinſel Appearance; which drew more Ridicule than Reſpect from all Men of Senſe; and after a little Heat, they ſeldom failed in adjourning to *Jenkins*'s, there to purſue their uſual Debates, how to improve whatever Miſchief they took in hand. —— Moſt of our labouring Men, and Artificers, were in full Employ at the Orphan-Houſe, ten Miles off;

off; ſo that Planting went on heavily, with a ſmall Number of ſuch as were leſt at home: And from what I yet ſaw, it did not appear to me, that we were to expect more than a Dozen, or thereabout, of the five-Acre Lots in the Neighbourhood of this Town, planted with Care (for ſuch as are planted with more Haſte than good Speed, and not well cultivated at firſt, as well as attended cloſely afterwards, I look upon to be of but very little Value.) Nevertheleſs, I had yet pretty good Hopes, that we ſhould find a while hence ſomething done, among ſome of the larger Tracts of Land, that would be worth obſerving; divers who occupied ſuch (ſome by Virtue of a Grant, and ſome in Expectation of a Leaſe, being permitted to go on) having ſet themſelves to Work in earneſt, with ſuch Help as they can get; which it were to be wiſhed they could find more of. 1740. March

Friday. Little Likelihood appeared of any Alteration in Favour of planting yet awhile (which Yeſterday I took Notice of) the firſt News I heard this Morning, being of an able Man voluntarily loſt; which looking ſomewhat like a Paradox, may need a little Explanation. The Man's Name is *John Sellier*, who holds a Freehold Lot here, by Virtue of his Marriage ſome Years ſince with the Widow *Tibeau*, who has a Son grown a good hard Youth, 28.

1740. March 28. and trained up to Labour by his Father-in-Law *Sellier*. This Lad ſeeing many other Boys, beſides Orphans, accepted into Mr. *Whitfield*'s Houſe, there to be inſtructed and maintained, in Conſideration of their Labour (which ſeveral of them were capable of undertaking a good Share of) whether through his Parents Leave, or any other Perſuaſion, does not appear; entered into that Houſe; where, after about a Month's Continuance, finding there was no Intermiſſion, but every Hour of his Life was fully taken up, betwixt Things temporal and divine; grew weary, and returned home to his Parents, liking it better to work for them, or any other Maſter where he got a Penny: But his Father-in-Law *Sellier* has ſhewn a different Way of thinking, and is grown lately ſo ſignal a Convert, through the Power of the Word as delivered by Mr. *Whitfield*, that he has bid adieu to all worldly Care; and reſolving from henceforth to be content with Food and Raiment for his Labour, has given himſelf up to Mr. *Whitfield*'s entire Diſpoſal for his Service, on the ſaid Condition of being fed and cloathed for Life. This Man has been as regular and orderly in his Behaviour, and Pains-taking in planting conſtantly, as moſt of the Inhabitants, according to his Ability; and what he did plant, was done carefully and well; wherein to to encourage him, the General was pleaſed to make him one of our Tything-men: He is a ſtrong, healthy Man, betwixt forty and fifty Years of Age; has left his Wife, *&c.* regardleſs of this Colony, to make one in building up the *New Jeruſalem:* Young *Tibeau*, who left that Station which his Father-in-Law has now taken, continues with his Mother; and it is to be hoped they will be able to plant their five-Acre Lot without him. Methinks, it is great Pity this Place ſhould be bereft of the Labour of ſuch Youth, who are of Age and Strength ſufficient to maintain themſelves.——But I muſt not run beyond the Length of my Tedder. 1740. March

Saturday. Mr. *Norris* who returned, baulked in his intended Paſſage (as noted on the 18th Inſtant) and waited ever ſince for the Opportunity of another Boat going, went off this Morning for *Frederica.* The ſame Day (after he was gone) it was commonly talked, that Mr. *Whitfield* would be going in few Days on another Progreſs among the Northern Plantations, in *Penſylvania*, *New-York*, &c. Capt. *Davis*, after ſo long labouring in vain, to fit out his Privateers, for want of Men and other Requiſites on that Occaſion, now began to turn his Thoughts other ways; and it was given out, that with the few Hands he had, he would go a trading Voyage to 29.

St.

1740. St. *Kitt's*, or ſome of the *Weſt-Indian* Iſlands.

March 30. *Sunday*. Mr. *Whitfield*, this Day, declared his Intention of leaving us for a while, preaching a farewel Sermon, in the ſame Manner as St. *Paul* exhorted the Elders of the Church in *Acts* xx. taking for his Text the 26th and 27th Verſes of that Chapter, and carrying the Parallel betwixt the Apoſtle and himſelf as far as it would go; ſignified, that he expected Perſecution wherefoever he went; therefore knew not, whether ever thoſe among whom he had preached the Goſpel here, ſhould ſee his Face any more, or not: However, as the Work was great which he had in hand, it muſt take up ſome Months, at leaſt, before he could return.

31. *Monday*. Received a Letter this Morning from Lieutenant *Kent* at *Auguſta*, brought by two or three Men newly come thence, who had left *Carolina* lately, complaining how hard a Matter it was for a labouring Man to live there, the Negroes doing all the Work: And Mr. *Kent* recommended them to me, to obtain ſome Land for them at *Auguſta*, from the General, where they had a great Deſire to ſettle (as indeed it was become very deſirable by many others, from the Goodneſs of the Soil.) I told them they came hither in a good Time, for that the General being gone to *Charles-*

Charles-Town, we now expected him back every Day. The reſt of Mr. *Kent*'s Letter was more diſpleaſing, informing me of an unhappy Accident that befel one of their Men lately at the Fort; who upon firing one of their little Pieces of Cannon, and the Gun burſting, had his Head ſtruck clean off. The remaining Part of what he wrote was, that from what he heard, he was doubtful leſt the *Cherokee* Nation ſhould fall off, and not perform what the General expected from them, in ſending him an Aid of ſeveral hundred Men, to march with him againſt the *Spaniards*. 1740. March 31.

Tueſday. Mr. *Mc Leod*, Miniſter at *Darien*, coming lately to Town in a Viſit to Mr. *Whitfield*, and to ſee this Part of the Country, which he was a Stranger to; there was a notable Ride out this Day, to the Orphan-Houſe, by a pretty many, who were deſirous to attend on that Occaſion, and ſhew their particular Regard to their Teachers. After ſuch Orders given there by Mr. *Whitfield*, as he thought proper, for carrying on the Work (which was in great Forwardneſs by ſuch a Number of Artificers and Labourers conſtantly employed) they returned to Town again in the Afternoon; where nothing was to be heard of worth Notice till Evening; when Mr. *Whitfield* (after expounding on the Leſſon for the Day out of the *New Teſtament*, April 1.

1740. April *ment*, as his uſual Manner was) took Occaſion to reproach his Audience with their Hardneſs of Heart, and little Marks which they ſhewed in Improvement of Grace; inſomuch that they came behind all, to whom he had preached the Word elſewhere; for he ſeldom failed of Numbers in thoſe Places, who followed him with Weeping, deſirous to know how they muſt be ſaved; but he found very few ſuch here; Thoſe few that had found themſelves prickt to the Heart, and began to be enlightened by the Holy Spirit, he charged to take Care of Backſliding; telling them they muſt expect many Trials and Temptations; to be ſcoffed at and derided, and probably perſecuted too; wherefore they muſt not forget to aſſemble and meet together, ſtrengthning and comforting one another: And for the reſt, he told us, he had often thought this Colony would never be ſuffered by Providence to proſper, till God had planted it with Seed of his own.——The Conſtruction of which I muſt humbly ſubmit to my Betters.

Wedneſday. About Eight this Morning Mr. *Whitfield* went on board his Sloop, accompanied with Mr. *Seward*, and taking with them Mr. *Haberſham*, formerly School-Maſter here, hitherto deputed by Mr. *Whitfield* to officiate in his Abſence; but now ſeemed choſen out for other Purpoſes elſewhere:

where: The Wind being fair, they ſailed immediately; and the Place they were ſaid to be bound to, was ſome Part of *Penſylvania*, but far ſhort of *Philadelphia*, to which Town they meant to travel by Land, gathering the Brethren together, and preaching the Goſpel in their Way: From *Penſylvania* they were to proceed to *New-York*, and ſo on to *New-England*; if my Information is right: By the ſame Information I learnt, that Mr. *Whitfield* had farther Views in taking up a Tract of Land in ſome one of the Provinces, and erecting a School or Nurſery for the Inſtruction of young Negro Children, in the Chriſtian Religion; which Works of ſo extenſive Piety, are moſt undoubtedly to be highly eſteemed: At the ſame Time it is to be wiſhed, that whilſt he is gone far off to make Proſelytes, he may retain a few charitable Thoughts at leaſt towards this poor Place, and not look upon all the Inhabitants, as Caſtaways not worth regarding; except the little Children which he has taken to himſelf, and about half a Score full-grown Perſons, Men and Women (ſome of which came with him, and a few others became early Adepts) who are diſtinguiſhed by the Name of True Believers; and ſeparating themſelves from among their Neighbours, they appear with a different Aſpect, and converſe as little as

1740. April 2.

may

1740. April 2. may be with any but one another.——But it would make a Volume to purſue this Theme, which I meddle with unwillingly in theſe ſhort Notes; having no Prejudice, or the leaſt Ill-will to Mr. *Whitfield*; but on the contrary, a Deſire to join with him in all Chriſtian Fellowſhip and Communion; as I have evidently ſhewn, though (I am ſorry to ſay) I have thought myſelf, on divers Occaſions, to be coldly received: Whatever Remarks, therefore, I may have made on this Affair, or may hereafter, it has been, and ſhall be, only the Reſult of what I think a conſcientious Diſcharge of my Duty, without any ſiniſter Views, or particular Reſpect of Perſons. Notice being brought me in the Afternoon, that ſome Perſon (unknown yet) had ſet Fire to a large Tract of old Canes, growing in the Swamp at the Weſt Side of the Town; which was become ſuch a terrible Conflagration, by reaſon of a ſtrong Wind driving it on, that nobody dared to go near it; I ſent immediately, and got what little Strength together I could, to do our Endeavours about it; when indeed we gave over all Pretence to extinguiſh it; but as there was a new Bridge that lay in its Way very much in Danger, which was built about a Year or more ſince, at an exorbitant Expence of the Truſtees; we applied ourſelves, if poſſible,

ſible, to ſave that from periſhing; and by taking timely Care, we ſo managed Matters, as to conduct the Flames clear on each Side, at ſome little Diſtance from it: After which, we had nothing to fear from its raging in thoſe Swamps; neither, if it threatned the upper Lands, was there a ſufficient Pabulum to maintain it. Theſe Fires are a common Practice in all theſe Countries, as well for deſtroying Vermin, as to allow young tender Graſs to grow for the Cattle: But I conceive it would need ſome Regulation. 1740. April

Thurſday. Moſt of my Time taken up this Day, in getting together Proviſions of all Kinds, to be ſent to my People at *Bewlie* by Water; being far round: Wherefore I thought beſt to ſend ſuch a Store as might hold out a few Months, and prevent my being too frequently called upon to ſupply their Wants, and interrupted at ſuch Seaſons when I could ill attend them. 3.

Friday. This being a Day much regarded by the Church of *England*, it was expected that it would have had ſome Notice taken of it, by ſuch as Mr. *Whitfield* had conſtituted to take Care of all divine Affairs here in his Abſence; but I was ſorry to find not the leaſt Regard ſhewn to it at Church, nor any Part of the particular Service appointed by the Rubrick, read; either Pſalms, Leſſons, or Collects. Though 4.

1740. April it is a ſad Truth that this Place has little Piety, to deſerve being looked on as a People zealous in good Works; yet it is to be hoped there may be ſome well-meaning Perſons in it, who find a Comfort in frequenting the Church, and joining in the publick Service, when duly performed; that are equally grieved when they ſee the Liturgy mangled, and giving Way to ——. We know not what next.

5. *Saturday.* Finding little abroad that required my Attention, I made the beſt Uſe of my Time at home, where my Pen and Ink ſeldom ſtood ſtill. In the Evening pretty late, the General arrived from *Charles-Town*, on his Way back to the South; whither he was haſting, and deſigned to make but a ſhort Stay here: There was little Room to have much Talk with him this Night; but we found him well ſatisfied with his Reception in *Carolina*, and the Aid he was aſſured of from thence: So that the Siege of *Auguſtin* was now again talked of, as a Thing certainly deſigned.

6. *Eaſter-Sunday.* Prayers appointed by the Church of *England* were read, Morning and Afternoon, by Mr. *Simms*, deputed by Mr. *Whitfield* to perform that Office in his Abſence, and who likewiſe was charged by him with the principal Care of the Orphans: Mr. *McLeod*, Miniſter at *Darien*; having

having not yet left the Town, was pleaſed to give us two Sermons after Morning and Evening Prayer. *Simms* was one who came from *England* lately in Company with Mr. *Whitfield*; had the Appearance of a modeſt young Man, and one of very few Words, eſpecially with any but of the Brotherhood; but whether he was a Butcher living in *Clare-Market*, or not (as it is currently ſaid here) who left all, by the Impulſe of the Spirit, to follow wereſoever he thought it called him, I can ſay nothing of; but the Truth or Falſity of it, may upon Enquiry be made eaſily appear; as alſo it may, whether one *Peryam*, another Inſtructor of the Orphans, was bred a Lawyer, and found out at a Mad-Houſe, from whence his Liberty was procured, that he might, with the greater Fervency of Devotion, unite among thoſe who are become approved Converts. 1740. April

Monday. The General was ſo thronged with Affairs of various Kinds, which he would allow himſelf but a ſhort Time to diſpatch whilſt here, that it was difficult to have Acceſs to him for Advice, in many needful Caſes, how to conduct myſelf hereafter. He was pleaſed now to deliver me a ſmall Packet, ſent from the Truſt, and dated the 28th of *September* laſt, which came by Capt. *Wright*, who brought with him the Box of Papers at the ſame Time, 7.

1740. April the Beginning of *January* laſt; which Box I have not yet: In this Packet was a Letter from Mr. *Verelſt*, by Order of the Truſt; Invoice of Goods on board that Ship; Notice for Perſons to claim, to be fixed in the Town-Court of *Savannah*, and Copy of the ſame to be publiſhed in the *South-Carolina* Gazettes, *&c.* And the Contents of the Box, not yet received, *viz.* a Deed-Poll relating to forfeited Lots: And alſo two hundred of the printed Reſolutions for the Inhabitants, relating to the Grants and Tenure of Lands, *&c.* Theſe Things could not be otherwiſe than a little ſurprizing at firſt; till I became aſſured in myſelf, that the General would certify it ſo to the Truſt, as to take off all Blame from me.

8. *Tueſday*, } Both theſe Days were en-
9. *Wedneſday*. } tirely taken up in attending the General, and receiving his Inſtructions, how to behave when he left us; which he intended the next Morning early; but a Boat arriving late in the Evening on *Wedneſday*, from *Auguſta*, which brought Letters importing, that Mr. *Eyre* was on his Way from the *Cherokees*, with a hundred choſen Men of that Nation, who were the Forerunners of ſeveral hundred more to follow; that he had moreover about ſeventy of the *Chicaſſaws* with him, and twenty white Men, Volunteers: And alſo being adviſed, that ſeveral Hundred

of the *Upper* and *Lower Creek* Nations were preparing to join him: Withal, that the Report of the *Chicaſſaw* Nation being deſtroyed by the *French*, and one of our principal Traders *(Thomas Andrews)* cut off among them, was a malicious, falſe, and groundleſs Report, ſpread to intimidate and diſcourage the People of this Colony: Such good and ſeaſonable News coming, occaſioned his Excellence to conſider farther, and incline to pauſe a little upon it, before he would ſet out. 1740. April

Thurſday. The Advices of Yeſterday had now ſo far wrought on the General, that he reſolved perſonally to go up the Country, in order to meet thoſe that were on their Way hither, and prevent their coming to this Town; which would create an unneceſſary Expence, and alſo retard them from making ſuch Expedition as he wiſhed: Wherefore he deſigned to alter their Rout, and point out the March they muſt make croſs the Country, over the River *Ogeechy*, to *Darien*, &c. which when he had ordered as he ſaw good, he purpoſed to take this Town in his Way South himſelf; by which Time he expected the Reinforcement from *Carolina* would begin to be on their Way to the Place of general Rendezvous, appointed by him at St. *John's* River. After having diſpatched many Orders and counter Orders, which ſo ſudden 10

1740. April of his Purpoſe, therefore muſt unavoidably produce; he ſet out in the Evening by Water up the River, having before ſent Orders for Horſes to be ready for him to mount, where he thought fit.

11. *Friday.* The General, upon delivering the Packet, as mentioned on *Monday* laſt, underſtanding from me what Orders the Truſt had been pleaſed to ſend, relating to my publiſhing the Notice to be given, that all Grantees of Lands were required to enter their Claims in one of the Town-Courts of *Georgia*, &c. for the more effectual Performance of which Publication, they had alſo directed me to get it printed in the *South-Carolina* Gazette: His Excellence was pleaſed now to tell me, that if the Truſtees had known the Circumſtance of Affairs at preſent here, he was ſure they would have thought farther of it: And directing his Diſcourſe in a particular Sort to me, aſked me if I did not know, that Dr. *Dale* was the Writer of that Gazette? Which I anſwered I did: Then he aſked me, what my Opinion of him was, with Regard to this Colony? To which I made no Scruple in ſaying, that I looked on him as one of the moſt inveterate Oppoſers of any good that might befal it; and that he was generally ſo eſteemed: Then his Excellence replied, how eaſy a Matter would it be for a Man of ſuch a Diſpoſition, that delights

delights in Scribbling and Scandal, to give ſuch a Turn to the true Intent of it, either by Addition or Omiſſion of two or three Words, as to render it ridiculous? And then he would be the firſt Perſon to print ſuch Remarks on it as he thought good. For theſe Reaſons he was pleaſed to ſay, that he thought it adviſable not to print it at *Charles-Town*, but to poſt up divers written Copies of it in the uſual Places of publiſhing any other Affairs in this Town that required it: Upon which, I did ſo this Day; and at the ſame Time (which was his expreſs Command) wherefoever I fixed one of thoſe Notices ſo written, cloſe by the Side of it I placed one of thoſe printed Anſwers, which the honourable Truſtees had long ſince given, to that notable Repreſentation, ſent by this Town and Neighbourhood, of Grievances which they thought they lay under. This was all I remembered fit to take Notice of: The Box, with thoſe other Papers often mentioned, remaining ſtill at *Frederica*, nothing yet can be ſaid farther of that. 1740. April

Saturday. Some Inhabitants of *Frederica*, who had been two or three Days here, on Buſineſs of their own, returned this Morning in the ſame Boat they came; and Mr. *M^c^Leod*, who had ſpent ſome Time among us, took the Opportunity, by the ſame Boat, of returning to his Care 12.

1740. April at *Darien*. In the Evening Mr. *Thomas Holmes*, one of our *Indian* Traders among the *Cherokees*, together with —— *Craig*, a *Carolina* Trader inhabiting at *New-Windſor*, arrived with Letters to the General from Mr. *Eyre*, and alſo to me (doubting where the General was to be found) whereby we were informed, that he was coming down with a certain Number of *Indians*, and twenty white Men (as before noted on the 9th Inſtant) to go on immediate Service under the General; and that they are to be followed by a good Body more: By the ſame Hand I had alſo Letters from Mr. *Wigan*, ſignifying the preſent State and Diſpoſition of the *Creeks*, among whom he had lived many Years a principal Trader; and alſo a Letter from Lieutenant *Willy* to the ſame Purpoſe: By all which it appeared, that ſome ill-meaning People had been tampering with the *Indians* of thoſe ſeveral Nations, and endeavouring to excite them to a Rupture; but (it was hoped) in vain.

13. *Sunday*. The Office of the Day was performed by Mr. *Simms*, appointed thereto by Mr. *Whitfield*; who read ſuch Parts of it as he ſaw good; but mangled, omitting the Pſalms, and ſuch other Parts as it may be ſuppoſed he thought unneceſſary. Towards Evening a Meſſenger arrived, with a Letter to Mr. *Jones* from the General, then at

at the *Uchee* Town, belonging to a Tribe of *Indians* ſo called; where he met the Body of *Indians*, *Cherokees*, &c. mentioned on *Wedneſday* laſt; and acquainting us, that they would purſue their intended March as far by Land as *Muſgrave*'s (i. e. *Matthews*'s) where he would have ſome Pettyaguas ſent to meet them on *Monday* Evening, and bring them thence on *Tueſday* to *Savannah*. 1740. April

Monday. The General arrived in his Cutter, about Three a Clock this Morning, at *Savannah*: About Eight, after taking a little Reſt, he converſed with ſuch as had received his Commands, and had any Matters of Conſequence to lay before him: In the Afternoon, the Pettyaguas which he had before ordered, were diſpatched up the River to *Matthews*'s; and nothing more happened memorable. 14.

Tueſday. I had the General's Orders to receive the *Indians* under Arms, with as many Freeholders as could readily be got together, other ſpare Men and Inmates being not allowed on this Occaſion: And upon Beat of Drum, we got ſoon together about forty; which indeed was more than expected, conſidering how many were abroad at work, ſome one Way, and ſome another, eſpecially at the Orphan-Houſe; and Minors alſo, who were not of ſufficient Stature, though judged capable of doing Guard Duty in their own Right, 15.

1740. April 15. were excluded here. At Eleven a Clock they landed, under the Conduct of Mr. *Eyre*, and Mr. *Samuel Brown* an *Indian* Trader of Diſtinction; when I received them; and the greateſt Part of the Town were gathered together, out of Curioſity, to ſee them: They were a Body of luſty, lively Fellows, with all their Faces moſt diſmally painted with Vermillion and Blue, variouſly, as each fancied, to make himſelf appear terrible (as is their uſual Cuſtom) and well armed with Firelocks and Hatchets: The Freeholders marched firſt, four in a Rank; then the *Indians* in the ſame Manner, with each Party a Drum in the Centre, which alternately beat the *Engliſh* March, till we came to the Court-Houſe, where the General ſat to receive them; and the Freeholders then forming two ſtrait Lines, the *Indians* paſſed betwixt them into the Houſe, and the Drums ceaſed: During the March up the Town, fifteen Pieces of Cannon were diſcharged: When they were all ſeated, the General talked kindly to them a while by an Interpreter, and they had Pipes and Tobacco given them, which they all took readily: After that was over, I had Orders to conduct them to the Place prepared for them to reſt in; which I did, in the ſame Manner as before; and there they found what neceſſary Refreſhment was provided, *&c.* After which, I diſcharged

diſcharged our People, to follow their own Buſineſs, and took my Leave. 1740. April 16.

Wedneſday. What I thought moſt worth regarding, was ſome private Intelligence I got, that there was a Combination carrying on, among our inceſſant Workers of Miſchief, to form another Repreſentation of Grievances, in a different Strain from their former, and of more dangerous Conſequence; foraſmuch as that was ſpeculative only, and imported divers Propoſitions, ſo far culpable, as they were the Production of a raſh Preſumption: But this (I underſtood) was intended to ſtrike at the Foundation of the executive Power in this Place, by heaping up Abundance of illegal and arbitrary Proceedings, deſerving immediately to be remedied; and laying them to the Charge of all thoſe in any Authority, who hitherto boldly withſtood their miſchievous Purpoſes; wherein even the General himſelf (if my Information proves true) will hardly eſcape their vile Calumny: It is ſaid moreover, that the People at *Darien* act ſecretly in Concert with them; and that an Agent from thence, whoſe Name I yet forbear mentioning (though I obſerved for ſeveral Weeks paſt his frequent coming and going to and fro) has been very buſy here, on this good Work. Among other Pieces of curious Politicks, I am told farther, they want an Officer to be created, under the

Title

1740. April 16. Title of Sheriff; but how far his Power is to extend, or be limited, I cannot yet learn; nor whether, in theſe Times of War, he is to be elective, Dictator-like, or not, is not yet revealed: But in caſe it comes out ſuch a finiſhed Piece as we may expect, it will then be ſeen what the Authors dare to drive at; which a little Time will ſhew. Late at Night arrived ſome Expreſſes; by one of which the General was adviſed, a large Body of the *Creeks* were preparing to march, and join his Excellence in the South: And by another he was informed, that ſeveral half Gallies, and Sloops, well armed and manned, came out of the Harbour at St. *Auguſtin*, and in a Calm attacked one of our Frigates of twenty Guns, commanded by Capt. *Warren*, who was upon a Cruiſe off that Place: That they fired ſeveral Shot at him, and with a nine Pound Ball went through and through his Ship betwixt Decks, killing one Man only: But the Captain ſo behaved, that they found a warm Reception; and after about twenty of their Men ſlain, they were glad to ſheer off; and not able to get in by the Way they came out, they took Shelter in a ſmall Cove near by, where they were pent up. About Two in the Morning the General diſpatched an Expreſs to *Charles-Town*, to haſten the Force he expected, and to acquaint the Commanders of thoſe Frigates that

that were ſtationed there, how needful it was for them to turn out, and give what Aſſiſtance they could in preventing any Succours getting in, or any uſeleſs Hands out of *Auguſtin*, where he began to grow impatient till he could make them a Viſit. 1740. April

Thurſday. Much Hurry, and crowding of Buſineſs, took up the whole Day: The General determining with himſelf not to loſe an Hour that could be ſaved, in ſetting forward the Operations of War, and putting himſelf at the Head of what Forces he had, with all poſſible Expedition: Wherein nothing happened particularly fit to be taken Notice of here. Capt. *Davis*, with his Snow and Sloop, were now all put to Sea from *Tybee*; but whither bound, very few knew. 17.

Friday. Orders being given for the *Indians* to embark on board the Pettyaguas which brought them, and ſufficient Proviſions for them on their Paſſage, *&c.* that was the Work of the Forenoon; and about Two a Clock they all ſailed, under the Diſcharge of eleven Pieces of Cannon: In little more than an Hour after, the General took his Cutter, and followed, expecting to overtake them at Anchor, as ſoon as the Tide they had with them was ſpent; for the Wind being ſoutherly, and againſt them, till they were paſt *Skeedoway Narrows*, they muſt depend on the Tide alone, 18.

unleſs

1740. April 18. unleſs it veered to a more favourable Point. Out of the eight Companies of fifty-two private Men in each, which were to be paid by the Government of *Carolina*, the General had engaged to raiſe two of them on this River, under the Command of Meſſieurs *Richards* and *La Feit*, appointed Captains: Which ſucceeded ſo well, that *Richards*, who lives at *Puryſburgh*, had that whole Town to follow him, leaving only Women and Children, with a few old Men, to keep Poſſeſſion at home; ſo that he had a Surplus to ſpare, towards forming the other Company; to which three or four were added from *Ebenezer*; and the Remainder, even this Town, in the low Eſtate it is, without all Doubt will make up; for we ſeldom fail of rambling Fellows among us, ſufficient for ſuch an Enterprize, and ready to ſhew their Bravery againſt the *Spaniards:* All ſuch, together with ſome of our young Men inhabiting here, readily and voluntarily ſhew their good Diſpoſition, by enliſting themſelves for four Months (which is the Time limited for this Expedition, and) within the Compaſs of which, the Succeſs againſt *Auguſtin* is expected to be known. In ſuch a Juncture, when we daily hear of divers Gentlemen, Volunteers, taking to Arms at their own Expence, from *Carolina* and elſewhere, in order to ſignalize themſelves againſt the Enemies

Enemies of their Country; it might have been hoped, that ſome of our reforming Gentry, in their Gold and Silver buttoned Coats, and gay Waiſtcoats, would have made ſome little Advance, beyond the Parade, which they daily tread here, and diſplayed their Abilities, *tam Marte quam Mercurio:* But herein only they are modeſt. 1740. April

Saturday. Being under a little Diſorder, by reaſon of an accidental Bruiſe in one of my Legs, I ſat all Day at home, where I never was at a Loſs to find Employment; and did not hear of any Thing abroad more than common. 19.

Sunday. Mr. *Simms* read the common Prayers of the Church regularly this Day, and a Sermon both in the Forenoon and after, ſtill ſetting forth the Neceſſity of a ſtrong Faith, *&c.* 20.

Monday. A Report had flown about for a Week paſt, that *Donald Stewart* (Maſter of a ſmall Sloop, often made uſe of as a Pilot, and a Freeholder) was caſt away with his Sloop, and drowned; but being contradicted by ſeveral, little Credit was given to it; till now it was unhappily confirmed. He was hired by ſome Perſons in this Town, who were on their Way thus far to ſettle at *Auguſta*, to go and fetch their Families and Effects from the Place where they had left them in *Carolina (vide* 21.

March

1740. April *March* 31.) On which Occaſion, this poor Man ſailing, within *Port-Royal Iſland*, in croſſing a Sound, under a hard Gale of Wind, ran upon ſome Shoals, and ſtaved his Veſſel, his Son and another eſcaping with their Lives; but himſelf and one Man more drowned.

22. *Tueſday*. One of the two Companies, appointed to be raiſed on the Banks of this River, being not yet compleat, which was to be commanded by Capt. *La Feit*; the enliſting Officer applied to me for the Guard-Drum to beat up for Volunteers; which I very gladly made him a Compliment of; hitherto no ſuch Means of Invitation having been uſed, but all that enliſted, came without a Call; but now the Town was grown ſo exceeding thin, the Orphan-Houſe taking off hence ſuch a Number one Way, and ſo many more going into the War chearfully and commendably another, that we were almoſt become uncapable of finding Hands ſufficient to carry on the ordinary Guard-Duty; and Planting was regarded by very few.

23. *Wedneſday*. A Boat was ſent off early this Morning to the General at *Frederica*, with an Expreſs from *Charles-Town*, by whom Mr. *Jones* and I wrote Letters needful. The ordinary Club, which meet at *Jenkins*'s, rode out, with Landlord at the Head

Head of them this Day, by Invitation, to an Entertainment provided for them at Mr. *Fallowfield*'s Plantation, about eight Miles off; where it may be preſumed, it was taken into Conſideration, what Steps farther to make in theſe dubious Times towards ſettling this Colony upon ſuch a Foundation as would beſt pleaſe them: It having been obſerved, that at theſe ſelect Meetings out of Town, uſually ſomething extraordinary has been the Subject Matter of their Deliberations; and it is not queſtioned, but their aſpiring Temper is ſomewhat offended, at a Rebuke one of their Fellow Workers lately met with from the General; who overtaking the Pettyaguas with the *Indians*, on *Friday* Night laſt, and eſpying on board one of them, a Man whom his Excellency thought not proper to mix with that Company, knowing him to be a cloſe Attender of the Club, and a buſy Perſon, often paſſing to and fro betwixt this and the South, which rendered him ſuſpicious of being employed to no good Purpoſes; he ordered the Maſter of the Pettyagua to ſet him aſhore that Inſtant, at the firſt Place of Landing; which happened to be on the Iſland called the *Iſle of Hope*, whereon Mr. *Fallowfield* is one of the three that are ſettled there, and where now this Company met: But whether or not it was only to celebrate the Feſtival

1740. April 23.

of

1740. April 24. of St. *George*, they beſt knew: Hoiſting up the *Britiſh* Flag, was all I thought needful in the Town of *Savannah*.

Thurſday. Enliſting of Men was now the principal Affair in hand; which had ſo drained the Town, that it was hard to find a Man more to enter: Wherefore it was reſolved by the Officer, to make a Viſit to the People at work about Mr. *Whitfield*'s Plantation at the Orphan-Houſe; which I would have nothing to ſay to, but left them to do as they pleaſed, being unwilling to ſhew the leaſt Diſcouragement in ſo important a Service; and not over-fond of meddling, where my appearing in it (I had Reaſon to apprehend) would be ill conſtrued as a Sort of Sacrilege, in breaking in upon ſuch a Work, carrying on for ſo pious an Uſe: Moreover, I knew it was a Matter much in queſtion among the Directors of that Work, whether or not it was lawful in the Sight of God, to take up Arms with an offenſive Intent, or on any Occaſion, but purely in Defence of our own Lives. In the Afternoon an Officer in the new-raiſed Troops of *Carolina*, arrived from *Charles-Town*, by the Way of *Puryſburgh*, with Letters expreſs from thence for the General, which was incumbent upon us to forward, with what Expedition we could: But indeed, the daily Demand upon us for Boats, and Men to to go in them, was ſo diſproportioned to our Abilities (being now ſo far bereft of People for ordinary Uſes) that we were hard put to it to do, what we wiſhed, more readily for the publick Service. One or two of the Letters now brought us for the General, I obſerved by the Superſcription, came from *England* by the *Charming Philly*, Capt. *Colebatch*; which gave me Hopes, that I might alſo have ſome thence for me fall into Mr. *Hopton*'s Hands at *Charles-Town*, who would not ſlip the firſt Opportunity he could meet with, of forwarding whatever he received. 1740. April

Friday. The Letters we received Yeſterday *per* Expreſs from *Charles-Town*, we ſent over Land by the Way of *Darien*; and other Letters for the General, which came by the South, expecting he was here, we ſent back alſo by the ſame Hand, together with more Letters now wrote from hence. The enliſting Officer ſtuck to his Purpoſe of Yeſterday, and marched with a few Volunteers, and a Drum attending him, to beat up for more Soldiers at the Orphan-Houſe, where he would find a Number of People; but what Diſpoſition any of them were in for War, or what Succeſs he met with, we yet had not learnt. What occurred in Town was not worth remembring. 25.

1740. April 26. *Saturday.* Capt. *La Feit*, and his Subaltern Recruiting Officer, taking Breakfaſt with me, I was informed by them what Succeſs they had attending Yeſterday's Expedition to *Betheſda* (which is the Name given to that Place by Mr. *Whitfield)* and it proved almoſt fruitleſs, one or two Fellows only taking on: They took Notice to me of the People in general there, being provided with one and the ſame Anſwer; which it was ſuppoſed was taught them to give, by their Employers, when invited to take Arms; which was, that they had good Proviſions, and a Place to ſleep in, with ready Money Pay for their Work, where they were, which they were not deſirous to change for the Hazard of being knocked on the Head, and the Certainty of being continually expoſed to bad Weather, either Heats, or heavy Rains. By reaſon of ſeveral Tythings now rendered incapable of doing effectual Duty on our Guard, for want of Hands ſufficient, it behoved me to make ſome new Regulation, for carrying on ſo neceſſary a Service: For when the utmoſt was done in our Power to raiſe Recruits, which might contribute to Action againſt our Enemies in the South; it was Time to conſider a little our own Safety, in being watchful with thoſe Freeholders which remained, that we might not be ſurprized by any Party of *Florida*

Indians ſtraggling, to come on our Backs, nor by any armed Boat coming up the River, ſculking to do Miſchief; who coming upon us unaware, and unprovided, might carry all before them; whereas on Diſcovery of approaching, imminent Danger, we yet hoped, by putting Arms into our ſpare Mens Hands, and calling in all others employed within little Diſtance, we might make a Stand with at leaſt one hundred and fifty Men, ſufficient to repel any ſuch Attempt: Upon looking carefully, therefore, over the Liſt of Freeholders, with the Conſtables; it was thought adviſable, that three or four of thoſe Tythings, with the feweſt Hands left in them, not competent to make a reaſonable Guard, ſhould be totally reduced for this preſent Occaſion, and the few Freeholders left in them, ſhould be divided among other Tythings, ſo as to make them ſufficient, and called upon to do Duty with them: This we apprehended could produce no Inconvenience, but muſt bring their mounting on Guard a little quicker about; but that could not be holpen, and was therefore ordered: As alſo the Orders before given, I now renewed in the ſtrongeſt Terms, requiring a frequent Patrole from the Guard every Night, and that the Conſtables would be careful in viſiting the Guard often, and making con-

1740. April 26.

1740. ſtant Report to me in Writing of what paſſed.

April 27. *Sunday.* Mr. *Simms* obſerved the Directions given him by Mr. *Whitfield*, in reading the Prayers of the Church, and a Sermon (out of what Author I know not) in the Forenoon, and after, maintaining the Doctrine of Juſtification by Faith alone, in ſtronger Terms than had been delivered yet; excluding from Heaven all who came not fully up to that Pitch of Faith, and ſuch might reſt aſſured of Sanctification next following, and of their being numbered among the Elect. In the Afternoon a Skooner from *Charles-Town*, laden with ſundry Stores for the Uſe of the Army, and bound for the South; having been out a full Week with contrary Winds; fearing they ſhould want Water, came up the River for a Supply of that, with Intent to go down again to-morrow, and wait for the firſt Wind at *Tybee*.

28. *Monday.* Volunteers no longer now offering themſelves to enliſt, and a few more yet being wanted to compleat the Company; what few Servants remained among us, who were the Property of private Perſons, had Temptations offered them, to exchange their preſent Service for one more valuable; which, without ſome Stop put to it, muſt have been of miſchievous Conſequence: And the General well know-

ing

ing that, had forbidden it: Moreover, instead of twenty-five Men, which his Excellency said he thought would be an handsome Quota for this Town, if so many could readily be spared, they had already enlisted upwards of thirty: Wherefore some of the Magistrates thought proper to represent to the Officers, that there was a Necessity of their interposing, to prevent great Injury accruing to Masters; for if indented Servants had the Liberty of going off on this Occasion, possibly there would hardly be one left in Town: Out of seven that remained with me, after the Loss of three by Death and Desertion, I made the Captain a Present of one for this Expedition, who was a lively Fellow at any Thing but what I most wanted him for, *viz.* Work; and all would have gone the same Way readily. Late in the Evening came Letters from the General, by the Return of a Boat lately sent to *Frederica*; wherein were some short Orders for Mr. *Jones* to observe, *&c.* but what was most acceptable to us, was telling us in few Words, "All goes well, "and the *Spaniards* desert daily."

1740. April

Tuesday. Most Part of this Day was taken up by me in going over a List of all the Inhabitants, and taking personally, from Tything to Tything, as true an Account of the State of each, as possibly I could, for the Satisfaction of the honoura-

29.

1740. April ble Truſtees: Which Work I had of late attempted ſeveral Times in vain, by reaſon of ſuch frequent Changes and Alterations happening, during ſome Months paſt, in this Town and Neighbourhood; inſomuch that it baffled my utmoſt Endeavours, to make out a Liſt perfectly correct; and even now, I cannot warrant but this may need ſome Emendation, before it is many Days out of my Hand.

30. *Wedneſday.* More Letters and Expreſſes from divers Parts arrived, for the General; among which one for me from Lieutenant *Willy* in the *Creek* Nation; ſetting forth ſeveral Attempts made by the *French*, to draw thoſe People, as alſo the *Chicaſſaws*, off from any Alliance with us, and what large Preſents they had made them, of Stores of all Sorts, for Food and Cloathing; and great Plenty of Guns, Ammunition, *&c.* endeavouring, at any Rate, to make Peace with the *Chicaſſaws*, who were ſtrongly attached to us, and whoſe Bravery in the Field they had experienced many Times to their own Coſt; and from what Aſſurances the General had received from them, they ſtill appeared firm in their Friendſhip with us, ſeveral of their People being gone to ſerve in the Wars under him, and more were expected to follow: Moreover, at this very Time, another ſmall Party of the *Chicaſſaws*, joined by as many *Euchies*,

chies, were on their Way down to the South, under the Conduct of one *Hewet*, an *Indian* Trader, who came to Town in the Night paſt, whilſt they followed after. So many Men as were liſted for Soldiers, living idle about Town, and frequent Diſorders happening from thence, by their getting drunk; it was much to be wiſhed that their Officers would ſend them away to their Duties; more eſpecially ſince it was found that the Authors of all Licentiouſneſs, and Contempt of the Civil Power, at our noted Club, were never wanting to encourage, and make Sport of, any Diſturbance given to our Peace and Quiet; ſo that every Thing tending to a Riot, appeared to be what they aimed at. 1740. April 30.

Thurſday. Having found no convenient Leiſure for about ſix Weeks paſt, to ſee what my People at *Bewlie* were doing; I choſe this Day to make them a Viſit; where I had the Satisfaction to ſee they had not been idle, but had planted as much Land, as could well be expected, in the Time they were there, conſidering what Work they had to do, at firſt ſitting down on a Plantation, in building convenient Huts, and other neceſſary Conveniences of Life; falling Abundance of large Timber, diſbranching that, whereof they had burned and deſtroyed great Part, and clearing the Whole from all Shrub-Wood, and other May 1.

1740. May 1. Impediments of Planting; beſides their farther going on, and adding to it daily: So that I had good Reaſon to hope, before the Seaſon of Planting was quite over, I ſhould be yet better pleaſed with my new Plantation. In my Return home, I ſtopped at the Orphan-Houſe, which I found carrying on with a great Number of Hands for various Uſes, at an unknown Expence; but undoubtedly it muſt be proportionable to the grand Appearance it already makes, by the two Wings that are now carried up and covered, intended for ſeveral Offices: The Body of the Dwelling-Houſe, which is hitherto carried up with ſubſtantial Brick-Work for Cellars, *&c.* to a certain Height, a little above the Surface of the Land, will be very large, and diſpoſed into ſuch Apartments as are, or ſhall be judged proper, each fronting Angle whereof is to have a Communication with the Offices in the before-mentioned Wings, whether by a Colonade, after the Manner of *Buckingham-Houſe*, or not, I have not learnt. Rain had been much wanted a long while, none falling ſince the Beginning of *March*; which dry Spring occaſioned ſuch as regarded Planting, to fear their Labour would prove fruitleſs; but we now happily found what we wiſhed for, great Plenty of it overtaking me in my Travel, and I was well pleaſed

pleaſed to get home in the Evening, thoroughly waſhed to my Skin. 1740. May 2.

Friday. A bleſſed Rain continued moſt Part of the Day, which confined every body at home: Towards Night Letters were brought me out of the *Creek* Nation from Lieutenant *Willy*, Mr. *Wiggan*, and others, by one *Finlay*; the Contents whereof were ſetting forth many Particulars, relating to the preſent dubious State and Diſpoſition of thoſe *Indians*, which it behoved me to lay before the General by the Opportunity that firſt offered. It ſeems old *Chigellie*, their chief *Mico* at preſent, had of late ſhewn an unuſual Coldneſs towards meddling in the Wars that we were engaged in againſt *Spain*; telling ſome of his People, that they had no Buſineſs to interpoſe among the white Mens Quarrels: Which Behaviour of his, it is ſuſpected aroſe from ſome *French* and *Spaniſh* Emiſſaries among them; but the main Body of his People were eagerly bent upon joining the General; and his Nephew *Malatchie*, who was the Son of old *Bream*, the former *Mico*, ſtuck cloſe to them, and put himſelf at their Head, reſolving in the firſt Place to go himſelf, and have a perſonal Talk (which is a Term they uſe) with the General at *Frederica*; and whither he was accordingly gone: After which, if he liked the General's Talk, he

1740. he would return and try who had the beſt Intereſt in his Country, he or *Chigellie*.

May 3. *Saturday.* Capt. *Heron* (now ſaid to be Major in the General's Regiment) arrived from *Frederick* Fort at *Port-Royal* in a ten-oar'd Boat, filled with Soldiers, having been ſent by the General to fetch a certain Number of the Company commanded by Capt. *Norbury*, to join the other Forces in the South; and he had brought away thence forty-two, what he had not with him, being in a Pettyagua that was coming after. Mrs. *Matthews* arrived in the Afternoon from the South, by whom came ſeveral Letters and Orders from the General, and withal, *Malatchie*, accompanied by three or four head Men, and noted Warriors of their Nation, who had been to get a Talk with the General, agreeable to what I noted Yeſterday; in which he had made ſuch quick Diſpatch, and was ſo well pleaſed, that he was now making the like Speed home, reſolved to put his Purpoſe in Execution; and if *Chigellie* oppoſed him, to cut off his Head: For the farther Explanation whereof, it ſhould be obſerved, that when old *Bream*, the Father of *Malatchie*, died, his Son was then a Youth; and thereupon *Chigellie* had the Power put in his Hands by the old Men, till *Malatchie* came to the Age of Maturity: During which Time, the young Man has ſignalized himſelf

himſelf to be a great Warrior, and behaved ſo well, that he is now looked on as the greateſt Man of that, or moſt other Nations; which makes him highly eſteemed among them: Nevertheleſs (he ſays) he never intended to take the Government out of old *Chigellie*'s Hands, but let him die poſſeſſed of it, had he ruled for the Good of his Country; but now, if he ſhews no longer Regard to the pleaſing his People, it is Time to put an End to his Power; and he thinks himſelf of Age ſufficient to take his own Right, being near Thirty: And as his Ability, as well as his Good-will to the *Engliſh*, is not to be queſtioned; ſo his Perſon is very engaging: His Stature but a little ſhort of ſix Foot, his Make clean, and perfectly well ſhaped from Head to Foot, as he appears when naked to his Skin; and when he puts on a Coat and Hat, his Behaviour is ſuch, that one would rather imagine from his Complaiſance, he had been bred in ſome *European* Court, than among *Barbarians:* At the ſame Time, though the Features of his Face were inviting, and ſhew Tokens of Good-Nature; yet there is ſomething in his Aſpect which demands Awe. By Mrs. *Matthews* we were moreover informed, that two Men of War were newly arrived at St. *Simon*'s; and that the General was preparing to ſet out in few Days for the appointed Place of Rendez-

1740. May 3.

vous:

1740. May vous: To whom I wrote by Capt. *Heron*, incloſing thoſe Letters I received for him on *Friday* laſt.

4. *Sunday.* About Two this Morning Capt. *Heron* went down the River, proceeding with his Men for the Camp: And about Eight *Malatchie* went up the River, with his Attendants, intending to ſtay a Day or two with Mrs. *Matthews*, whilſt a Scarlet Coat, *&c.* with other Preſents for him by the General's Order, were making ready. Mr. *Simms* read the Prayers of the Church, and Sermons on the ſame conſtant Topick of Faith and Free Grace.

5. *Monday.* Nothing of any Kind happened within my Obſervation worth remembring; ſo that I had full Leiſure at home, to take ſuch Matters in hand, as required Diſpatch, to be ſent for *England.*

6. *Tueſday.* Some of our few Freeholders left, beginning again to grow ſlack in their Duty of keeping a good Guard; upon looking over the Defaulters returned to me by the ſeveral Tything-men, I had them ſummoned before the Magiſtrates; when we made the Pockets of thoſe that were moſt culpable, pay for their Neglect; for it was Time now to be ſtrict: And whereas divers of our Tythings were grown much thinner than others, and too weak to make a competent Guard; it was thought beſt, in this Caſe of Neceſſity, to vary a little

little from the ordinary Cuſtom, and by reducing two or three of thoſe Tythings, who had perhaps not more than two or three Freeholders occupying them, in the Out-parts of the Town, and joining ſuch with another Tything, which was a little ſtronger; by ſo doing, I found, upon a careful Calculation, that we could make out eighteen Tythings capable of doing conſtant Duty round, with an Officer and eight Men; which I would be content with, inſtead of ten that was the original Eſtabliſhment; but a leſs Number would not be ſufficient, ſome of the Guard having my Orders to keep the Patrole conſtantly going round the Town in the Night: This being reſolved, I took Care to ſee Liſts made out, and given to the ſeveral Tythingmen, of the Names of thoſe eight Men appointed to do Duty under each of them; which would make a Round of eighteen Days before they mounted again, and could not be thought hard: But it is not to be underſtood from hence, that every Night produced freſh Men, many of our People doing frequent Duty upon Hire, or otherwiſe, for others, who perhaps lived remote, or had Avocation on ſuch Buſineſs, as induced them rather to pay a Man for ſtanding in their Stead, than ſhewing any eager Diſpoſition to perſonal Service, unleſs

1740. May 6.

an

1740. an Alarm were to call them out in good Earneſt.

May 7. *Wedneſday.* Two or three *Indian* Traders arrived from the *Creek* Nation, in order to renew their Licences; by whom I had another Letter from Mr. *Wigan*, relating to ſome farther Apprehenſions they were under of Diſturbances ariſing among them: But as *Malatchie* was now preparing to be with them ſoon, whoſe Fidelity we could rely on, we promiſed ourſelves, and were very confident, that all Doubts of that Sort would ſoon vaniſh. One of Mr. *Fallowfield*'s Boys, from his Plantation in the *Iſle of Hope*, came and brought me a Letter, which he ſaid was left the Day before, by Mr. *Hird* of *Frederica*, who was paſſing by in a Boat for *Carolina:* Upon opening it, I found it was a Letter from Mr. *Vereſt*, dated the 22d of *October* laſt, which (he ſaid) he took the Opportunity of writing by a Ship with Stores of War for the General; and I knew that muſt be Capt. *Wright* in the St. *George*, whoſe Name has been ſeveral Times mentioned before on ſome ſuch like Occaſion: It happened, indeed, to be only a private Letter, acquainting me, that he had ſeen my Son then newly arrived in *England*, who he thought knew of no immediate Opportunity of writing to me; wherefore he very kindly ſent me himſelf what he thought would

would be the firſt Advice I ſhould have of his being well; but therein he happened to be miſtaken ſeveral Months, which is of leſs Significance, ſince it proved of no Detriment to the Publick; but inevitably it muſt recur to my Thoughts, what I formerly noted, concerning what I was to expect by that Ship, *&c.* whereto I ſhall add no more now. — About Noon arrived a trading Boat from *Charles-Town*, bound up the River (—— *Johnſon* Patroon) by whom I had Letters from Mr. *Hopton* of the 29th and 30th *ult.* acquainting me, that he had ſent by that Boat three Boxes, one of which directed to me, came out of *England* in the *Colcheſter* Man of War, Capt. *Symonds* Commander; who meeting with bad Weather, and receiving great Damage in his Rigging, was forced to put in at *Virginia*; but had ſent that Box by Sir *Yelverton Peyton*, Commander of the *Hector*, bound for *Charles-Town*, from whom Mr. *Hopton* had received it, and now ſent it by this firſt Conveyance to me: In which Box I found a good and welcome Parcel of Stationary Ware, a large Packet for the General, and ſeveral other Letters; among which one from the Secretary, Mr. *Martyn*, to me, and one from Mr. *Verelſt*; both dated the 5th of *December* laſt; together with ſundry Papers, relating to Mr. *Robert Williams*'s Accounts, which

1740. May 7.

1740. May which were to be examined, *&c.* Mr. *Hopton* farther wrote me, that the other two Boxes now ſent, came a few Days before by Capt. *Somerſet*, a trading Ship; one of which was for *Peter Joubert*, a Freeholder here; and the other was directed for *Ebenezer:* I was moreover informed by Mr. *Hopton*, that there were yet in his Cuſtody two more Boxes, or Caſes, which alſo were brought by Capt. *Somerſet*, but one of them more eſpecially, being of great Weight, and the Patroon of this Boat therefore not caring to take it in, being already deep laden; I might expect them both by *Peter Emery*, who was coming this Way very ſoon. Beſides this, Mr. *Hopton* referred me to ſeveral Particulars, which he had wrote me of the 21ſt paſt; when at the ſame Time he ſent me (as he now wrote) ſome Letters from Mr. *Verelſt*, by Enſign *Tolſon* to *Port-Royal*, and engaged him to forward them from thence: But as yet I had no farther Tidings of any ſuch Letters.

Thurſday. Capt. *La Feit* intending to carry off what Men he had raiſed, for the South, this Evening; the Fore-part of the Day was wholly taken up by me, in writing divers Letters that Way; which, together with the Packet I received Yeſterday, for the General, I committed to the Care of *James Carwils*, one of our Freeholders,

holders, who had been an old Soldier, and formerly a Serjeant in the Army, and was now going, not a lifted Soldier, but a Volunteer, to be diſpoſed of as his Excellence ſaw good; and as there was Room enough to employ experienced Men, among theſe yet undiſciplined, there was little Reaſon to doubt of his being kindly accepted. It was no ſmall Trouble to the Captain and his Officers, to get his Men together, out of the ſeveral little Holes in Town, where many of them had been too long debauching themſelves; ſo that the Tide being far ſpent, they were obliged to wait, after their being on board, till the next Tide ſerved; when they went off before Morning. 1740. May

Friday. A Skooner in the Service of the Province of *Carolina*, arrived here from *Port-Royal* by Order, to take in Major *Richards*'s Company, who were expected down from *Puryſburgh*, and ſo to the general Rendezvous in the South, where the Forces intended for this Expedition were now drawing together apace. By this Skooner I had the Packet ſent by the Hands of Enſign *Tolſon*, to be left at *Port-Royal*, and forwarded from thence; as Mr. *Hopton* had wrote me in his Letter of the 21ſt of *April*, which accompanied this Packet, as noted by me on *Wedneſday* laſt: Under which Cover I found a Letter to the General, one to Colonel *Cook*, and one to another Perſon 9.

1740. May in the Regiment; beſides two for myſelf from Mr. *Verelſt*, one of the 10th, and one of the 12th of *December*; all which came by Capt. *Somerſet*, who had been four Months from *England*, in the *Carolina* Packet, on his Paſſage, laſt from *Madera*.

10. *Saturday*. Capt. *La Feit* and his Men now gone, and all ſpare Hands, for the Camp; the Orphan-Houſe alſo drawing off a conſiderable Number, very few remained in Town, to be ſeen in our Streets; from whence little could be obſerved.

11. *Sunday*. Mr. *Simms* went on in executing the Office appointed him by Mr. *Whitfield*, reading the Prayers and Sermons before Noon and after; wherein we found always hitherto the Subſtance the ſame, with very little Diverſity of Phraſe from ſuch former Diſcourſes; which many People ſeemed to grow weary of hearing.

12. *Monday*. Mr. *Upton* came to Town from the South, and brought us the News of the General's being gone, with what Forces he had ready, to Fort *Franciſco del Pupa* (taken a while ſince from the Enemy) upon the River St. *Juan*'s, being the Rendezvous appointed, where others from divers Parts were daily joining him. In the Evening Major *Richards* arrived at *Savannah* from *Puryſburgh*, with Part of his new-raiſed Company, the other Part being ſent off ſome Time before; and with theſe he was

to proceed to-morrow in the Skooner appointed, as noted on *Friday* laſt. All well-meaning Peoples Hearts were now full of good Wiſhes for Succeſs in this Enterprize, of ſo great Importance for the Security of his Majeſty's Dominions in theſe Parts, and the Enlargement of his Power, to bridle the Pride of the haughty *Spaniard.* 1740. May

Tueſday. His Majeſty's Declaration of War againſt *Spain*, which had lately been publiſhed in moſt of the neighbouring Parts, but never yet here, was by the General's Order read this Day, with due Solemnity at our Guard-Houſe, in Preſence of the Magiſtrates, all the Town-Officers, and moſt of the Inhabitants, under a Diſcharge of all our Cannon, with chearful Acclamations of the People; wherein the new-raiſed Men, under Command of Major *Richards*, joined us; and in the Evening they proceeded Southward, in the Skooner before provided: But before their going off, a little Ruffle happened between our Magiſtrates and the Major, on the following Occaſion. Mr. *Groneau*, one of the Miniſters of *Ebenezer*, coming to Town a Day or two ſince, on ſome Buſineſs, with a Boat rowed down by ſome of their own People, as uſual, came to me complaining, that Major *Richards* had impreſſed one of his Men into the Service, and took him by Force aboard the Skooner, 13.

1740. May 13. intending to carry him off; whereupon I recommended him to the Magiſtrates, who I told him I was ſure would not ſuffer a Freeholder of this Colony to be carried away againſt his Will: Accordingly upon hearing the Complaint, and finding it to be juſt, (for the Man was aboard on the Deck, with two Men as a Guard over him) they ſent two Tything-men to demand the Fellow's Appearance before them aſhore, where they themſelves then ſtood, that they might enquire into the Truth, the Veſſel lying faſt at the new Wharf: But ſeveral of the liſted Men obſtructed them in their Way, and ſet up a great Shout, crying out to their Comrades, *Couragio:* Whereat the Magiſtrates ſeeing themſelves ſo comtemned, called particularly to one of the Tything-men (known remarkably for a robuſt, daring Man) and bad him lay hold on one of the moſt inſolent among them, and to bring him before them; whereupon *John Lyndal* the Tything-man inſtantly collar'd him, and betwixt him and his Partner, they brought him up the Hill, when the Magiſtrates directly committed him into Cuſtody: Upon which the Major then appeared, and offered ſome Words in Juſtification; which made it rather worſe: Wherefore ſeeing it in vain to contend, he gave up the Man again to Mr. *Groneau*; and upon aſking it as a Favour,

vour, the Magiſtrates gave him his Soldier out of Cuſtody. So Peace was concluded, and the Service went forward. 1740. May

Wedneſday. After ſeveral Days waiting for an Opportunity to ſend the General that Packet which I received on *Friday* laſt, with ſeveral other Letters encloſed, for Colonel *Cook*, &c. I took Occaſion by Mr. *John Pye*, one of our Clerks, now going by the General's Order from hence, to tranſmit it all to his Excellence. Several Matters of Controverſy and Litigation being at this Time brought before the Magiſtrates, aſſembled on that Occaſion at the Stores, I thought it proper to attend them there, at their Deſire, more eſpecially having ſomewhat to offer to their Conſideration, which I conceived would require it: Among the reſt, one *Marmaduke Canon*, an Orphan, and Freeholder here, happening to be ſeen now in Town, I had him brought before them, that due Enquiry might be made concerning him, and the Way of Life he was in, many Stories, and uncertain Reports, often paſſing, which we wanted to get to the Bottom of; and it may not be improper to make a ſhort Minute here, how it appeared to us upon Examination. The Boy was taken by Mr. *Cauſton* (with the Allowance and Approbation, it may be ſuppoſed, of his Brother Magiſtrates at that Time) into his Houſe, 14.

1740. May 14. with Intent to maintain him; for which undoubtedly his Maſter had Reaſon to expect ſome Service from him: This commenced ſeveral Years ſince, long before I ſaw *Georgia* in the Year 1736; at which Time I obſerved him there a lively Youth; from which Period, Mr. *Cauſton* then beginning his Improvements at *Ockſtead*, the Boy was ſent thither, and there employed in hard Labour, as others were; where he has continued ever ſince, excepting when ſent to Town on an Errand. Upon Mr. *Whitfield*'s coming with thoſe Powers lately from the honourable Truſtees, to take all the Orphans under his Care, Mr. *Cauſton* was the only Perſon who refuſed to comply, and perſiſted in not ſurrendring him; though ſome others, who had equal Pretence, gave up theirs, howſoever againſt their Inclination. The Boy now appeared much dejected, looked poorly, and in miſerable Rags, weeping: Upon aſking him whether or not he was miſuſed, he ſeemed under a Terror, not daring to complain; but it was alledged by ſome of the Byſtanders, that his Miſtreſs tyrannized over him with great Cruelty, whilſt his Maſter gave little Heed to Things of that Kind. He was grown a tall Lad, at leaſt five Foot high, and could hardly read his Primer: I aſked him whether or not he had received a Gun, which I ordered to be be delivered to him, by the General's Direction; who told me I ſhould give a light *Indian* Gun out of the Stores, to each Orphan Boy that was capable of handling it, who was a Freeholder, that they might be trained, in their younger Years, to do Guard-Duty; which would become habitual, and teach them to be ready in Defence of their own Property: This I had obſerved, and ſuch of them as I allowed of, were delighted at it: And upon my telling this Boy, that I muſt not loſe a Soldier, but that he muſt appear this very Evening with his Gun, upon Guard, it being his Turn to come on; and that he muſt go home, and fetch it from his Maſter, acquainting him that he came by my Order; he promiſed to do ſo, and went his Way; returning in the Evening with his Gun, and did his Night's Duty with the reſt very orderly. 1740. May

Thurſday. Young *Canon*, on his Appearance this Morning, and declaring his Deſire of leaving Mr. *Cauſton*, and putting himſelf under Mr. *Whitfield*; one of the Perſons who were left in Charge of the Boys by Mr. *Whitfield*, was ſent for by Mr. *Jones*, to whom the Lad was delivered, and he took him with him. All was huſht and quiet now in Town, and every body following their own Buſineſs, without any Thing happening extraordinary. 15.

1740. May 16. 17. *Friday*, *Saturday*. } The only Occurrence I found to obſerve theſe two Days was, that ſome Boats from *Carolina* ſtopped at *Thunderbolt*, waiting an Hour or two for the Tide in their Way South; wherein was Colonel *Barnwell*, with near thirty other Gentlemen; who acquainted us, that near thirty more were gone at the ſame Time in the *Tartar* Pink, all Gentlemen Volunteers, to ſerve under the General in this Expedition.

18. *Sunday*. Mr. *Simms* continued to read the Prayers of the Church, and Sermons, as before.

19. *Monday*. *John Rea*, who went lately Patroon of a Boat to *Charles-Town*, returned from thence, and brought with him what Mr. *Hopton* had committed to his Care, that he had lately received by the Ship *Ann and Marianna*, Capt. *Campbel*, newly arrived, *viz.* ſeveral Packets of Letters, and a Box containing Blank Sola Bills to the Value of 1000 *l.* Sterling, with many Letters encloſed therein, and Packets to me for the General, and divers other Perſons near him: All which it was incumbent on me to haſten forward as ſoon as might be; as I would alſo take Care to ſee what came for others in this Neighbourhood duly delivered to them: Among the reſt, there was a Packet for Meſſieurs *Bolzius* and *Groneau*, at *Ebenezer*; and Mr.

Mr. *Hopton* took this Opportunity of ſending another of thoſe three Caſes which came for them in Capt. *Somerſet*'s Ship, as noted on *Wedneſday* the 7th Inſtant; but the largeſt was yet in Mr. *Hopton*'s Cuſtody, till he could find a ſuitable Conveyance. What Letters came for me were two from Mr. *Verelſt*, one of the 28th of *December*, and the other of the 25th of *February* laſt: In the former of which was encloſed Copy of Mr. *Robert Ellis*'s Account, *&c.* and the latter contained Matters of the utmoſt Importance, relating to the Truſt; which, to be ſure, my Duty and Fidelity required me to pay the ſtricteſt Regard to, and to purſue the Inſtructions ſent me, with all Diligence. By this I now partly underſtood what was meant in that Letter, and Paſſage therein, then hinted to me (as noted on the 22d of *March* laſt) wherein the Writer acquainted me, that it was currently reported the Parliament would make an Enquiry into the State of this Colony; which many People ſeemed to ſpeak lightly of, as if it was likely never to come to any Good.—— Theſe are ſome of the Fruits of our deteſtable Club, who have ſo long been labouring to get the Direction of all into their own Hands; reſtleſs under any but their own headſtrong Will, which produced that memorable Repreſentation, calculated (I am fully

1740. May 19.

1740. May fully convinced) purely to ſet *Williams* and *Tailſer* at the Head of the Negro Trade, which they meant to be the ſole Importers of; and finding themſelves therein miſtaken, Malice and Revenge ſucceeds to ſuch a Degree, that their whole Study appears to be making Miſchief at any Rate, and even the utter Deſtruction of the Whole, were it in their Power, would give them Pleaſure: But let them take Care, leſt they trip in their Career, and fall headlong at once.

20. *Tueſday.* Mr. *Brownfield* called on me, and ſhewed me a Letter he had received from my Son, which came not in any Packet directed to me, but (as I obſerved) was directed to the Care of one *Mackenzie*, Merchant in *Charles-Town*; from whom Mr. *Brownfield* had it, and it was dated the 28th of *December*. The Subſtance of it was to inform him, of a Deſign carrying on, to obtain a parliamentary Enquiry into the bad State of this Colony, *&c.* which he made no Scruple to inform him, he was, among others, a Promoter of, and profeſſed, that what he did therein, he did not deſire ſhould be concealed, for that he meant it openly and publick. This, without any Thing elſe to employ my Thoughts, was more than ſufficient for one Day's Diſquiet; whereof none can judge, but ſuch only as have the Misfortune to deal with an

an unruly Son of his own. At our laſt parting, and frequently before, too well knowing the Impetuoſity of his Temper, I begged and conjured him to promiſe me not to meddle in any Affairs relating to the Colony, or to keep Company with any, whom he knew to have Pique or Ill-will againſt it: For I knew *Robert Williams*'s Intention was, to be in *London* in the Winter; and as I alſo knew, that there was a Familiarity betwixt them here, my Heart foreboded that no Good would come of their meeting in *London*, being not unlike in Warmth, but very unequal in Craft. He knew my Opinion of all that Set of People very well, and how narrowly I obſerved all their Proceedings here; which he often, when with me, would blame them for (in good Earneſt I verily believe at that Time) and engaged to me in the moſt ſolemn Manner to keep at a Diſtance from all ſuch Company, mind his own private Affairs only, and return to me in the Winter. What a Shock, therefore, muſt an old Man feel from ſuch a Blow given by his own Son? No Letter from him to frame any Excuſe to me for what he has done, or to offer at any Vindication of himſelf (and ſo far, perhaps, he judges right, that it is inexcuſable) but the World, nevertheleſs, will not fail to cenſure the Father as an Adviſer in this, however contrary to his

1740. May 20.

1740. May his conſtant Profeſſion, his open Zeal, and even to his Oath; which muſt render me infamous, unleſs the honourable Truſtees pleaſe to entertain more kind and charitable Thoughts of my Simplicity; which from the many Inſtances of their paſt Benevolence towards me, it would be a Crime in me not to hope for their Continuance of.

21. *Wedneſday.* Yeſterday's Affair ſat ſo heavy upon my Spirits, that it rendered me incapable of Action; nor could I ſhake off that Pain of Mind which I laboured under, all this Day; wherein it ſo happened, that no Tranſaction in this Place, was of ſuch Conſequence, as to need any Remark of mine.

22. *Thurſday.* Our Court met, as *per* Adjournment; ſat an Hour or two; little to be done; and adjourned farther to the 7th Day of *July* next. This being the Seaſon of the Year, when the *Indian* Traders uſually came to renew their Licences; two of them, newly arrived, were this Day with me; one of whom, that had laſt Year taken Licence from *Carolina*, doubting he was not well warranted from thence to trade in thoſe Towns therein named; now threw it up, and deſired a Licence might be granted him from *Georgia*.

23. *Friday.* Another Party of Gentlemen Volunteers paſſed this Day by *Thunderbolt*, on their Way to the General, which renewed

newed my Sorrow, in thinking how much more commendably my Son might have been ſo employed, than in what he has been buſied about at *London*, or elſewhere in *England*. Conferring with ſome *Indian* Traders, and adjuſting Matters with them, in order to obtain new Licences, or Permits, to continue their former for a Year longer; took up much of my Time this Day. Mr. *Jones* acquainted me, that he had taken a Reſolution (after conſidering well what I had ſhewn him, of Mr. *Verelſt*'s writing to me from the Truſt, in his Letter of the 25th of *February*) to go South, and wait on the General, and take his Advice, as well on that, as divers other Matters now depending: To which I had no Objection at preſent, but deſired him to be as expeditious in his Return as poſſible; for that he knew how daring and inſolent our good People at *Jenkins*'s were lately grown, even to the Caſting out Threats againſt all who oppoſed them. 1740. May

Saturday. Being diſappointed in my Expectation of ſending off a ſmall Packet for *England*, which I had got ready in a Hurry, dated the 14th Inſtant, and been forced to keep by me ever ſince I prepared it, directed to the Truſt's Secretary, Mr. *Martyn*; I now ſent it away by the *Carolina* Scout-Boat, *Thomas Biſwick* Patroon, who was bound to *Port-Royal*, where he 24.

engaged

1740. May 24. engaged to deliver it ſafely to Mr. *Wire*, whom I knew to be a conſtant Correſpondent there, with Mr. *Hopton* of *Charles-Town*, and would be careful in ſending it to him, together with a Letter accompanying it, that I wrote to Mr. *Hopton:* So very difficult was it now become, for me to carry on a regular Correſpondence any where; all Boats here, and hereabout, being impreſſed for the publick Service in the South. This Afternoon I had a full Inſtance given me, what the preſent Diſpoſition was of our miſchief-making Cabal: Mr. *Tailfer*, attended by *William Sterling*, and Landlord *Jenkins* himſelf, thought fit to call on me; the firſt as the principal Catechiſt to examine me; and the other two as able ſeſquipedarian Evidence, qualified in a tumultuous Manner to promote an Uproar; if they were of Opinion that I acted clandeſtinely, and kept back any Thing from them, that the Truſtees required me to communicate. Being therefore interrogated, what Letters and Orders I received from the Truſt in their laſt Packet; and whether, among other Things, I was not enjoined by them to lay divers Affairs relating to the preſent State of the Colony, in open Court before them, for their being enabled to give ſuch Anſwers to them as they thought proper? Without diſputing by what Authority they took upon

upon them to take ſuch Examination of me; I told them plainly, that whilſt I continued to ſerve the Truſt in my preſent Station, I ſhould never think myſelf ſubject to give any Anſwer at all, to what they demanded in the firſt Place, of knowing what Orders or Letters I received at any Time, but ſuch only as immediately required it: And as to what they more particularly inſiſted on, *viz.* my expoſing to publick View thoſe Affairs before-mentioned, I ſaid flatly, that I had received no ſuch Orders; wherein I conceived I departed not from ſtrict Truth: For upon reading over again and again thoſe Orders to myſelf, I cannot any Way put ſuch a Conſtruction upon them, as would oblige me to it; neither can it (I think) be juſtly ſuppoſed that the Truſtees meant to have it ſo; which would be an effectual Means of defeating the Purpoſe they intended by it, and would put it out of the Power of well-meaning Men to diſintangle Truth from Error, were theſe good People to have the Preference of all in ſcanning over thoſe Particulars, which more eſpecially the Truſtees expect ſhall be ſet in a true Light; towards which we are not to look for any Help from them. They had little more to ſay to me at preſent, viſibly much out of Humour; and ſo they left me, with this farther Admonition, that if I had no ſuch Orders from the

1740. May 24.

1740. May the Truſtees yet, moſt undoubtedly I ſhould very ſoon: By which I might underſtand, that their Intelligence came from good Hands, near the Fountain-Head.

25. *Whit-Sunday.* Mr. *Simms* went on in reading the Church Service, and two Sermons, Morning and Afternoon, upon the Reſurrection. Mr. *Jones* determining to ſet out to-morrow on his Expedition Southward; this Evening I committed thoſe Packets to his Care, which I received lately by *John Rea* from Mr. *Hopton*, who had them out of the *Ann and Marianne*, Capt. *Campbel*, from *England*; with which I wrote alſo to the General himſelf, encloſing divers Papers needful.

26. *Monday.* This Holiday-Time (a Word made uſe of by ſeveral of my Acquaintance) I was inclinable to comply with the Mode, and take a Day or two to myſelf: Wherefore I took a Ride to *Bewlie*, to ſee how they went on at that Plantation, where I had not been ſince the 1ſt of this Month: And upon my telling Mr. *Jones* that it was twelve Miles by Land, and at leaſt thirty by Water, and that the Boat in its Way to *Frederica* muſt paſs very near by us there, he was perſuaded to ſend the Boat round, and take Horſe with me to *Bewlie*, where he might refreſh himſelf: He did ſo, and the Boat came thither four or five Hours after us; from whence he proceeded in

in her as ſoon as the Tide would admit, which was not till near Night; and then, not willing to ride through the Woods ſo far alone home, I choſe to ſtay all Night where I was, having a very good Roof over my Head; and making a good Neſt of Palmeta Leaves, whereon was laid a Blanket, I laid myſelf upon that, and ſlept very heartily. 1740. May

Tueſday. No Want of Diverſion to employ my Time and Thoughts: It was a Pleaſure to ſee my Corn coming on, and other Things that were planted, very promiſing, the live Stock increaſing, and all hitherto in a hopeful Way: Beſides the Amuſement it gave me, in forming Schemes for many future Improvements in Gardening, and more curious Cultivation of Land, for the Production of Vines, Mulberries, Cotton, *&c.* of all which, I had provided a ſmall Nurſery, in the little five-Acre Lot near home. Mr. *Mercer*, and another Neighbour or two, who had Improvements in thoſe Parts, calling on me in the Afternoon, we travelled home together, and got to Town in very good Time in the Evening. 27.

Wedneſday. No Appearance of any Thing at preſent to diſturb our Quiet; every body followed his own Buſineſs; and all I had to obſerve was, that Mr. *Bradley*'s Door being locked up, it was not doubted 28.

1740. May 28. but he was gone off to *Carolina*, where he had been for a good while paſt providing for a Retreat; even before thoſe Orders came from the Truſt, requiring him to give good Security, for his not going out of the Province, till his Accompts were made up: Which the Magiſtrates demanding of him, and often putting him in Mind of, being unwilling (if poſſibly it could be avoided) to commit him to Priſon; and plainly ſeeing, that he could find not one Man to appear for him (ſuch was the Opinion that every body had of him) they indulged him, upon making large Promiſes, and giving his Parole of Honour, to appear when required, ſo far as to enjoy his Liberty of walking the Streets, and employing himſelf about his Accompts, *&c.* but upon his aſking ſeveral Times for a Permit to take a Boat (which is ſtrictly expected from every body) and that being not granted him, he now took Leave without aſking, and went off clandeſtinely by ſome back Way. It has been ſufficiently proved, that had he ſtaid here ever ſo long, he would have done nothing towards clearing up any Doubts, or Objections, that might be made, but make new Obſtacles continually: Wherefore there remained no other Method of going on, in Behalf of the Truſt, but to ſtate it as well as it could be done, from his own Accompt delivered in, com-

comparing it with the Store Books, and leaving proper Room for him (if he thought fit) to make any Remarks of his own, upon any Part where he thought himſelf aggrieved. This being ſo done, and ready to receive any ſuch Remarks of his, I am apt to think he found it pinch too cloſe for him to evade coming to an Iſſue; wherefore he left it upon our Hands, as not worth his farther Care, or Notice.— A Man of ſuch a finiſhed Character, that he moſt eminently merits a due Appellation! 1740. May

Thurſday. Nothing ſtirring that was new, and no Intelligence from the Camp for a little while paſt; it was Time to expect ſome framed at home would be ſent out, and paſs currently; which had often ſucceeded to the Wiſh of the Publiſhers, whoſe principal Buſineſs it was, to ſpread Terrors, that might diſcourage weak People, and keep them under continual Alarm: No leſs now than four or five of our People who were gone to War, were ſaid to be killed by the Enemy, who lay in Ambuſh for them; but where or when, none could tell: Nevertheleſs the Report went about ſo ſtrongly, that ſome good Wives bewailed the Loſs of their Huſbands with Tears; and I found it no eaſy Matter to undeceive them preſently, till the firſt Flaſh of the Report was pretty well paſt, 29.

1740. May and I found convincing Arguments to ſhew them there was no Truth in all they heard, but it was contrived with only a wicked Deſign, *&c.* which at length pacifying *them*, I was not well contented myſelf, to ſee three or four audacious Perſons daily going on *impunè*, to diſturb the Minds of the People, which they made their Paſtime and Delight: But if I can luckily fix upon one of them, with good Proof, to be the Author of ſpreading ſuch falſe News, I ſhall not doubt but the Magiſtrates will find Law ſufficient to reſtrain them for the future, as well as give them their Demerits for what is paſt.

30. *Friday.* Nothing occurred of any Moment, but every body wiſhed for ſome Intelligence what was doing in the South, to clear up thoſe Doubts which had for ſome Days paſt ariſen among us, by the Means before-mentioned, which I could find no Grounds for.

31. *Saturday.* The Time was now come, when Truth muſt appear, by the Arrival of a Perſon who came immediately from the Camp *(William Ewen)* who had formerly been a Servant in the Stores, and now came away in haſte from Mr. *Houſton*, whoſe Employment was to deliver out Proviſions to the General's Regiment; ſo that he brought no Letters from the General, but made Report, on his own Knowledge,

in Subſtance as follows, *viz.* That the General was broke up from the late Camp on the Main, oppoſite to the Iſland St. *George*, and advanced nearer the Enemy: That upon receiving Intelligence there was a large Cow-Pen not far off, which had more than a thouſand Cattle belonging to it, ſuppoſed to be the King of *Spain*'s own, for the Uſe of the Gariſon of *Auguſtin*, and defended by a Fort called St. *Diego*; his Excellence reſolved to take that in, and accordingly marched to attack it, making uſe of a little Stratagem, as well as Force: Which was, by appointing three or four Drums together beating here and there in divers Places in the Woods, and now and then a few Men appearing ſuddenly, and then withdrawing out of Sight again; which the Enemy in the Fort were ſo confounded at, not doubting but they were inveſted by a greater Number of Troops than we really had, they made but a feint Oppoſition, by firing a few Guns over our Mens Heads (which whether ſo intended or not, is uncertain) and upon being ſummoned to ſurrender, they did not long heſitate ere they did ſo, on Condition of being treated as Priſoners of War, and (what they principally inſiſted on) not to be delivered into the Hands of the *Indians* with us; which was granted; and they were in Number forty-ſix *Spaniards*, and four Negroes,

1740. May 31.

1740. May 31. groes, moſt of whom were ſent on board our Men of War, only the Commander had his Liberty to walk to and fro in the Camp, on his Parole given to the General; and one other, ſaid to be a Gunner, and upon good Examination found to be an expert one, upon his Requeſt to take on in our Service, the General readily accepted of him; and from what private Intelligence he got of him, ſhews him great Countenance; a very agreeable Inſtrument at this Seaſon. The Camp is now ſaid to be within thirteen Miles of *Auguſtin*, and the General has been ſeveral Times to view it, at a very little Diſtance: Great Numbers of Boats of all Kinds and Sizes lie ready for any Service, within the Mouth of the River St. *Juan*, and two Men of War (the *Phœnix* and *Flamborough)* without all, to protect them; ſome being employed in fetching Mortars, Bombs, and other Stores of Ammunition to the Camp, from *Frederica*, and where elſe they had been landed: Several other Men of War are conſtantly cruiſing, to prevent any one getting into, or coming out of *Auguſtin*; wherefore it is preſumed we ſhall now ſoon hear of the Town's being actually beſieged, which all our Troops are briſk and intent upon: In the mean Time, after ſuch a prodigious Seizure of Cattle, our People eat roaſt Beef in Plenty, and are likely to do

ſo

ſo a while to come, as well as mount *Spaniſh* Horſes, which they alſo took great Numbers of. 1740.

Sunday. All Fears being now blown once more over, ſuch as were ſo diſpoſed, went quietly to Church, to hear the Prayers read by Mr. *Simms*, and two Sermons, as uſual. June 1.

Monday. Advice being brought me by *Jacob Morris*, an *Indian* Trader among the *Cherokees*, who arrived late laſt Night, that he had brought down with him out of that Nation twelve Men, whom he had left at Mr. *Matthews*'s, and deſired I would ſend a Conveyance for them hither; I aſſured him no Delay in the Service ſhould be imputed to me, which was in my Power to prevent: But the great Difficulties we lay under for want of Boats here, which were moſtly employed already in the South, muſt unavoidably check ſuch Expedition in many Caſes, as otherwiſe we ſhould readily make: Soon after, we made Shift to get a Boat however, to go up thither, large enough to bring them all down with the next Tide. In the Afternoon I received Letters from Lieutenant *Willy*, in the *Upper Creeks*, and Mr. *Wigan*, a Trader in the *Lower Creeks*, both ſetting forth divers Artifices uſed by the *French* Emiſſaries to create a cold Indifference in that Nation towards us: Whereof Notice has before been taken (*vide May* 2, 3 and 7.) but as *Ma-* 2.

1740. June *latchie* was not arrived, who was every Day expected, when theſe Letters were wrote that I now received; we expect his Preſence among them, on his Return, will alter the Face of Affairs there very ſoon. In the Evening the Boat came down with thoſe *Indians* from *Matthews*'s, whom I received in the accuſtomed Manner of greeting, went with them to the Houſe provided for them, and took Care that they had Proviſions of Meat, Drink, Pipes and Tobacco, to their Content, after the Rate which had always been allowed.

3. *Tueſday.* A Riot happening lately in the *Lower Creek* Nation, by ſeveral unlicenſed Traders inſulting ſome of thoſe legally appointed, wounding, aſſaulting, and binding two or three, and threatning immediate Death to them: For which Violence, Endeavours have been uſed to ſeize the Offenders, but hitherto only two of them have been laid hold on; one of whom was catcht at *Frederica*, or near it, whoſe Deſerts the General will beſt judge of: Another, ſince taken up in the Nations, was now brought down a Priſoner here, whom the Magiſtrates have taken in hand; and finding that he was not a Fomenter of the Miſchief, but came at the latter End of the Fray, they thought fit to accept of Bail for his Appearance at our next Court, he offering ſuch as was unexceptionable.

tionable. Two or three others, the moſt culpable, are yet ſought after, and it is hoped, through Mr. *Kent*'s Diligence at Fort *Auguſta*, they will be apprehended in a little Time. My immediate Care at preſent, was to haſten away thoſe few *Indians* that came laſt Night; wherein I would not loſe an Hour willingly: But we were now left in ſuch a low State, without almoſt any Boats or Hands to row them, all our Strength on the Water being employed in the South, that it was not inſtantly in my Power to ſend away this Handful of People after them; but I would leave no Stone unturned, till ſome Expedient or other might be found, to accompliſh my Purpoſe. Mr. *Williamſon*, newly arrived from *Charles-Town*, called on me in the Form of a Viſit; and falling of courſe into ſome Talk of what paſſed ſeveral Months ſince, relating to the Recorderſhip, *&c.* I aſked him, whether or no at that Time he did not tell me, in caſe he had been in my Place, he muſt have acted as I did? which he now confeſſed; but told me the Caſe was ſince altered, by Mr. *Chriſtie*'s going off: To which I replied, that the whole Affair having at that Time been laid before the honourable Truſtees, I could not perſuade myſelf to think, it would become me, to take the leaſt Step farther in it, till I received their Orders fully thereon: And

1740. June 3.

it

1740. June it was well known, that the utmoſt Extent of my Office, was to be a Vehicle of their Commands, which ſome People fancied the Title of, the Truſts Letter-Carrier, was a ſynonymous Term for *(vide May* 6.) We parted in good Humour; and in the next Place I was to expect what an extraordinary Council held at *Jenkins*'s would produce.

4. *Wedneſday*. Having Intelligence, that Capt. *Davis* was come into the River at *Tybee*, after much Time loſt at *Charles-Town*, his Men being impreſſed into the Men of War, and himſelf engaged in much Controverſy at Law, which put a full End now to any farther Thoughts about Privateering: He therefore purpoſed to make the beſt of his Way to the General in the South, hoping, that as he had ſhewn him many Favours, he would receive him kindly, and admit the Sloop he had with him into the publick Service, among ſo many others employed. This I thought a providential Piece of good News for us, whereby it was hoped we might get theſe *Indians* off our Hands, which we were at ſo much Loſs about before; and therefore I wrote a Letter immediately to the Captain, and ſent it by the ſame Perſon who came up, and brought us this News, (which was *Eliſha Foſter*, one of our Freeholders, that ſailed with him in ſome Office) deſiring that we might have the Benefit

Benefit of ſuch a Conveyance, which would be ſhewing a ready Diſpoſition to promote the Service, and making a Compliment to the General, which without Doubt he would take kindly; and that they ſhould be no Expence to him, for they ſhould be fully victualled from hence. This I conceived was ſo reaſonable a Requeſt, that I aſſured myſelf it could not be refuſed; but muſt wait for his Anſwer. In the mean while, the Devil had been hard at Work in finding out freſh Means to diſturb Peoples Minds, with Rumours of ſtrange Things we were to ſee very ſoon, namely, that his Majeſty being made ſenſible of the Hardſhips which his Subjects of this Colony labour'd under, he was determined to put an End to the Truſt, and would eſtabliſh ſuch Rules, and Forms, as he ſaw proper to be obſerved, under a new Governor, whom he would appoint. Howſoever ridiculous this muſt appear to Men of good Underſtanding, yet there were not wanting ſome honeſt Men of the common Rank, who in a Sort of Conſternation came to be informed of the Truth of what they had heard, expecting I would tell them *all the Truth*; but when they found I had nothing to ſay to it, but laughed at them, for ſuffering themſelves to be ſo eaſily impoſed on, when they ſo well knew from whence theſe vile Stories ſo frequently

1740. June 4.

1740. June frequently ſprang; they went away with equal Shame in themſelves, as Indignation at the Authors, whom they beſtowed their Curſes upon bitterly. This is looked upon by many People as the utmoſt Stretch of Politicks our Wiſeacres of the Club have attempted, vain as it is, but deſigned to try how well it would reliſh among us. Whether or not Mr. *Williamſon*'s Preſence added any Weight to their Deliberations, does not appear to us without; but undoubtedly they are all big with the Expectation of ſomething that is to come to paſs (very ſoon, as they give out.)

5. *Thurſday.* The Relict of *John Weſt*, a while ſince deceaſed, died this Morning, after a ſhort Illneſs; but whether ſhe was a Widow or Wife, many People doubted; though ſhe cohabited with Mr. *William Kellaway*, a Trader and Freeholder in this Town; and it was ſaid they were privately married by the *French* Miniſter at *Puryſburgh*, which ſome queſtioned the Truth of. Mr. *Whitfield*, to the Surprize of moſt People, came to Town in a Boat from *Tybee*, where he left his Sloop that he ſailed in from *Penſilvania*, and was a Month or two ſooner than expected. Upon my making him a Viſit in the Afternoon, to bid him welcome; he told me, that he had collected upwards of 500 *l.* Sterling for the Uſe of the Orphan-Houſe, on his preaching

ing ſeveral Sermons, notwithſtanding the Oppoſition he met with: Whereat obſerving it was what I ſeemed to take particular Notice of; he farther added, that he ſhould not think himſelf a Preacher of the Goſpel, unleſs he met with Oppoſers: I underſtood he had travelled by Land to *New-York* from *Philadelphia*, and back again; after diſpatching his Friend, Mr. *Seward*, firſt to *Old-England*, before he himſelf viſited the *New*; which he told me was in his Intention the latter End of this Summer, after he had tarried a while here. His Sloop, that he came in, was fully loaden with Proviſions of all Sorts, for Food and Cloathing, and ten Paſſengers (Men and Women) of divers Trades, uſeful to his Purpoſe, *viz.* Taylor, Shoemaker, Glazier, *&c.* In the Evening (after pauſing and heſitating a while) he buried the Corpſe that died this Morning; but after it was in the Ground, and the Service over, he made a Sort of Declamation againſt a looſe and debauched Life and Converſation; not ſparing the Deceaſed, as one who had given publick Scandal to good People, by her Deportment for ſome Time paſt: Mr. *Kellaway*, her ſuppoſed Huſband, being at preſent attending the General, as an Interpreter of the *Spaniſh* Language, which he is a good Maſter

1740. June 5.

1740. Maſter of, having lived among them ſeveral Years in Time paſt.

June 6. *Friday.* This Morning early *Peter Emery*, with his Boat, arrived from *Charles-Town*, to whom Mr. *Hopton* had committed the Care of the following Particulars, which he wrote me came by the *Charles*, Capt. *Haramond*, on *Sunday* the 1ſt Inſtant, and were now delivered to me, *viz.* a large Box directed to the General, and a Letter with it for him; a Box of a leſs Size directed to me, wherein were Blank Sola Bills to the Value of 1000*l.* Sterling; and with it divers Letters for Meſſieurs *Jones*, *Parker*, *Fallowfield*, *Chriſtie*, *Bolzius*, &c. and among others, one for me from Mr. *Verelſt*, importing the Orders and Directions of the Truſt to be obſerved by me: Withal a new Conſtitution, appointing Mr. *Parker* firſt Bailiff, and revoking that which was formerly ſent Mr. *Chriſtie:* Alſo a Conſtitution appointing *John Pye* to officiate as Recorder, during the Suſpenſion of *Thomas Chriſtie*; and Revocation of Mr. *Williamſon* from that Office: Moreover, a Grant of three hundred Acres of Land to the Rev. Mr. *M^c^Leod*, Miniſter of *Darien*, for the Benefit of him and his Succeſſors, dated *October* 10, 1739, together with a Counterpart for him to execute, *&c.* I loſt no Time in delivering out the Letters, whereat I obſerved ſome People appeared as if thunder-

thunder-ſtruck, finding themſelves ſo defeated in their Deſigns: For it was evident beyond Contradiction, that had the Scheme ſucceeded, which ſome few had formed in their Imaginations, the whole Determination of all Matters would have reſted in the Will of our political Club, who knew how to lead two of thoſe as they pleaſed, who they expected would ſit on the Bench of Juſtice; Mr. *Fallowfield* by too often frequenting that Company, imbibing many Notions tending to create much Diſturbance in this Place, and had of late ſhewn himſelf a Creature of theirs, whom he adviſed with on all Occaſions: But I am unwilling to ſay more of that now, hoping he will ſee his Error, when he finds it in vain to ſet himſelf in Oppoſition to two of his Brethren; either of whom he is in no Degree comparable with, in Underſtanding or Judgment: And if Mr. *Williamſon*'s being among us for ſo many Days paſt, was owing to an Opinion that about this Time the Truſtees Orders would come for eſtabliſhing ſuch a Court of Juſtice, as he and a few others looked for; I ſaw no Obſtacle now to his returning when he pleaſed to *Carolina*, till he ſaw Matters go more to his Liking. As to myſelf, nothing could be of equal Comfort to me, under my preſent Anxiety of Mind, with the kind and tender Regard which Mr. *Verelſt*

1740. June 6.

1740. *relſt* wrote me the honourable Truſtees expreſſed on that Occaſion.

June 7. *Saturday.* Having received a Letter from Capt. *Davis*, readily conſenting to what I aſked of him a Day or two ſince, relating to his Conveyance of thoſe *Indians* to the South, that were lately come hither, I ſent them off this Day in a ſmall Sloop, to be put by her on board the Captain at *Tybee*, namely, eleven *Cherokee Indians*, and nine *Chicaſſaws*, together with their Conductors, and a few other white Men that accompanied them out of their Nations, making in all about thirty Men: And with them I ſent the Box that I had newly received for the General; as alſo the Letter that came with it; together with Letters, and various Diſpatches to his Excellence, from myſelf, and others in theſe Parts; all which I charged Mr. *George Currie* with the Care of, whom I always had looked upon as a ſedate, ſober Perſon, to be confided in: Which is more than I can ſay of many of our *Indian* Traders, that are too much addicted to a looſe Way of Living. This Afternoon I entertained myſelf by looking into my little Plantation and Nurſery near the Town, where I ſpent a few Hours; which, though ſo nigh, was more than I could find Leiſure to do for a Fortnight paſt.

Sunday.

Sunday. Mr. *Whitfield* appeared to be returned to his Miniſtry here, with double Vigour; and after reading the Common Prayer, what he delivered *extempore*, as well in Prayer as Sermon, ſeemed to be with uncommon Vociferation and Waſte of Spirits; enforcing the Doctrine of original Sin, and the Neceſſity of a Regeneration, Converſion, and Juſtification by Faith in Chriſt, *&c.* otherwiſe Hell was ready to receive us. It matters little how far I thought all he ſaid was ſound Divinity; but unleſs he abates ſome of his Threats to keep Heaven Gates ſhut, againſt all whom he ſhall think unworthy to enter in, I fear the Conſequence will be bad. 1740. June 8.

Monday, } The violent Heat of Wea- 9.
Tueſday. } ther more than ordinary, 10.
which People felt for a few Days paſt, made the moſt Hardy ſubmit to it, and leſſen their Labour: And I found ſuch Influence from it on my own Spirits, that every Thing I attempted becoming irkſome, I acquieſced in an indolent State, as others did, waiting a little refreſhing Change of Air: My Thoughts, however, were not aſleep, but ſufficiently buſied about thoſe weighty Matters, which thoſe Letters contained, lately ſent me from the Truſt; and I began now with ſome Impatience, to look for Mr. *Jones*'s Return from the General, after more than a Fortnight's Ab-

1740. June ſence, that we might join in our Endeavours, to anſwer what was required. By a Boat arrived this Day *(Tueſday)* from *Port-Royal*, we learnt, that Capt. *Davis*'s Sloop at *Tybee*, with the *Indians* on board, was not yet ſailed thence; but the Captain told him he intended to put to Sea this ſame Night; whereat I began to grow a little uneaſy, wiſhing him gone.

11. *Wedneſday.* This Day we had Intelligence again of another Riſing of the Negroes in *Carolina*, which, unleſs ſoon ſuppreſſed, has the Appearance of greater Danger than any of the former; foraſmuch as this broke out near *Charles-Town* itſelf, about *Aſhley* River, *Dorcheſter*, and the circumjacent Parts, where at leaſt a hundred and fifty were got together in Defiance: But as they were yet unprovided with Arms, and there was no Corn on the Ground ripe, for their Subſiſtance, it was hoped they would quickly be diſperſed: And the Country being all alarmed and in Purſuit of them, they had already taken about fifty, whom they were daily hanging, ten in a Day. Such dreadful Work, it is to be feared, we may hear more of in Time, in caſe they come to breaking open Stores to find Arms, as they did the laſt Year; and are able to keep the Field, with Plenty of Corn and Potatoes every where; and above all, if it is conſidered,

how vaſtly diſproportionate the Number of white Men is to theirs: So that at beſt, the Inhabitants cannot live without perpetually guarding their own Safety, now become ſo precarious. What Inference may be drawn from hence, with relation to this Colony, will be beſt done by the honourable Perſons who make the Welfare of *Georgia* their Study. I had this Afternoon the Pleaſure of ſeeing a Beginning made, of a Work long wiſhed for, *viz.* building a Church at this Town, a few Load of Stones being brought, and laid down in the Place where it is intended to ſtand. 1740. June

Thurſday. This Day began with the melancholy News of more Duelling, at the Camp in the South, and the fatal Conſequence of it. Enſign *Tolſon*, of Capt. *Norbury*'s Company, having a Quarrel with Mr. *Eyles*, a Surgeon in the Army, they fought; and the latter was killed on the Spot; a Man of very good Skill in his Profeſſion, and well eſteemed. Not many Days after, *Peter Grant*, lately of this Town, and a Freeholder, afterwards made Naval Officer at *Frederica* by the General, and ſince changing, to be a Cadet in the Army; having a Quarrel with one Mr. *Shenton*, a Cadet likewiſe; which Mr. *Shenton* endeavoured (as far as he well could) to avoid deciding by the Sword; but the other admitting of no Terms of Reconciliation, *ib.*

1740. June they fought, and the Aggreſſor dropt dead. Theſe Tidings came by a ſmall Boat, on its Way from the Camp to *Charles-Town*, which ſtopt and left it at one of our Out-Plantations; and is looked on with great Pity: It is not very long ſince Enſign *Leman*, in a Rencounter, being wounded in his Leg, and a Mortification enſuing, he was forced to ſuffer an Amputation, and ſupply its Place with a wooden one. Surely our Enemies will hear this with Pleaſure. After three or four Days Detention at *Tybee*, by contrary Winds, I was now adviſed, by a Boat from thence, that Capt. *Davis*, with the *Indians* lately taken by him on board his Sloop, ſailed Yeſterday to the South; which I was very glad to hear. In the Evening Mr. *Jones* arrived from thence, having been about ſeventeen Days on this Expedition.

13. *Friday.* In frequent Conference with Mr. *Jones*, I learnt the General's Opinion in divers of thoſe Matters which had been laid before him, for our better Conduct; and withal, his Excellency's near Approach to the Fortreſs of *Auguſtin*; wherein various Conjectures were made, whether they ſhould meet with an obſtinate Defence, or the contrary; but a very little Time now, would let us ſee the Event, which every good Man had much at Heart. It was obſervable, that ſince the Anſwers I had

had given to thoſe Queſtions, demanded of me on the 24th *ult.* thoſe Examiners, or ſome of the ſame Fraternity, were often on Horſeback, taking a Progreſs through moſt of the Plantations, as well near, as more remote, looking on themſelves as Surveyors, and Inſpectors, appointed ſo to do; and it was not improbable, that their Correſpondents in *England* had ſo adviſed them, in order to ſee how well the different Reports would agree, which muſt be expected from hence hereafter; when without Doubt no Pains would be wanting in them, to accumulate Abundance of Grievances, to obviate any Poſitions, or Sentiments offered, by Perſons who retain a juſt Opinion of the impartial Proceedings of the honourable Truſtees. 1740. June

Saturday. A Sloop from *New-York* (—— *Tingley* Maſter) arrived with ſundry Sorts of Proviſions for Sale; but no Beef, or Pork; which being greatly wanted, we were much diſappointed in our Expectations, not knowing which Way to come at any this Summer Seaſon: Wherefore, after ſome few Things of leaſt Value were taken off his Hands, he deſigned to proceed with the Bulk of his Loading to the Army in the South, conſiſting of Flour, Rice, Biſcuit, ſtrong Beer, Wine, *&c.* which would be welcome there, to make uſe of with their choice Food, that they were lately 14.

1740. June ſo happily ſupplied with at St. *Diego* from the *Spaniards* (much Good may it do them.) As for us here, though it is too early yet to meet with Beef that is thorough fat; we are obliged for Subſiſtance to kill now and then a Steer, perhaps once in ten Days, which we debet ourſelves with as Caſh, and ſell out, to the People who are able to pay for it, in ſmall Pieces, for immediate Uſe; otherwiſe it will corrupt, Salt not availing to cure during theſe Heats. I cannot paſs over this, without offering my poor Opinion humbly thereon to the honourable Truſtees (as I think I have done ſome Time formerly) that if they would pleaſe at a proper Seaſon in the Winter, or early in the Spring, to ſend us a Veſſel of pretty good Burden, laden in *Ireland* with good Beef, ſome Tallow, a little Butter, and nothing elſe; it would be gladly received, and accounted for as Caſh, and put us out of all Anxiety about Meat, which we always ſuffer at this Time of Year, for about four or five Months, when it is not to be had for Money by the moſt induſtrious among us, otherwiſe than as I have ſaid.

15. *Sunday.* Mr. *Whitfield* performed the Divine Service, with ſuch a devout Emotion of Spirit, as nobody could juſtly blame him for: After which he dwelt a while on *extempore* Prayer (as uſual;) and in his Preach-

Preaching, I was very glad to obſerve him more temperate in his Utterance, than ſometimes he appears: Nor did I think his Reaſoning a Jot the leſs enforcing, without Ranting. 1740. June

Monday. Another Set-out this Morning, with two or three of our new-appointed Inſpectors from *Jenkins*'s, to make what Obſervations they thought proper, and report to their Principals, how they found Matters at their Return: Which without Doubt they meant to apply to a right Uſe, for perfecting the Work of Reformation, which they had ſo long been labouring in, for the Good of the Colony. Late in the Evening Mr. *Whitfield* took Boat up the River, to make a Viſit at *Ebenezer*, accompanied by Mr. *Groneau*, one of the Miniſters there, who was come hither to wait on him. I could not find any Thing elſe all this Day to make Remark of. 16.

Tueſday. The Weather happening to be rainy, was a little Baulk to our Inſpectors, who thought it beſt to repoſe themſelves at Mr. *Fallowfield*'s Plantation theſe two Days; where it may be preſumed they found Matter in Diſcourſe, to make farther Improvement on in due Seaſon: All we could know of their Proceedings was, that they returned home again this Afternoon, as wiſe as they went. Spending an Hour or two with Mr. *Jones* at the Store (as I frequently 17.

1740. June 17. uſe to do) he told me Mr. *Whitfield* had made him a Viſit there the Day before, complaining to him, that he thought himſelf hardly uſed by him (Mr. *Jones)* during the Time of his Abſence in the Northern Provinces; by taking away one of the Orphans out of his Houſe, in an authoritative Manner, whereas he could have no ſuch Authority; which might in Effect deſtroy the Deed of the Truſt to him. Mr. *Jones* alledged the General's poſitive Orders to him, to do what he did: But that availed little with Mr. *Whitfield*, who ſaid he was reſolved to write thereupon to the Truſt. Wherefore, being no Party myſelf in this Affair, it may not be amiſs to recollect what I remember about it.——— *Mellidge*, a Freeholder here, and one of the firſt forty, at his Death left ſeveral Orphans, whom the General (then only Mr. *Ogletborpe)* ſhewed particular Marks of his Favour to, for their Father's Sake, whom he looked on as a valuable Man; and in the Proceſs of a few Years, the eldeſt Boy proving to be an active, diligent, and well-grown Youth, he was become ſerviceable, in many Caſes, to his good Patron, and employed by him variouſly, as Occaſion required: The eldeſt Siſter began now likewiſe to be capable of managing the Houſe at home, and guiding the young Family: Whereupon the General

neral laſt Spring encouraged them to begin, and try what they could do about Planting, intending ſeemingly thereby to ſhew, what might be expected from Boys, if encouraged, and well looked after. About that Time it happened, that Mr. *Whitfield* came, with the Power which the Truſt had granted him, for taking the Orphans under his Care; among whom the Younger of theſe two Brothers *(Mellidge)* was taken by him for one, leaving the Elder at home; who complained, that his Brother being taken from them at this Time, when he could be of ſo much Uſe; it would be a Means of breaking up a Family that were now come to the Point of ſhifting for themſelves: Which agreeing exactly with the General's Thoughts (then at *Frederica)* he ſent Orders to Mr. *Jones*, to take the young Lad home to the Family, which now would be no Charge to the Publick: And on that Occaſion was pleaſed to write his Sentiments relating to the Orphans; which (as I remember) I encloſed Copy of to Mr. *Verelſt*, for the Peruſal of the Truſt; whoſe Opinion we ſhall now hope for, upon Mr. *Whitfield*'s laying this Caſe before them. 1740. June

Wedneſday. A profound Quiet; and nothing ſtirring all Day worth taking Notice of. 18.

Thurſday.

1740. June 19. *Thurſday.* After having at ſundry Times conferred with ſome Perſons, whom I thought I could repoſe the greateſt Confidence in, relating to what the Truſt had been pleaſed to impart to me, of the Parliament being appealed to, by ſome of our Malecontents, who ſought all Ways to give them Trouble: And by Degrees informing ſuch as I knew to be open-hearted, well-meaning People, what Means the honourable Truſtees propoſed, to defeat their malicious and baſe Deſigns, namely, by our atteſting the Truth, of what we knew to be ſuch, in ſeveral Articles they had ordered to be laid before us: (In the doing whereof it behoved me to act with the utmoſt Caution, leſt a *Judas* ſhould be found among us) I thought as little Time as poſſible ſhould be loſt in reducing ſome of our Thoughts into Writing: For which Purpoſe I conceived, that three or four at a Time meeting, would be ſufficient; who were ſtedfaſt to the Truth, and utterly averſe to all ſuch Clamour as they ſaw made of late; which they rightly apprehended muſt produce great Miſchief, if ſuffered to go on: Thus in ſome Meaſure prepared, I reſolved, in a Day or two more, to make a Beginning, and try whether or not we could produce ſomewhat towards the Support of Truth, at leaſt as valid as what our woful Patriots brought forth at *Jenkins*'s, to to diſguiſe it. Mr. *Williamſon*'s Stay ſo long among us here, gave Occaſion for various Reports (now in other Folks Turn) to fly about, and aſſign ſome Cauſe for it, right or wrong: Some ſaid he was ſending for his Wife to come to him; from whence others concluded, that *Charles-Town* was too hot for him —— at this Seaſon; and ſuch Stories ſtill improving as they go, a great many Things were talked of to his Diſcredit; which, without ſure Grounds, I would not, in common Charity, be the Reporter of; Time will diſcover greater Myſteries than this. 1740. June

Friday. The *New-York* Sloop that arrived here laſt *Saturday*, after diſpoſing of a few ſmall Wares, which were of little Value; and intending to ſail for the South this Day, I wrote by her to the General, *&c.* giving my Letters in Charge to Mr. *Minis*, a *Jew* Freeholder of this Town, to whom the Loading was conſigned. Two or three *Indian* Traders, wanting to renew their Licences, and pretty much fluſtered in Drink (which is pretty common among them) took up more of my Time this Day with their Impertinence, than I could well afford. 20.

Saturday. To purſue my Deſign of *Thurſday* laſt, with as little Delay as poſſible; I now called to my Aſſiſtance three ſuch as I had no Doubt of their Qualifications 21.

1740. June 21. tions or Good-will, to promote that neceſſary Piece of Service, namely, Meſſieurs *Parker* and *Jones*, firſt and third Bailiffs, and *Mercer*, firſt Conſtable: When we ſpent a few Hours together, in an hearty Concurrence of Opinion on what was under our Conſideration; which we hoped, in due Time, to reduce into ſuch Form, as we might be able to juſtify to every Perſon unprejudiced, who had a real Diſpoſition to maintain Truth: And at parting we reſolved to meet again, and communicate our Thoughts to each other, as often as conveniently might be. Mr. *Jones* afterwards, in Diſcourſe on various other Matters betwixt ourſelves, ſhewed a great Diſlike of ſeveral of Mr. *Whitfield*'s late Proceedings; more eſpecially with Regard to calling his Authority in Queſtion, concerning what he did lately about young *Mellidge* (which I took Notice of on *Tueſday* laſt) and Mr. *Whitfield*'s having wrote a Letter to the Truſt thereon, complaining of Mr. *Jones*, without acquainting him that he intended ſo to do, before their late Conference on that Affair; which Mr. *Jones* reſented very much; and I plainly found, by his warm Expreſſions, it was likely to come to an open Rupture between them: One, on all Appearance, ſetting little Value on any Power, either eccleſiaſtical or civil, which claimed a Superiority over

over him; and the other, not much heeding what Obedience was paid to Church Government, reſolved not to abate one Iota of what he thought due to the Civil Magiſtrate. 1740. June

Sunday. Mr. *Whitfield* ſtuck cloſely to his Vocation, in praying and preaching *extempore*, as was his Cuſtom, after the appointed Service was firſt read: But the Surplice for ſome Time paſt ſeemed to be laid aſide as uſeleſs. The Morning Service was on one of the Beatitudes, concerning hungring and thirſting after Righteouſneſs; which he treated of to very good Purpoſe a while; till at length he had wound himſelf up into one of his ordinary Rhapſodies, touching a New Birth, Conviction, Converſion, Free Grace, Juſtification by Faith, *&c.* which, be the Subject what it would, all his Diſcourſes terminated in: And now he told us plainly, that unleſs we were ſo far advanced in the Knowledge of Chriſt, as to have a full Aſſurance that we felt the Holy Spirit move within us, we were as uncapable of hungring and thirſting after Righteouſneſs, as the Stones in a Wall; without which, nevertheleſs, we were all in a reprobate State, *&c. &c.* In the Afternoon he took St. *Paul*'s Words to *Timothy*, in his 2d Epiſtle, 3d Chapter, and 12th Verſe, for his Subject: Wherein addreſſing himſelf to thoſe few particularly, 22.

who

1740. June who were his ſtrickeſt Diſciples, and ſcarcely allowed themſelves to converſe with any that had not found the Spirit yet upon them, he ſhewed what the Word Perſecution imported in its full Latitude; and that from the Apoſtle's aſſerting, all who will live holy muſt ſuffer Perſecution, it was plainly begun already, in oppoſing the Doctrine he taught, and ridiculing the converted Saints, who endeavoured to live up to it: Bidding *them* be of good Cheer, to ſtand faſt together as Brethren: And as for himſelf, he was expecting all cruel Treatment from his Adverſaries, who were ſet on by the Devil; all which he was ready to undergo. This Point he had lightly touched on, twice or thrice before; but now he was grown more vehement; which occaſioned ſome Talk after Church was over, ſeveral Conſtructions being put upon it; and among others, Mr. *Jones* would needs have it, that *he* was one pointed at, next under the General himſelf.

23. *Monday*. From the Time of my Arrival here in the Truſt's Service, on *November* 1, 1737, I had divers Times notified the Danger I apprehended from the Decay of the Sea-Mark at *Tybee*, leſt it ſhould come to Ruin for Want of timely Care to prevent it, which would bring a Reproach from all the trading People in theſe Parts, for ſo ſhameful a Neglect, and alſo might prove

prove of very bad Conſequence to many: But all I could ſay upon it, proved of no Effect, ſome publick Work or other ſtill taking Place, as more immediately needful; inſomuch that not any Survey had been taken of the Condition it was in; till now, upon the Truſt's making particular Mention of it, in their late Letter; and thereupon my urging it again, it was agreed by Mr. *Jones* and me to go down this Day; as we did; and taking ſufficient Workmen with us, who were competent Judges of the State it was in; it was very grievous to me to hear every one of them declare, that it was not in the Power of Man now to repair it, it was ſo far gone to Ruin: And it would hardly have been thought credible by me, what I now ſaw myſelf, how greatly the Deſtruction of it was increaſed, ſince the laſt Time I ſaw it, which was in *October* laſt, when I conceived it might have been ſomewhat holpen; and ſo I reported it at my Return, after going on board Capt. *Thompſon*, at that Time there: But every Part, both of the upper and lower Work, was now ſo periſhed, and all the Joints become ſo rotten, that it was rather to be admired it yet ſtood as it did, many of the Braces frequently dropping; and it muſt now be expected, as ſoon as the ſtrong North-Weſt Winds come, which we uſually look for in

1740. June 23.

1740. in Autumn, it muſt tumble all together.
June Under theſe melancholy Apprehenſions we returned home.

24. *Tueſday.* The Heat of the Weather abating, which had confined me at home all Day; towards Evening, in my Walk to catch a little Breeze of Air, I accidentally met Mr. *Williamſon*, who ſoon found ſomething to ſay to me; and ſo we fell into Diſcourſe from one Thing to another; wherein he took Pains (as I thought) to make me believe, how much better Opinion he had of *Georgia*, where he once lived, than *Carolina*, where the Buſineſs he was in obliged him at preſent to be reſident: Then he inveighed againſt the Vanity of the Inhabitants, and the inveterate Ill-will they almoſt in general bore to this Colony; which they would talk of with great Contempt, though at the ſame Time they were under ſtrong Apprehenſions, that in a few Years it would outdo them in Trade and Manufactures too, who in ſuch a Length of Time had attained to nothing but Rice. I told him, in my Turn, that we were under no Pain at ſeveral of our People deſerting this Place, laſt Year particularly; moſt Part of whom have experienced, to their Coſt (ſome with the Loſs of their Lives) what an unhappy Change they made: Some are eſcaped out of their Miſery there, and returned to poor *Georgia*, glad

glad to be admitted again to work for their Bread among us; and one Family or two more, as I am adviſed from them, are purpoſing the like juſt now. I could not refrain from adding, that if we can be ſo happy to get Poſſeſſion of *Auguſtin*, I did not doubt but we ſhould quickly ſee ſome of the fine Folks at *Charles-Town* looking out for a Place to ſit down in, more in the Way of a *Spaniſh* and *Weſt-India* Trade, than where they are; and might be glad to ſubmit to the Conſtitution of *Georgia*, which ſo much Pains had been taken to explode. He replied, that he was firmly of that Opinion; and whatever ſome might think of *him*, he would not quit what Intereſt he had in Land here, for 200 *l.* Sterling: Then he told me, that I gueſſed right in what I ſaid; for that to his Knowledge, ſeveral were hunting about for Titles of Grants of Lands, run out here formerly; and among others, he ſaid the Attorney-General had ſent his Service to me by him, and adviſed me, as a Friend, not to be at any farther Expence in making Improvements, as I was going on at my Plantation; for that he had a good Title to a large Tract of Land there (I think he ſaid a Barony) wherein mine, which I held from the Truſt, was included: I ſmiled, and deſired him to return my Compliments to that Gentleman; and to aſſure him,

1740. June 24.

1740. June him, I ſhould not ſtop my Hands at *Bewlie*, nor be in any Pain about the Title to it; and ſo we parted. —— *Fas eſt & ab Hoſte doceri.*

25. *Wedneſday.* Very little worth taking Notice of; But I found, upon ſome Talk I had with Mr. *Jones*, that no good Underſtanding was yet to be looked for, betwixt him and Mr. *Whitfield*; for that he had ſent this Morning to one of Mr. *Whitfield*'s principal Actors to come to him, whom he had diſcourſed with very freely, and plainly told him divers Things, wherein he thought Mr. *Whitfield* to blame, as to his outward Conduct and Behaviour, eſpecially with reſpect to the General, whoſe Name, at any Time when mentioned, he ſeemed to make light of; and if it was made uſe of in any Inſtance, where his Approbation was judged needful, Mr. *Whitfield* commonly would expreſs his Diſlike of it, by ſaying —— What have I to do with the General? or Words to that Effect: Seeming to inſiſt on it, that in all Caſes he ſhould have Regard only to the collective Body of the Truſtees. Mr. *Jones* added farther (as he ſaid to me) that he could not but take Notice of Mr. *Whitfield*'s going on ſo unadviſedly as he did, in paying ſuch an *extravagant* Price for Stones, which were now bringing, in order to begin building a Church, without ever conſulting,

ſulting, or adviſing, with any one but himſelf; when he knew he was directed by the Truſtees, to confer with me thereon; and the General moreover had directed both him (Mr. *Jones)* and me, to be aſſiſting to him in promoting that Work; eſpecially in the Laying out and Diſpoſal of the 150*l.* lately advanced towards it from the Truſt, who, as Guardians of all the Benefactions for that Purpoſe, have moſt undoubtedly a Right to appoint Officers of their own, to inſpect and controll the Diſburſement thereof, *&c. &c.* All which, the Perſon whom it was ſaid to, was charged to acquaint Mr. *Whitfield* with; and it is to be preſumed he did ſo. Here it may be proper to explain the Occaſion of the Word *extravagant* being made uſe of as above. One *William Gough*, a Freeholder here, who near two Years ſince left this Place, and went to *Carolina*, taking up his Abode at *Port-Royal*, where he made a poor Shift to live, by teaching little Children to read; had it nevertheleſs ſtill at heart, to return again ſome Time or other to *Savannah*, where he hoped to ſee more Proſperity; on which Account, to preſerve his Claim, he took Care that his Guard-Duty ſhould be performed duly: For which End he left the Care of his five-Acre Lot to *Duchee* the Potter, who in Lieu of Rent would provide for the ſaid Duty; and has conti-

1740. June 25.

1740. June nued ſo to do: But *Duchee* having before made ſome Trial what that Lot would produce, found in it a plentiful Quarry of Iron Stone; went to work upon it, and turned out a conſiderable Quantity of ſuch Stone; which was then looked upon as a Rarity; and he ſold a great deal of it to divers People for various Uſes; ſome for building Chimnies, and ſome for other Purpoſes; at the Rate of two Shillings *per* Load, and at one Shilling *per* Load for digging, beſides Carriage; by which he got a pretty deal of Money: And that put ſome others upon Experiments, whether or not the like could not be found in their Lots: Among whom, Mr. *Mercer* happened to find ſome on his Lot, at leaſt equally good with the other; which he offered to any one that would dig it, and fetch it away, at Sixpence a Load; and which we intended to make uſe of at that Rate, for ſuch publick Work as we were directed to carry on, *viz.* about the Houſe lately Mr. *Bradley*'s, *&c.* and would exceedingly differ from the Rate which Mr. *Whitfield* was to get them at from Mr. *Duchee*.

26. *Thurſday.* An odd Humour being lately ſprung up among ſome of our People for Horſe-Racing, ſeveral Days ſucceſſively; it gave me a Jealouſy of ſome farther latent Deſign; when I obſerved it was promoted by that deſperate Crew, whoſe whole Study

Study and Employment was to diſturb the Quiet of the Place, and keep the Spirits of the Well-meaning in a continual Flutter. The Horſes were ordinarily mean and low-prized, ſuch as are moſtly adapted to common Uſes, for Hire, *&c.* the Riders alſo ready, for Payment in Drink, to contribute to the Diverſion: The Race a little more than a Quarter of a Mile, from the Gate of the publick Garden, to the Midſt of *Johnſon's-Square.* This anſwered the Purpoſe of the Bettors (Dr. *Tailfer* and his Aſſociates) very well, and occaſioned a Gathering together of a Number of People, idling; among whom, a great Number of Children, in the Way of Danger (as I thought.) After the Race was over, it was very remarkable, that inſtead of going to *Jenkins's*, *Tailfer* directed the Bets to be ſpent at another publick Houſe; for this Reaſon only, as I could find; becauſe he could there find more People to talk to, than at their Club; ſeveral not ſcrupling to go here, who would have thought it a Scandal on themſelves to be ſeen in their Company at the uſual Place of their meeting. Seeing Matters thus carried on, I had the Curioſity to try if we could not penetrate farther into what they were doing: Wherefore Mr. *Jones* and I went in the Evening to the ſame Houſe (Mr. *Parker* being out of Town at his Plantation;) and

1740. June 26.

1740. June 26. taking a little Room adjoining to this Aſſembly, we called for a Glaſs of Wine, ſitting to obſerve what paſſed: Where we ſoon diſcovered what I gueſſed to be their Buſineſs; and could hear diſtinctly their Prolocutor, diſplaying his Parts moſt vehemently to his Audience, in a long Harangue; to ſhew how grievouſly ill-uſed this poor Colony had been, for a great while paſt, through the arbitrary Proceedings of thoſe who had the Government of it: And now at laſt, after all, they could imagine, that People were to be ſweetened by ſome trifling Amendments which they thought fit to make, in relation to the Inheritance of their Lands: But he would make it appear it was the baſeſt Tenure in Chriſtendom; and that it was not in the Power of any Man living to be ſafe in what he held, it being liable to ſuch a Multitude of Forfeitures, which the Grantors would, at their Pleaſure, take Advantage of: But he hoped in few Months to ſee a new Leaf turned over, and that Juſtice would be done by a ſuperior Power: And as for thoſe Tools who worked under them here (meaning, without Doubt, ſuch as had the Execution of the Truſt's Commands) it was in vain for them to conceal their Inſtructions; for all muſt now very ſoon come to Light, *&c.* with Abundance more ſuch like Ribaldry, too long to dwell upon here; all tending to inflame his Hearers, and excite Diſturbances. I could not find, however (with all this Contrivance) that any Perſon of good Character had joined their Company; only two or three looſe, idle Fellows, were got among them, who had more Regard to their Share of Drink in the Wagers loſt, than to the Doctor's Eloquence: But the ſtanch Members of the Club ſtuck together, as at other Times. After about an Hour's Stay, my Companion having no longer Patience to bear ſuch Roaſting among others; we walked off, and left them to make what they pleaſed of it. 1740. June

Friday. The ſame Humour of Horſe-Racing going forward, my Apprehenſions increaſed, of the Conſequence proving pernicious, from ſuch mad, tumultuous Work; and I could not forbear imparting my Sentiments of it to Mr. *Jones*, as a Magiſtrate; recommending a Stop to be put to it, as a Breach of the Peace; by their publiſhing an Advertiſement, forbidding ſuch illegal Aſſemblies; which undoubtedly ought to be deemed ſo, in the Heart of the Town, how warrantable ſoever they might be at a Diſtance out of it: Wherein he ſeemed to be tacitly of my Opinion; but no other Magiſtrate being then to be found, it reſted for the preſent; and the Sportſmen, as Yeſterday, took a plentiful Cup in the Even- 27.

1740. ing, imbibing (I fear) but little Good under ſo ſignal a Conductor.

June 28. *Saturday.* Capt. *Patrick Mackay*, going for *Charles-Town*, I wrote ſome Letters by him to Mr. *Hopton*, and others. Meſſieurs *Whitfield* and *Jones*, coming (in outward Appearance at leaſt) to a better Underſtanding, I was invited, with Mr. *Jones*, to Dinner at the Parſon's, where he acquainted us with his Intention of going the Beginning of the Week for *Charles-Town*: But whether he ſhould go farther, or not, he was not fully determined, for that he purpoſed to be back again here in about three Weeks. Private Information was brought me this Afternoon, that a Paper, ready drawn at *Charles-Town*, full of more ſad Complaints againſt our chief Rulers, and inferior Magiſtrates alſo, was ſecretly crept into this Place, with Intent to be handed about, and to get as many Names to it, as could be had among our Malecontents: But what Title it bore, whether it was by Way of Petition, or Remonſtrance, my Informer could not yet learn; only he promiſed to uſe his beſt Endeavours to get farther Knowledge about it very ſoon, *viz.* whoſe Framing it was, what the Subſtance of it, and whom it was intended to be preſented to. One of this Kind of Productions, I before took Notice of, was beginning to appear about the Middle of *April* laſt; but by by what Means it proved abortive, I could never learn. 1740.

Sunday. The publick Service was duly obſerved, as uſual; and Mr. *Whitfield* gave an inſtructive Diſcourſe on the barren Fig-Tree. After Church we had the ill News, by a trading Boat juſt arrived from *Charles-Town*, of a ſharp Action that happened lately near *Auguſtin*, wherein we loſt about ſeventy Men; and it was related thus, *viz.* That Colonel *Palmer*, a Gentleman of good Fortune in *Carolina*, and an old Officer there formerly, but now not commiſſioned in this new-raiſed Regiment, and ſerving as a Volunteer, was appointed by the General, with the Command of about a hundred Men, to take Poſt at a certain Diſtance from the Town, towards the Land: That in the Morning, about Day-break, or before, a Body of five or ſix hundred *Spaniards* out of the Town attacked them; when they defended themſelves bravely a while, and repelled them twice; but being over-powered with Numbers, a great Slaughter enſued, and two Thirds of our Men fell by the Sword; but not without making the Enemy pay dearly for their Lives: Among the Dead was Colonel *Palmer* himſelf, the Remainder making what Eſcape they could: And it is ſaid farther, that a great Number of the Enemy, at leaſt twice as many as on our Side, were ſlain. June 29.

1740. June ſlain. Thus we had it told us by the Patroon of this Boat: But as we ſeldom find the Reports from that Neighbourhood verified in all Parts, and moreover having not the leaſt Intelligence of any Thing like it ſent us from the General's Camp (which ſeems very ſtrange) we are willing to hope the next authentic Account we have from thence, will make ſome Abatement of this diſagreeable Story, and render it more favourable.

30. *Monday.* Lieutenant *Kent* from Fort *Auguſta*, arrived this Morning, by Permiſſion, for a few Days, to adjuſt divers Matters, relating to his own private Affairs, as well as conſult the Magiſtrates in ſome Affairs concerning the Civil Power, wherein he met with frequent Embarraſſment how to put it in Execution; there was ſuch Jangling among the Traders, and often Attempts of Violence with one another, to decide Controverſies by Force, rather than ſubmit to any Judicature; having committed the Care of the Fort to a Serjeant under him, whom he could well confide in, during his Abſence: He alſo had with him three Men, that he brought Priſoners, whom he had lately taken, after a diligent Purſuit; and were Part of thoſe who committed that notorious Riot in the *Creek* Nation ſome Time ago *(vide June* 3.) but one or two of the moſt criminal were got out

out of his Reach, and fled to *Charles-Town*; which they looked on as a ſafe Aſylum againſt all Proſecutions from *Georgia:* Theſe who now appeared, found good Bail for their ſo doing again at our Court, near at hand now, and to abide the Judgment of the ſame. Mr. *Whitfield* went off for *Carolina* about Noon, taking one only Companion of his Houſhold with him (Mr. *Simms)* after having conſtituted Mr. *Haberſham*, to perform the Office of the Church in his Abſence, and Mr. *Brownfield* chief Steward of the Whole, who now gave himſelf up wholly to that Care, appointing *William Ewen* to manage his own private Affairs, about keeping Stores, who had formerly been Mr. *Cauſton's* principal Agent in delivering out thoſe of the Publick: Since which, the ſaid *Ewen* went on very induſtriouſly with a fifty-Acre Lot at *Skeedoway*; but now all was given up to promote a Work thought to be of greater Importance; which was the Caſe with many others, not only of this Town, but of *Hampſtead*, *Highgate*, and divers Places beſides; ſo that the Work at the Orphan-Houſe ſeemed to be the great Gulph which ſwallowed up moſt of our common People, whether Artificers, Labourers, or Planters, that thought it more preferable to be ſo employed; which made the Town become thin indeed. The Humour of Horſe-Racing

1740. June 30.

1740. Racing was yet kept up; but they thought fit to alter the Scene, and carry on the Show a little out of Town.

July 1. *Tuesday.* Three or four more *Indian* Traders took up good Part of my Time this Day; which I could not well ſpare, from being employed about what I was directed to uſe my beſt Diligence in, to get ready ſuch a State of the Colony, as the Truſtees could abide by the Truth of, in any parliamentary Enquiry, *&c.* and therein my daily Employment ſhould be doing ſomething towards it. Mr. *Cauſton* having for ſome Months paſt forſaken the Town, and retired to *Ockſtead*, it has often been reported among us, that he was in a decaying State of Health; which (it is to be feared) a great Anxiety of Mind has contributed to; and now we heard from thence, that he was ſo waſted away, and weak, it was believed his Life was near an End.

2. *Wedneſday.* Mr. *Mackenzie*, a Store-Keeper at *Auguſta*, ſtopping here, in his Way home from *Charles-Town*, confirmed the bad News, as he had it there, which was reported to us by one of the trading Boats thence, on the 29th paſt, of the Loſs of a great many Men; who (it was alſo ſaid) ſold their Lives at a dear Price, taking Payment of the Enemy by the Death of more than two hundred of them

them ſlain; which they could ill ſpare: The Loſs is ſaid unhappily to fall heavieſt (on our Side) upon the Men of this Colony; moſt of thoſe that were killed being either of the *Darien* People, or of our Troop of Rangers, or other ſmall Parties; none of the regular Forces, or of the *Carolina* Regiment, having any Share in the Action. This rather quickens than abates the Reſolution of the Beſiegers, who are now animated with a Spirit of Revenge; and we hear, that a large Battery of heavy Cannon had begun to play on the Town. During theſe Tranſactions, we of this Place can come at very little News that is certain, to be relied on, having not had any Intelligence from the General ſince Mr. *Jones*'s Return; and what we more admire at is, that not any Letters come thence from any of our People to their Friends. 1740. July

Thurſday. After a pretty long Continuance of exceeding hot Weather, we were bleſſed this Day with a plentiful Rain, but accompanied with terrible Thunder and Lightning, which laſted a great Part of the Night following; whereby the Earth, and all thereon, was much refreſhed; and ſuch as had Employment for a Pen and Ink, were ſure to be undiſturbed by any Avocations from home, or giving Attention to what was doing abroad. 3.

Friday,

1740. July 4. 5. *Friday*, *Saturday*. } Being under ſome Indiſpoſition, I would not allow myſelf the Liberty of being abroad; but Meſſieurs *Parker*, *Jones*, &c. now and then calling on me, we conferred betwixt while on the principal Affair at preſent in hand, to make what Progreſs in it we could: Wherein I wiſhed for better Abilities, than I found myſelf endued with, ſo to illuſtrate the Truth, as to vindicate the Truſtees Honour, and expoſe the Malignity of thoſe who attempted to impeach it. Thinking it of little Significance now, to puzzle my Thoughts farther, in putting together thoſe Fragments which I had been collecting, in order to lay the State we were in before the Truſt, when the State of the Colony was expected ſo fully to be explained and laid open to them with our utmoſt Care and Diligence, at this Time to be uſed: I choſe rather to make up a Packet, with my Journal to this Time, and other Papers, *&c.* together with a Letter to Mr. *Verelſt*, which might be ready at any Time to ſend off, when Opportunity offered; and which indeed was all I attempted theſe two Days.

6. *Sunday*. Mr. *Haberſham*, in Mr. *Whitfield*'s Abſence, read the Prayers of the Church, and Sermons before Noon and after, out of ſome old Author; wherein, tho' the Language was ſomewhat antiquated, the

the Doctrine was good, tending to promote Piety and Virtue. 1740.

Monday. Our Court met this Day, as *per* Adjournment, and ſat, to determine ſeveral Controverſies among ſome of our Keepers of Stores at *Auguſta*, and ſome *Indian* Traders who dealt with them; wherein I obſerved a Propenſity pretty equal on both Sides, to over-reach one another, and ſcramble which of them ſhould gain moſt. Attending the Court before Noon, and ſome of the Traders after, who came to renew their Licences, took up moſt of my Time all Day. July 7.

Tueſday. The Court went on with ſuch Matters as they could not well avoid hearing; much of the ſame Significance as Yeſterday, and worth little Notice from me: But what elſe occurred there, I thought required my particular Remark, being what poſſibly one Day or other I may be called to account for: When the Court was about riſing, an Attempt was made, by two or three, to interrupt them in a clamorous Manner, and demand an Entry of their Claims to ſuch Lands as they held: Which they received an Anſwer to in the ſofteſt Manner, to pacify them as far as might be, *viz.* that they would readily concur in ſo doing; but they apprehended, from what I had ſome Time ſince acquainted them with, that there was a Box directed to me, 8.

ſent

1740. July 8. ſent from the Truſtees, wherein were divers Papers, printed, intended to be diſperſed by me for the Satisfaction of the People, relating to the future intended Tenure of Lands; and among other Things in the ſaid Box, a Deed-Poll relating to forfeited Lots; which printed Papers concerning the Tenure of Lands, and Deed-Poll relating to forfeited Eſtates, they had never yet ſeen, and that they ſhould have expected ſome plain Inſtructions thereon, when I publiſhed the Notice that I received from the Truſt for the People to enter their Claims; but all appeared dark to them, as Matters now ſtood; and they were fearful leſt they might commit ſome Error, *&c.* reſerving them to me at laſt, to explain the whole Progreſs (or rather I ſhould ſay Obſtruction) of my putting in Execution the Orders ſent me from the Truſt, concerning this important Affair; wherein the one only Step I have been able to take about it, has been publiſhing the Notice in our Town which was written and encloſed from the Truſt, about Claims, *&c.* and even that I never received till the 7th of *April* laſt, tho' the Letter it came in, was dated the 28th of *September* laſt; and no Box, or other Thing relating, has yet ever come to my Hand; of all which I took proper Notice on the ſaid 7th of *April*, and 11th *Ditto*, in this Diary; as I had ſeveral Times before ſore in divers preceding Articles, and now I related the Whole fully to them, for their Satisfaction; being ſorry to hear it even whiſpered by ſome, that they found, if any Benefit was intended them, it by ſome Means or other was ſure to prove abortive: And foraſmuch as all Claims to be made purſuant to this Notice muſt be before the 28th of *Auguſt* now drawing near, I recommended it to the Magiſtrates to make another ſhort Adjournment of the Court, that farther Conſideration might be timely had of it; for I greatly feared, that this Check given to their Expectation from the honourable Truſt, might be a Sowering to ſome, who had hitherto readily acquieſced in all Determinations from them; whereupon the Court adjourned to the 1ſt of *Auguſt*. 1740. July

Wedneſday. About Two a Clock this Morning, I was knocked up by a Party of about eight or nine People, who fled from Mr. *Whitfield*'s Works at the Orphan-Houſe, terrified with the Apprehenſions they were under, of two Boats full of *Spaniſh Indians* coming upon them in the Night; for that two of their young Men who were fetching ſome Lime in a Boat the Evening before, were purſued by thoſe *Indians*, and in their Fright fearing to be taken by them, they got aſhore, and run to their Comrades at the ſaid Works; 9.

1740. July 9. whereupon theſe People now made what Haſte they could, to give us Information of it, bringing the two young Men with them: I went inſtantly to ſee what Poſture our Guard was in, ſending, at the ſame Time, our Magiſtrates Notice, and to the Conſtables to meet me: I was glad to find the Guard waking and alert, and immediately alarmed the Town, by Beat of Drum to Arms, which in leſs than a Quarter of an Hour brought betwixt thirty and forty together (and but few more could be expected on the Spot, conſidering where, and how many of our Freeholders were daily employed) I then ſent out two Patroles, with an Officer and ſix Men to each, to take a Round at a little Diſtance from the Town, appointing them where to join, and return, *&c.* After the two Lads had been examined by the Magiſtrates (who ſtood to what they had before reported) upon a Conſultation had, ſeven or eight of our moſt expert Cattle-Hunters were ſent out on Horſeback to ſcout about thoſe Parts, and ſee if any farther Diſcovery could be made, and in ſuch Caſe to give us immediate Notice. In this Poſture we continued till about Ten a Clock, when on a ſudden we were well informed, by two or three Perſons coming one after another from *Thunderbolt*, *Skeedoway*, and that Neighbourhood, that the *Indians*, whom the two Lads

Lads took to be Enemies, were no other than ſome of thoſe our Friends who live near us, and who at this Time were out a hunting on thoſe Iſlands, and the adjacent Coaſt: We were alſo farther aſſured, that they had ſpoke with them, at the Place where their Camp was laſt Night, and where they made Fires to dreſs their Veniſon: Which Circumſtance alone is ſufficient to demand Belief of their not being Enemies; for it is a Rule among all of them, when they go to War, to make not the leaſt Fire, which would diſcover them, and ſpoil their Deſigns, that are always projected to attack their Foes, when they do not look for them.——Thus all this imagined Storm blowed over, and every body went to their Homes in Peace. 1740. July

Thurſday, } Very little ſeemed worth 10.
Friday. } Regard now among us, in 11.
Compariſon of what great Things we were daily expecting ſome Intelligence of from the South; from whence (to our Admiration) no authentick Account had for a long Time paſt come to our Hands; but during theſe two Days, ſeveral private Letters were received by ſome of our People, from their Friends thereabout; which Letters came round about, having been as far as *Port-Royal*, and moſt of them agreeing, in the Main, on what Advices we got before, in the Manner I took Notice (the 29th of

1740. *June*, and 2d of *July*;) but variouſly told now, as the Writers got Information, none of them having been perſonally in that Action. It was paſt all Doubt, that it was a great Slaughter on both Sides; our People fought very bravely, and grown deſperate, ſeeing themſelves ſo over-powered, ſold their Lives at a dear Rate, at leaſt double the Number of the Enemy being ſlain, Sword in Hand, to what fell of our Men. It fell heavy upon our Party of Rangers, who were a Set of gallant, brave, young Men; and behaved ſignally well: But the moſt bloody Part of all fell to the unhappy Share of our good People at *Darien*, who almoſt all to a Man engaged, under the Command of their Leader *John Mackintoſh (More)* a worthy, careful Director among his People at home, and who now ſhewed himſelf as valiant in the Field of Battle, where calling on his Countrymen and Followers to follow his Example, they made ſuch Work with their broad Swords, as the *Spaniards* cannot eaſily forget: This is certainly an unhappy Accident, not more however than the Chance of War often produces; and therefore it behoves us ſtill to look forward, whence it is to be hoped, ere long, we ſhall find a different Story to tell, all Accounts confirming, that the Siege of *Auguſtin* goes on ſucceſsfully by Sea and Land; that we are Maſters of the Harbour, where are ſeveral

July 10. 11.

veral warlike Gallies, *&c.* that muſt fall into our Hands; that we are firing at the Fort from a Battery of heavy Cannon; that we had thrown a hundred and ſixty Bombs, whereof not more than ſix or ſeven had miſſed falling into the Caſtle, *&c.* and it is ſaid the General declared, that he expected ſoon to be Maſter of the Place. *N. B.* The above-mentioned Attack is ſaid to have been on *Sunday* the 15th of *June.* 1740. July

Saturday. We now at length attained to ſome more ſatisfactory Account, than any yet to be depended on, of the late Action with the Enemy, by Means of a Letter from Mr. *Patterſon* at *Frederica* to Mr. *Jones*; which Letter had taken a Round alſo to *Port-Royal*, as well as all others of late, that were wrote from the South to this Place; the Bearers being ſome of our *Carolina* Gentry for the moſt Part, who went as Volunteers, and made more Haſte to return home, than was for their Credit, carrying with them the News of this Miſadventure, which they reported in ſuch Colours, as their Fright ſuggeſted, few or none of them having been Witneſſes of it; which ſtruck a Damp upon ſome weak Minds that are apt to take the firſt Impreſſion too deep. What Mr. *Patterſon* wrote Mr. *Jones* was authentick, being Copies of the General's own Letters to the Magiſtrates of *Frederica*, and to Mr. *Mc Leod*, 12.

1740. July 12. Miniſter of *Darien:* Wherein, the Bravery of our People is ſet forth to their Honour, and the Loſs of Men much leſſened, from what was at firſt given out; which the General ſays he expected would be by a Parcel of runaway Cowards, many being ſince come in that at firſt were ſaid to be ſlain. Colonel *Palmer*, a Gentleman in good Eſteem, is among the Dead; but *John More Mackintoſh*, the Leader of the *Darien* People, together with ſome of his Countrymen, and ſome alſo of the Rangers, are Priſoners in the Town; whence, his Excellence writes, he does not doubt but to releaſe them ſoon: In the mean while he was pleaſed to write a Letter to the Governor, by a Flag of Truce, telling him, that he expected the Priſoners ſhould not be ill treated; for that in caſe they were, he would hang up every Priſoner he had before the Gates of the Town; of which he had a great Number: Whereupon the Governor ordered our Men that were taken, to write to the General; who acquainted him, that they were kindly uſed.—And now we are imagining Things near a Criſis at *Auguſtin*; which raiſes our Expectations daily, of ſuch Advices from thence, as will preponderate all paſt that was diſagreeable. It was not an Obſervation of my own only, but the like made to me by ſome honeſt Men, that during the

the Obſcurity which the Truth of theſe Things lay under, our common Diſturbers took great Pains, with a Kind of Sneer, to publiſh what they thought fit, in a frightful Manner, as what their Friends had (I know not from whence) wrote them they might depend on, ſeemingly full of deep Concern for poor *Georgia:* All which, any Man of common Underſtanding could eaſily ſee thro': But the Light now appearing through that Cloud, it was yet more remarkable, that the counterfeit Sorrow which they had then put on, now viſibly became real; and when other Folk grew chearful, they ſo far forgot themſelves, as to look ſullen and out of Humour: What Inference may juſtly be drawn from hence, I chuſe to ſubmit to thoſe who are the beſt Judges. 1740. July

Sunday. Mr. *Haberſham* performed the Divine Service, Morning and Afternoon; reading after it two Sermons, one exhorting to a due Obedience of God's Laws, and the other ſetting forth his Omnipreſence: Both (I thought) better adapted to a Reformation of Life, than ſuch nice Points concerning Juſtification, which were ſo often taken in hand. 13.

Monday. The laſt Week carried off moſt of our *Indian* Traders, and Store-Keepers at *Auguſta*, who had ſpent a little Time with us: Lieutenant *Kent* alſo returning 14.

1740. July 14. Yeſterday to his Command at the Fort there; and among others, Mr. *Williamſon* likewiſe at length thought fit to go back to *Charles-Town*, after having employed himſelf here a long Time paſt, doing what Miſchief he could in promoting falſe Rumours, and concerting Meaſures with our wicked Crew, how moſt effectually to alienate the Minds of well-diſpoſed People, from ſhewing a due Regard to the good Intention of the honourable Truſtees, whoſe Deſigns for the Welfare of the Colony they always talked of in an ironical Stile, or in ſuch a Manner as to be on their Guard, leſt any Expreſſions ſhould drop from them, which if animadverted on, they might have Cauſe to repent of; for they well know what they may expect, if they openly dare to revile thoſe in the higheſt Authority over us. It now appeared, that the principal Cauſe of *Williamſon*'s coming hither, was in Expectation that his Uncle *Cauſton* was dead, or dying; that ſo he might be ready to take Poſſeſſion of what he could; but Mr. *Cauſton*, tho' grown very weak, yet leaving Room for his Friends to entertain ſome Hopes of his Recovery, gave him a cold Reception, and blamed his Conduct very much (as I am informed) for meddling ſo much as he did, with the Affairs of the Colony, and allowing himſelf the Liberty of cenſuring the Acts of the Truſtees; much leſs would *Cauſton* be perſuaded by him, to be a Partaker in thoſe wiſe Councils, which were carrying on among them at their Club; for (to give *Cauſton* his Due) he had more Penetration than all of them put together, and could ſee afar off what their Politicks would end in: Whereat the other enraged, left him; and coming to Town, let looſe all the Scandal he could think of againſt him at *Jenkins*'s, giving him the Title of both Fool and Knave, for not concurring with them, in appealing to the Parliament againſt the Truſtees, who had dealt ſo hardly with *him:* Which *Cauſton* was ſo provoked at, that when the other came a few Days after to ſee him, he forbad him his Houſe, and ordered the Doors to be ſhut againſt him. Our Court ſitting ſoon after, he then turned Sollicitor, in a Cauſe or two to be heard betwixt ſome of our *Indian* Traders, *&c.* But being timely admoniſhed, thought it ſafeſt not to appear as a Pleader; tho' he confidently affirmed, that he had the Truſt's Leave to practiſe as an Attorney. From thence-forward, as well as before, he buſied himſelf as an Inſpector among our ſelf-elected ones, riding frequently to and fro, to note what he imagined would make for his Purpoſe; and at going off, left this Memento behind him; that he had made himſelf ſo far Maſter of all the Settlements,

1740. July 14.

Planta-

1740. July 14. Plantations, and Families, in the Province; how many, and whom they conſiſted of, and what every one was employed about, that he ſhould get a faithful Account ready againſt the next Enquiry into the State of the Colony, to confront any ſent by other Hands, and prevent Gentlemen from being miſled. What paſſed betwixt him and me, towards the latter End of his Miſſion here, I think not worth remembring; but upon meeting him once or twice accidentally, and his attempting to obtrude a Queſtion or two upon me, which I took to be enſnaring, I told him, that I thought ſuch Queſtions would be beſt anſwered before Witneſſes, as (he knew) had been practiſed by him and his Friends upon *me*; and ſo I turned my Back on him. Lieutenant *Kent*, in his Way home, meeting with a Letter ſent to him out of the *Cherokee* Nation, thought it proper to be ſent hither; that if we ſaw it needful, we might tranſmit it to the General: It came to us this Morning, and was from *Lodowick Grant*, a Trader in that Nation; who wrote him, that there were eighty of thoſe People lately marched out in two Parties, on what Deſign, at firſt not known; but it proved to be againſt the *French*, whom they attacked as they were coming up the River to *Terriqua*, in three Perriaguas, two of which they plundered and deſtroyed: What

What the Conſequence may be we know not, but think it forebodes no Ill to the *Engliſh*. In the Evening Mr. *Fallowfield* came to Town from his Plantation on the *Iſle of Hope*; which it may be proper to take Notice here, is a Name given it by the Settlers thereon, who are Meſſieurs *Parker*, *Fallowfield*, and *Noble Jones*: It is a Peninſula, cut off from the Main with a very little Iſthmus, which by a ſhort Fence makes the Iſland an entire Poſſeſſion to them; and it is equally divided betwixt them, which they hold by Leaſe (or Expectation of ſuch) from the Truſt, having occupied it two or three Years, and made conſiderable Improvements: The Iſle of *Skeedoway* lies without it, and betwixt them is the Way that all Boats paſs to and fro, betwixt us and the South. —— What News Mr. *Fallowfield* brought was very ſurprizing, *viz.* that about Noon there was a Boat paſſing from the Camp towards *Carolina*, wherein was young Mr. *Delagal*, a Lieutenant in the General's own Regiment: That upon hailing the Boat, and aſking what News? *Delagal* told him, the General was intending to draw off his Forces from before *Auguſtin*, and make them another Viſit in *October* next; which being ſomewhat ſtartled at, he would have aſked him ſome more Queſtions, but that he thought *Delagal* was ſhy, and ſeemed unwilling

1740. July 14.

1740. July willing to talk any farther with him; but as the Men lay upon their Oars, he called on them haſtily to pull away, which they did. What he obſerved farther was, that he ſaw a Gentleman under the Awning, who lay ſtill, and did not ſhew himſelf. Upon this Report made to us, and ſo many odd Circumſtances attending it (among others I ſhould not forget that the Rowers appeared to Mr. *Fallowfield* not to be natural-born Subjects, being of a black and ſwarthy Complexion, ſomewhat of the Mulatto Kind) various were our Conjectures, too many to name: But moſt were of Opinion, that *Delagal* was not well warranted to give ſuch Intelligence. Nevertheleſs it muſt needs leave us under much Perplexity of Thought, till we could come at the Truth.

15. *Tueſday*. The dark Account we had laſt Night of Matters at *Auguſtin*, which came by that Boat Mr. *Fallowfield* had ſpoken with, ſeemed to vaniſh, with the Light of another Day: Two of the Men who rowed in her, who thro' much Sweat and Toil appeared with dirty Faces, and were taken to be Mulatto's, landing not many Miles off; this Morning we found one of them to be an *Engliſhman*, who had lived ſeveral Years up in the *Cherokee* Nation; and talking that Language perfectly, was made uſe of by the General as an Interpreter

terpreter with them at the Camp; where those *Cherokees* having a peculiar Sickneſs among them, whereof ſeveral of them had lately died, the reſt, with the General's Leave, were returning home, and were on their Way hither; to which Place this Man was ſent as a Forerunner, to make Preparation againſt their Arrival; the other, who was his Companion, was an inſignificant, little, old Fellow, a Sort of Jack Pudding at *Auguſta*, whom the Inhabitants there made uſe of on Occaſion in a ſervile Manner, and he was maintained out of their Plenty; to which Place he was now returning, together with this People; but what Motive carried *him* to War, I am not able to gueſs from theſe two; we made ſhift to underſtand, that the General finding Bombarding to have very little Effect on the Works of the Fort, which were made Bomb Proof, had put ſome of his heavy Artillery on board the Men of War, who now (according to the Uſage of those Countries) were obliged to ſtand farther off to Sea, fearing leſt in caſe of a Hurricane coming upon them at this Seaſon (the uſual Time of expecting ſuch) they ſhould be catcht, and not able to get out from the Bay; that the Enemy lately made an Attempt of ſallying with a Party of Horſe, but were ſoon glad to make haſte in again; ſeveral of the Horſes carrying only their Saddles,

1740. July 15.

1740. July Saddles, without any Riders. That the coming away of theſe *Cherokees* would not be miſſed, for their Room would be more than ſupplied by three hundred from the *Creek* Nation, who were within few Days March of the Camp when theſe left it; and that the General ſeemed determined to carry on the Siege; which I muſt own I could hardly believe; unleſs he meant to turn it into a Blockade, and wait the coming of more Force from other Parts (as it was of late pretty much talked of) under the Lord *Cathcart*. The Perſon in the Boat who did not ſhew himſelf Yeſterday, we now heard was Colonel *Barnwell* of *Carolina*, whom the General had been friendly with; and it was not doubted but both he and Lieutenant *Delagal* had with them ſome particular Orders and Inſtructions from his Excellency. Thus all was pretty well again, and moſt Folk muſt talk about what few of them underſtood.

16. *Wedneſday*. *Peter Emery* arriving laſt Night with his Boat from *Charles-Town*, brought me a Box ſent me by my Son from *England*, with ſundry Neceſſaries that I wanted, which came by a Ship newly come in, as Mr. *Hopton* wrote me; but no Letter, except one, adviſing me of the Contents. This Day produced nothing relating to the Publick worth regarding.

Thurſday,

Thurſday. The whole Attention of all People this Day, was to the various Reports that came by ſeveral Perſons returning to *Carolina* from the Army; who in their Way home dropt ſuch Accounts of Matters here and there among our Out-Settlements, as were very inconſiſtent, and much diſagreeing; ſo that the Truth could not yet fully be come at, but gave Occaſion of a great deal of Talk at random to no Purpoſe. 1740. July 17.

Friday. Capt. *Tingley* arrived this Morning from the South, where he had been to diſpoſe of his Cargo (*vide June* 14.) and with him came Mr. *Abraham Minis*, a *Jew* Freeholder here, whom the Cargo was conſigned to, and who was looked on by all of us, as an honeſt Man: Wherefore we could make no Scruple of giving Credit to what was now told us, as real Fact. The Action which happened upon the Enemy's ſallying out in the Night, and attacking our Party early in the Morning, ſo often canvaſſed amongſt us here, differed very little in Circumſtances from what we had heard; and it was very ſharp; but the Number ſlain was too much magnified on our Side; for out of about one hundred and thirty, which the Party conſiſted of, it is now ſaid that forty were killed, and ten taken Priſoners; among the firſt of whom, Colonel *Palmer* was one; and among 18.

1740. July 18. mong the latter, Capt. *John Mc Intoſh More*, the Principal of the *Darien* People; the reſt making their Eſcape. It is agreed by all, that the Enemy ſuffered twice as much; for our Men finding themſelves encloſed, fought deſperately, and made their Way thro' and thro' them, Sword in Hand: But the certain Loſs they ſuſtained, is not to be diſcovered; for remaining Maſters of the Field a-while, they buried their Dead, leaving us to do the ſame by ours; which we did ſoon after: But to countervail the Loſs of Colonel *Palmer*, the principal Commander of the *Spaniards* there was killed at the firſt Onſet, when our Men maintained a briſk Fire for ſome Time, before they engaged Hand to Hand; and it is ſtill ſaid the *Spaniards* were upwards of five hundred. They made a faint Attempt very lately of ſallying with a Party of Horſe, to perform ſome farther Exploit: But the General was ſo well provided for them, that they made more haſte back, than they had done ſo far, and a great many Horſes were ſeen to have left their Riders; as we were before told by thoſe two Men whom we talked with on laſt *Tueſday*; and what the ſame Men then told us of the General having ſhipped off his Artillery, and his Reaſons for ſo doing; as alſo of the Men of War ſtanding off farther to Sea, for Fear of a Hurricane, was now confirmed: Moreover,

over, the General ſeeing his Men beginning to grow ſickly, and finding little more could be done, reſolved to turn the Siege into a Blockade (as I imagined would be the Caſe) till they were recruited with good Health, and ſome additional Strength, intending after *Michaelmas* to have ſomething more to ſay to them: In the mean Time, he was marched, with his little Army, to his former Camp at St. *Juan*'s. 1740. July

Saturday. The only Thing that came farther to my Knowledge worth obſerving from the South, was, that Capt. *Davis*, whom on many Occaſions, I have formerly at ſeveral Times, for a whole Year paſt, taken Notice of, as a Man, in my Opinion, carrying on dark Purpoſes, which I did what in me lay to obſtruct, by the Aſſiſtance of the Magiſtrates; which produced a great Clamour from our Patrons of Liberty at the Club, charging us with acting illegally, *&c.* (the Particulars whereof were noted in my Journal of *Sept.* 10, 11, 12 and 13, 1739; and again on the 18th Ditto:) But the General coming among us again ſoon after, very much approved of what we had done (as noted on the 24th Ditto;) tho' afterward upon Aſſurances of his Fidelity, he was pleaſed to grant him a Commiſſion to act as a Privateer; which he never did; his Character was ſuch among the Sailors, that he could never get 19.

1740. July Hands ſufficient for that Purpoſe: This Man now lying with his Sloop near St. *Auguſtin*, in Expectation of being employed, as many other were, by the General, we are now informed is taken into Cuſtody by his Excellency's Order, for ſending off two of the *Spaniſh* Priſoners, in his own Boat, into the Town of *Auguſtin*, by whom the Enemy would get the beſt Intelligence they could wiſh.——But I muſt not anticipate what Evidence will appear, nor the Conſequence.

20. *Sunday*. Mr. *Haberſham* continued to perform the Office of Reader of the Divine Service, and a Sermon in the Forenoon and after, with good practical Doctrine; till in the Concluſion his Author left a Diſreliſh to all he had ſaid, by denouncing Damnation to all who were not juſtified by Faith.

21. *Monday*. I had waited now ever ſince the 28th of laſt Month, to get a little farther Account, if I could, of the Paper, which I had private Intelligence of that Day, was ſent among us from *Charles-Town*; but I could not find that its Poiſon had operated upon any worth naming: It was ſent to the Care of the Wife of *Edward Townſend*, whoſe Huſband keeps a Perriague, and is at preſent employed among others by the General. *Probably* ſhe may be better known by the Name of

Hodges

Hodges (her former Huſband) and it is very well known how exceeding kind Mr. *Oglethorpe* was to her, and her Family, for ſeveral Years; notwithſtanding all which, ſhe has, to an inconceivable Degree, moſt ungratefully upon all Occaſions, reviled her kind Benefactor, and given herſelf moſt unwarrantable Liberties with her Tongue to defile his Character; which he uſed to hear of with Contempt, and beneath his Notice: But Mr. *Brownfield* marrying her Daughter, he foretold would be a Means of his becoming tainted with the Sourneſs of that Family; which I fear was too true a Prediction; for he is unhappily fallen into the ſame Way of thinking with Regard to this Colony, as other of our Malecontents are (or I ſhould rather ſay was one of the earlieſt of them) but ſecretly, and avoiding all publick Clamour: But this good Mother-in-Law of his, expoſes the Bitterneſs of her Heart continually, as far as ſhe dares, and her Houſe was a long while the Place of Reſort for ſuch as delighted in her Way of Railing, and would take a Part in it themſelves; till at length a ſuperior Genius prevailed at *Jenkins's*, which this was obſcured by; but the Woman ſtill retaining the ſame Faculty of ſcattering what Venom ſhe can, the Author of this doughty Piece judged ſo far right, that ſhe would be a Well-wiſher to it at leaſt: Wherefore

1740. July 21.

1740. July 21. it was depoſited with her, to ſee what good Uſe ſhe could make of it; and ſtiled no leſs than An humble Petition to the King and Council, ſetting forth what terrible Hardſhips the People of this Province laboured under, *&c.* as the Author's fertile Genius thought fit to diſplay; who was ſaid to be Mr. *Bradley*, as my Informant told me, who averred that he knew it to be his Son's Hand Writing: But this Cockatrice Egg was cruſhed, and not allowed to come to Maturity, by our ſupream Divan; who would ſuffer no Interfering in thoſe weighty Matters, which they alone were ſufficient for. Found an Opportunity of ſpending a little Time at the five-Acre Lot near the Town, good Part of which I had converted to particular Uſes, as a Nurſery for greater Purpoſes: The little Quantity of Corn growing there, I thought no farther worth my preſent regarding, than to obſerve, that ſince the Time I firſt began planting, I had never known ſo promiſing an Increaſe as now, of that Grain, and alſo Potatoes; ſo that the like proving pretty general, I thought it great Pity that all thoſe who were grown weary of perſevering in Cultivation, would now ſee Cauſe to wiſh their Patience would hold out longer. After taking much Pleaſure in ſeeing divers other Things come forward, ſuch as Vines, Mulberries, Cotton, *&c.* I returned home, not

not without wiſhing for ſuch a Receſs oftener; for it was more than a Month ſince my laſt Viſit there. 1740. July

Tueſday. What paſſed at the Time of our Court's adjourning on the 8th Inſtant, relating to the ſeveral Claims being received, which divers were deſirous to make, and for which Purpoſe I obtained a farther ſhort Adjournment to the 1ſt of *Auguſt*, gave me much Uneaſineſs, leſt any Defect of Duty ſhould in the End be imputed to me; wherefore I thought it proper to fix up publick Advertiſement, ſigned by me, to give all People Notice, that Whereas the Court now ſtood adjourned till the 1ſt of *Auguſt*, it would then ſit, and be ready to receive Claims from all Perſons who had any to make for Lands, *&c.* held under the Truſt, provided they ſpecified where their Lots lay which they claimed, and that the Perſons ſo claiming ſigned the ſame: This was all that I could think of in my Power to do towards it at preſent. Much Buzzing began again to appear in our Town (among moſt People indeed now) ſince the News came of the General's having withdrawn a little from the Fortreſs of *Auguſtin*; from whence it was not unreaſonable to infer, that whilſt the General had a watchful Eye over the Enemy by Land, they might poſſibly ſend out Row-Gallies and Launches, *&c.* by Sea, 22.

1740. July with which they might very much annoy the Coaſt, and make Depredations on our Out-Settlements lying all along that Way, of which mine ſtood foremoſt on a Point facing *Uſſibaw Sound:* Nevertheleſs, I could diſcover no Terror among the Generality of our People, who were moſtly of Opinion, that whatever Miſchief might fall on the moſt remote Parts, that lay expoſed, they would ſcarcely venture ſo far up as *Savannah*, and run the Riſk of being intercepted: Wherein I concurred with them; and after giving what Orders I found neceſſary, for a ſtrict Inſpection into every individual Man's Arms, and for a Diſtribution of what Powder and Ball was proper; as alſo ſpecial repeated Orders touching the Guard, *&c.* all appeared in good Temper, whom it might be expected from, but *ſome* nothing would ſatisfy.

23. *Wedneſday.* Whilſt my Thoughts were employed as uſefully as I could for the Publick, in the Station appointed me, it was not amiſs to have ſome Regard likewiſe to my own little Affair: And having not ſeen *Bewlie* ſince *Whitſuntide*, which was now eight Weeks ago, I rode out to make them a Viſit there, and ſee what Diſpoſition my little Family were in, under ſuch daily Rumours there. I found eight Acres of Land as well filled with Corn, Peaſe, and Potatoes, as I could wiſh, all thriving, and

and likely to do well: More I could not expect to ſee planted this Year, conſidering what Time they began, and how many Kinds of Works they had upon their Hands at firſt ſetting down. The Men were eaſy, and their preſent Work was to erect another Edifice, partly for holding Corn, and partly for divers other Uſes; after which, in the next Place, I purpoſed to ſet up a Dwelling-Houſe, in ſuch a Manner, that it might be for a comfortable Reception of myſelf and a Friend at any Time, as well as whomſoever I thought fit to live in it. Upon aſking my People, whether or not they would allow the *Spaniards* to come aſhore and eat the Fruits of their Labour; they promiſed me very chearfully, to ſhew them they would not part with all for Nought; and having with them two Fuſees of my own, and two Muſkets that I ſent them from the Stores, which I aſſured them they ſhould not want Ammunition for, they engaged to behave manfully, if it came to a Trial: And knowing him that was appointed by me their Overſeer, to be a briſk Man, I was pretty confident in them that they would not ſet an ill Example to my next Neighbours there, by running away ſooner than they were forced. 1740. July

Thurſday. Hard Thunder-Showers falling in the Evening, ſtopped me at *Bewlie* till this Morning, and then I ſet out home- 24.

1740. July 24. ward, in Company with my Neighbour *Mercer:* We called in our Way at *Betheſda* (the Name given to that Place by Mr. *Whitfield)* next adjoining to *Bewlie*, where I ſaw great Things done ſince I viewed it laſt: The principal Houſe was a grand Edifice; the Deſign of the Apartments within I am not Maſter of; they were in ſuch Forwardneſs, as to be ready for raiſing the Roof this Week; it is all well cellared underneath; the Foundation Walls are of Brick, which riſe ſeveral Foot higher than the Surface of the Land, and the Rooms of both lower and upper Story are of good Height: As we approach it, are ſix good, handſome Edifices, three of each Side, for the following Purpoſes, *viz.* a Work-houſe for Women and Children, oppoſite an Infirmary of the like Dimenſions; next a Kitchen, oppoſite to it another of the ſame Size, for Waſhing, Brewing, *&c.* the other two I was not yet informed what Uſes they were deſigned for. Thence travelling on, we got home about Nine a Clock in the Morning; where I found about thirty of the *Cherokee Indians*, arrived the Day before from the Camp, being thoſe whom we expected, from the Account we had of them, as noted on the 15th Inſtant. They continued very ſickly and weak, and one of them died this Evening: They were conducted hither by Meſſieurs *Samuel Brown*, and

and *Jacob Morris*, two Traders in that Nation. The Heats were now grown ſo violent, that very few attempted to ſtir abroad; and I was contented to ſit ſtill, as others did, not hearing of any Thing that required Action without Doors. 1740. July

Friday. Indolence prevailed with moſt People, which I took my Share of; and avoiding any Buſineſs abroad, I found ſufficient always at home to employ my Time and Thought there, in getting forward what I had to do. Mr. *Whitfield* returned in the Afternoon from his Expedition to *Carolina*; but what Succeſs he met with there, in preaching, to promote the great Deſigns he had in hand, I yet heard nothing of: Before his Coming, we had various Reports of the Oppoſition he met with from Mr. *Garden*, Miniſter at *Charles-Town*, who (it is ſaid) by Virtue of a Power from the Biſhop, cited him to appear, and anſwer for many Doctrines which he preached that were not orthodox, and alſo for his irregular Proceedings, which gave ſo great Diſturbances to the publick Peace, as well as Diviſions among Families: To all which Mr. *Whitfield* gave but little Heed; but offering to partake of the Sacrament, Mr. *Garden* refuſed him, *&c.*——The certain Truth of theſe Things, we may probably ſoon be better informed in. 25.

Saturday.

1740. July 26. *Saturday.* Our Declaimers of the Club, finding thoſe Terrors, which they ſcattered among the People, did not operate ſo effectually as they expected, ſeemed reſolved to try what Example would do; and it was publickly given out, that *Tailfer* and Landlord *Jenkins* were preparing to ſend their Wives and Families out of Harm's Way, into ſome other Province, I know not where, intending to follow, when they judged a proper Time. Theſe cannot be numbered ſurely among our defenſive Men, nor any who have the like Faculty of ſmelling Danger at a Diſtance; of ſuch it is to be hoped there are but few, if ſuch theſe are. I really think it would be for the Benefit of the Colony, that they all left it, notwithſtanding the Decreaſe of People for ſome while paſt; for if they do not think their Property worth defending, I know not what Good can be expected from them; and moſt certainly a ſmall Band, well united, is of more Force than a looſe one more numerous, but eaſily diſperſed.

27. *Sunday.* Mr. *Whitfield* attended on the Service of the Church, as uſual; but being in a weak State of Health (ſuppoſed to be occaſioned by the Fatigue he underwent in his late Progreſs) he was not able to preach in the Forenoon; and in the Evening Service he was obliged to break off, and return home.

Monday.

Monday. Every Day now brought forth ſome new Report or other, touching the preſent Situation of Affairs in this Colony, and how far any Danger from the Enemy might affect us in theſe Parts: But I found the Generality pretty equanimous, and in no wiſe fond of giving Credit to many Falſhoods that were frequently publiſhed to affright Families (for Women will always have their Fears:) On the contrary, it was pretty evident with what Pleaſure any News was received, which imported a Probability of acting in a little Time offenſively againſt the *Spaniards:* Such was the Report of this Day, that came by a Boat from *Carolina:* Whereby we were informed, that a Ship arrived at *Charles-Town* from *Cowes*, brought Intelligence, that there was a very conſiderable Body of Soldiers, that were draughted out of ſeveral ſtanding Regiments lying in the Neighbourhood of *Portſmouth*, when he came away, deſigned to embark ſoon, to enable General *Ogletborpe* to carry on his Enterprizes againſt the Enemy. Whether there was any Foundation for this, or not, tho' much doubted, yet it is ſcarce credible how much all were enlivened by it, whom any Regard was due to: And on this Occaſion, looking over our Liſt of Freeholders, I thought even in this our low Eſtate I could mark out about ſeventy of them, who would be ready to defend their Country, and ſtand

1740. July 28.

1740. July ſtand to their Arms in good Earneſt, if Occaſion called them out for that Purpoſe; and it is of the Freeholders only, Inhabitants in *Savannah*, that I now ſpeak: For upon reckoning all the ſpare Men, and Servants, *Dutch* and *Engliſh*, belonging to the Town, there may be found more than enough to double that Number, excluſive of *Highgate*, *Hampſtead*, &c. and the Town of *Ebenezer* alone is able to furniſh betwixt fifty and ſixty good Men.

29. *Tueſday*. Capt. *Tingley*, who lately returned from the South, where he had diſpoſed of his Cargo, intending this Evening to proceed homeward for *New-York*; it would now be ſeen how many took this Opportunity, by Flight, to leave us; as we were told to expect Abundance would (by thoſe who would be glad to ſee it.) I took Care, as I uſed to do, to be exactly informed who went; and as Permits were refuſed to none who were weary of ſtaying here, excepting ſuch only as had juſt Demands upon them, which were yet unſatisfied, and no Perſuaſion, much leſs Compulſion, had been uſed to ſtop any body againſt their Inclination; there could be no truer Teſt, whereby to judge of the People's Diſpoſition than this. And behold it ended all in what follows: 1. *Joſeph Stanley*, a Freeholder ſuperannuated, weak and paſt any Labour; his Wife left him, and

and went to *England* three Years ſince, and he now went to a Relation, who he expects will keep him in his old Age: He never did any Thing towards maintaining himſelf by Planting whilſt here. 2. *Jacob Bernal*, a *Jew*, of no viſible Way of Livelihood. 3. *Hiam Bendannoon*, ditto, with his Wife and two ſmall Children. And laſt of all (thank God) the eminent Mrs. *Townſend* thought fit to leave us, whoſe Tongue has been a Nuſance to this Town ever ſince I knew it; taking her young Daughter with her now, and had not Patience to wait her Huſband's Return home from the South, where he with his Perriague had been employed; and what Loſs the Colony ſuſtains by ſuch a Deſertion, of whom no one has been a Grain of Corn the better for, I leave to our wiſe Men of the Club to diſcuſs, being paſt my Diſcovery. *N. B.* None of theſe now going off, were reckoned in that Number of ſeventy in Yeſterday's Notes. 1740. July

Wedneſday. A Skooner paſſed by *Thunderbolt* from the South, wherein was ſaid to be about eighty of the *Carolina* Regiment, on their Return home; which Regiment, from all the Reports we had, proved of little or no Uſe to the General in carrying on the Siege of *Auguſtin*, being always turbulent and diſobedient to Orders, many Inſtances whereof were notorious, but not 30.

proper

1740. July 30. proper to be noted here, before due Enquiry made into all thoſe Things, which it is expected will be in another Place, ere long; moſt of the gay Volunteers run away by ſmall Parties, baſely and cowardly, as they could get Boats to carry them off during the Time of greateſt Action; and Capt. *Bull* (a Son of the Lieutenant-Governor) who had the Command of a Company in that Regiment, moſt ſcandalouſly deſerted his Poſt when upon Duty, and not ſtaying to be relieved regularly, made his Flight privately, carrying off four Men of his Guard with him, and eſcaped to *Charles-Town*; for which he ought in Juſtice to have been tried as a Deſerter; but he was well received at home; and upon the Aſſembly's meeting, his Brother was choſen Speaker of that Houſe, in the Room of Mr. *Pinckny*, who was lately gone off (ſo the *Carolina* Gazette terms it) with two others of particular Note and Diſtinction in that Province, namely, Meſſieurs *Wragg* and *Whitaker*; the firſt one of the moſt conſiderable Merchants there, and the other a noted Lawyer, choſen by the Council to fill the Place of Chief Juſtice, till there ſhould be one duly appointed by his Majeſty: It is ſaid they are gone to *New-York*, to look for ſome Place to ſettle on, where they may be more eaſy, not liking (it ſeems) the Situation of Affairs at preſent, where they were.

were.—— If Half that we hear of theſe People proves true, it will afford Room for many Inferences, which I would not be too haſty in making till we know a little farther. 1740. July

Thurſday. Nothing to be heard of now from all Quarters, but Abundance of flying Reports concerning the late Tranſactions before *Auguſtin*, which were ſo different, that in giving too eaſy Credit to, a Man would moſt probably ſoon find himſelf deceived: One only Report, every one who wiſhed well to the Place, was in Hopes would prove true; which was, that we might expect the General here in a Fortnight, and then we might aſſure ourſelves many Truths would be laid open, which yet lay concealed. Mr. *Whitfield*'s Sloop came in from *Carolina*, by which ſeveral of his Diſciples in thoſe Parts came; but whether it was purely on a Viſit, or that any of them had a Deſign of continuing among us, was not known; tho' the latter did not ſeem likely yet a-while, one of them being an Anabaptiſt Teacher. 31.

Friday. Purſuant to the Court's Adjournment on the 8th *ult.* to this Day, for the Reaſon then given, they now met; when about ſeventy Freeholders delivered in their ſeveral Claims to ſuch Lots as they held, *&c.* But foraſmuch as many others did not appear, either thro' Ignorance, or Miſtake, Auguſt 1.

or

1740. Auguſt or other pardonable Occaſion, that none might think themſelves hardly dealt with, the Court adjourned farther for a Fortnight to the 15th Inſtant. Nothing elſe material to take Notice of.

2. *Saturday.* Mr. *Whitfield* not coming to Church this Morning (occaſioned, as it is ſaid, by the late Indiſpoſition continuing upon him) Mr. *Haberſham* read the Confeſſion, Lord's Prayer, and a Chapter out of the Goſpel; after which the Preacher before taken Notice of, advanced to the Deſk (there being yet no Pulpit) and naming the five firſt Verſes of the ſecond Chapter of the firſt Epiſtle of St. *Peter*, for his Text, he proceeded to give us a Sermon, ſetting forth the ſame Doctrine we were taught for a long while paſt, concerning the Neceſſity of a New Birth, and being endued with that vital Principle in our Hearts here on Earth, without which no one could enter into Heaven, being altogether carnal and void of ſaving Grace: After Sermon ended *extempore*, he made uſe of a long Prayer in the ſame Way; wherein he gave Thanks to God for the great Progreſs, and wonderful Succeſs which the Publication of the Terms of Salvation had met with, from that Inſtrument whom he had made uſe of in theſe Parts, and who (he prayed) might be as a Poſt of Iron, or Wall of Braſs, in Defence of the Truth he contended for, *&c.*

Sunday. Divers of the *Carolina* Strangers, who came laſt Week, continuing with their Wives, *&c.* among whom Mr. *Jones*, Miniſter at *Port-Royal*, was one; Mr. *Whitfield* had two Divines with him on the Bench this Day, when Mr. *Jones* read the Prayers of the Church, who is a Man of a very good Character, and orthodox Principles: Mr. *Tilly*, the Anabaptiſt Teacher, ſat as an Auditor only, and Preaching was the Part which Mr. *Whitfield* took to himſelf, the like before Noon and after; when he ſeemed to exert himſelf in a particular Manner, labouring to make good the Doctrine, which more eſpecially he had taught hitherto. 1740. Auguſt 3.

Monday. Having in vain waited for a Month or more paſt, to find a ſafe Conveyance of a Packet to *Charles-Town*, deſigned for the Truſt, which I made up on the 5th of *July*; but hearing of no Boat going that I could confide in, till now, when I underſtood a fair Opportunity offered to-morrow, I reſolved to do what I could, in getting another Packet ready, to be ſent in Company with the former; and that was my chief Employment this Day. 4.

Tueſday. What with one Hindrance or another, which unavoidably ſometimes called me aſide, I found this Day ſhort enough to finiſh what I took in hand Yeſterday; but at length putting an End to it, and Mr. 5.

1740. August *Jones* likewiſe having got ready what he had to ſend, I put it all up in a ſmall Box, together with my former Packet of the 5th *ult.* and in the Evening delivered it to the Patroon of the Boat *(Peter Shepherd)* whom I had Confidence in, and who was to ſet off with the next Tide about Three in the Morning; by him I alſo ſent another Box for Mr. *Eyre* (one of the honourable Truſt) wherein were Sundries left in Charge with me by his Kinſman, a Cadet in the Army in the South; and with the Boxes I wrote to Mr. *Hopton*, as uſual. Mr. *Whitfield*, with the Company about him, taking Horſe early to go and view what was doing at *Betheſda* (where they ſpent the Day;) after the Morning Leſſon was read at Church by Mr. *Haberſham*, Mr. *Tilly*, the Anabaptiſt, ſupplied the Place of an Expoſitor on the ſecond Chapter of the *Epheſians*.

6. *Wedneſday*. Returned now to my former Taſk, how to ſet the preſent State of the Colony in its due Light before the honourable the Truſtees, as they required: Wherein I met with ſuch Contrariety of Opinion, among divers whom I converſed with, touching ſome of thoſe Queſtions that were to be reſolved, that it was a great Difficulty how to reconcile them, ſo as to make one uniform Contexture of the Whole; which I had ſtrong Inclination to do, that as little Diſſenſion as poſſible might appear

appear among thoſe, whom I knew to be Perſons of a good Diſpoſition towards the Colony; and ſuch as I knew too well to expect they could be brought into any Meaſures but thoſe they had been projecting I know not how long paſt, I was determined not to have any Thing to ſay to them. In the Afternoon arrived Colonel *Vanderduſſen*, Commander of the *Carolina* Regiment, which had been in the Service at *Auguſtin*, with whom he was now on his Return to *Charles-Town*; and with him were ſeveral of his Officers: They had been beating the Sea ſeveral Days againſt a contrary Wind, without getting forward; for which Reaſon they came aſhore here for ſome Refreſhment. By Converſation with the Colonel, I was informed of ſeveral Things which I was a Stranger to before, and found him as ready as others, to condemn the daſtardly Behaviour of many of thoſe runaway Volunteers, and to expreſs a Reſentment againſt the ill Conduct of ſome of his own Officers; but from what he ſaid, I underſtood he was himſelf on very good Terms with the General, whom he ſpoke of with all due Honour and Deference; but it raiſed a Concern in us to be told by him, that the General was in ſo ill a State of Health at *Frederica*, as he was at the Time when he now left him, being (as he ſaid) reduced to an extraordinary Weakneſs, by

1740. August 6.

1740. August a continual Fever upon him, with ſome Intermiſſion, for two Months paſt; during which Time his Spirits ſupported him under all Fatigue; but the Diſappointment of Succeſs (it is believed) now galled him, and too great Anxiety of Mind preyed upon him.

7. *Thurſday.* Colonel *Vanderduſſen*, and ſome of his Officers, ſhewing a Deſire of viewing the Town, and Parts adjacent, which they were Strangers to, and admired the pleaſant Situation of; I walked with them to ſhew what I thought moſt worth their Notice; and upon ſome of them ſeeming to expreſs a great Pity, that ſo fine a Place made no faſter Advances towards Perfection, I could not refrain from addreſſing myſelf to ſuch among them, as I knew to live in the Neighbourhood of *Port-Royal*; and ſaying (in Return) that I alſo thought it great Pity, ſo commodious a Place as *Beaufort* was, ſhould ſeem at a Stand; for that in ſo many Years as I have known it, I did not diſcover the leaſt Increaſe of Inhabitants; but the ſame Show of a few ſtraggling Houſes ſtill appeared as when I firſt ſaw it: And as for *Charles-Town*, it was well known by ſome old People yet living, how many Years that Town lay in a languiſhing State, with little Hopes of Recovery: The ſame Obſervation was to be made on *Penſilvania*, now one of the moſt flouriſhing

riſhing Provinces in theſe Parts, from being almoſt in Deſpair of ever riſing, *&c.* and I made no Doubt, *Georgia* would alſo find the Way to its true Intereſt in a little more Time; tho' I ſhould never expect it would conſiſt in planting of Rice, which I apprehended they began to grow weary of now in *Carolina*; when it was apparent that as the Rate of Intereſt of Money was at 10 *per Cent.* unleſs Rice would bring 40*s.* *per* Hundred, the Planters muſt be ruined; and the Increaſe of that Product is grown ſo exorbitant, that for two Years paſt it will not exceed 30*s.* From all which I might naturally have inferred, that the Zenith of that Province's moſt flouriſhing State muſt certainly be paſt, unleſs they turn their Strength, as *Georgia* muſt, to ſome different Uſe from what is paſt. After ſome little inoffenſive Raillery among us on this Occaſion, I dined with them, as did alſo Mr. *Jones*; and towards Evening they took themſelves Boats, and went down the River to the Tender which they came in. 1740. Auguſt

Friday. Little paſſed worth Notice. Mr. *Whitfield*'s Weakneſs continued upon him, which he had brought on himſelf by ſuch an exceſſive Vehemence in preaching and expounding: He was ſometimes obliged to break off, unable to proceed; nevertheleſs I underſtood he was preparing to ſet out very ſoon on another Progreſs Northward, in- 8.

1740. August tending now to viſit *New-England* and thoſe Parts. Mr. *Jones* (the Miniſter of *Port-Royal)* left us this Evening, with his Wife, and went home, to the Diſappointment of many who wiſhed to have heard ſome of his Doctrine; but why they did not, I could no ways learn: The other Strangers, who with their Wives came hither more than a Week ſince, to hear the Word from Mr. *Whitfield*, deſigned (as I heard) to attend him till he departed hence, ere they returned to their ſeveral Homes in *Carolina*. By a freſh Account this Day from *Ockſtead*, we heard, that Mr. *Cauſton* was ſo far waſted as to leave his Friends little Hopes of ſurviving it much longer.

9. *Saturday*. Mr. *Tilly*, the Anabaptiſt Teacher, ſupplied Mr. *Whitfield*'s Place, in expounding a Part of the Scripture; for which he made Choice of the third Chapter to the *Philippians*, at uſual Time of Morning Service: The enſuing Day produced nothing particularly remarkable.

10. *Sunday*. Mr. *Haberſham* read the Prayers of the Church, and Mr. *Tilly* again preached. In the Afternoon the Congregation found ſome good Doctrine, from a regular Divine of the Church, Mr. *Jones* of *Port-Royal*, who went hence on *Friday* Evening, but meeting with a croſs Paſſage, was forced to return hither about Noon, and now gave the People a good Sermon, exhorting them to

to have a lively Faith in Chriſt, to lead virtuous Lives, and to put their Truſt in God's good Providence for all Things needful. 1740. August

Monday. Mr. *Whitfield* officiated at the Morning Service in his uſual Manner, but was yet very weak: About Noon Mr. *Noble Jones* arrived here laſt from *Frederica,* and brought many Letters thence for divers of our People; beſides a Letter from the General to Mr. *Jones* and me each: Whereat I conceived much Pleaſure, having not had the Honour of any from his Excellency for ſeveral Months paſt; neither could I well expect it, as Affairs ſtood: He was pleaſed to acquaint me, that he had ordered the Bearer, *Noble Jones,* to raiſe ten Men for a Guard and Scout-Boat; and that he was to receive his Orders from me, where principally to have a watchful Eye, that ſo we might have timely Notice, and not be ſurprized; and the like Caution was taken in divers other Parts, the General well knowing how very much the Safety of both theſe Provinces is expoſed to the Enemy's Half Galleys, with a wide-extended Frontier towards the Sea; hardly to be defended by a few Men; wherefore we muſt wiſh that our Frigates, which are ſtationed to cruize on this Coaſt, may be alert in their Duty alſo, and not lie aſleep in Harbour, which I have known in former Times has been laid to the Charge of ſome Commanders; 11.

1740. August 11. but far be it from me to ſuſpect any of our preſent Captains can be guilty of ſo diſhonourable an Indifference towards the Preſervation of theſe Countries. The Men that came now with *Noble Jones* (in Number upwards of thirty) were all *Georgia* Men, moſtly of *Savannah Town*, and liſted voluntarily here, towards compleating the *Carolina* Regiment, which was one Cauſe of *Noble Jones*'s having a Lieutenant's Commiſſion therein; and now their Time is near expired, the Colonel *Vanderduſſen* required all of them to proceed with the reſt of the Regiment for *Charles-Town*, to be paid off; but the General foreſeeing, that if they went thither, very few of them probably would return hither again, except ſuch as were married, moſt of the reſt being young Men, who were eaſy to be ſeduced; and moreover a pretty many Servants among them, both *Dutch* and *Engliſh*, who had their Maſters Leave to go, but not thereby to take the Remainder of their indented Time to themſelves: For theſe Reaſons they were all of them put on one Bottom, under this Officer's Care, who was charged by the General to ſee them all ſafe aſhore on this Place; and if any Doubt aroſe at *Charles-Town* concerning the Pay due, he would ſee that looked into; and *Noble Jones* was to go on himſelf to to *Charles-Town*, to ſignify the General's Sentiments to the Government there. 1740.

Tueſday. I found nothing ſtirring all this Day that deſerved particular Notice; ſome of our *Carolina* Strangers, who found themſelves pretty well repleniſhed with the Spirit, which they thought abounded from the Doctrine they had learnt here, now left us; and Mr. *Jones* the Miniſter of *Port-Royal* alſo, who was defeated in his Endeavour to return home laſt Week, attempted it again this Morning: But Mr. *Tilly* being found uſeful during Mr. *Whitfield*'s Weakneſs, continued yet as a Helper, and Fellow Labourer. August 12.

Wedneſday. The extream Heat of Weather more than common, for ſome Days paſt, had ſuch an Influence as to throw me into a little Diſorder, which would not admit of my cloſe Attention to any Buſineſs at preſent; neither did I hear of any Thing material to obſerve abroad. 13.

Thurſday. This Morning began with a very ſurprizing Piece of ill News; that the *Spaniſh* Priſoner, whom the Magiſtrates committed above a Year ſince (*vide* 29th and 30th of *July*, 1739.) upon ſtrong Preſumption of being a Spy, together with an *Iriſhman* his Companion, under the Term of a Servant; and whom, under Apprehenſions of a War likely to break out ſoon, the General had given Orders 14.

to

1740. August 14. to be continued in ſafe Cuſtody: They both broke out of Priſon this laſt Night, and were fled: Some ſtrong Grounds of Suſpicion ariſing ſeveral Days before, of their having a Deſign to make ſome Attempt that Way; the Magiſtrates ordered them to have Irons put on, for their better Security; which upon View a few Days after, were found ſo near ſawn off, that they might readily get quit of them; upon which freſh Irons were ordered, and withal an Iron Belly-band, with a Chain fixed in a Staple driven into the Floor: Notwithſtanding all which Precaution, and they being alſo locked into a cloſe Cell, they found Means to wrench the Staple of that Lock, and got into the outer Priſon, where in a moſt incredible Manner they got free alſo from their Fetters and Chains, and before Morning found Means to get out at the Top of the Priſon Room, by ſome of the Timber-Work being raiſed up, which could not be done but by ſome Help from without; nor could they have effected what they did within, had they not been ſupplied with proper Materials, by ſome Villains who aſſiſted them; and out of Hatred to the Authority by which this Colony ſubſiſts, are wicked enough to turn Parricides, and wiſh to ſee Deſtruction brought upon the Whole: Theſe are ſome of the Fruits of that ſeditious Club which infeſted

infeſted this Place; and though I would not, without plain Conviction, charge any of that Aſſembly with being perſonally aiding in ſo deteſtable an Act, I can very readily believe the Perpetrators of it to be well-inſtructed Diſciples of theirs, ready at all Times to obſtruct (as far as in them lies) every Thing done, however legally, which does not ſuit their Humours; and now more eſpecially upon miſſing a little while that Succeſs, which was immediately expected at *Auguſtin*, I made no Doubt but we ſhould ſee more and more daring Attempts made in various Shapes, to irritate People (if poſſible) to commit ſome Outrage or other; and that very ſoon too. All was done that could be thought of, in the Power of thoſe in Authority, to endeavour retaking theſe Fugitives, and Men ſent every Way on Horſeback, and Foot, and by Water, to try if any Diſcovery could be made; but as to my own Part, I own, that my Hopes were very ſmall about it; being poſſeſſed with an Opinion, that it was an Affair concerted by ſuch as had good Skill, as well as Will, to conduct it. And the Conſideration of an enraged and provoked Enemy being broke looſe, capable of giving the *Spaniards* ſuch Information at this Time, of all Circumſtances here, muſt needs quicken the Apprehenſions of divers good People among us, whom

1740. August 14.

1740. August whom I look on as valuable Men, and diſpoſed truly to give Proof at any Time of their firm Attachment to the Colony.

15. *Friday.* The Court ſat again, as *per* Adjournment, and received Claims from all who brought any ſuch, for what Lands they held under the Truſt, which were as many, or more, than at their laſt Sitting. Great was our Expectation of what would be the Succeſs of their Endeavours, who were gone in Purſuit of the Goal Breakers; but yet it proved vain.

16. *Saturday.* What happened this Day among us, I thought a pretty plain Indication of my Imagination not being without ſome Foundation, from whence ſuch Thoughts aroſe on *Thurſday* laſt: For two or three of our *Indian* Traders, who took up their Lodging at *Jenkins*'s (who are generally, with a few Exceptions, a debauched, diſſolute People) having continued in Town ſomewhat longer than uſual, and got intimate with our Club Gentry there, who had taught them the Way of railing againſt all publick Tranſactions of this Place, and talking with Contempt in whatever Company they kept, of the Magiſtrates, and all in any Authority; it was no more than might be expected, if ſuch Inſolence ſhortly broke out into Action, and open Defiance of all Power whatever. Accordingly Meſſieurs *Parker* and *Jones*, having

ſummoned one of theſe Traders to appear before them, and anſwer the Complaint of a certain Keeper of Stores at *Auguſta*, who was a well behaved Man, and ready to make it appear how grievouſly he had injured him, and fraudulently attempted to carry off a great Quantity of his Goods: The firſt Step taken by him was an abſolute Diſobedience of their Warrant, which put them under the Neceſſity of ſending the Conſtable to bring him by Force; which was no ſooner done, but two more of his Comrades followed after him; and when the Magiſtrates attempted to examine into the Truth of Things, with all due Temper, they were interrupted in a ſcandalous Manner, and ſet at nought by them all three, ſwearing, curſing, and daring them to do their worſt, refuſing to ſubmit to any Determination of theirs, and even to lay aſide their Hats in Token of allowing them to be Magiſtrates, though they well knew it. One of them was audacious enough to diſcover the Venom of his Heart, by bitter Imprecations, and declaring, that he hoped to ſee this curſed Town ſhortly in Flames, which nothing ſhould extinguiſh but the Blood of the Inhabitants; for which he was immediately, and moſt deſervedly, ſent to Priſon: Another of them, in the Time of his Ranting, ſhaking his Fiſt at Bailiff *Parker*, and threat-

1740. August 16.

1740. August 16. threatning to call him to Account for theſe Things to-morrow, it was thought proper to ſend him to the Cuſtody of the Guard, for preventing of Miſchief: And in his Way thither he attacked the Conſtable, who being a Man of Spirit, and a good Officer *(viz. Samuel Mercer)* he ſoon ſhewed him he was miſtaken in his Man, and delivered him a Priſoner; which in a little Time brought ſome of his Club Acquaintance to pay him a Viſit there, being a Perſon in much Eſteem among them, and looked on by them as an able Railer, and Maker of Miſchief; wherefore they came not empty-handed, but brought both Wine and Landlord *Jenkins* himſelf with them, to keep up a good Heart in him. The third (who was the firſt Occaſion of this Uproar) refuſing to come to any Terms of Agreement whatever with his Adverſary, or to comply with any Thing propoſed by the Magiſtrates, wherein they ſought all Ways poſſible to give him Contentment, as far as Juſtice would permit; but he continued obſtinate and inflexible, bidding them do their worſt; though they would have been content with his giving his own Bond to come to a fair Account with the Complainant in any reaſonable Time; or would even have accepted of his entering into a ſingle Recognizance for his Appearance at any Seſſions three or four Months hence; but

but refuſing to accept of any ſuch Indulgence, and perſiſting ſtill in his contumelious Behaviour, there was no avoiding the Neceſſity they were under of committing him; which they did, to the ſame Place where they had ſent his incendiary Companion. During theſe Tranſactions, another Fellow (a Stranger, who has ſome Concern among theſe Traders) came ſaucily up to the Centry upon Guard, who would not ſuffer him to go in without Orders; and in an impudent Manner, with Abundance of Oaths, telling the Guard to their Teeth they were a Pack of Scoundrels, and that he, and a few more ſuch, as he knew where to find, would come and drive them all into the River: The Officer of the Guard laid hold of him, and bringing him to me, I ſent him to the Magiſtrates to get his Demerits with the others; but it appearing he was pretty much gone in Drink, and an honeſt Man of the Town being near who knew him, upon Security given for his Appearance at a proper Time, he was diſmiſſed; but after the Magiſtrates had done, I thought ſomething farther neceſſary for me; for on one Occaſion or another, obſerving a pretty many People gathered together, and it growing a little late in the Night, I was not without ſome Apprehenſions of a yet greater Feud ariſing; wherefore I ſent to the Tything-man next upon

1740. August 16.

1740. August upon Duty, ordering him immediately to bring his People with him, which I waited till he did; and then doubling the Guard, and leaving ſtrict Orders to prevent any Diſturbance, a little after Midnight I went home. No News yet of the Runaways.

17. *Sunday.* One of our Neighbour *Indians* coming to Town this Morning, and hearing of what had happened of the late Eſcape made by the two Priſoners, told us, that he met two ſuch Perſons as were deſcribed, about four Miles off, on the Path leading to *Palachocolas*; by which we found they had been lurking near, if not in Town, till they thought the firſt Heat of Purſuit was a little over; and now upon the ſame *Indian*'s telling us, he believed it was not too late to overtake them, wherein he would give what Aſſiſtance he could, by tracking, *&c.* we ſent out immediately freſh Parties, Horſe and Foot, in Queſt of them, under his Guidance, with freſh Hopes of Succeſs. Mr. *Whitfield* did his Office of praying and preaching this Morning, but was in a very weak State; and in the Afternoon was forced to go out of Church as ſoon as he came in, leaving Mr. *Haberſham* to read the Prayers, and Mr. *Tilly*, the Anabaptiſt, to perform the reſt; who after an *extempore* Prayer of more than an Hour, and a Sermon of as great a Length, diſmiſſed his Audience; a great Part of which (if

(if I miſtake not) would have choſen rather to have ſtaid at home. Whether he, or who elſe, was appointed by Mr. *Whitfield* to perform the Duty of a Miniſter here, during his Abſence, I know not; but notwithſtanding the low State he was in, I found he was determined to leave us in a few Days, and go to the Northern Provinces: For in a Kind of a farewel Sermon that he gave us in the Forenoon, when he recommended us all to the Grace of God, and in a particular Manner charged thoſe of his own Houſe how to behave as well towards each other, as the Children he left under their Care; he ſignified that he believed it would be a long while ere he ſaw us again: And indeed unleſs he got a little Recovery of Strength ſoon, which was ſo waſted by his inceſſant Labour and Vehemence in preaching, I much doubted whether or not he would live to come back. 1740. August

Monday. I could not learn any Thing, during the Courſe of this whole Day, that deſerved Notice from me here: The Purſuers of the Fugitives not yet returning, we knew not what to expect. A fine Shower of Rain falling, was exceeding delightful and refreſhing, the Heats for a while paſt having been more than ordinary violent; nevertheleſs the Town had the great Bleſſing of Health to a Degree far 18.

1740. August beyond its Neighbours croſs the River in *Carolina*, which it was to be wiſhed might not be impaired, as the Fall came on, through the immenſe Quantity of Peaches growing every where, which our People have long eaten with Greedineſs, alike with the Swine, that have in great Part been fed with them. All Peace and Quiet again, and *Saturday* Night's Ruffle forgot for the preſent.

19. *Tueſday*. Mr. *Whitfield* went on board his Sloop very early, about Three in the Morning, falling down the River on his intended Voyage Northward, and taking with him Mr. *Simms* only of his own Houſhold, to attend him in his Travels; divers others, Men and Women, Strangers, went Paſſengers as far as *Charles-Town*, who had a good while been his Diſciples here, and now returned to their ſeveral Homes in *Carolina*; Mr. *Tilly* alſo took the ſame Opportunity, and left us; *Robert Gilbert* (one of our Freeholders, and Magiſtrate laſt Year) with his Wife, were the only Perſons who went with them, which they could give no good Reaſon for; not that their Loſs is of any great Significance, for he was originally a Seller of old Cloaths in *London*, here a botching Taylor, and no Planter, but a ſober, quiet Man, doing no Harm, nor much Good, more than doing his own perſonal Guard-Duty; and if

if I am rightly informed, he hath formerly received many diſtinguiſhing Marks of Favour, very ſolid ones too, from Mr. *Oglethorpe*; for he came in a very poor State; but howſoever hard Thoughts ſome Folks may have conceived of *Georgia*, it is plain he has found it a Place where he could live and make Money; whereof he is not wanting to carry with him to *Penſilvania*, to which Place he thinks himſelf directed by the Spirit, which mixed with ſome Ingratitude, I think to be his preſent Compoſition. The next Movement of any of our ſettled Inhabitants, it is expected will happen among our reſtleſs Gentry of the Club, ſome of whom, namely, Dr. *Tailſer* and *Jenkins*, I have before taken Notice were preparing to ſend off their Wives and Families; but that not yet being done, it is now publickly given out, that they themſelves alſo are preparing to go with them, and were putting their Goods on board a ſmall Sloop lying near, formerly built by Mr. *Robert Williams*, but never yet employed, whereof another of the Club was to go Maſter on this Occaſion, whoſe Skill in Navigation is ſuppoſed not to be great; and when I ſee this come to paſs, I ſhall think the Colony happily delivered from the moſt miſchievous Set of People that ever ſat down in it; for it muſt inevitably cauſe a Diſſolution of that So-

1740. August 19.

1740. August ciety when their great *Pan* is gone; nevertheleſs as they all ſtand Debtors in ſome Degree or other on the Truſtees Books, it is to be expected they muſt come to an Account before they are ſuffered to depart; though probably that may, among others, be termed an arbitrary and tyrannical Act.

20. *Wedneſday.* Some of our Purſuers being returned *re infectâ*, who went out on *Sunday* laſt, and others yet continuing abroad, after tracking them as far as the River *Oguchee*, we did not deſpair utterly of their coming up with them. One of the Perſons taken into Cuſtody on *Saturday* laſt, being diſcharged from the Guard on *Monday* Morning, upon aſking Pardon for his Offence, and finding Sureties for the Peace; another of them was this Day diſcharged out of Goal, upon his Submiſſion likewiſe, and complying with what was at firſt required of him, confeſſing he found himſelf miſtaken in ſome whom he expected to take his Part, that in this Time of Need would not ſo much as appear to be his Bail; from whence it was pretty evident who had been the Inſtigators of that Diſturbance, as we judged at that Time; but the third ſuperlative to the others, with his Menaces of Flame and Blood, the Magiſtrates thought proper to detain till he was made a little more ſenſible

ble of his Crime. What fell out more in the Day, was of no Moment. 1740. August 21.

Thurſday. The reſt of the Horſemen now returned from their Purſuit of the Goal-Breakers, all agreeing in one Opinion, that they could not have paſſed the *Oguchee* River, but they muſt have made ſome Diſcovery of it; but the Swamps and Thickets on this Side were ſo impenetrable, that no Good could be done by attempting to look into them; and thereupon ſome of our *Indians*, which they had with them, undertaking to guard all thoſe Places of difficult Acceſs, and to watch them narrowly if they lay hid there (as was ſuppoſed) what Hopes we now had remaining, were built upon the Diligence of thoſe *Indians*. Mr. *Jones* calling on me this Afternoon, and conferring a while (as we frequently uſed to do with one another) was gone not far from my Houſe, when a Gun went off; and he returning immediately, aſked me if I knew whence that Shot was, for that it was with a Ball, which he heard whiz very near him: He went away again but a little Way, when another Shot was made from the ſame Quarter, with a Ball alſo, and that I heard clearly paſs over my Head as I ſtood at the Gate of my Yard looking out; whereupon I called on Mr. *Jones* (not yet out of Sight) and when he came, upon laying theſe

1740. August 21. Things together, we thought the Circumſtances attending it were pretty remarkable; wherefore Mr. *Jones* taking the Tything-man with him, who is a Smith, and whoſe Shop is over-againſt the Backſide of my Houſe, in one of the Planks of which Shop one of theſe Balls lodged that were now fired, they went directly and ſeized the Fellow, who was yet ſtanding on, or near the ſame Spot from whence he had fired, and had his Gun again ready loaden; it was juſt without the Skirts of the Town; the Houſe where I live at preſent is in *Huck*'s Tything, N° 9. in *Percivall* Ward, not far from the Court-Houſe: The Diſtance of Mr. *Jones* from me was as far as N° 6. in the ſame Tything, when the firſt Shot paſſed by him, on his Way home: Upon Examination, the Fellow owned that he was not ſhooting at any Mark or other particular Thing whatever, but only diverting himſelf with his Gun; when we aſked him whether he thought it a reaſonable Diverſion or not, to ſtand without the Town and fire Ball into it, levelling his Piece directly: He had nothing to ſay more, than that he did not mean any Harm: But Mr. *Jones* not ſatisfied with that Anſwer, and which I neither could think a very ſufficient one; he committed him for the preſent, and took the Gun from him, which I was told afterwards was found to be loaden with Drop Shot (the ſame as is commonly uſed in killing of Deer) by which it looked as if he reſolved to make ſure of ſome Miſchief the next Diſcharge, the two laſt that he made paſſing ſo near each of us, though at ſo wide a Diſtance as we then were from one another. The Fellow was a Servant to *Phelps* a *Scotchman*, who for a Year or two paſt had rented a Houſe in Town, where he kept Store of Cloth, and other like dry Goods, and was one of the moſt active and buſy Men of our Club, being the ſame whom the General ſhewed ſuch a particular Mark of his Diſpleaſure to, as noted in my Journal of the 23d of *April* laſt; and of late finding his Behaviour narrowly watched, he thought it beſt to withdraw to *Charles-Town*, quitting his Houſe, where he had little Store left; and this Man was appointed to ſtay here, waiting his farther Orders. Divers of our People, beſt affected, are apt to draw Inferences from this, which I cannot readily join in; for how malicious ſoever the Maſter may be, I am unwilling to think he had a particular and perſonal Antipathy towards me, or that his Servant would, at any Inſtigation, perpetrate ſo baſe and wicked an Act, as to deſtroy a Man in cold Blood, who had never injured him, and hardly knew him.

1740. August 21.

1740. August 22. *Friday.* The Court ſat again, to receive Claims from any who brought them, whereof divers yet came in. Mr. *Currie* (an *Indian* Trader) went privately out of Town, as the Magiſtrates were informed, to the Orphan-Houſe, where ſome of Mr. *Whitfield*'s People had promiſed to aſſiſt him with a Boat, to carry him to the General at *Frederica*, with Intent to make Complaint to his Excellency of the hard Uſage which ſome of his Fraternity had met with in thoſe Proceedings againſt them, as noted on *Saturday* laſt & *ſeq.* but the Magiſtrates were under no Apprehenſion of his Diſpleaſure, for having done no more than their Duty on ſuch an Occaſion, when the publick Peace was at Stake, and their lawful Authority ſet at nought.

23. *Saturday.* This Day I devoted wholly to my little Ville at *Bewlie*, where I ſpent it with Pleaſure, having not ſeen it ſince the 23d paſt: The principal Work now in hand was ſetting up a little Edifice of ſomewhat better Sort than any yet done, as Neceſſity required hitherto; for I was alſo deſirous to frame a ſmall Habitation, commodious for myſelf and a Friend with me, when I ſaw it during my own Time, and uſeful to ſuch afterward as were to take Poſſeſſion. After a pretty hot Day, I choſe to return pretty late in the Evening, having the Benefit of a bright Moon, and heard of nothing ſtrange when I came home.

Sunday.

Sunday, St. *Bartholomew*. Mr. *Habersham* now ſupplying Mr. *Whitfield*'s Place during his Abſence, he read the Prayers, and a Sermon before Noon and after; but out of what Author I knew not; it ſeemed to be entering upon a freſh Round of the Doctrine of Regeneration, Converſion and Juſtification, beginning again with our Saviour's Conference with *Nicodemus*. Having no freſh Intelligence ſince *Thurſday* of what Succeſs might be expected relating to the Recovery of thoſe Goal-Breakers, we began now to deſpair of any Good. 1740. August 24.

Monday. In the Afternoon arrived *Peter Emery* with his Boat from *Charles-Town*, and brought with him two Packets from the Truſt, which were committed to his Care by Mr. *Hopton*, who alſo wrote me a Letter, ſignifying his having received them about a Week before, and acquainting me, that a new Poſt-Maſter being lately appointed, he ſuffered no Letters to be brought aſhore, but what he fetch'd himſelf; wherefore all Letters and Packets, for the future, muſt be paid for; and that he was now obliged to pay 20*s*. Currency (*i. e.* Half a Crown) for theſe two; he wrote me likewiſe, that the two Boxes I ſent him lately, one directed to Mr. *Verelſt*, the other to *Robert Eyre*, Eſq; as ſpecified in my Letter to him of the 5th Inſtant, he had delivered to the Care of Capt. *Samuel* 25.

Ragly

1740. August *Ragly* of the *Betty*, taking the Captain's Receipt for them, which he had incloſed to Mr. *Verelſt* in a Letter; but was obliged to mention in the Receipt 10*s.* Sterling to be paid for Freight of them, or he would not take them and ſign it. In each of theſe Packets I found one for the General, with various other Letters to ſundry People, one to Mr. *Jones*, and two ſhort ones to myſelf of the 24th of *April* and the 5th of *May*, referring to divers Papers incloſed from Mr. *Verelſt*, &c. I ſent abroad all that came to hand for other People, and the Contents of what Mr. *Jones* and I receiv'd gave Occaſion of our Conference good Part of the Evening; when we concluded upon it, that one of us would go and wait on the General ourſelves in a Day or two, with thoſe Packets for him, having not ſeen or heard from him for a good while paſt; and it was highly needful to inform him of divers Things paſſed here of late, that we might be adviſed the better *ore tenus.*

26. *Tueſday.* Mr. *Cauſton* being brought to Town a few Days ſince in a very weak State, hoping that Change of Air, and the Converſation of his Friends might contribute towards his Recovery; I had the Opportunity of delivering him his Letter from the Truſt, whereof I had received a Copy. He was reduced, indeed, to the Shadow of a Man, and there appeared little Room

Room of his Amendment, otherwiſe than from him with whom all Things are poſſible. It was again given out, that Meſſ. *Stirling*, *Grant* and *Douglas*, had received in that Letter which I delivered them from the Truſt, a ſatisfactory Anſwer to what they had requeſted, touching their ſettling on *Wilmington Iſland*; which I knowing of could ſay nothing to: But as Dr. *Tailfer* was preparing now in Earneſt to leave us, and that Club muſt thereby come to an End, I apprehended no ill Conſequence, provided they were under a Covenant to cultivate Land, as well as raiſe a live Stock, which, perhaps, was their Aim only. 1740. August

Wedneſday. Much Talk now of Dr. *Tailfer*'s Preparation to leave us ſoon, together with his cloſe Adherents; and more than ordinary Pains having been taken by them ſince the Siege of *Auguſtin* being raiſed, to ſet forth the deſtitute and indefenſable State this Colony was left in, and that we might ſurely expect the Enemy to come ſoon upon us; I made no Doubt but I ſhould find this doughty Club, at their Breaking entirely up, go off with ſome little Train of puſillanimous Attendants: My Wiſhes at the ſame Time were, that they might not leave one among us behind them ſo actuated by the like Spirit of Diſcord, as to be capable of propagating more Miſchief. 27.

Thurſday.

1740. August 28. *Thurſday.* *Noble Jones* being in Town, whom the General had given the Command to of a Scout and Guard-Boat, with ten Men, to watch the *Narrows* at *Skedoway*, and who was to take his Orders from me as Occaſion might happen; I had many Things to ſay to him thereon, concerning a Boat which I had in my Eye at *Puryſburgh*, that was to be ſold, and I conceived would very fitly anſwer our Purpoſe, wherein I gave him proper Directions, as I alſo did about getting able and good Men for the Uſe intended (*vide* 11th Inſtant;) moreover acquainting him, that as it was probable I might go South very ſoon, to wait on the General, I ſhould in ſuch Caſe, on my Return, expect to find his Boat and Men at their proper Station; and therefore recommended to him to uſe all poſſible Diligence in ſo neceſſary a Piece of Service; which he promiſed.

29. *Friday.* The Packets for the General having lain in my Hands ſince *Monday*, and ſeeing no Opportunity offer to ſend them; upon conferring with Mr. *Jones* upon it, I obſerved he had it in his Intention, to be the Bearer of them himſelf; but having not waited on the General in the South for more than a Year paſt (which Mr. *Jones* had divers Times) and withal having a more than ordinary Deſire at this Time, to conſult his Excellency on thoſe arduous

arduous Points, which the Truſtees in their Letters (of late received) had required me to be very explicit in, and for that Reaſon they had deſired me to crave his Help; I thought proper not to be too free with my Compliments at preſent, but ſaid plainly to him, that I thought it was my Turn; at which he acquieſced, and a Boat was ordered to be ready againſt the Morning Tide, very early. Dr. *Tailfer* now alſo began to ſend off his Goods and Luggage on board a ſmall Sloop lying at the Wharf, in order to proceed for *Charles-Town* in a Day or two, as it was ſaid. 1740. August

Saturday. I took Boat at Three in the Morning, having with me Mr. *Clee*, who had ſome ſmall Affair of his own to tranſact at *Frederica*, &c. and knowing him to be well ſkilled as a Pilot to ſteer, and moreover an inoffenſive Companion, I was glad of him in both Capacities. *Noble Jones* was to go out of Town in the Morning on Horſeback, to meet me at his own Plantation, which is within a Mile or two Diſtance from the Guard-Houſe: We arrived at his Houſe about Nine, and he came ſoon after; when we went together to the Watch-Houſe; which I found in pretty good Order; but with little more Expence and Labour, it would be very uſeful, and capable of Annoyance and Defence; and after a little Time ſo ſpent, we 30.

went

1740. August — went on with our Boat, and reached *Bear Iſland* that Evening, where we went aſhore, reſted during the Night; and,

31. *Sunday*, very early, we went forward, and reſted that Night on *Sapiloe Iſland*, not venturing too far, by reaſon the Wind aroſe, and began to blow hard.

Septemb. 1. *Monday*. Arrived at *Frederica* about Sunſetting; when underſtanding the General was in but a weak State of Health, ſeldom converſing with any more than needful; and being myſelf alſo pretty much diſcompoſed and fatigued, I ſent him his Packets by Mr. *Hawkins*, and aſked his Leave to wait on him in the Morning; whereupon he was ſo good to ſend me a Bottle of Wine, and a Bottle of Cyder: And the beſt Compliment I had to make him in Return, was to acquaint him I had a Bottle of *Savannah* Wine at his Service, made there, which I had brought with me, to preſent it with my own Hand from the Maker.

2. *Tueſday*. I did ſo in the Morning; when I was readily admitted, and kindly received; but wiſhed to have found his Excellency in better Health, for a lurking Fever that hanged on him for a long Time paſt had worn away his Strength very much; ſo that he indulged himſelf pretty much on his Bed, and ſeldom came down Stairs, but retained ſtill the ſame Vivacity of Spirit in Appearance to all whom he talked

talked with, though he choſe to converſe with very few; wherefore I never was urgent to ſpeak with him, when I called to aſk his Servants how he did (which was pretty often) but only left my Name, *&c.* waiting for the Time when he found an Inclination to talk with me of the Buſineſs I came about, which he very well knew. From this Day, during my Abode there, it was in vain for me to attempt keeping a daily Journal, which muſt have been *pro formâ* only, and filled with incoherent Trifles, not worth remembring. One Day I took to go and make a Viſit to the Camp at the South-Eaſt End of St. *Simon*'s, and paid my Reſpects to Colonel *Cook*, Major *Heron*, and ſome other Officers whom I knew, which is about eight Miles from *Frederica* by Land, but by Water (as I went) it is much farther round: Four Companies were here ſtationed, and the other two are at *Frederica* with the General, who are alſo encamped without the Lines of the Town, which the General is fortifying, by caſting up a Trench, and making proper Works at due Diſtances. I was glad to ſee the Men ſo ſoon and well recovered from the Sickneſs which they brought with them from *Auguſtin*, very few of them being now unfit for Service, and the Companies much fuller than I expected, wanting little more than a fifth Part to recruit the

1740. Septemb. 2.

1740. Septemb. the Whole; though the Company which marched at the Beginning of the Summer from *Port-Royal*, to join them, had loſt ſo many by Sickneſs, Accident of drowning, Deſertion, *&c.* that it wanted near half its Complement at their firſt taking the Field. From theſe two Camps, Detachments are made to ſupply the Out Gariſons near the Frontiers, *viz.* St. *Andrew*, *Fort William*, *Amelia*, St. *George*, &c. in Proportion to their Strength, and they are relieved as thought fit by the General. After nine or ten Days, his Excellency growing ſtronger, began to talk more cloſely of Buſineſs; and by Degrees taking the Affair into Conſideration, which principally occaſioned my waiting on him, I collected his Sentiments in many Things that I wanted to know, and withal informed him how far I could atteſt and maintain the Truth of divers Things which would need it: Many Things were diſcuſſed during the laſt few Days of my Stay, too long to enter into again here, but not fit to be forgotten by me; ſo having gone through what was requiſite, having the Pleaſure of parting with his Excellency in a much better State of Health than I found him, I took my Leave; and,

17. *Wedneſday*, about One o'Clock, we put off again with our Boat for *Savannah*, and reſted that Night at our former Camp on *Sapiloe*.

Thurſday.

Thurſday. We proceeded, and by the Help of a fair Wind we reached *Vernon* River; a little Way within the Mouth of which was *Bewlie*, where I took the Opportunity of looking into what was doing; but was ſorry to find ſo much Sickneſs among them; one of my beſt Servants ill; as was alſo my Overſeer's Wife, whilſt he himſelf newly gone to Town for ſome Help, was alſo taken ill there. 1740. Septemb. 18.

Friday. It was Noon this Day before the Tide would admit of our going on, with the Wind againſt us; and then we proceeded, after leaving the beſt Directions among them that I could, with Promiſes of remembring them farther, of which they ſhould have Tokens as ſoon as I got home. On our Way, we met with the Scout-Boat at her proper Station, which was appointed to guard that Paſs of *Skedoway Narrows*; and it was a Satisfaction to me to find the Orders I left with *Noble Jones (vide* the 28th of *Auguſt)* ſo well obſerved: After rowing a few Miles farther, the Wind holding contrary, we were oblig'd to come to an Anchor, and wait another different Tide coming, to carry us on, ſo we dozed in the Boat a-while; and putting forward again about Eleven at Night, we arrived at *Savannah* about Three or Four o'Clock in the Morning, being about the 19.

1740. Septemb. 20. ſame Hour we left it juſt three Weeks ſince.

Saturday. The firſt News I met with this Morning, as ſoon as abroad, was a full Completion of what I foreſaw would come to paſs, as I noted it on the 27th *ult.* For ſoon after I went South, the Doctor and his Crew made their Way North (it is ſaid) to *Charles-Town*; his Attendants or Followers ſoon after, were *Grant*, *Douglas*, *Sterling*, *Baylie*, and (to make the Set compleat) Landlord *Jenkins*, with his Wife alſo. It is needleſs to ſay what inſtigated theſe People, who have ſufficiently ſhewn their good Diſpoſition for ſome Years paſt. Thus we at laſt ſee an End of that curſed Club, which has ſo long been the very Bane of this Place, and which might have been happy ere now, had not the poiſonous Influence of that Crew blinded their Underſtandings. It is ſaid that the Fear of the *Spaniards* was what drove away theſe next following (all likewiſe ſince my going from home) *viz.* Dr. *Nunez* and his Son *Daniel*, *De Lion*'s Wife, *Pye*'s Wife (Siſter to Mr. *Brownfield*) our Conſtable *Duchee*'s Wife; their Huſbands yet ſtaying to wait a farther Event; and *Penroſe*'s Wife went off in Defiance of hers; a notorious Termagant, whom I ſuppoſe he thinks himſelf well rid of: On the contrary,

contrary, I this Day received the bad News of my own dear Wife's Death. 1740. Septemb. 21.

Sunday. Mr. *Haberſham* read the Prayers and Sermon in the ſame Way as before. Towards Evening *Laughlan M^c^Intoſh* alighted at my Door, and gave me a diſmal Relation of what had happened at Fort *Argyle*, upon the River *Oguchee:* Which in Subſtance was, That having been ſome Days abſent from the Fort on Buſineſs, partly at *Savannah* and elſewhere; on his Return thither laſt *Thurſday* Evening, he found the Doors all open, what Cheſts or Boxes were within rifled, much Blood ſpilt on the Bed, Floor, *&c.* and his Dog wrapt up in a Blanket with his Throat cut; from whence he concluded, that a Man and Woman Servant, whom he left there, were both murdered. How it happened that ſo few Hands were left there, or why he himſelf, who had the Charge of the Place, left them ſo defenceleſs, it was not a Time for me to enter into an Enquiry of; but I ſoon called the Magiſtrates, together, that due Examination might be taken of all Circumſtances which could be come at: And then he depoſed, that they had found the Servant-Man's Body floating in the River a Mile or two lower, with no Head to it, which was ſuppoſed to have been cut off; but they could find no Token of what became of the Maid: He ſaid, that

1740. Septemb. 21. when he went thither on *Thurſday* laſt, he had in Company with him *William Francis* of this Town, who was appointed one to keep Gariſon there; and before he came thence now, two or three other Men arrived there, under the ſame Appointment: It was obſerved, that during his Examination, he appeared very much diſordered, by an uncommon Flutter of Spirits, which raiſed a Jealouſy there was ſomething more than ordinary which he had not diſcovered; wherefore it was thought beſt to defer a farther Examination till to-morrow; and in the mean while a watchful Eye was appointed to be near him, as a Companion, that he might not ſlip out of Town, whilſt at the ſame Time he knew not himſelf to be under Confinement. Various were Peoples Conjectures on this Occaſion, and indeed the whole Town was alarmed, moſt Part of them concluding, that it muſt be ſome *Indians*, but what *Indians* they could not tell, unleſs our own Friends and Neighbours, which there were not the leaſt Grounds to ſuſpect. My own Thoughts (which divers concurred with me in) were, that the *Spaniſh* Doctor, and the *Iriſhman*, who broke Priſon, and eſcaped hence (as noted the 14th of *Auguſt*, *&c. ſeq.)* finding themſelves under great Difficulties how to ſubſiſt, and make a thorough Eſcape, had joined themſelves to ſome Negroes lately fled

fled from *Carolina*, who were wandring Southward (as of late many of them had deſerted; inſomuch that there was a Party of Horſe appointed always to ſcout on the Banks of the River, and guard the Paſſes out of that Province) and theſe ſo joined very probably might attempt ſuch an Act, eſpecially when they would meet with no Oppoſition; and what induced me the rather to incline to this Opinion was, that among the ſeveral Particulars of Plunder carried off, which chiefly conſiſted of Eatables, I took particular Notice they had taken a Quire of Writing-Paper, which could be of no Uſe to an *Indian*; and moreover it is to be obſerved, that when an *Indian* kills, he always takes the Scalp alone; but the Negro moſt commonly takes the whole Head. We were next to wait for what farther Diſcoveries we could come at to-morrow. 1740. Septemb.

Monday. The Magiſtrates now met again, and took Depoſitions in Form of what *Laughlan M^c^Intoſh* had to ſay; which he made Affidavit of: And finding him very abſtruſe in many Things, and differing from what he had reported Yeſterday; they became more ſuſpicious than before, that ſomething at Bottom was not right; wherefore Mr. *Parker* the Magiſtrate, and Mr. *Mercer* the Conſtable, offering voluntarily to go to the Fort themſelves, and endea- 22.

1740. vour to find out the Truth of the Whole,
September. it was ſo agreed at my Houſe; and as their readieſt Way to come at it, was up the *Oguchee* from the Mouth of it, they purpoſed to go by Land to *Noble Jones*'s Plantation; to whom I wrote an Order to be aſſiſting to them, with his Guard-Boat, and proper Hands; and accordingly they ſet out ſoon after. In the mean while proper Means were uſed to amuſe *Laughlan*, and keep him in Town, till we ſhould get ſome Report from *Parker* and *Mercer* how they found Matters at the Fort.

23. *Tueſday.* I thought every Day now loſt that was not chiefly employed in forwarding the great Work in hand, to ſet the preſent State of the Colony in a due Light before the Truſtees, as they had required for ſome Time paſt; and therefore having got ſome of the principal Materials together, in the beſt Manner I could, it muſt next be my Care to get it perfected with all poſſible Expedition; and ſo I reſolved.

24. *Wedneſday.* Nothing happened that required my taking Notice of in the Town, or abroad elſewhere, which I was not ſorry for, having enough to do at home every Day for ſome Time coming; and ſuch Confinement happened now to be alſo requiſite, on Account of a lame Leg that I brought home with me from my late Expedition, which was occaſioned by a trifling Acci-

Accident of a Bite from one of our flying Inſects (of which there is great Variety in this Part of the World) which occaſioned a ſmall Swelling, from whence enſued an extream Itching, and that was attended with Scratching, which added to the Venom; and the Skin being thereby a little broke, an Humour immediately followed it; ſo that maugre what Mr. *Hawkins* applied to ſtop it at *Frederica*, from the Bigneſs of a Pin's Head, it ſoon became a Sore as broad as a Man's Hand, as it yet continues; but by the Help of innocent cooling Things made uſe of now, and proper Reſt, I hope ſoon to ſee it healed. 1740. Septemb.

Thurſday. Meſſieurs *Parker* and *Mercer* returned; and having examined, upon Oath, the Perſons whom they found at the Fort, and made the beſt Enquiry they could, upon comparing the ſeveral Affidavits together, it was found, that in the main Points they agreed all. *Peter Emery* at this ſame Time having his Boat freighted with ſundry Goods bound for *Frederica*, Mr. *Jones* and I both wrote Letters to the General, adviſing him of what was needful in many other Caſes, as well as in this, delivering all to *Emery*'s Care, and recommending it to *Laughlan M'Intoſh* to go in the ſame Boat, and relate all to the General himſelf; and ſo he reſolved to do. 25.

1740. Septemb. 26. *Friday*, } Confinement at home be-
27. *Saturday*. } ing doubly neceſſary now, as well on Account of my Lameneſs, as to get forward what I had in hand; I ſtuck to it, and heard of nothing abroad that required my Attention theſe two Days.

28. *Sunday*. A Preſbyterian Divine, who arrived from *Carolina* ſome Days ſince, preached to the Congregation before Noon and after; but my Infirmity would not admit of my going to hear him.

29. *Monday*. Freſh Intelligence being brought us this Evening, that the *Spaniſh* Doctor, who with his Companion broke Priſon, and eſcaped hence ſome Time ago, had been ſeen that Morning near the Cow-Pen at *Old Ebenezer*; we began to conceive again more Hopes of Succeſs in our Endeavours to take them; wherefore upon Conſultation had, we made Choice of three of the moſt active and expert Men in the Woods that we had, to ride out well armed and provided with Food, to try what they could do; and for their Encouragement, a Reward of 20*l.* Sterling was promiſed upon catching them, or proportionable for either; being now pretty full in Opinion, that the late Murder and Plunder at Fort *Argyle* was perpetrated by that Crew; one at leaſt, if not more, having lately joined them; but who, we could not tell.

Tueſday.

Tueſday. The Perſons appointed rode out this Morning in Purſuit of thoſe Villains; and I reſted in the ſame Poſture at home as before, doing what I could in employing my Pen to a right Purpoſe. 1740. Septemb. 30.

Wedneſday. Still confined at home. Mr. *Cauſton* having ſpent a few Weeks in Town, for the Benefit of converſing with ſome of his old Acquaintance, thereby hoping to get a little Strength; during his Continuance here had the Misfortune to loſe his Son (his only Child) who was taken in one of thoſe intermitting Fevers, which are pretty frequent in this Part of the World, at this Time of the Year, whereof very few die; and being of a weak Conſtitution, it carried him ſoon off, which ſo affected his Father, that he returned mournfully to *Ockſtead*, ill able to ſuſtain his Grief. October 1.

Thurſday. Nothing came to my Knowledge from abroad worth Notice, but every body following their own Buſineſs, as I did mine, and hoped ſoon to be on my Legs again. 2.

Friday. At length the Time was come which brought the News we wanted, of thoſe Villains being taken; two of thoſe Men we ſent out returning this Day, and acquainting us, that they came upon them about twenty-five Miles beyond the Cow-Pen at *Ebenezer*, at a Place called *Mount Pleaſant*, or the *Uchee* Town (from ſome of 3.

thoſe

1740. October

thoſe *Indians* inhabiting thereabout) on the River *Savannah*, and is the uſual Place of croſſing it to the *Palachocolas:* Here the Rain had driven them for Shelter into a Hut, and our Purſuers ſurprizing them, they were ſecured without Reſiſtance; tho' they had Arms with them, which they took at Fort *Argyle*, and where they readily confeſſed they had murdered that Man and Woman, and made Plunder of what they liked. After binding them ſafely, they left them under the Charge of one of their own Company, joined with ſeveral other well known truſty Perſons, whom they met on their Paſſage by Water to *Savannah*, where they were bound; and it was a convenient Opportunity of ſending the Priſoners with them, whom we were to expect to-morrow; but they utterly denied having any third Perſon in their Company, as it was reported.

Saturday. Great were all Peoples Expectations of ſeeing thoſe Priſoners brought down, which were in Cuſtody, as they that took them reported to us Yeſterday; but one of their Guard being a principal *Indian* Trader among the *Creeks* and *Uchees*, we judged he might be detained a little by his Buſineſs with them, before he ſet out for *Savannah*; and ſo we would look for them to-morrow. A *New-York* Sloop, *Samuel Tingley* Maſter, arrived with Store

Store of Proviſion for Sale, which effectually put a Stop to one current Lie, that our late Deſerters had ſpread before their Departure; that all Provinces looked on us as a Place given up for loſt, and none of them would deal with us any farther for any Support: At the ſame Time the ſaid Maſter told us, that he himſelf heard ſome of thoſe that went thither from hence, complaining already how much dearer they found it living there than here, and beginning to wiſh they had not been ſo miſled. In the Evening Mr. *Cambel* returned, who went hence for *London* with Captain *Thompſon*, and arrived at *Charles-Town* about a Fortnight ſince; where he fell ill, that Place of late being grown very ſickly again: And he told me, he had brought ſeveral Packets for the General, which he had ſent to *Frederica*, by a Boat going that Way; and that he had alſo one for me from Mr. *Verelſt*, which he had during his Illneſs delivered to another Boat, under the Care of *Young Germain*, who was the Patroon bound hither; but that Boat being ſomewhere detained (as he imagined) was not yet arrived with the ſaid Packet, and he got hither by another Conveyance, before her, which gave me ſome Uneaſineſs: He farther told us, that ſeeing ſome of our late Club at *Charles-Town*, they aſked him if he was not

1740. October 4.

1740. October 4. not mad to go again to *Savannah*, where all People that were left were ſtarving, and the Place muſt ſoon be depopulated? So inceſſant were their vile Tongues employed in uttering their Venom againſt this Colony.

A

STATE

OF THE

Province of *Georgia*,

Atteſted upon Oath in the Court of *Savannah*, *Nov.* 10, 1740.

THE Province of *Georgia* lies from the moſt Northern Stream of the River *Savannah* (the Mouth of which is in the Latitude of 32 Deg.) along the Sea-Coaſt, to the moſt Southern Stream of the *Alatamaha* (the Mouth of which is 30 ½ Deg.) and Weſtward from the Heads of the ſaid Rivers, reſpectively in direct Lines to the South Seas.

THIS

THIS Province was Part of *South-Carolina*; but the Eaſtern and Southern Parts of it, inhabited by the *Creek Indians*; the Northern by the *Cherokees* and *Chickeſaws*; the Weſtern by the *Chactaws*; the *Blewmouths*, and other *Indian* Nations, to the *South-Sea*. The *Creek Indians*, who always acknowledged the King of *England* for their Sovereign, yet made War with the People of *Carolina*, to obtain Satisfaction for Injuries done by their pedling Traders: The War was concluded by a Peace, which obliged the People of *Carolina* not to ſettle beyond the River *Savannah*; and no *Engliſhman* was ſettled within this Diſtrict, that we know of, when the firſt Colony of *Georgia* arrived. The Country was then all covered with Woods. Mr. *Ogletborpe* agreed with the *Indians*, and purchaſed of them the Limits mentioned in the Treaty.

THE Town of *Savannah* was laid out, and began to be built, in which are now 142 Houſes, and good habitable Huts. The Soil in general, when cleared, is productive of *Indian* Corn, Rice, Peas, Potatoes, Pumpions, Melons, and many other Kinds of Gourds, in great Quantities; Wheat, Oats, Barley, and other *European* Grains, 'tis found by divers Experiments, may be propagated in many Parts (more eſpecially in the Uplands toward *Auguſta*) with

with Succeſs. Mulberry-Trees and Vines agree exceeding well with the Soil and Climate, and ſo does the Annual Cotton, whereof large Quantities have been raiſed; and it is much planted: But the Cotton, which in ſome Parts is perennial, dies here in the Winter; which nevertheleſs the Annual is not inferior to in Goodneſs, but requires more Trouble in cleanſing from the Seed. Cattle, Hogs, Poultry, and Fruit-Trees of moſt Kinds, have increaſed even beyond Imagination.

SHIPS of about three hundred Tons can come up to the Town, where the Worm (which is the Plague of the *American* Seas) does not eat; and the River is navigable for large Boats, as far as the Town of *Auguſta*, which lies in the Latitude of 33 D. 5 M. and is 250 Miles diſtant from *Savannah* by Water; ſmall Boats can go 300 Miles further, to the *Cherokees*.

THERE is already a conſiderable Trade in the River; and there is in this Town a Court-Houſe, a Goal, a Store-Houſe, a large Houſe for receiving the *Indians*, a Wharf or Bridge, a Guard-Houſe, and ſome other publick Buildings; a publick Garden of ten Acres cleared, fenced, and planted with Orange-Trees, Mulberry-Trees, Vines, ſome Olives which thrive very well, Peaches, Apples, *&c.*

IT

It muſt be confeſſed, that Oranges have not ſo univerſally thriven with us, as was expected, by Reaſon of ſome ſevere Blaſts by Froſts in the Spring; yet divers with proper Care have preſerved them; and as we ſee them grow and thrive well, with many of our Neighbours of *Carolina* to the Northward, we are convinced that they will with us alſo, as ſoon as we are become more perfect in the Knowledge of propagating them in a right Manner; in order to which frequent Experiments are making; and we have already diſcovered not only what Kind of Soil agrees beſt with them, but alſo that they flouriſh moſt when they grow under Foreſt Trees, whereby we imagine they are protected from Blaſts; and 'tis obſerved, that they take no Harm from the Droppings of any, except the Pine; which ſuffers nothing to grow near it, unleſs of its own Kind.

Notwithstanding the Quantity of Silk, hitherto made, has not been great, yet it increaſes, and will more and more conſiderably, as the Mulberry-Trees grow, whereof there are great Numbers yearly planted.

Vines likewiſe of late are greatly increaſed, many People appearing to have an Emulation of outdoing their Neighbours; and this Year has produced a conſiderable Quantity of very fine Grapes, whereof one

Planter

Planter in particular made a Trial, to ſee what Kind of Wine they would make, which he put into a large Stone-Bottle, and made a Preſent of it to the General; who upon taſting, ſaid he found it to be ſomething of the Nature of a ſmall *French* White Wine, with an agreeable Flavour; and ſeveral Perſons here, who have lived formerly in Countries where there are a Plenty of Vineyards, do affirm, that all young Vines produce ſmall Wines at firſt, and the Strength and Goodneſs of it increaſes as the Vines grow older.

THREE Miles up the River there is an *Indian* Town, and at ſix Miles Diſtance are ſeveral conſiderable Plantations: At ten Miles Diſtance are ſome more, and at fifteen Miles Diſtance is a little Village, called *Abercorn.*

ABOVE that, on the *Carolina* Side, is the Town of *Puryſburgh*, twenty-two Miles from *Savannah*; and on the *Georgia* Side, twelve Miles from *Puryſburgh*, is the Town of *Ebenezer*, which thrives very much; there are very good Houſes built for each of the Miniſters, and an Orphan-Houſe; and they have partly framed Houſes, and partly Huts, neatly built, and formed into regular Streets; they have a great deal of Cattle and Corn-Ground, ſo that they ſell Proviſions at *Savannah*; for they raiſe much more than they can conſume.

THIRTY Miles above *Ebenezer*, on the *Carolina* Side, lies the *Palachocolas* Fort: Five Miles above the *Palachocolas*, on *Georgia* Side, lies the *Euchee* Town (or *Mount Pleaſant)* to which about a hundred *Indians* belong; but few of them ſtay now in the Town, they chuſing rather to live diſperſed. All the Land from *Ebenezer* to the River *Briers* belongs to thoſe *Indians*, who will not part with the ſame, therefore it cannot be planted.

ONE hundred and forty-four Miles above *Mount Pleaſant*, on the *Carolina* Side, is *Silver Bluff*, where there is another Settlement of *Euchee Indians:* On both Sides of the River are Fields of Corn planted by them.

THIRTY Miles above *Silver Bluff* is *New Windſor*, formerly known by the Name of *Savannah* Town, or *Moore*'s Fort, where there are but two or three Families on the *Carolina* Side, and a ſmall Fort.

SEVEN Miles above *New Windſor*, on the *Georgia* Side, lies the Town of *Auguſta*, juſt below the Falls; this was laid out by the Truſtees Orders in the Year 1735, which has thriven prodigiouſly; there are ſeveral Warehouſes thoroughly well furniſhed with Goods for the *Indian* Trade, and five large Boats belonging to the different Inhabitants of the Town, which can carry about nine or ten thouſand Weight of of Deer-Skins each, making four or five Voyages at leaſt in a Year to *Charles-Town*, for exporting to *England*; and the Value of each Cargo is computed to be from 12 to 1500*l.* Sterling. Hither all the *Engliſh* Traders, with their Servants, reſort in the Spring; and 'tis computed above two thouſand Horſes come thither at that Seaſon; and the Traders, Packhorſe-men, Servants, Townſmen, and others, depending upon that Buſineſs, are moderately computed to be ſix hundred white Men, who live by their Trade, carrying upon Packhorſes all Kinds of proper *Engliſh* Goods; for which the *Indians* pay in Deer-Skins, Bever, and other Furs; each *Indian* Hunter is reckoned to get three hundred Weight of Deer-Skins in a Year. This is a very advantageous Trade to *England*, ſince it is moſtly paid for in Woollen and Iron.

Above this Town to the North-Weſt, and on the *Georgia* Side of the River, the *Cherokees* live, in the Valley of the *Appelachin* Mountains; they were about five thouſand Warriors; but laſt Year it is computed they loſt a thouſand, partly by the Small-Pox, and partly (as they themſelves ſay) by too much Rum brought from *Carolina*. The *French* are ſtriving to get this Nation from us, which if they do, *Carolina* muſt be ſupported by a vaſt Number of Troops, or loſt: But as long as we keep the Town of *Auguſta*, our Party in the *Cherokees* can be ſo eaſily furniſhed with Arms, Ammunition and Neceſſaries, that the *French* will not be able to gain any Ground there.

THE *Creek Indians* live to the Weſtward of this Town. Their chief Town is the *Cowetas*, two hundred Miles from *Auguſta*, and one hundred and twenty Miles from the neareſt *French* Fort. The *Lower Creeks* conſiſt of about a thouſand, and the *Upper Creeks* of about ſeven hundred Warriors, upon the Edge of whoſe Country, the *French* Fort of *Albamahs* lies: They are eſteemed to be ſincerely attached to his Majeſty's Intereſt.

BEYOND the *Creeks* lie the brave *Chickeſaws*, who inhabit near the *Miſſiſipi* River, and poſſeſs the Banks of it; theſe have reſiſted both the Bribes and Arms of the *French*, and Traders ſent by us live amongſt them.

AT *Auguſta* there is a handſome Fort, where there is a ſmall Garriſon of about twelve or fifteen Men, beſides Officers; and one Reaſon that drew the Traders to ſettle the Town of *Auguſta*, was the Safety they received from this Fort, which ſtands upon high Ground on the Side of the River *Savannah*, which is there one hundred and forty Yards wide, and very deep; another Reaſon was the Richneſs

and

and Fertility of the Land. The great Value of this Town of *Auguſta* occaſioned the General to have a Path marked out, through the Woods, from thence to *Old Ebenezer*; and the *Cherokee Indians* have marked out one from thence to their Nation, ſo that Horſemen now can ride from the Town of *Savannah* to the Nation of *Cherokees*, and any other of the *Indian* Nations, all on the *Georgia* Side of the River; but there are ſome bad Places which ought to be cauſewayed and made good, and which the General ſays he has not yet Capacity to do. This Road begins to be frequented, and will every Day be more and more ſo, and by it the *Cherokee Indians* can at any Time come down to our Aſſiſtance.

At *Old Ebenezer* there is a Cow-Pen, where the Truſtees have a great Number of Cattle, and 'tis hoped with Care they will amount to ſix or ſeven hundred Head in another Year: But they were much neglected, there not being Horſes or Men ſufficient to drive up the young and outlying Cattle.

This is the Situation of the Settlements upon the River, at the Mouth of which lies the Iſland of *Tybee*, with the Light-Houſe, which has been of the greateſt Uſe to all Ships falling in with this Part of *America*. But from *Savannah* Southward, there are ſeveral Plantations (beſides the Villages of *Hampſtead* and *Highgate)* ſeveral of which are ſettled by ſuch of the Inhabitants of the Town, as being able to purchaſe Cattle, have petitioned for Leaſes of Lands, and are ſettled upon thoſe Lands by the General's Permiſſion, until the Truſtees Pleaſure be known concerning the Leaſes: The Terms they propoſe, is the Leaſe to be for twenty-one Years, renewable every ſeven Years, upon paying one Year's Purchaſe of the improved Value; the firſt ſeven Years to be free, and no Fine paid for the firſt Renewal. Beſides theſe Settlements, there are ſome others of five hundred Acres *per* Grant from the Truſt, which extend as far as the *Ogeechy* River; upon which River lies *Fort Argyll*, in ſuch a Situation, as is intended thereby to command all the Paſſes in that Part of the Province.

THE next is *Darien*, where the *Scots* Highlanders are ſettled; the Buildings are moſtly Huts, but tight and warm; and they have a little Fort: They have been induſtrious in Planting, and have got into driving of Cattle, for the Supply of the Regiment, *&c.* but this laſt Year moſt of them going voluntarily into the War, little was done at home, where their Families remained.

BELOW

Below the Town of *Darien*, is the Town of *Frederica*, where there is a ſtrong Fort, and Store-Houſes, many good Buildings in the Town, ſome of which are Brick; there is a Meadow near adjoining that is ditch'd in, of about three hundred and twenty Acres, of which there is good Hay made. The People have not planted much there this Year, occaſioned by the War ſo near their Doors, and being chiefly Tradeſmen, who make more by working, or ſelling to the Camp, than they can by Planting. There are ſome little Villages upon the Iſland of St. *Simon*'s, and ſome very handſome Houſes built by the Officers of the Regiment; and there has been Pot-Herbs, Pulſe, and Fruit, produced upon the Iſland, of great Uſe towards ſupplying the Town and Garriſon: But Corn, Beer, and Meat, they have from elſewhere.

Between this Iſland and *Jekyll Iſland*, is an Inlet of the Sea, called *Jekyll Sound*, which is a very fine Harbour, and is one of the beſt Entries the *Engliſh* have to the Southward of *Virginia*. This is an excellent Station for Ships to cruize on the *Spaniards*, it commanding the homeward-bound Trade, which muſt come through the Gulph of *Florida*, and near St. *Simon*'s; the Entry lies in 31 D. 10 M. The Place is barred, but upon the Bar there is Water ſufficient every Tide to carry in Twenty-

Gun Ships; and taking the beſt Opportunity, Forty-Gun Ships may be carried in to refit; — a great Conveniency to a Squadron in this Place. Upon *Jekyll Iſland* there is but very little good Land, not above three or four hundred Acres, the reſt being ſandy Sea-Beach. Mr. *Horton* has his Lot upon this Iſland, and has made great Improvements there. To the Southward of *Jekyll* lies the Iſland of *Cumberland*, and the Fort of St. *Andrew*'s, ſituated upon a fine commanding Ground; and on the S. E. of the ſame Iſland, is another ſtrong Fort called *Fort William*, which commands *Amelia Sound*, and the inland Paſſage from *Auguſtine*. The next Iſland is *Amelia*; beyond that is St. *John*'s, one of the *Spaniſh* Outguards; and between forty and fifty Miles from that is *Auguſtine*.

We are now fully acquainted with the Colony, and what it will produce; the inland Part is hilly, till it riſes into Mountains, where all Kinds of Timber grow. Near the Sea the Ground is more level and flat, where Laurels, Cedars, Cyprus, Bays, and Live Oak, are of the Size of Timber-Trees: Among the Shrubs, ſome of the principal are Pomegranates, which will grow well in Hedges, Myrtle, prickly Pears, Shumach, Saſſafraſs, China Root, ſeveral Sorts of Snake Root, *&c.* There is commonly black Mould in the low Lands;

Lands; the riſing Ground is frequently Clay, where Oak and Hickery moſtly grow; as it alſo does in a great Part of the flat Land that is dry, where Walnut, Aſh, Gum-Tree, Oak of ſeveral Kinds, Hickery, Beech, wild Cherries, *&c.* are in great Plenty to be found. The higher Lands are of a ſandy Surface, where Pines uſually grow, all Parts producing Trees of ſome Kind or other, except the Savannahs, and Marſhes, which bear Graſs; and many of the low Land Swamps covered with Canes, which are excellent Feed for Cattle in the Winter. Where the Oak and Hickery grow, the Soil is in general of a ſtrong Nature, and very well eſteemed for Planting, being found by Experience to produce the beſt Crops of *Indian* Corn, and moſt Sorts of Grain, except Rice, which thrives beſt in ſwampy Ground: This is only ſpoken of the lower Parts of *Georgia*, which reaches from the Sea-Shore to the Foot of the Hills, being a flat Country of ſixty or ſeventy Miles, or more, in Breadth. The Hill Country is very different, there being Marble, Chalk, Gravel, Rocks, and all the ſame Variety of Soil that is in *Europe*; with reſpect to the Proportion of the different Kinds of Soil, it cannot be given, unleſs the Whole were ſurveyed; but the *American* Dialect diſtinguiſhes Land into Pine, Oak and Hickery, Swamp, Savannah,

nah, and Marſh. Near the Town of *Savannah* we have found Stone, which is dug for Building; as there is alſo good Clay, whereof Bricks are made; and a Pottery Work is carried on with Succeſs, where common Ware for moſt Uſes is made in good Plenty, and exported to the neighbouring Provinces; and the Maſter, who is of an enterprizing Genius, has undertaken, as ſoon as he has made proper Furnaces, to make a ſuperfine Sort, of ſuch as ſhall not be inferior to *Porcelian* itſelf; but a little Time will diſcover his further Performances.

THE Coaſt is low, with a hard, ſandy Beach: When we approach it at twenty-five Leagues Diſtance, we find Ground in twenty-five Fathom Water, and it ſhoals gradually to the Shore; the Sounding being ſo regular, makes it a ſafe Coaſt to fall in with, having good Anchoring all along, and no Rocks. The Mouths of the Rivers *Savannah* and *Alatamaha* make a great Number of Iſlands, and the Entries between them form good Harbours. To the Southward of *Tybee* are the following Entries, *viz. Waſſaw*, *Oſſebah*, St. *Catharine's*, *Sapello*, *Doboy*, St. *Simon's*, which is the North-Entry to *Frederica*; *Jekyll Sound*, which is the South-Entry to *Frederica*, to which Place the Channel is navigable, from the ordinary Place of Anchoring in the

the Sound, for Ships of a good Burden up to the Town.

THE Staple of the Country of *Georgia* being preſumed, and intended to be, principally Silk and Wine, every Year confirms more our Hopes of ſucceeding in thoſe two, from the great Increaſe (as has been before obſerved) of the Vines and Mulberry-Trees, wherein Perſeverance only can bring it to Perfection. Several other Things might be produced, and perhaps more immediately profitable to the Planters; but it is apprehended, that it is not any Buſineſs of this Colony, nor any Benefit to the Trade of *England*, to interfere with what other *Engliſh* Plantations have produced, ſuch as Rice, *&c.*

As the Boundaries of the Colony are now known, together with the Climate, and Manner of Agriculture, more might be done henceforward in one Year, than could in ſeveral Years before we attained to that Knowledge; but our People are weak, being decreaſed, by great Numbers having been decoyed away to other Colonies: Many having taken to Idleneſs, upon ſhutting up the Store went away; but thoſe who ſtayed, and now remain, are ſtill a Body of the moſt valuable People, that find Means to live comfortably, ſome by their Trades, ſome by Planting, and raiſing live Stock, and ſome by their Labour,

bour, either by Land or Water; and one of thoſe remaining, are worth three that left us, for ſuch Work: And if an Embarkation was to come in with the next Year, it would be of great Service to the Colony, the *Saltzburghers* wiſhing for more of their Countrymen, and having been very induſtrious.

THE Perſons ſent from *England* on the Charity were of the Unfortunate, many of whom have by their Induſtry proved that they deſerved better, and have thriven; many alſo ſhewed they were brought into thoſe Misfortunes by their own Faults; and when thoſe who quitted their own Country to avoid Labour, ſaw Labour ſtand before their Eyes in *Georgia*, they were eaſily perſuaded to live in *Carolina* by Cunning, rather than work: This has been a great Misfortune alſo upon many Perſons, who brought over Servants indented to ſerve them, for a certain Number of Years, who being picked up in the Streets of *London*, or ſome ſuch Manner, their Maſters found them unfit for Labour, and many of them took ſuch Opportunities as they could get, to deſert and fly into *Carolina*, where they could be protected. Indeed, good and bad which came from *England*, were moſtly Inhabitants of Towns there; but ſuch ſeldom turn out good Huſbandmen with their own Hands; yet ſome of them proved very uſe-

uſeful in a new Colony, ſince they moſt readily compoſe Towns, which is the firſt Thing neceſſary to be a Receptacle for new Comers: And from thence, when all Demands of Labour, for Building and Trade are ſupplied, the laborious People may enlarge into the Country, and raiſe Proviſions for the Uſe of the Towns: Whereas, if the firſt were all labouring Countrymen, they would naturally diſperſe to the moſt fertile Land, and perhaps ſucceed for a While; but for Want of Neighbourhood and Markets, would force moſt of them to remove, and the Country remain little or nothing the better improved, as it happened in *Virginia*, till the Government, with great Difficulty at laſt, raiſed Towns in that Province.

It ought not here to be paſſed over, how ready the Country is to receive a Number of *German* Families, accuſtomed to Huſbandry, ſuch as uſually come once a Year down the *Rhine* to *Holland*, and embark thence for *America*, or the *Eaſt-Indies*; ſome of theſe we have already had Experience of, inſomuch that the People here would take off a good Number of them: And it would be of great Service (as we apprehend) to this Colony, at preſent, to ſend a Ship over, loaden with *Germans*, on the ſame Terms Mr. *Hope* does to *Philadelphia*, only taking Care that Proviſions for

for them on their Paſſage be more plentiful, and that they are leſs crowded than on board his Ships: The Terms are, they pay Half their Paſſage themſelves on embarking, and ſix Weeks after their Arrival, to pay the other Half, which they generally do, with private Contracts to People; but in caſe they do not, then they may be bound by the Ship's Maſter for four or five Years, if they are above twenty-one Years of Age; but if under, they may be bound until the Age of twenty-one if Men, and eighteen if Girls. It muſt be at the ſame Time confeſs'd, that divers of theſe Foreigners have, during the Time of their Servitude, ſhewn themſelves of a dogged Diſpoſition, ſurly and obſtinate, diſcovering an Averſeneſs to their Maſters Orders, which proceeds (as we imagine) from a Diſlike of their being ſubject to Strangers; whilſt others again have behaved well; but it may be alledged with Truth, that when, or wereſoever among us, any of them have worked for their own Benefit, they are indefatigable, and out-done by none, which joined with great Parſimony, fits them for excellent Settlers when free.

To enable the induſtrious *Engliſh* Settlers to go on with Planting, who are truly deſirous of cultivating Land; we humbly conceive nothing could be a greater Inducement to it, than that the honourable

Truſtees

Truſtees would pleaſe to import yearly, ſo long as they ſee good, a Number of *Engliſh* or *Welch* Servants, ſuch as are uſed to hard Labour in the Country, and Strangers to *London*, to be contracted with in *England*, to ſerve the Truſtees for five Years, from two to four Pounds yearly Wages, according to their Ability, for finding themſelves in Apparel. Thoſe Servants, on their Arrival, to be hired by the Inhabitants for one Year, the Perſon hiring to pay over and above the contracted Wages, one Pound yearly to the Truſtees, ſo that in five Years the Paſſage-Money will be paid. And to enable the Planters to pay the ſaid Wages, it is humbly propoſed, that a Bounty be ſettled on every Product of the Land, *viz.* Corn, Peaſe, Potatoes, Wine, Silk, Cotton, Flax, *&c.* to what Value the honourable Truſt ſhall judge meet to be limited in the following, or any other Manner, *viz.* For the firſt Years the ſaid Bounty to be payable for Corn, Peaſe, Potatoes, *&c.* only; and thenceforward to ceaſe wholly, and the Reſidue of Years wherein any Bounty ſhould be allowed, to be payable only for Silk, Wine, Oil, *&c.* by which Means the Planter ſo aſſiſted might be able to live, whilſt at the ſame Time he propagates Vines, Mulberry-Trees, *&c.* from which he can expect no immediate Benefit before

they

they come to ſome Maturity. A Rule to be made, that they who hire the ſaid Servants ſhall employ them only in Plantation-Work of their own, and not let them out at Hire to work at handicraft Trades, or any other Buſineſs, *&c.* That each Servant ſhall ſerve one whole Year; and if they part at the Year's End, he ſhall find himſelf another Maſter within Days to ſerve for one Year alſo, and ſo on to the End of their reſpective Times to ſerve; by which Means good Maſters will not want good Servants, and 'twill be a great Means to make other Maſters become good, in order to get good Servants, or elſe be content with the bad, or none. If any Diſputes ariſe between Maſters and Servants, ſuch to be determined by the Magiſtrates, according to the Laws of *England*, wherein the Magiſtrate concerned as a Party ſhall not appear as a Judge, or offer to interfere with the Opinion of the others, but acquieſce in their Determination, if it happens to be in Favour of the Servant, whom they ought to defend from cruel Uſage, and where they find ſuch evil Treatment either thro' too ſevere Correction, or want of ſufficient wholſome Food, according to the Cuſtom of the Colony, the Magiſtrates to have Power of vacating ſuch Services, and obliging the Servants to find another Maſter.

THE

THE kind Intention of the honourable Truſtees to extend the Tenure of Lands in the Manner propoſed (as ſignify'd to their Secretary here) gave great Satisfaction to all reaſonable Perſons who ſeem'd to deſire no more, and only wiſh to find that ratify'd, which they apprehend to be not yet done, and that occaſions ſome Anxiety about it.

WHETHER theſe Helps, or whatever other, the honourable Truſtees ſhall be pleas'd to afford us, the Ability of the Inhabitants to ſupport themſelves muſt ſtill in a great Meaſure depend on the Induſtry and Frugality of each. Divers in the Province who underſtand Planting, and are already ſettled, provided they can attain to ſome live Stock, can and do ſupport themſelves. Men working for Hire, Boat-men, Pack-horſe-men, *&c.* ſupport themſelves very well, if they will work; and more ſuch would, were they to be found. Shopkeepers, Tradeſmen, and Artificers, ſuch as Tallow-Chandlers, Soap-Boilers, Braſiers, Sadlers, Shoemakers, Tanners, *&c.* live very well on their Buſineſs here, and many more might, were there more Merchants to import Goods for ſupplying the *Indian* Traders, which would increaſe the Reſort to *Savannah*; whereas thoſe Traders are now obliged to get the greateſt Part of what they want from *Charles-Town* in *Carolina*. New Planters, and ſuch as go on upon particular

Improvements, ſuch as Wine, Silk, *&c.* will need ſome Aſſiſtance. Magiſtrates, Conſtables, and Tything-men, and others whoſe Time is taken up in the publick Service, require ſome Allowance for the ſame. It is alſo needful for the Well-being of the Colony, that Roads ſhould be maintain'd: Poſts for communicating of Letters, and Forts upon the Frontiers, as well towards the *Indians* as *Spaniards*, be ſupported: As likewiſe other publick Works, which the People here are in no Degree able to bear.

When the Eaſt Part of the Province of *Georgia* was taken Poſſeſſion of under the Truſtees Charter by Mr. *Ogletborpe*, according to the Limits of the *Britiſh* Dominions in *America*, Forts were erected upon the Extremities to keep up Marks of Poſſeſſion: The Strength and Materials were of ſuch a Nature, as the Men he had with him could make, and ſufficient for Defence againſt any Strength that could be brought againſt them by the neighbouring *Indians*, or *Spaniards* in *Florida*.

The firſt Foundation of the Colony was upon Tenures, by which each Lot was to be occupied by a Freeholder, obliged to take Arms for the Defence of the Colony; and this Militia, with the Aſſiſtance of our friendly *Indians*, held the Colony againſt all Attempts of the *Spaniards* from

Auguſ-

Auguſtine, who alarmed them almoſt every Spring, pretending a Claim, and therefore a Right to invade, without being ſaid to infringe the Peace; but did not take one Foot of Ground from us.

In the Beginning of the Year 1738, great Preparations were made at the *Havannah*, and Troops were ſent from thence and *Old Spain* to *Auguſtine*, for the taking Poſſeſſion (as they call'd it) of that Part of *Carolina* in which *Georgia* was comprehended, and which they gave out belong'd to them. Upon the Truſtees having early Notice of theſe great Preparations, they applied to his Majeſty to take upon him the Protection of the Colony, which in its Infancy was unable to repel ſo great a Force. His Majeſty thereupon ordered a Regiment to be raiſed, and poſted on the *Spaniſh* Frontiers, ſince which the War is broke out, and that Regiment, with the Aſſiſtance of Troops and *Indians* raiſed in *Georgia* and *Carolina*, in Conjunction with a Squadron of Men of War, attack'd *Auguſtine*, and after raiſing the Siege of that Place, remain'd in the Poſſeſſion of the Frontiers, as before the War; but for the Defence of the Colony now, it is neceſſary to have Veſſels that can act in ſhoal Water, on ſo large and extended a Frontier towards the Sea, and Rangers who can ride the Woods; as alſo Artillery, and all other

Things neceſſarily appertaining thereto, and Means for augmenting our Fortifications equal to the increas'd Strength of the *Spaniards.*

Savannah, Nov. 10, 1740.

WE whoſe Names are hereunto ſubſcribed, being duly ſworn in open Court, do declare, that the above State of the Province of *Georgia* is true, according to the beſt of our own Knowledge, and from the moſt certain Informations we could obtain from others; and do deſire, that the Seal of this Court may be affixed thereto.

* Pat. Graham	George Johnſon
* Joſ. Fitzwalter	Samuel Parker
* James Carwells	Thomas Palmer
* Thomas Upton	William Stephens
* Giles Becu	Henry Parker
* Thomas Egerton	Thomas Jones
* Thomas Cundell	Samuel Mercer
Anthony Camuſe	James Campbell
John Burton	John Rae
Joſ. Pavey	Noble Jones
Robert Hainks	Thomas Young
John Mellidge	Thomas Ellis.
Tho. Bayley (Smith)	

N. B. Thoſe ſeven mark'd with *, at their own voluntary Deſire, were admitted to ſign it, and were ſworn before the Magiſtrates out of Court.

The

The Depoſition of Lieutenant George Dunbar, *taken upon the Holy Evangeliſts, before the Recorder of the Town of* Frederica, Jan. 20, 1738-9.

THIS Deponent ſays, That he arrived in *Georgia* the Beginning of *June* laſt, with the firſt Detachment of General *Oglethorpe*'s Regiment; and from that Time, to the Beginning of *Auguſt*; all the Carpenters of the ſaid three Companies, and a certain Number of other Soldiers, were employ'd in building Clap-board Huts for the ſaid Companies, and the other Soldiers were employ'd in unloading Veſſels and Boats loaded with Clap-boards, and other Neceſſaries for Building, and Proviſions of different Kinds, often up to their Necks in Water: They were alſo employ'd in carrying Clap-boards, *&c.* upon their Backs to the Camp, in clearing Ground from Roots of Trees, *&c.* for a Parade, burning the Wood and Rubbiſh upon it, carrying of Bricks, and burning Lime: And the Artiſts who were excuſed from theſe Works, wrought at their own Trades, without ſtanding ſtill, by Reaſon of Heat. The Hours of Labour were from Day-Light, till between Eleven and Twelve; and from between One and Two, and ſometimes between Two and Three, till

Dark. All that Time the Men kept ſo healthy, that often no Man in the Camp ailed in the leaſt, and none died except one Man, who came ſick on board, and never worked at all; nor did I hear, that any of the Men ever made the Heat a Pretence for not Working.

And this Deponent further ſays, That he has been often in *America*, and frequently heard, that in the Negro Colonies, the Hire of White Men is more than that of Negroes. And this Deponent knows, that in *South-Carolina* White Ship-Carpenters and Caulkers have about one Third more Wages than a Negro of the ſame Trade or Profeſſion, this Deponent having often paid Wages to both; and alſo knows there is the aforeſaid Difference in many Handicrafts, and verily believes it is ſo in all; and affirms, that the ſame is owing to the White Men exceeding the Negroes in the ſame Profeſſions, both in Quantity and Quality of their Work.

George Dunbar.

Sworn before me the
Day and Year above
written,

Francis Moore.

Extract

Extract of a Letter from Mr. Thomas Jones *at* Savannah *in* Georgia, *to the Truſtees Accomptant, dated* July 1, 1741.

THE Truſtees *German* Servants in general behave well, and are induſtrious: Of theſe, eight or ten Families are more remarkably ſo, and have this laſt Year purchas'd a good Stock of Cattle, ſome having ſix Cows, the leaſt two; and each having a Garden, where they raiſe ſome Corn, Peaſe, Pompions, Potatoes, *&c.* which with the Milk of their Cows is the chief Part of their Food: They are at little Expence in Cloathing; but this expoſes them to the Envy and Hatred of our Negro-Mongers, and ſuch who ſeek the Extirpation of the Colony, as well as of the drunken, idle Sort amongſt us.

I AM informed by *Francis Harris* and *William Ruſſell* (who are very converſant with them, and can talk the *German* Tongue) That they have lately joined, in a Letter writ and ſent to their Friends and Acquaintance in *Germany*, perſuading them to come to *Georgia*, where they may, by their Induſtry, live in greater Plenty, and more comfortably than they can elſewhere.

THESE Servants are very deſirous, That (when the Time of their Service is expired) they may have Lands allotted them within twelve or fifteen Miles of *Savannah*; where they may bring Things by Land-Carriage in a Vicinage, and that they may make one common Fence (as the People of *Ebenezer* have done) and be affiſting to one another.

The Copy of a Letter from the Reverend Mr. Frederick Michael Ziegenhagen, German *Chaplain to his Majeſty, dated at* Kenſington, January 11, 1741-2, *and ſent to the Truſtees for Eſtabliſhing the Colony of* Georgia *in* America.

GENTLEMEN,

HAVING ſeen Paragraphs in Print repreſenting the *Saltzburghers* as being uneaſy with their Settlement at *Ebenezer* in *Georgia*, and deſirous to remove therefrom; and fearing ſuch Reports (if credited) might give juſt Offence to your Honours their Guardians, as well as to their Benefactors in *Germany*, and thereby deprive them from having yours, and their Favours continued.

I THOUGHT it my indiſpenſible Duty to acquaint your Honours, That by all the Letters and Journals I have received ſince their Settlement at *New Ebenezer*, they have expreſs'd quite different Sentiments;

and not to trouble you with many Particulars, I beg Leave herewith to incloſe you two Extracts of the lateſt Accounts I received from them in *November* laſt.

Extract of a Letter from the Reverend Mr. Boltzius *at* Ebenezer, *dated the* 23*d of* July, 1741, *to the Reverend Dr.* Francke, *Profeſſor of Divinity at* Hall.

"TOGETHER with theſe ſpiritual "Bleſſings, and the ſalutary Ef-
" fect of the Word of God to the Con-
" verſion of many Souls, we enjoy alſo
" this Year, by the Mercy of God, many
" temporal good Things.

" THE preſent War, and the Burden of
" it, hath not affected us yet, and we
" don't feel the leaſt of it; and in the
" great Dearneſs the Colony ſuffered laſt
" Year, we have not been in Want of
" neceſſary Proviſions. As to the preſent
" Year, we have a very hopeful Proſpect
" of a good Harveſt, every Thing in the
" Fields and Gardens growing ſo delight-
" ful, as our Eyes hardly have ſeen in this
" Country before. * If *Iſaac*, by the Bleſſ-
" ing of the Lord, received from what he
" had ſowed, an hundred Fold, I believe, I
" dare ſay, to the Praiſe of the great Mercy
" of God over us, our *Saltzburghers* will
" get

* Gen. xxvi. 12.

" get thouſand Fold, notwithſtanding that
" the Corn, when it came out of the
" Ground, was eaten quite up two or three
" Times by the Worms, of which nobody
" can hardly form a right Idea, except he
" ſees it with his own Eyes. Wheat, Rice,
" and other Grain, muſt be ſowed very
" thin, becauſe each Grain brings forth
" fifty, an hundred, or more Stalks and
" Ears. The Land is really very fruitful,
" if the Sins of the Inhabitants, and the
" Curſe of God for ſuch Sins, doth not
" eat it up, which was formerly the
" unhappy Caſe of the bleſſed Land of
" *Canaan.*

" And I am heartily ſorry to acquaint
" you, that I don't find in ſome of the
" Inhabitants of the Colony, a due Thank-
" fulneſs for, and Contentment with the
" many Benefits beſtowed on them for ſe-
" veral Years together; although thoſe who
" are induſtrious, and will labour for their
" Maintenance, may, as we do, live con-
" tentedly, and ſubſiſt under the Bleſſing
" of God, promiſed by St. *Paul*, *Heb.* xiii.
" 5. *I will never leave thee, nor forſake*
" *thee.* Which Bleſſing the Idle and Un-
" thankful are not intitled to."

Extract

Extract out of the Journal of Mr. Boltzius, *Miniſter of the Goſpel at* Ebenezer *in* Georgia.

"THE 10th of *Auguſt*, 1741. We "have this Year Plenty of Peach-"es, and as this Fruit doth not keep, "ſome of our People try to make a cer-"tain Sort of Brandy of them, others "give them to the Swine: This is more "than any body could have promiſed to "himſelf, or others, ſome Years ago. Even "at this Time, when I am writing this, a "Man brings a large Diſh of blue Grapes "to me, grown wild in the Woods; they "are of a ſweet Taſte, and pretty like "our *European* Grapes; that I am very "apt to believe, the wild Vine-Trees, if "properly managed, would give good "Wine. Thanks be to our gracious God, "who gives us here every good Thing for "our Support.

"The 9th of *September*, 1741. Some "Time ago I wrote to an honoured Friend "in *Europe*, That the Land in this Coun-"try, if well managed and laboured, brings "forth, by the Bleſſings of God, not only "hundred Fold, but thouſand Fold; and "I this Day was confirmed therein. A "Woman having two Years ago picked "out of *Indian* Corn, bought at *Puryſ-*

"*burgh*,

" *burgh*, no more than three Grains of
" Rye (called here *German* Corn) and
" planting them here at *Ebenezer*, one of
" theſe Grains produced an hundred and
" ſeventy Stalks and Ears, and the three
" Grains yielded to her a Bag of Corn as
" large as a Coat-Pocket, the Grains where-
" of were good and full grown; and ſhe
" deſired me to ſend Part of them to a
" kind Benefactor in *Europe*. One of our
" *Saltzburghers* brought to me alſo a like
" Bag of Beans, all grown out of one
" Bean.

" TRUE it is, notwithſtanding the Fer-
" tility of the Land, the firſt Tillagers of
" it muſt undergo and ſtruggle with great
" Difficulties; but them that come after
" them will reap the Benefit thereof, if
" they go on to do their Labour in the
" Fear of God.

" THE Land is able to provide every
" good Thing, and more particularly is
" Paſturage very plenteous."

INDEX

INDEX

TO THE

SECOND VOLUME.

A.

ABERCORN, an Account of the Village Page 215
Amelia Island attack'd by the *Spaniards* 197
Auguſtine, Account of an Action at the Siege 428, 435, 447. An Account of raiſing the Siege 444, 448

B.

BARNWELL, Col. goes with others from *Carolina* to the Siege of *Auguſtine* 376
Baylie, an Account of him, and his Intentions to leave the Colony 209. Leaves the Colony 498
Bernal, *Jacob*, a *Jew*, without any viſible Way of Livelihood, leaves the Colony 461
Bernandoon, *Hiam*, another *Jew*, leaves the Colony ibid

Bradford,

Bradford, a Thief who had eſcap'd from *Georgia*, demanded at *Charles-Town* 10. Committed to Priſon at *Savannah*, and eſcapes by the Keeper's Negligence 32

Bradley kills one of the Truſt's Steers without any Authority for it 6. Requir'd to deliver up every Thing in his Cuſtody belonging to the Truſt 11. Sends away his Goods to *Charles-Town* 23. Kills and ſells the Truſt's Cattle 93. Call'd upon again by the Magiſtrates to deliver up the Truſt's Effects 103. Quits the great Houſe built by the Truſt's Servants 172. His Intentions to go off to *Carolina* 190. Stopt by his Creditors 200. Permitted to go 205. Requir'd to give Security not to leave the Colony till his Accounts are made up 257. Goes off privately without giving Security 386

Brixy, Maſter of a Sloop, confin'd upon Suſpicion of Murder 60. His Trial and Conviction 67. His Execution 82

Brooks, *Francis*, kill'd in a Boat by a Party of *Spaniards* 294

Brownfield appointed by Mr. *Whitfield*, in his Abſence, Steward of the Orphan-Houſe 427

Bull, Col. his Relation of the Orders given to the Captains of the Men of War 134

Bull, Capt. deſerts his Poſt at the Siege of *Auguſtine* 462

Bunyon builds a Boat at *Abercorn* 215

C.

CADOGAN, Enſign, returns from *Charles-Town* with Diſpatches about the Supply granted

granted by the Aſſembly for carrying on the War 282
Cambel, his Account of the Malecontents diſſuading him at *Charles-Town* from going to *Georgia* 507
Canon, *Marmaduke*, an Orphan and Freeholder at *Savannah*, an Account of him 373
Cargo of Flour and Cheeſe ſpoilt 53
Carolina Regiment, their Behaviour at the Siege of *Auguſtine* 461
Carwils, *James*, a Freeholder of *Savannah*, goes a Volunteer to the Siege of *Auguſtine* 368
Charle-Town, a contagious Sickneſs in it 135, 146
Chriſtie, his Complaints of *Thomas Jones* 9. His Conduct in relation to Capt. *Davis* 125, 136. His Commiſſion for firſt Bailiff of *Savannah* ſuſpended 159. His Conduct relating to a Copy of the Court Proceedings 184. A further Account of him 187. His Conduct about *Wiſe*'s Effects 190, 192. Demands of Mr. *Stephens* the Conſtitution appointing him firſt Bailiff 226. Produces an Account to Mr. *Jones*, making the Truſt Debtor of 100*l.* to him 235. His Commiſſion for firſt Bailiff of *Savannah* revok'd 398. Leaves the Colony in order to come to *England* 309
Coates, his Death at *Charles-Town* 135
Commiſſioners for examining the Truſt's Accounts, their Proceedings 86, 91, 96, 99, 103, 108, 117, 119, 234, 238
Conn, a Sailor, examin'd about an Information of the Soldiers Deſigns againſt General *Ogletthorpe*, and ſent to the South 3
Cookſey ſettles at *Charles-Town* 57

Court

Court at *Savannah*, their Proceedings 160, 165, 205, 239, 255, 311, 431
Cozens tried for a Murder, and convicted 68, His Execution 83
Currie, *George*, his Character 400. A further Account of him 488
Cuthbert, Capt. his Death and Character 193

D.

DALE, Dr. of *South-Carolina*, an Enemy to the Province of *Georgia* 340
Davis, Capt. a remarkable Controverſy between him and *Pope* the Maſter of a Ship 24. His Sloop ſtopt from going to *Auguſtine* 123. Endeavours to eſcape with her 125. Put under Confinement 136. Diſcharg'd upon giving Security not to go to *Auguſtine* 144. Turns his Sloop into a Privateer 145. Sails upon a Cruiſe againſt the *Spaniards* 236. Returns to *Savannah* 279. Taken into Cuſtody for ſending off two *Spaniſh* Priſoners to *Auguſtine* 450
Delgraſs, his Death at *Charles-Town* 135
Deſborow, his Death at *Charles-Town*, with his two Sons 146
Douglaſs, an Account of him, and his Intentions to leave the Colony 209. Leaves the Colony 498
Ducbee undertakes to build a Wharf at *Savannah* 39
Dyſon, Chaplain to General *Ogletborpe*'s Regiment, his Death 132

E.

INDEX.

E.

EVANS, a young Man, kill'd by an Accident 53
Ewen, *William*, leaves off cultivating his Lot to work at the Orphan-Houſe 427
Eyles, Mr. Surgeon to the Regiment, kill'd in a Duel by Enſign *Tolſon* 403
Eyre, Mr. ſent by General *Oglethorpe* to the *Cherokee Indians* 146. Returns to *Savannah*, his Conduct relating to the *Indians* 206. Goes to the South 210. Goes again to the *Cherokee* Nation 265. Brings a large Body of them to the Siege of *Auguſtine* 338, 342, 344

F.

FAllowfield ſworn in ſecond Bailiff at *Savannah* 159. An Account of his Conduct 236. Viſited by the Club of Malecontents 351. His Conduct relating to a Schooner ſeiz'd 241, 245, 248. His Plantation on the *Iſle of Hope*, an Account of it 443
Fennel, Capt. his Relation of the Poſture of Affairs at *Havannah* 78. Arms a Sloop to go to *Jamaica* 176
Foſter, *Eliſha*, a Tything-man, his Conduct in relation to Capt. *Davis* 126, 222. Goes a privateering with Capt. *Davis* 236
Freeholders, the Appearance of them at *Savannah* 81. Seventy of them deliver in their Claims of Lots to the Court 463. Seventy others deliver in their Claims 476
French, Col. *Bull*'s Account of their Deſigns 107.

107. Lieutenant *Kent*'s Account of their marching againſt the *Chicaſſaw Indians* 219. A Body of them attack'd, and taken Priſoners by the *Cherokee Indians* 442

G.

GARDINER kill'd by an Accident 213
Garrett, an Account of him 222
Gilbert, his Complaint of the *Moravians* 100. Leaves the Colony, his Character 482
Gough, *William*, an Account of him 419
Graham, *Patrick*, his Marriage at *Savannah* 303
Grant, an Account of him, and his Intentions to leave the Colony 209. A further Account of him 309. Leaves the Colony 498
Grant, *Peter*, a Cadet, kill'd in a Duel by Mr. *Shenton* 403

H.

HABERSHAM appointed by Mr. *Whitfield*, in his Abſence, to officiate for him 427
Hetherington goes off privately to *Charles-Town* 309
Holmes, his Death at *Charles-Town* 135
Horſe-Racing ſet up by the Malecontents in *Savannah* 420, 423, 427
How, *Robert*, leaves the Colony to come to *England* 101. Returns to *Georgia* 229
Hunt, Capt. refus'd Leave to diſpoſe of his Cargo, Rum being Part of it 37

INDEX.

J.

JENKINS, Truſtee for the Orphans, delivers up his Truſt to Mr. *Whitfield* 270. An Account of his Conduct 382, 458. Goes away from the Colony 498

Indians, *Chicaſſaw*, take a large *French* Boat with Goods and Letters 188. A Party of *Chicaſſaws* and *Euchies* come to *Savannah* to join General *Oglethorpe* 199. *Cherokee*, an Account of their intending to attack the White Men among them 72

Jones, *Lewis*, an Accomplice in a Murder, makes his Eſcape 74. Taken in *Charles-Town* 113

Jones, *Noble*, returns to *Savannah* after the Siege of *Auguſtine*, with ſeveral Volunteers 472. Appointed with a Guard-Boat to watch the *Narrows* at *Skeedoway* 492. His Conduct approv'd of 497

Jones, *Thomas*, his Difference with the Magiſtrates 6. Goes to *Frederica* 47. Returns to *Savannah* 62. Sworn in third Bailiff at *Savannah* 159. His Complaints of Mr. *Whitfield* 412, 418

Iron Stone, Quarries of it found 420

K.

KENT, Lieutenant, a Letter from him recommending ſome Men to be ſettled in *Georgia* 330. Comes to *Savannah* about the Conduct of the Traders at *Auguſta* 426

Kitt committed for ſeditious Practices, and makes his Eſcape 61

L.

LAFEIT appointed Capt. of a Company to be paid by the Government of *Carolina* 348. Goes with his Company from *Savannah* to the South 369

Leman, Enſign, his Duel with Enſign *Sutherland* 237

Letters receiv'd from the Truſt 34, 38, 49, 73, 139, 154, 210, 230, 243, 337, 367, 370, 376, 398, 489

Letters ſent to the Truſt 39, 58, 84, 132, 145, 202, 276, 315, 381, 466

Levett tried for Murder, and convicted 68. Repriev'd 83

Lyndal, *John*, the Pindar, Regulations made for his Conduct 85. His Conduct relating to a Freeholder preſs'd by Major *Richards* 372

M.

MACKINTOSH, Capt. his Deſign of going home to *Scotland* 279. Surrenders the Command of *Palachacolas Fort* to his Brother 296

Mackintoſh, *John More*, Priſoner at *Auguſtine* 438

Mackintoſh, *Laughlan*, his Relation of a Murder at *Fort Argyle* 499. The Murder confeſs'd by the *Spaniſh* Spy and an *Iriſhman* 506

Magiſtrates of *Savannah*, their Conduct about the Adminiſtration of *Cuthbert*'s Effects 194. Their Conduct relating to a Freeholder preſs'd by Major *Richards* 371. Their Conduct relating to the Inſurrections of Negroes in *Carolina* 129

Malatchie,

Malatchie, one of the *Creek Indians*, his Conduct 361, 362
Malecontents, their Remarks on the Truſtees Anſwer to their Repreſentation 216. Their Reports about the *French* attacking the *Chicaſſaw Indians* 381. Their Reports about the King's diſſolving the Truſt 395. A further Account of them 405, 407
Matthews, *Jacob*, goes to the South to prevent any Hoſtilities againſt the *Spaniſh Indians* 1. Inſults Mr. *Jones* at the Store-houſe 280. A further Account of him 289
McLeod, Miniſter of *Darien*, Grant of Land for him and his Succeſſors 398
Mercer, his Care of the Effects of *Little*, an Orphan 275
Militia at *Savannah* ſettled 162
Montaigut, Mr. his Death and Funeral 186
Moravians, their Cruelty to *How*'s Daughter 101
Muer, his Death at *Charles-Town* 135.

N.

NEGROES in *South-Carolina*, an Inſurrection of them 129, 402. A Negro ſold by Auction at *Savannah* 298
Nelſon, a Mate of a Ship, examin'd about the Soldiers Deſigns againſt General *Oglethorpe* 3
Norris, Mr. the Rev. comes to *Savannah* 38. His Uneaſineſs about Mr. *Whitfield*'s being ſent to *Savannah* 41. His Complaints of *Thomas Jones* 110, 172. Goes to the South 182
Nunez, Dr. and his Son, leave the Colony 498

INDEX.

O.

OGLETHORPE, General, his Orders to Bailiff *Parker* about a Waſte of Stores 16. Comes to *Savanuah* 62. Goes to viſit the *Indian* Nations 67. Returns from the *Indian* Nations 142. His Account of the *Creek Indians* 143. His Proclamation in *Savannah* for ſtopping runaway Negroes 151. Orders Capt. *Thompſon* to ſail to St. *Simon*'s 155. Inſpects the five hundred Acre Lots 171. Returns to the South 182. Takes *Fort St. George*, and garriſons it 224. Takes two Forts on St. *Juan*'s River 263. Recommends to Mr. *Stephens* to forward the Building of the Church 297. Goes to *Charles-Town* 316. His Letter to Mr. *Jones* about the Management of the Orphans 321. Returns from *Charles-Town* 336. Returns to the South 346. Takes *Fort Diego* 389. Raiſes the Siege of *Auguſtine* 449. His Sickneſs 494

Orphan-Houſe, an Account of it 319, 320, 360, 454

P.

PALMER, Col. kill'd at the Siege of *Auguſtine* 438

Parker, his Complaints of *Thomas Jones* 9, 31, 33. His Cattle maim'd 124. His Conduct about *Dyſon*'s Effects 133. His Character 138. Appointed firſt Bailiff of *Savannah*. 398

People clear the Town of *Savannah* and the Com-

Common from Weeds, *&c.* 161. Number of them 162
Periam deputed by *Whitfield* to take Care of the Orphans in his Abſence 337
Plantations, an Account of them near *Savannah* 96
Pope, a Controverſy between him and Capt. *Davis* before the Magiſtrates 24
Potter appointed Conſtable at *Savannah* 163. His Conduct and Character 219. Goes a privateering with Capt. *Davis* 236. His Death 313
Pye, *John*, his Commiſſion to act as Recorder during the Suſpenſion of *Chriſtie* 398

R.

RANGERS, a Company of them appointed by General *Oglethorpe* 193
Richards appointed Captain of a Company to be paid by the Government of *South-Carolina* 348. Goes with his Company from *Puryſburgh* to the South 371
Rum, People drunk with it inſult the Peace-Officers 92

S.

SALTER, a Tything-man, ſtops Capt. *Davis*'s Baggage 126
Savannah Town, a remarkable Proof of the Healthineſs of it 75
Saw-Mill at *Old Ebenezer* blown up 113
Scooner, *Spaniſh*, ſeiz'd and ſecur'd at *Tybee* 225, 229, 240
Scroggs, Lieutenant, ſecures the Effects of Capt. *Cuthbert*

Cuthbert 193. Robb'd at *Savannah* 208
Sellier turns Methodiſt, and leaves the Colony 328
Servants, runaway, protected in *South-Carolina* 9
Shannon, a Soldier, committed for treaſonable Practices 90
Simms deputed by *Whitfield*, in his Abſence, to take Care of the Orphans 336
Sloop built in *Georgia* 113
Sloop from *Philadelphia*, belonging to Mr. *Whitfield*, arrives at *Savannah* 228
Spaniſh Launch ſtopt at *Tybee* 70
Spaniſh Spy confin'd 76. Eſcapes with his Servant from Priſon, an Account of it 473, 480. He and his Servant murder two Perſons at *Fort Argyle* 499. Is taken again 505
Stanley, *Joſeph*, leaves the Colony 460
Stephens, Mr. his Acconnt of a Diſpute between his Son and *Thomas Jones* 18. Settles a Diſpute between the Pindar and other Perſons 22. His Conference with *Parker* about iſſuing Sola Bills 46. Receives a Commiſſion to examine, with Meſſ. *Jones* and *Parker*, the Truſt Accounts 49. His Reaſons for refuſing to ſign for the iſſuing of Sola Bills 64. His Son ſets out for *England* 80. His Account of a Quarrel between *Parker* and *Thomas Jones* 106. Commiſſion'd by General *Oglethorpe* to command the Militia 163. His Account of his Plantation 166. His Speech to the Conſtables, Tything-men, *&c.* 169. His Account of *Hamerton*'s Bill for 200*l.* being refus'd Payment 177. His Conduct relating to the Militia and Guard-Duty 249, 272, 286, 354, 365. His Account of the People's Planting about *Savannah*

nah 285, 327. His Account of a Box of Truſt-Letters directed to him being detain'd by Mr. *Hawkins* at *Frederica* 287, 301, 313. His Account of the Growth of Oranges in *Georgia* 295. His Conduct in relation to the Artillery 299. His Account of a Letter from *Williamſon* relating to Mr. *Chriſtie*'s Conſtitution of firſt Bailiff 304. His Account of his Plantation by *Vernon* River 317, 359, 385, 454. His Account of the Growth of Cotton 325. Fixes up Advertiſements for Grantees of Land entring their Claims 340, 453. His Remarks upon his Son's Conduct in *England* 378. His Converſation with *Williamſon* about the Recorderſhip 393. Sends off a Party of *Indians* to aſſiſt at the Siege of *Auguſtine* 398. His Opinion about ſending Proviſions from *Ireland* 406. His Converſation with ſome Perſons about forming a Repreſentation of the State of the Colony 410. Calls to his Aſſiſtance for the ſaid Work Meſſ. *Parker*, *Jones* and *Mercer* 411. His Account of the Light-Houſe at *Tybee* 414. His Converſation with *Williamſon* about the Colony 416. His Account of a Paper of Grievances fram'd by the Malecontents 424. His Relation of an Action at *Auguſtine* 425. His Account of the Increaſe of Rice in *South-Carolina* 469. In Danger of being kill'd by a Servant of *Phelps*'s 485. Goes to General *Oglethorpe* at *Frederica* 493. His Account of the Regiment 495

Sterling, *William*, his Conduct 382. Leaves the Colony 498

Stewart, *Donald*, Maſter of a Sloop, drowned within *Port-Royal* Iſland 349

T.

T.

TAILFER, Dr. his Endeavours to form a Company of Volunteers 147. His Conduct with the Malecontents 183, 378, 382, 421, 458. Leaves the Colony 498

Thomas, Monſieur, an Engineer, arrives in the Colony 98. His Death 146

Tomo Chichi promiſes to go and reſtrain the *Creek Indians* from committing any Hoſtilities againſt the *Spaniards* 2. His Death and Funeral 153

Townſhend, Mrs. her Conduct and Character 450. Leaves the Colony 461

Traders, *Indian*, apply for Licences at *Savannah* 40, 45, 47, 63, 366, 380. Their Conduct at *Auguſta* 426. Some of them inſult the Magiſtrates at *Savannah*, and are ſupported by the Club of Malecontents at *Jenkins*'s 476. Unlicens'd, their Riots in the *Lower Creek* Nation 392

Tything-men, the Number of them at *Savannah* ſettled 162, 168

U.

VAnderduſſen, Col. his Reſentment at the Behaviour of ſome of his Officers and the *Carolina* Volunteers 467. Is pleas'd with the Town of *Savannah* 468

Vernon, Mr. his Arrival at *Savannah* 178

Vines ſent to *Georgia*, ſpoil'd for want of Care in packing them 4. Thrive beſt near the Sea 192

Volunteers at *Savannah* inliſt for ſome Months

to ſerve at the Siege of *Auguſtine* 348, 350
Upton diſpoſes of his Land near *Frederica*, and gets another Grant on *All-honey Iſland* 47. Detain'd in *Georgia* by a Warrant upon Capt. *Norbury*'s Account 131. His Boat caſt away 203. Suſpects it to be done with Deſign 211. Carries on a Trade between *Georgia* and *Charles-Town* 266

W.

WAR between *England* and *Spain*, News of it arrives in *Georgia* 120. Declaration of it publiſh'd at *Savannah* 371
Warren, Capt. attack'd by ſeveral *Spaniſh* Half-Gallies and Sloops 346
Weſt, his Death 75
Whitfield, Mr. arrives at *Savannah* 243. His Conduct relating to the Orphan-Houſe 248, 251. Harangues the Grand Jury 256. A Lot of five hundred Acres deliver'd to him 259. Takes two Orphan Servants of *Parker*'s from him 271, 277. Forbid by General *Ogletborpe* to take away any Orphans from their Maſters 295. Charges Mr. *Norris* with preaching falſe Doctrine 305. His Conduct at *Charles-Town* 320. His Diſcourſe to the People 332. Leaves the Colony *ibid.* Returns again 396. His Conduct relating to *Mellidge*, an Orphan 408. Goes to *South-Carolina* 427. Cited by Mr. *Garden*, Miniſter at *Charles-Town*, to appear, and anſwer for his Doctrine 457. Returns to *Savannah* ibid. Goes a Progreſs to the Northern Provinces 482
Wigan, a Trader among the *Lower Creeks*, his Letter

Letter about the Attempts of the *French* to draw off the *Indians* from the *Engliſh* Intereſt 391

Williamſon, his Conduct about the Recorderſhip of *Savannah* 179, 183. His Commiſſion for Recorder of *Savannah* revok'd 398. His Conduct at *Savannah* 440

Willy, Lieutenant, his Letters about the Attempts of the *French* to draw off the *Indians* from the *Engliſh* Intereſt 358, 361, 391

Wright, who had eſcap'd out of Priſon, taken, and ſent by Lieutenant *Kent* from *Auguſta* 52

FINIS.